# Learning and Community

Susan G. Solomon
*Louis I. Kahn's Jewish Architecture:*
*Mikveh Israel and the Midcentury American*
*Synagogue*

Amy Neustein, editor
*Tempest in the Temple: Jewish Communities*
*and Child Sex Scandals*

Jack Wertheimer, editor
*Learning and Community: Jewish*
*Supplementary Schools in the Twenty-first*
*Century*

Carole S. Kessner
*Marie Syrkin: Values Beyond the Self*

Leonard Saxe and Barry Chazan
*Ten Days of Birthright Israel: A Journey in*
*Young Adult Identity*

Jack Wertheimer, editor
*Imagining the American Jewish Community*

Murray Zimiles
*Gilded Lions and Jeweled Horses: The*
*Synagogue to the Carousel*

Marianne R. Sanua
*Be of Good Courage: The American Jewish*
*Committee, 1945–2006*

Hollace Ava Weiner and Kenneth D.
Roseman, editors
*Lone Stars of David: The Jews of Texas*

Jack Wertheimer, editor
*Jewish Education in an Age of Choice*

Edward S. Shapiro
*Crown Heights: Blacks, Jews, and the 1991*
*Brooklyn Riot*

Marcie Cohen Ferris and Mark I. Greenberg,
editors
*Jewish Roots in Southern Soil: A New*
*History*

Kirsten Fermaglich
*American Dreams and Nazi Nightmares:*

*Early Holocaust Consciousness and Liberal*
*America, 1957–1965*

Andrea Greenbaum, editor
*Jews of South Florida*

Sylvia Barack Fishman
*Double or Nothing? Jewish Families and*
*Mixed Marriage*

George M. Goodwin and Ellen Smith, editors
*The Jews of Rhode Island*

Shulamit Reinharz and Mark A. Raider,
editors
*American Jewish Women and the Zionist*
*Enterprise*

Michael E. Staub, editor
*The Jewish 1960s: An American Sourcebook*

Judah M. Cohen
*Through the Sands of Time: A History of*
*the Jewish Community of St. Thomas, U.S.*
*Virgin Islands*

Naomi W. Cohen
*The Americanization of Zionism, 1897–1948*

Seth Farber
*An American Orthodox Dreamer: Rabbi*
*Joseph B. Soloveitchik and Boston's*
*Maimonides School*

Ava F. Kahn and Marc Dollinger, editors
*California Jews*

Amy L. Sales and Leonard Saxe
*"How Goodly Are Thy Tents": Summer*
*Camps as Jewish Socializing Experiences*

Ori Z. Soltes
*Fixing the World: Jewish American Painters*
*in the Twentieth Century*

Gary P. Zola, editor
*The Dynamics of American Jewish History:*
*Jacob Rader Marcus's Essays on American*
*Jewry*

# Learning and Community

## Jewish Supplementary Schools in the Twenty-first Century

*Edited by* JACK WERTHEIMER

BRANDEIS UNIVERSITY PRESS
*Waltham, Massachusetts*

Published by University Press of New England
Hanover and London

Brandeis University Press
Published by University Press of New England,
One Court Street, Lebanon, NH 03766
www.upne.com

Printed in the United States of America
5  4  3  2  1

Library of Congress Cataloging-in-Publication Data
Learning and community : Jewish supplementary schools in the twenty-first century /
edited by Jack Wertheimer.
   p. cm. — (Brandeis series in American Jewish history, culture, and life)
Includes index.
ISBN 978-1-58465-770-5 (pbk. : alk.paper)
   1. Jewish religious education of children—United States.  2. Jewish religious schools—
United States.  I. Wertheimer, Jack.  II. Series
BM103.L373  2009
296.6'80830973—dc22      2009000998

 UNIVERSITY PRESS OF NEW ENGLAND is a member of the Green Press Initiative.
*The paper used in this book meets their minimum requirement for recycled paper.*

# Contents

Contributors                                                                          vii

Introduction                                                                           xi

## I. Innovative Small Schools

Chapter 1   Kehillah                                                                    3
            *Isa Aron with Nachama Skolnik Moskowitz*

Chapter 2   The Power of Their Commitments: Lessons for the                           47
            Jewish Community from a Small Synagogue School
            *Susan L. Shevitz with Marion Gribetz*

Chapter 3   Between Entrepreneurship and Jewish Mission:                               79
            The Making of a Chabad Hebrew School
            *Jack Wertheimer with Serene Victor*

## II. Re-Thinking Large Suburban Congregational Schools

Chapter 4   Belonging Before Belief                                                   113
            *Harold Wechsler with Cyd Beth Weissman*

Chapter 5   Adath Shalom Religious School: Strengths,                                 145
            Challenges, and Transitions
            *Randal F. Schnoor with Billy Mencow*

Chapter 6   Innovating Inside the Box: An Ongoing Process                             176
            to Improve a Congregational School
            *Susan L. Shevitz with Marion Gribetz*

Chapter 7   Promoting a Counterculture                                                207
            *Harold Wechsler with Cyd Beth Weissman*

Chapter 8   Beit Knesset Hazon: A Visionary Synagogue                                 236
            *Isa Aron with Nachama Skolnik Moskowitz*

## III. High School Models

Chapter 9   Western Hebrew High: A Place for Social                                   277
            Belonging and Personal Meaning
            *Randal F. Schnoor with Billy Mencow*

Chapter 10  Putting the School Back into the Supplementary                            308
            Jewish High School
            *Jack Wertheimer with Serene Victor*

Conclusion                                                                            347

Index                                                                                 363

Research for this project was sponsored by the Avi Chai Foundation, which has taken a strong interest in strengthening Jewish education in the United States. The research team is grateful to the foundation for its support and encouragement. During the course of the project, we received much helpful advice from Yossi Prager, North American director of the foundation and Deena Fuchs, the foundation's communications director.

# Contributors

**Isa Aron** is Professor of Jewish Education at the Rhea Hirsch School of Education, HUC-JIR, Los Angeles, where she teaches courses in teaching, philosophy of education, and organizational change. She was the founding director of the Experiment in Congregational Education, a project of the RHSOE, now in its sixteenth year. She continues to serve as the senior consultant to that project, which works with synagogues throughout the United States, helping them become congregations of learners and self-renewing congregations, and to re-imagine their religious schools. She is the author of *Becoming a Congregation of Learners* and *The Self Renewing Congregation*, both published by Jewish Lights Publications. She is currently engaged in a study of the long-term impact of synagogue change efforts, together with Steven M. Cohen, Lawrence Hoffman, and Ari Y. Kelman, which will be published in 2009.

**Marion Gribetz** is on the faculty of the Shoolman Graduate School of Jewish Education at Hebrew College in Newton, Massachusetts. She is also managing director of Gribetz Mencow Consultants, an independent consulting firm specializing in improving Jewish education. She has published, researched, taught, and consulted in all areas of Jewish education.

**Billy Mencow** founded Kolbo, Inc. in 1978, which grew into the nation's most innovative retailer of Judaica. Billy's new career in Jewish Education began as the high school coordinator at Temple Emunah in Lexington, Massachusetts, and as the director of post-graduate studies for the Solomon Schechter Day School of Greater Boston. He moved on to central agency work, and coordinated the Youth Educator Initiative (now YESOD) at BJE Boston. Billy has since served as director of Camp Ramah in New England from 2000 to 2005, and as associate director of the Bureau of Jewish Education in Boston. Billy currently consults to Jewish educational institutions in the United States and Israel in the areas of strategic planning and team building.

**Nachama Skolnik Moskowitz** is the senior director, as well as the director of curriculum resources at the Jewish Education Center of Cleveland. She has been a day school principal, congregational school director, and camp educator. Nachama is nationally known and respected for her curricular work and is the author of numerous student materials and teacher resources, including *The Ultimate Jewish Teacher Handbook* (ARE, 2003).

**Randal F. Schnoor**, a sociologist, teaches at the Centre for Jewish Studies at York University in Toronto. He is co-author, with Alex Pomson, of *Back to School: Jewish Day School as a Source of Meaning in the Lives of Adult Jews* (Wayne State University Press, 2008) and of the chapter titled "Bringing School Home" in the forthcoming *Jewish Day Schools, Jewish Communities: A Reconsideration* (London: Littman Library of Jewish Civilization). His research on Jewish identity has been published in academic journals such as *Sociology of Religion, Canadian Ethnic Studies*, and *Canadian Jewish Studies*. Since 2005 he has served as president of the Association for Canadian Jewish Studies.

**Susan L. Shevitz** is an educational consultant with a particular interest in congregations, religious pluralism in Jewish education, and patterns of leadership. She has served as an associate professor at Brandeis University, as a senior research associate at its Mandel Center for Studies in Jewish Education, and as an instructor at the Rabbinical School of Boston's Hebrew College, where her teaching has focused on the organizational contexts of rabbinic work as well as leadership. Recent publications include a review of efforts to improve congregational education over the last decade ("Don't Conduct, Improvise: New Approaches to Changing Jewish Schools," in Paul Flexner and Roberta Goodman, eds., *What We NOW Know about Jewish Education*) and "Building Community in a Pluralist Jewish High School," in Alex Pomson and Howard Deitscher, eds., *Jewish Day Schools, Jewish Communities*, The Littman Library of Jewish Civilization.

**Serene Victor** is lecturer and faculty leader of the DeLeT/MAT Program at Brandeis University. Previously, Serene was consultant for synagogue education for the United Synagogue of Conservative Judaism. She has served as education director at a large Conservative congregation, designed and directed a national institute for new school directors, supervised interns in the Hornstein Program in Jewish Communal Service at Brandeis University, and served as a mentor for new graduates of the Davidson School of

Education at the Jewish Theological Seminary. An alumna of the Mandel Teacher Educator Institute (MTEI), Serene received an honorary doctorate from the Jewish Theological Seminary.

**Harold Wechsler** is a professor of education at the Steinhardt School of Culture, Education, and Human Development, New York University. He co-directs Steinhardt's doctoral program in Education and Jewish Studies. His publications include *Jewish Learning in American Universities: The First Century* (with Paul Ritterband), *Access to Success in the Urban High School: The Middle College Movement*, *The Transfer Challenge*, and *The Qualified Student: A History of Selective College Admission in America, 1870–1970*. He also edits the annual *Almanac of Higher Education* for the National Education Association and co-edits the *ASHE Reader on the History of Higher Education* (with Linda Eisenmann and Lester Good-child). He is the 2008 president of the History of Education Society.

**Cyd Beth Weissman,** is the director of the New York Re-Imagine Project of the Experiment in Congregational Education (ECE) of the Rhea Hirsch School of Education of Hebrew Union College, where she also teaches Organizational Dynamics and Curriculum on the New York campus. Prior to her work with ECE, Cyd worked as the director of education at Congregation Beth Am Israel, Penn Valley, Pennsylvania, where she was a member of a team that created one of the earliest Shabbat-centered communal models of education. Her recent publications include: "Professional Development Requires a Discipline for Seeing Wholes," in the forthcoming book, *What We NOW Know About Jewish Education*; and *Vision by Evolutionaries and Revolutionaries*. Cyd also teaches for the Legacy Heritage Fund.

**Jack Wertheimer** is professor of American Jewish history at the Jewish Theological Seminary and serves as a consultant to the Avi Chai Foundation. In the latter capacity he has directed a project on the changing role of Jewish education in the American Jewish community, which culminated in an edited volume, *Family Matters: Jewish Education in an Age of Choice*. He has also completed a number of studies for the foundation on Jewish supplementary education, including most recently a census report. He directed this project on ten supplementary schools that work.

# Introduction

Jewish supplementary schools[1]—programs that meet on weekends and/or weekday afternoons when students have completed their general studies schooling and that enroll the majority of children receiving a Jewish education[2]—carry a heavy burden of responsibilities. Parents who enroll their children, congregations that invest large amounts of their financial resources in their schools, and religious and communal leaders who look to these programs to nurture the next generation of engaged Jews expect supplementary schools to deliver all or most of the following: a serviceable knowledge of Hebrew sufficient to enable students to perform at their Bar or Bat Mitzvah ceremony at age 13 and participate in religious services thereafter; an introduction to Jewish holidays and religious rituals; learning about the Biblical narrative and the trajectory of Jewish history; a personal connection to the Jewish people and appreciation for Israel; exposure to good Jewish values; and perhaps most important, positive feelings about being Jewish. All of this must be accomplished during anywhere from three to six hours of classes a week, meeting for under thirty weeks per year. Schools are also expected to attain these multiple goals even though the majority of students are in their care for no more than five years.

Since it is impossible in so short a time to address all of the learning objectives itemized above, schools make trade-offs. Most invest their energies first and foremost in imparting positive feelings about being Jewish by creating a warm and welcoming environment so that children will come to associate Jewish life with positive feelings; they also try to expose their students to joyful experiences of Jewish holidays and rituals. As to more substantive learning outcomes, some schools lavish considerably more attention on teaching synagogue skills as compared to teaching about Jewish history or Israel. In some, classes focus mainly on holidays and ritual observances, while other schools embrace a mission to teach Hebrew language reading or Jewish approaches to ethical issues. The choices can be wrenching.

Moreover, the challenges facing supplementary schools do not end with the paucity of time at their disposal. Here are a few of the more common obstacles impeding the work of these schools:

• The supplementary nature of the education imparts a message to young children about the limited importance of the enterprise. As parents are swept up by the social pressure to involve their children in sports, the arts, entertainment, tutoring, and other after-school activities, pressures mount to limit Jewish education even more, pressures that grow exponentially when teenagers are enthralled by the college chase. The fact that supplementary education takes place after school and grades do not "count" shapes the perception of children as to what is truly important.

• Teaching in supplementary schools is primarily part-time work and comes with meager compensation, which means that few schools employ educators with very much time to invest in remaking the system. The relatively low pay available to educators and the shortage of well-trained teachers result in a huge turnover in school directors and teaching faculty. This, in turn, limits the continuity of school programs. Even the finest schools must scramble to retain excellence when key personnel retire or move on to other positions.

• Sixty percent of schools enroll fewer than one hundred students and are under the auspices of small synagogues. This limits their ability to fund their schools, hire full-time directors, or provide enhancements. Lacking a critical mass of students and the budget to support anything other than a bare-bones, often volunteer, staff, smaller schools cannot even contemplate offering a richer array of programming.

• Many congregations continue to tie synagogue education to the Bar/Bat Mitzvah celebration, thinking this gives them leverage with families. It probably does, but the consequence is a distortion of Jewish education, which becomes focused on a one-time performance, rather than enculturation to a "way of life." It also reduces Jewish education to a coercive experience that families must endure—that is, they are instructed to attend a set number of religious services over the course of the year prior to the Bar/Bat Mitzvah. The linkage also places a strong emphasis upon the acquisition of skills needed at the event, rather than the broad range of education necessary to live as a Jew.

• As schools redefine themselves, they risk creating increased confusion about their actual mission. Indeed, quite a few educators now regard it as a terrible mistake even to speak of the synagogue program as a school, when in fact it is more akin to a setting of informal education, such as a camping experience. The newly revamped schools, they contend, should be measured against other settings of informal education, not seen as venues for cognitive learning and skill building. Still other educators claim they are accomplishing both goals—the cognitive and the affective. But which is the priority?

- Because most schools are based in synagogues, they are highly dependent upon the good will and support of the rabbi and congregational leadership. Quite a few of the former understand the importance of Jewish education and are also aware of the centrality of the school for recruiting and retaining members. But in some congregations, resentment builds because members without children in the school are heavily subsidizing those families that do make use of the congregational school through the high membership dues they pay. School budgets and the allocation of personnel resources within the congregation are a source of tension.
- Supplementary high schools have not been able to achieve their maximal impact because of ongoing turf battles. When based within congregations, they are hard-pressed to offer enriched programming, and they suffer from drastically limited school hours. They seem more effective when under communal auspices or when they serve a consortium of congregations, but rabbis are reluctant to relinquish "their" teens to programs not housed in their own synagogues, perhaps feeling that synagogues can best socialize teens by connecting them with personal role models.
- The distance of national organizations from the local scene and the limited influence of those organizations on the day-to-day running of schools force each school to invent its own curriculum or tailor a pre-existing one to the capabilities of its personnel. This generally is not a prescription for excellence, although some schools have transcended this challenge by investing large resources in their improvement.
- Most important: graduates of supplementary schools have claimed they learned little, found classes highly repetitious from year to year, and in the main felt little incentive to continue their Jewish education beyond the age of 13. In fact, the drop-off after grade 7 is shocking, and by grade 11 only small percentages of students are still enrolled. The record indicates that children are voting with their feet.

With all these limitations, it is not surprising that supplementary schools have come under intensive scrutiny by educators and communal leaders. The mood was particularly grim during the 1970s and 1980s when observers called for dismantling supplementary schools in favor of all-day Jewish schools, centrally coordinated communal schools, or even family education programs. Not surprisingly, the steady drumbeat of criticism led to serious demoralization among practitioners.[3]

Beginning in the 1990s, though, a new can-do spirit began to inspire experiments to rethink and improve what supplementary programs might accomplish. Benefiting from a modest injection of funding, several new initiatives have sought to engage individual schools in intensive revitalization programs, provided teachers with continuing education, and spurred the creation of innovative models and new configurations mixing formal and informal education.

The present study, conducted under the auspices of the Avi Chai Foundation, was designed to scrutinize a number of supplementary school models that have emerged in recent years.[4] Employing a method in the tradition of Sara Lawrence Lightfoot,[5] who created a qualitative methodology for studies in education called "portraiture," and building upon Elliot Eisner's belief in the ability of the "connoisseur" who by virtue of prior expertise can assess a school in a limited amount of time,[6] this project brought together a small group of knowledgeable observers to take a close look at a set of Jewish supplementary schools. Over the calendar year 2007, a team of ten researchers—five academics and five experienced educators with backgrounds in school administration—observed ten schools. The research team examined factors that go into the making of reasonably good supplementary programs—their school culture, professional and lay leadership, teaching staff, curriculum, extracurricular activities, and attention to parents and family education. Each school was studied by a matched partnership of one academic and one seasoned educator with the expectation that a binocular view would improve our understanding of what makes these schools tick.

In selecting these schools, my colleagues and I sought out a variety of settings differing in size, region, denominational affiliation, and approach. Three are under Reform auspices, two are Conservative congregational schools, one is Reconstructionist, and one a Chabad school; two are community high schools and one is a nondenominational, independent school. One school has under 50 students and another two have under 140 students; the rest have anywhere from 150 to 400 or more students. Four schools are located in Middle Atlantic states, two in New England, three in the West, and one in the Midwest. This study makes no pretense of having selected a representative sample of the total universe of supplementary schools, particularly as we have only limited information about that universe. Rather, we were guided to these schools by a number of informants who are knowledgeable about schools in various locales and under different auspices. Moreover, we intentionally sought out schools reputed to "work": we were looking for models of reasonable success, not failure.

Once we selected our sample of schools, we considered a number of questions: (1) How does each school define its main objectives and how does it seek to achieve them? (2) What do class sessions look like? (3) Does the school have a distinctive approach to Jewish supplementary education? (4) How does the school bring together its major components—mission, curriculum, personnel, professional and lay leadership? (5) What kinds of resources does the school marshal and from where are they drawn? (6) How self-reflective are the key players in the school and how well do they work together? (7) To what extent does the school hold itself and its staff accountable for delivering an effective Jewish education? (8) What can others learn from this school if they seek to improve their own programs?

Each chapter of this study presents one distinctive school. Since the aim has been to understand how each school came to take its particular course, these portraits devote attention to the key leaders, both educators and lay leaders, who have shaped the school. Within these chapters, the reader will be able to observe vicariously what goes on in classes and how the key personnel interact with one another and with the students. Readers will be able to examine curricula and in one case exam questions and answers. They will be able overhear the voices of students, parents, and educators as they reflect on the meanings they attach to the school and its programs. And to some extent, readers will be able to discern the impact of the school on students.

By focusing on schools that work, this study offers no judgment about the condition of supplementary Jewish education overall. Currently, there is no basis on which to evaluate the roughly two thousand Jewish supplementary schools in the United States. Indeed, even finding ten effective schools proved complex because no central clearinghouse of information on supplementary schools exists. The project team relied upon the informed judgment of observers around the country to identify schools worthy of study—and even then it rejected schools of high repute that were undergoing a major transition in educational leadership or seemed to have stagnated. Thus, this is emphatically *not* a report on the state of the field. Nor does this book address the larger question of whether the time has come to invent a better system of part-time Jewish education. This study also does not draw any conclusions about the relative merits of this type of educational experience as compared to other forms of Jewish schooling.

What it does aim to illuminate are a number of issues of concern to supplementary schools and their supporters. Among the questions addressed by individual chapters are:

- How can a school maximize every moment of its time with students who attend only once a week for three hours?
- How can a small school lacking in resources, including trained teachers, still manage to give its students a good Jewish education?
- What types of experiential learning can a school foster to help students learn to pray, treat one another with respect, and identify strongly with the Jewish people?
- What kind of Hebrew can be taught and what are attainable goals?
- What should school heads be expected to do and not to do?
- How can high school programs offer serious study while continuing to attract overextended students?
- What is gained and lost when a supplementary school functions as a school with academic expectations?
- How might a supplementary school define its learning expectations and insure that its educators attain those objectives?
- What constructive roles can parents play to help turn a school around?
- What is the role of the senior rabbi? How involved must the rabbi be?
- What are the types of learning we can hope students will take away from a supplementary school experience?
- What broader lessons can we learn from the cumulative findings presented by these portraits? (This question is addressed explicitly in the Conclusion.)

The primary purpose of this volume is to explain how some supplementary schools deliver a reasonably effective Jewish education, whether in conventional ways or by taking their programs in unexpected directions. We have sought to bring to life some bold new approaches and to give voice to the flesh and blood students who populate these schools and the adults who work to create a worthwhile setting for Jewish education—teachers, administrators, clergy, parents, and volunteer leaders. As will become evident, no single lever will make a school successful; rather, the efforts of educators, teachers, synagogue personnel, curriculum designers, and lay leaders all have an important role to play in shaping the school program and setting. Nor is there only one way to deliver a reasonably good Jewish education: schools of different sizes, denominations, and styles can have a positive impact. There are a variety of ways to impart a love of Jewish living and learning. The research team encountered some quite compelling and moving examples. By capturing what is happening in ten interesting schools around the country, this volume hopes to shed light on what can be accomplished in supplementary Jewish schools under the best of circumstances.

## Notes

1. The field of supplementary Jewish education suffers from an inadequacy of precise language. To some, the term supplementary is offensive because it downgrades Jewish education to secondary status. But the term preferred by some today, complementary education, confuses more than clarifies. Older terms such as congregational education miss the mark because some programs are independent of synagogues; religious school is inadequate to cover schools that do not teach Judaism; and Hebrew school hardly does justice to programs that predominantly teach subjects other than language. Moreover, the use of the word school may also do a disservice in setting up expectations of formal study that cannot be met by part-time supplementary Jewish education.

2. Student enrollments in supplementary schools still exceed those of Jewish day schools by approximately 230,000 to 172,000 in grades K–12, but that margin has narrowed considerably over the past 50 years.

3. I have detailed the downward spiral of these schools in Jack Wertheimer, "Jewish Education in the United States: Recent Trends and Issues," *American Jewish Year Book*, 1999, pp. 37–42

4. Other efforts included an overview of recent trends and a census. The former appeared under the title, *Recent Trends in Supplementary Jewish Education* (2007), and the latter as *A Census of Jewish Supplementary Schools in the United States, 2006–2007*, published in 2008. Both can be downloaded at the website www.avichai .org.

5. Sara Lawrence-Lightfoot, *The Good High School: Portraits of Character and Culture* (New York: Basic Books, 1983). An outstanding recent example of a study presenting a portrait and analysis of a Jewish supplementary school in its synagogue setting is Joseph B. Reimer's *Succeeding at Jewish Education: How One Synagogue Made It Work* (Philadelphia: Jewish Publication Society, 1997).

6. Elliot W. Eisner, *Re-Imagining Schools: Selected Works of Elliot Eisner* (London and New York: Taylor and Francis, 2005).

# I. *Innovative Small Schools*

# CHAPTER 1

# Kehillah

ISA ARON AND NACHAMA SKOLNIK MOSKOWITZ

At 3:30 on a Wednesday afternoon the *Anafim* (fourth and fifth graders) at Kehillat Ha'ir are gathered around the table in their classroom for *kibud* (snack). On the table are water, slices of apple, and some pita bread. With only minimal direction from Shimon Feld, their teacher, the students say three *brachot* (blessings), one for the water, one for the fruit, and a third for the bread. As they munch on their snacks, the following conversation takes place:

*Shaul:*[1] Shimon, why is the *brachah* (blessing) over water just the general *brachah* over everything?

*Rina:* Yes, water is really important; it is the source of life, especially in Israel. Why doesn't it have its own *brachah,* just like bread and wine do?

*Shimon:* Well, my answer is pretty complicated—bread and wine were "high tech" things for their own times. There were many steps involved in making them. So we are partners with God in making them, and they deserve a special *brachah.*

*Yoav:* If bread and wine were so high tech, what about cheese?

*Shimon:* Cheese is complicated . . . it's actually made with the intestines of animals.

*Dena:* Why isn't there a *brachah* over meat?

*Shoshi:* Nobody should eat meat.

The conversation weaves in and out—who eats meat and who is vegetarian, which meats are kosher and which aren't. The atmosphere is quiet and calm. Everyone seems to be listening, or, if not listening, at least quiet. Of the fifteen students present, about eight or nine are actively participating. A few others have turned their backs to the table, or are staring into space; but, every once in a while, one of them chimes in with a question or a comment, evidence that they've been following the conversation closely. At 3:48 Shimon glances at the clock, sees that the time for *kibud* is just about over, and says: "OK guys, *ahat, shtayim shalosh* (one, two, three)." In unison, the students launch into an abbreviated and tuneful version of *birkat hamazon* (grace after meals).

This brief vignette captures the essence of Kehillah: the conversation was both serious and easygoing; the tone was light, but the ideas deep. Though the teacher's response to the initial question was complex, the students remained engaged without any external prompting.

While the conversation was spontaneous, the groundwork for it had been meticulously laid. Kehillah is a carefully constructed hybrid of the formal and the informal; of the norms of home and the norms of the classroom; of the teacher-led and the student-led. Kehillah has taken the elements of the supplementary school (the subject matter), the summer camp (the role of the counselor and the fun routines), and the after-school program[2] and woven them together into a unique and fascinating whole.

And there is one additional, crucial thread—a vision of community. To quote Kehillah's website: "To think of Kehillah as only a Hebrew school/afterschool misses the essence of what makes [us] special. Though Hebrew school and after school are still at the core of what Kehillah does, since its beginning, Kehillah has become a community."

In Hebrew, the word *kehillah* means "community," and the overall goal at Kehillah is to create community, among the students, the teachers, and the parents. The children in *Anafim* could engage Shimon in this kind of conversation because they have known him for years; before he became their teacher he was a member of their community, and they were members of his.

As Shimon puts it, Kehillah's assumption is that "serious Jewish learning always happens in community, so by carefully creating community we create a viable environment for learning." Below we will elaborate upon this assumption and others, but we will begin, first, with some basic information about this one-of-a-kind institution.

# Some Facts about Kehillah

Before its expansion in 2008, Kehillah had two independently incorporated, but educationally interconnected sites, one urban (Kehillat Ha'ir[3]), the other suburban (Kehillat Haparvar). Kehillat Ha'ir was founded in 1991 by a parent looking for a way to maintain her children's Hebrew skills after a year's sabbatical in Israel, and Melanie Fried, a former Young Judean who had been working in the field of after-school care. In its early years it was as much an after-school facility as a provider of Jewish education. However, as the school became committed to paying its teachers higher salaries, and hiring curriculum coordinators as well, it priced itself out of the after-school childcare market (it charges approximately $50 more per month than local after-school facilities for each day of the week that the student attends). Today, the vast majority of students attend two days a week (the minimum requirement) and are strongly encouraged to enroll on either Monday or Tuesday and Wednesday or Thursday, so that they are in sync with the curriculum. In 2006–07 Kehillat Ha'ir also had a Friday program for the half-dozen students who needed aftercare that day.

Kehillat Haparvar was founded in the fall of 2003 by parents who had heard about Kehillat Ha'ir. The two sites are separately incorporated and have very different parent populations, as will be discussed below. Their core beliefs and structure are identical, and they utilize the same curriculum, working together on its revisions and enhancements.

In keeping with the value of community, Kehillah is small by design. In the 2006–07 school year Kehillat Ha'ir had a total of 114 students K–12. Some have speculated that with a little effort they might add many more students—perhaps even doubling in size—but space constraints and the difficulty of finding qualified teachers keep them from expanding. Kehillat Haparvar had 66 students in 2006–07 and 80 in 2007–08. It anticipates having 100 students in grades K–6 by the time the current students' younger siblings are ready to join; preferring to limit its size, it maintains a waiting list for new families. The families in Kehillat Ha'ir vary greatly in terms of religious observance, intermarriage, synagogue affiliation, sexual orientation, economic bracket, and whether or not both parents work. Kehillat Haparvar's families are somewhat more homogenous—three-fourths are affiliated with either a synagogue or a *minyan*, and only a handful are intermarried.

Tuition at Kehillat Haparvar is $3,000 per year for two days; at Kehillat Ha'ir it is $3,600 for two days.

The daily schedule at Kehillat Ha'ir for pre-K through grade 8, is as follows:

2:00 - *Z'man Chofshi*: kids arrive and have "free time"

3:00 - *Z'man Bachutz*: "outside time"

3:30 - *Z'man Kibbud*: "snack time"

3:50 - *Z'man Ivrit*: "Hebrew time"

4:40 - *Z'man Yahadut*: "Judaica time"

5:25 - *Z'man Shirah*: "song time"

5:45 - *L'hitraot*: "goodbye and we'll see you soon"

The schedule for Kehillat Haparvar is slightly different, in accordance with the public school schedule in the surrounding suburban townships. When there is sufficient interest and available staff, Kehillat Ha'ir runs a very low-key program on Friday afternoons, as a service to the parents who require daycare.

Both schools meet in the basements of local churches, which, in both cases, have been remarkably accommodating. The hallways and classrooms are filled with Kehillah's materials: Hebrew signs, holiday illustrations, lists of Hebrew vocabulary and grammatical forms, posters made by teachers, and, of course, the work of students. Nearly every sign is in Hebrew and all are made by either the staff or the students. The classrooms, too, have a "cozy" atmosphere, each with a sofa, tables and chairs; there are no desks. The very small and crowded offices are rather informal as well.

Part of the reason for Kehillah's casual ambiance is that a very small portion of its budget is devoted to maintenance. While the urban site has a custodian, in the suburban site members of the *tsevet* (staff) do their own vacuuming and empty their own trash cans at the end of the day.

## Kehillah's Vision and Assumptions

Kehillah's space and the informality serve as a kind of screening device for families and staff; anyone comfortable pulling up his or her own folding chair in the office on the initial visit will fit right in.

But just as spontaneous should not be confused with unthinking, *heimish* should not be confused with haphazard. Underlying the informality are two carefully articulated assumptions. First and foremost is that at this "compelling part of the day" children require both structure and freedom; they should be challenged, but also given the chance to be themselves. This embrace of seeming contradiction yields what Shimon (who, in addition to being a teacher was, in 2006–07, the coordinator of the *Yahadut* [Judaica] curriculum) refers to as "the Kehillah tone: It's playful and lively. It's sophisticated and rich." As Miriam Berg, director of Kehillat Haparvar, puts it, "Kehillah is proof that you can have education that is both incredibly rigorous and incredibly fun."

In contrast to other supplementary schools, the "teaching day" at Kehillah begins when the children arrive. Melanie says: "Teaching here isn't just teaching *Yahadut*, just teaching *Ivrit*. We talk about this all the time that teaching begins from the moment the kids get off the bus or the moment they are dropped off from their car pool. From the moment you are asking them *ma nishma* (how are things going?) your teaching has begun. Whether they are playing [the game] 'Battleship' in Hebrew on the rug, that time of day is just as important as *z'man Ivrit*."

According to Tom Steiner, a career changer who teaches at Kehillah while studying to be a cantor and an educator, this combination of formal and informal gives Kehillah an advantage over the schools in which he has previously taught: "These are all things that I didn't have in my prior religious school teaching experience: Really taking the time to talk about kids, what their needs are, who their friends are, who is more sociable, who needs a different kind of help. We try to really focus on not just the outstanding and most troublesome kids but also the kids who could, in other systems, kind of fall through the cracks."

Parents too appreciate this quality. A board member at Kehillat Haparvar notes: "It's not that they are coming here and just learning. They come here and now they are out on the playground together, just the way they are with their public school friends . . . So it's just an extension of their life with their friends in our neighborhood at school . . . Like you are here and you're living and then you're learning and then you're playing and you're eating, you're dancing, you're singing—really like camp—really like free-flow camp, I think." As this mother suggests, Kehillah resembles a summer camp, in which free play and directed learning are interwoven. This easy flow between the structured and the unstructured serves as the fertile ground for the sprouting of spontaneous but significant discussions, such as the discussion of *brachot* recounted at the beginning of this chapter.

The mix of high purpose and playful expression is possible because of Kehillah's commitment to the value of *kavod*, respect. To quote the website: "We emphasize community building through the practice of *kavod*, respect, in all aspects of our lives—respect for oneself, for others, and for the environment and space that we share and in which we live and learn. The children are recognized and acknowledged by their teachers and their peers for acts of *kavod*. *Kavod* is a cornerstone at Kehillah from which all the curriculum is built."

We will have more to say about the way the value of *kavod* is expressed in the classroom and in the way Kehillah treats its teachers. But first, we need to explain Kehillah's second key assumption—that in order for students to become part of a learning community, their teachers, too, must form a learning community. This expectation is communicated to prospective teachers at their very first interview, and is part of what attracts the "right" teacher. Melanie explains: "So that's part of the draw . . . you are not just . . . teaching and leaving. You are becoming part of a learning community. And that's part of the interviewing process, meaning that when I'm talking to prospective teachers they are hearing that working in Kehillah means you are making a commitment to your own learning, your own learning about teaching and your own learning in terms of *Ivrit* and *Yahadut*. And that working here as a teacher means you are joining a community."

The creation of each year's community of teachers begins in the fall with an eight-day orientation attended by everyone, veterans and newcomers alike. Once the school year begins, teachers study the curriculum at an adult level before thinking about how to translate it for their students. In addition, they study their teaching—in individual reflection, with their mentor, and as a community. To quote Melanie: "So when teachers accept a job here they know that I will be in and out of their classroom all the time. They're going to be observed, they're going to be talking about their teaching, They're going to be reflecting on their teaching. This is going to be a lot of work. They are going to be very exposed. So for the people who choose to work at Kehillah, and who we hire, that has become an attractive piece of working at Kehillah, which doesn't mean that it's not scary and not vulnerable, but that is an attraction."

Bina Gibson, one of the teachers at Kehillat Haparvar, appreciates the principle of "making teaching a community property": "I look forward to our *tsevet* [staff] meetings. It's fun, in a way, to be able to exchange ideas. I build off of other people's ideas . . . Having that open forum to discuss ideas and to see what other people are doing really makes a difference."

Organizational theorist Edgar Schein argues that the culture of an organization is most effective when the observed regularities ("the way we do things around here") reflect the norms that are stated, and are not contradicted or undercut by any shared tacit assumptions (underlying, though not fully stated, beliefs).[4] From this perspective, Kehillah's culture seems particularly cohesive and healthy. Its central values, community and *kavod*, are stated on its website, referred to often, written into the curriculum, translated into a variety of activities, conveyed to teachers both implicitly and explicitly, and form the subtext of much of what goes on in the classrooms.

As if creating community and inculcating the value of *kavod*, were not complicated enough, Kehillah also teaches two subjects more formally— *Ivrit* (Hebrew) and *Yahadut* (Judaica). Not surprisingly, Kehillah's approach to both of these subjects is as carefully reasoned as it is unconventional, as will be discussed below. At this point, we simply want to note that, like everything else about Kehillah, its goals for its students are also complex. On the one hand, there are meticulous rubrics that chart each student's progress in *Ivrit*. On the other hand, Kehillah's ultimate goal is for the students to appreciate the depth and complexity of Judaism. Shimon puts it this way: "My *Anafim* [fourth and fifth graders] that I teach, they think that the Jewish tradition is important . . . Even if in four years time they can't remember a single one of those key words that I taught them this year, but they have a sense that the Jewish tradition is deep and meaningful and accessible to them, then I think we've not done too badly . . . Everyone speaks the language of . . . teaching them to be lifelong learners, . . . but what is the thing that's going to make someone want to return to it? Having a set of tools to return to is important, but so is having a conviction that there's something worthwhile to be returned to."

With all this as an introduction, we will examine in greater detail Kehillah's *tsevet*, its curriculum, its governance structure, and its work with parents. Throughout, we will discuss the challenges Kehillah faces.

## Kehillah's Tsevet

### Senior Members of the Tsevet

Understanding Melanie Fried's background helps one understand just how she became the founder of Kehillah. Melanie grew up in East Lansing, Michigan, where her parents helped found a small congregation that relied for many years on its members to do everything. Growing up, both she and her siblings were very involved in Young Judea. Upon graduation from college, she became a kindergarten teacher; and after teaching for a number of years, she moved to the city in which Kehillah is located, to do graduate work in education. In order to support herself in graduate school, she worked in an after-school program. She says, "I just completely fell in love with that time of day—it's a very compelling time of day for me. Because the kids had been in school all day and they still needed to be away from home because their parent or parents were working. And the challenge of making that time of day worthwhile for them and making that time of day a time that the kids felt known, cared about, and felt like they were continuing to learn. That turned me on."

While the early background of Miriam Berg, the director of Kehillat Haparvar, does not seem as though it would have led her to Kehillah, the trajectory of her post-college interests does. As a child, Miriam attended a Conservative religious school and a JCC camp, both of which she recalls as "fine, but not particularly compelling or exciting." Her interest in Judaism grew, however, as she became increasingly active in the student-run Hillel at the small liberal arts college she attended; this led her to spend her junior year in Israel. While at college, "I taught Hebrew school to make a little money, but it was pretty clear to me that it was not at all educationally interesting. It was a sort of typical bad experience doing it." Much more compelling was the teaching she did in a program called Upward Bound and a number of other urban and rural poverty programs. Upon graduation, Miriam moved to the city and began teaching at Citizen Schools, an after-school program for middle school children.[5] Here is her story about how she ended up at Kehillah:

> I met this woman who said, "What are you doing next year?" And I said, "Oh, I don't know." And she said, "There's this program that I think you should go check out." And I said, "I do *not* teach Hebrew school. I'm an educator. I care about education. I do not teach Hebrew school." And she said, "No, you really need to check it out. It's in your neighborhood, this woman is amazing—the director. You need to meet her, and I really just think it would be a good place for you." And so for whatever reason I called Melanie . . . Melanie said, "Why don't you come by?" And I said, "I'm not interviewing, because I don't teach Hebrew school." And she said, "Okay, but just come and say hello." And so I stormed in . . . "I don't teach . . ." And that was seven years ago. So I guess I do teach Hebrew school, it turns out.

While teaching part-time at Kehillat Ha'ir, Miriam studied for her master's degree in education at a local university and did some work at a center for Jewish education at another university. As Kehillat Haparvar was in formation, Miriam and other staff at Kehillat Ha'ir were brought on as consultants; after the first director at the new site didn't work out, Miriam assumed the position of director.

What Melanie and Miriam have in common is their early experience in "do-it-yourself" Jewish institutions, and, of course, their work experience in after-school programs. Unlike either of them, Shimon Feld was always on a path to becoming a Jewish educator. He grew up in England, where he was active in one of the Reform youth movements. His major in college was "academic studies of the Jewish tradition"; he went on to do an M.A. in Judaic studies at the Hebrew University in Jerusalem. He followed a girlfriend (who later became his wife) to the United States, and began working part time at Kehillat Ha'ir. After two years he became the coordinator of the *Yahadut* curriculum, which, combined with teaching, is a full-time job. Two years after that, when Melanie announced her intention to leave Kehillah, Shimon was appointed director of Kehillat Ha'ir, beginning in the 2007–08 school year.

Not apparent from these more formal biographies is how much both Miriam and Shimon have benefited from Melanie's mentoring. Kehillah's vision of a teacher-community meant that both of them met with her regularly, individually, as well as in meetings of the whole *tsevet*. Miriam and Shimon became good friends, and work together a great deal on the *Yahadut* curriculum.

A fourth senior member of the *tsevet* during 2006–07, Dalia Levy, was born in Israel, and earned a B.A. in psychology and the humanities, and an M.A. in cinema from Tel Aviv University. Like Shimon, she followed a boyfriend to the United States. She worked part time for the Jewish Organizing Initiative, where the director, knowing that Dalia would need additional part-time work, referred her to Kehillah. As a teacher, Dalia's interest in Kehillah's Hebrew curriculum grew. She took a number of courses with the Hebrew professor who is the architect of Kehillah's Hebrew program (more on this below), and attended workshops at a local day school. Two years ago she became the coordinator of the curriculum in *Ivrit*. She too works closely with Miriam (Kehillat Haparvar being too small to afford full-time curriculum coordinators, Miriam fulfills those roles).

There is a fifth senior member of the *tsevet*, who, in 2006–07, only worked part time—Beth Davids, who does teacher supervision at Kehillat Ha'ir. Beth, like Melanie, has a Young Judea background: she learned of Kehillah through the mother of one of her campers. She began teaching at Kehillah in 1997, and has filled a variety of positions, including curriculum coordinator. Like Miriam, Beth did graduate work in education while teaching at Kehillah.

## The Teachers

The practical implications of Kehillah's two foundational principles, connecting the formal and informal and creating a community of learners, are far reaching, and make Kehillah different from the typical Jewish afternoon program. In order to maintain a connection between the more unstructured parts of the afternoon (when students play outside or hang out indoors) and the more structured times (*z'man Ivrit* and *z'man Yahadut*), teachers at Kehillah must be fully present for the entire four hours. There are no "playground monitors" at Kehillah, and teachers are not busy at the copying machine or telephone while the children are present. Rather, they are hanging out with the children: greeting them (in Hebrew), engaging them in conversation, playing board games, and doing art projects.

In keeping with the value of community, all teachers work four days a week.[6] Moreover, teachers are paid for planning and supervision meetings that take place before the children arrive, as well as for time spent creating and reproducing materials; this amounts to 24–26 hours a week.

Beginning teachers are paid approximately $20.00 an hour, with increases as they gain more experience. Because Kehillah has no secretarial staff, clerical functions are divided among those teachers who are interested in earning additional income. In the 2006–07 school year the *tsevet* of Kehillat Ha'ir (which has been in existence long enough to have both middle school and high school programs) numbered thirteen. In addition to the director and the curriculum coordinators, who all worked full time, there was a fourth full-time employee, a recent college graduate who coordinated the *Tichon* (high school) program and performed various secretarial functions. Kehillat Haparvar, whose enrollment (and hence budget) was much smaller, had a *tsevet* of seven. Only the director worked full time. Two additional members of the *tsevet* worked thirty hours per week; they coordinated the family programs and helped with budgeting and administration.

All members of the *tsevet* are eligible to receive health benefits through a state-wide program for the staff of nonprofit institutions, though in Kehillat Ha'ir those who are not full-time must pay into the system. In 2007 the board of Kehillah Haparvar voted to pay 40 percent of the health-care premiums for part-time members of the *tsevet*, and 90 percent of the premiums for full-time members.

Kehillah's teachers are all college graduates; aside from that, their backgrounds vary. Some are taking time off before starting graduate school; others are already in graduate school; still others are part-time moms. At

Kehillat Ha'ir a number of the teachers are Israeli born; in fact, one Israeli teacher came to the United States in order to teach at Kehillah. Most teachers stay two or three years. Those who stay longer typically move up to take on additional responsibilities, such as curriculum development or family education.[7]

## Vignettes of the Teachers in Action

Kehillah's vision of the ideal teacher is very ambitious: s/he should care deeply about both the children and the subject matter; participate fully in the community; and have the skills to teach in a facilitative, engaging way, rather than a more directive, authoritative one. This is a very tall order, especially given the transient nature of the teacher population. In this section we will describe two classes we observed: one flawlessly executed and achieved its goals, the other, though engaging, failed to achieve its goals.

On a May afternoon, in the week before Shavuot, Bina Gibson met with 11 *Anafim* at Kehillat Haparvar. They had spent the past three weeks studying about the different meanings of "Israel," and this was the penultimate session of this unit. After some preliminaries, Bina asked:

*Bina:* What do you need to do to help your partner study a text?

*Leora:* Share your ideas.

*Dvora:* I know—use examples.

*Bina:* Nice. Remember the activity we did with the last text we studied, when we talked about how to disagree with *kavod*? We did it on the board. [Students nod their heads]

*Bina:* I am going to give you sheets, put you in *hevruta* [study partners]—to see what you think, then see what your partner thinks, and then there are questions to answer.

Bina counted the students off by six, so each would have a partner; she took the eleventh student as her partner. She gave instructions in English, interspersed with the Hebrew words Kehillah students are familiar with: "Each *hevruta* should have a *daf* [page], and you can go to the *shulchan* [table] or to the *shatiach* [rug]."[8] The worksheet Bina distributed contained the Biblical story of Jacob wrestling with the angel (Genesis 32:25–33), with two questions at the bottom:

- How do you understand the text? How is it different from how your partner understands it?
- Do you think it is important that Jews are called Israel? Does this differ from how your partner understands it?

The students went right to work, and soon you could hear a pleasant buzz around the room. Ten minutes later, Bina called them together: *"Anafim,* can we sit in a *ma'agal* [circle]? I want to briefly discuss. *B'maagal* [in a circle]. Leah, I need you not on that *kiseh* [chair]." Once they were settled, she proceeded:

*Bina:* This is an interesting story. What does Jacob get his name changed to?

*Students:* Israel.

*Bina:* It's interesting, this is the fourth week that we have talked about *Yisrael.*

The students reviewed what they had discussed in previous sessions. Bina asked, "What is this story about?" One of the students summarized the story concisely. Bina continued:

*Bina:* We are part of *Am Yisrael.* What does this story mean to us?

*Leah:* Israel is important to the Jews.

*Bina:* But it's not just the state . . .

*Leah:* It's the people too.

*Bina:* Noa said something interesting while we were studying together . . .

*Noa:* It's not necessarily a physical wrestling.

*Bina:* In this case it was a physical struggle. But often Jews struggle with things, like *kashrut.*

Bina described her own internal debates about buying a nonkosher turkey sandwich in the student cafeteria at her graduate school. She then returned to a short story she had begun reading during *z'man kibud,* a story for young readers about a girl who struggles with her Jewish identity.

This brief teaching segment seems so simple, but only because Bina is so skilled. She did not talk *at* the students, but facilitated a discussion, much like a discussion one might have among adults. Bina paid close attention to what the students were saying. This enabled her to bring Noa's comment into the discussion, and to help Leah self-correct, showing that she understood that Israel was more than a country.

In keeping with Kehillah's philosophy, Bina felt comfortable sharing with the class her struggles about keeping kosher. In her individual *hevruta* study, Bina said, at one point: "Do you remember how we talked at the beginning of the week how Sarai and Avram changed their names? Those who choose Judaism are blessed, and they get to change their names." The students know that Bina grew up not knowing anything about Judaism; that she (like some of them) comes from a mixed marriage; and that she, like Avraham, Sarah, and Ya'akov, changed her name. And one final thing to note—Bina had no classroom management problems. She gave instructions effortlessly, weaving in a number of basic Hebrew terms; and the students responded with alacrity.

In contrast, the following lesson of *Nitzanim* (second and third graders) in Kehillat Haparvar, was taught by Brad Green. The class had been reading *My Name is Rachamim*, the story of a boy's escape from Ethiopia to Israel. Brad said, "We're going to learn that wherever Jews are, we are supposed to take care of each other." He asked a boy to read what was written on the board in both Hebrew and English: "All of Israel is responsible for each other."

*Brad:* Why were these people in Ethiopia in danger, from what we've read so far in the book?

*Dvora:* They had no water.

*Brad:* What was the word with an F?

*Several students:* Famine.

*Brad:* We're going to learn some more about them. Sometimes Jews are in danger.

*Jonathan:* Not me.

*Brad:* That's great, but in other parts of the world, Jewish people are in danger. Here it's . . .

*Avi:* Like Adolf Hitler.

*Brad:* Yes like that.

*Gal* [picking up on Avi's comment]: It was about our religion, but I still don't get that.

*Brad:* The State of Israel is able to help other communities, other Jewish communities that are in danger. At the end of class today, we will finish the book. The book says that the Israeli government flew planes into certain parts of Africa. Special soldiers walked in the desert and snuck them out of their land. Almost like the Passover story.

*Yaffa:* Isn't that what's happening in that place in Africa. Like Darfa [*sic*]?

*Brad:* Darfur.

*Yaffa:* Aren't there Jewish people there?

*Brad:* There might be.

Brad was so intent on telling the students the message of the book that he either ignored or gave facile responses to a number of student comments, for example, those about Hitler and Darfur. While these comments were tangential to the discussion, they were thoughtful and deserved either a thoughtful reply or a promise that this subject would be taken up later.

More problematic was the activity that followed, in which Brad took the students upstairs to the auditorium, where they constructed an obstacle course. Brad introduced the activity in the following way:

*Brad:* Everyone will start here. We're going to pretend we are like the Beta Yisrael, who needed to walk past dangers like robbers, thieves, soldiers.

*Noam:* Like the Underground Railroad.

*David:* Like the subway.

*Brad:* Kinda like that. I will put everyone into pairs. Remember that everyone is escaping . . . to meet the planes that would take them to Israel.

They set up the obstacle course, and Brad explained that they would work in pairs, one student blindfolded, the other one guiding him or her through the maze. Brad asked, "Are there any questions about how the game works?" After each pair had crawled through the obstacle course twice, Brad gathered them in a circle, asking, "Using your thumbs, how did you think you did?" The students indicated thumbs up, and Brad asked why.

*David:* People are working together really good and having fun.

*Yaffa:* She did a really good job guiding me.

*Brad:* How did it feel to guide other people to safety?

*Avi:* I was the boss.

*Noam:* I didn't want them to bash into something because they would get hurt.

*Dvora:* It was, like, if they were blind somebody would have to guide them through.

*Student:* It felt like it was your responsibility, so they wouldn't fall down.

*Brad:* This was to help us think about what it means to be responsible for others.

*Jonathan:* It's almost like playing Game Cube. You're guiding them around to places you can see, but they can't. The people can see, but not really.

*Brad:* How do you think it might have felt for those who needed to walk through the desert?

*Students calling out:* Hungry, tired, sad.

*Brad:* Okay, put things into the boxes and put them under the table and then sit on the rug.

The goal of the obstacle course was to give the students an experience of helping one another, to reinforce the message that Jews are responsible for one another. Unfortunately, the message was undercut by the fact that the students had so much fun doing the activity, and that Brad himself referred to it as a game. At the end he was given an opportunity to drive his message home, when the students told him how good it felt for them to guide one another; but he failed to pick up on these comments and make the connection for them. And finally, contrast Brad's instructions with Bina's. While she effortlessly used Hebrew words, his instructions were entirely in English.

## *Working with the Teachers*

Kehillah is fully aware of the limitations of its teachers, and invests a great deal in supervising and supporting them. Four members of Kehillah's senior *tsevet* participated in a national teacher educator initiative. Many of the ideas and approaches promoted by that program reinforced their natural instincts and what they had learned in graduate school. Because the four of them spent so much time together thinking about teacher support and supervision, they were in a perfect position to experiment with new approaches to professional development, and learn from their experiments. The following structure for teacher development is the result.

As mentioned above, the year begins with an eight-day orientation, whose purpose is to create a community and to work on some of the challenges of teaching at Kehillah. During these eight days, members of the *tsevet* learn together, bond with one another, and begin to create their own *brit* (covenant), articulating their responsibilities to one another. They also learn about Kehillah's unique approach to *Ivrit* and *Yahadut*, work on the curriculum, and discuss how to facilitate classroom activities with *kavod*. Once school is in session, teachers can expect to have weekly meetings of the tsevet, regular supervisory meetings focusing on teaching skills, as well as planning meetings regarding *Ivrit* and *Yahadut*.

Part of the planning meeting for *Yahadut* involves an adult level exploration of the topics about to be taught. Beth explains the reasoning behind this: "If the teacher hasn't engaged with the content on their own in some way, found some kind of meaning . . . and conviction about it, they're not going to be good. Then it's less exciting to students—they get something that is pediatric." Supervisory meetings are usually devoted to problem solving. For example, a teacher was having trouble with one of her students, so she was given an assignment to observe him as he played during *z'man chofshi* (free time). Miriam explains this assignment: "I wanted her to get to know him outside of the classroom, where he was quite difficult. Who does he choose to sit next to? We gave her a whole list of questions for her to observe, and then she came back and she could talk about him in a different way."

In this way, and many others, the directors and (in Kehillat Ha'ir) the teacher supervisors support and challenge the teacher. But they realize that they are asking teachers to stretch a great deal. As Beth says: "While we were in [the teacher educator program] we were given a continuum of teacher development, and I studied it for a while, and started laughing, because [at Kehillah] we were asking new teachers to be at the intermediate or advanced level, conceptually and practically. So we have tried to figure out how to better support the teachers we are able to bring in for twenty-six hours a week."

We observed Miriam working with Tom on classroom management with his Hebrew class, *kitah hey* (level five). Miriam had videotaped a prior class, in which the students had worked individually on their own projects. This type of activity is difficult for many teachers to manage, and most avoid it, either teaching to the whole class or presenting the students with very limited choices. But Kehillah takes seriously Howard Gardner's theory of multiple intelligences, and aspires to give students a range of activities from which to choose. So Tom and Miriam were viewing the video together, to see where the students had gone off-task, and to discuss how Tom could manage such a complicated situation better the next time.

They saw on the video that one of the students across the room from Tom had asked him for directions, and that, without moving, he had answered her very loudly, which distracted some of the other students. After Tom noted that he should have crossed the room instead, they viewed this segment another time, focusing in on how Tom, who is over six feet tall, seemed to loom over his students. Miriam suggested that Tom stoop down to make eye contact with them: "Think about your body in space. If you drop down, you can reach the specific kid. See how that feels the next time." After discussing some details related to the assignment, it occurred to Tom that giving oral instructions for a complicated activity was not the most efficient thing to do.

*Tom:* The question is, how much of my words are wasted? Maybe I should print something out? Like put it on the board . . .

*Miriam:* That's one way. That would solve the problem of them not doing it because they don't have the instructions. But why on the board? Why not type? Type out the four steps . . . so they don't have to ask you again.

*Tom:* Yes, I agree.

*Miriam:* That's one thing, but you will still need to give individual directions.

Through repeated viewing of this videotape Miriam helped Tom develop an awareness of his presence in the classroom, and gave him some suggestions for how to manage the class in a positive, facilitative way, rather than a negative, punitive one. As she reflected on her work with the teachers, Miriam commented: "I think of Kehillah as a professional development school in a lot of ways. To me it's one of the main things that I'm working on, not just for the kids but for the teachers themselves."

Sometimes, all the supervision Kehillah can offer doesn't seem sufficient. Beth reflects: "There are teachers who we know are mediocre, and then the question becomes: Is it worth it to try to induct a new person who knows nothing about the Kehillah model, which is a long learning curve, or to hold onto the mediocre teacher . . . and, to a certain point, accept their mediocrity?" Ultimately, Beth believes, Kehillah can live with the mediocre teacher when the other members of the *tsevet* are strong: "A student at Kehillah is coming into the environment in total—it's not as though their experience is limited to a particular teacher. There is an overall cultural net. A mediocre teacher here and there . . . we put a lot of effort into elevating that, but then we say well OK, as long as in total there is a strong *tsevet* we will feel successful."

## Creating Community in the Classroom

The next sections will delve into the *Ivrit* and *Yahadut* curricula, but before that we will discuss an activity that every *kvutzah* engages in at beginning of the year—the creation of a classroom *brit* (covenant).[9] It took three weeks for Bina Gibson's *Anafim* to complete their *brit*:

> The first week we talked about the three different kinds of *kavod* [respect] that we focus on: *kavod la'atzmi* [respect for oneself], *kavod la'aherim* [respect for others], and *kavod la-sviva* [respect for the environment]. We took these categories and tried to decide what was important to the students. We did this in various ways. For example, we had everyone write down on a sheet some of the rules and boundaries. We also used a text from the Rambam as a springboard. It took a while to figure exactly how to phrase [our *brit*], to see that it was rooted in a text.

When it was finished, they hung a copy of their *brit* in a prominent place. Then they created three dials with scores ranging from 1 to 120, one for each type of *kavod*.

> We talk about them every day: *Kavod la'atzmi*—sometimes they suggest to me that we should raise the meter, because they were working really hard by themselves, or they had a good discussion, or they respected someone else's opinion when it was different from theirs; other times I see and highlight positive or negative points. *Kavod lasviva* is typically done at the end of the day, during *z'man lenakot* [cleanup time]. *Kavod la'acherim* is generally a synopsis of what happened in class; it's a good opportunity to review what happened that day, and then I can ask them how they did today. They're really honest; sometimes they say, "I don't think we had a good day today."

Every class in Kehillah has a *kavod* meter of some sort, some more elaborate than others; some (that of the youngest group) with fewer words and more pictures, and some (that of the oldest group) with more words.

# The *Ivrit* Curriculum

## *Modern, Not* Siddur *Hebrew*

As noted above, Kehillah's schedule includes two formal teaching blocks, one in *Ivrit* and one in *Yahadut*. It should come as no surprise that Kehillah's approach to each of them is unique.

Nearly all congregational schools teach *siddur* (prayerbook) Hebrew, since the synagogue is where s/he will encounter Hebrew most often, and since the students will read from the *siddur* at their B'nei Mitzvah service. Kehillah, in contrast, does not see preparation for B'nei Mitzvah as one of its goals. As Miriam explains: "I'm much more interested in what does it mean to be thirteen and make Jewish choices, and have a Jewish vocabulary, and know your history and what that means to you now, and feel like a speaker of the language? That's who I want thirteen-year-olds to be. And my belief about that is that if they can do all that, they are going to do just fine that morning. They are studiers of text and deep thinkers of issues, and so they'll write their *dvar torah* just fine. We don't do that with them, but we study a whole lot of text with them and so they know how to do it. We don't teach them to lead services or chant from the *siddur*, but reading Hebrew is pretty comfortable for them."

Kehillah has chosen to teach Modern Hebrew, for the reasons Miriam enumerates: "because it's a living language and kids naturally like learning it. It's fun. *Siddur* Hebrew isn't fun. It's not compelling. It's not the compelling part of prayer—you want to know what you're saying, but the work of figuring out what you're saying isn't the compelling part. If you're not instinctually prayerful, it is hard."

Though the focus of the curriculum is on modern Hebrew, students encounter prayers from the *siddur* as part of the *Yahadut* curriculum, and in the decoding exercises that are integral to the *Ivrit* curriculum. They have an opportunity to practice prayers at the end of the day when they are in *Benayim* (middle school).

In order to teach Modern Hebrew, Kehillah creates a Hebrew environment throughout the afternoon: teachers greet students in Hebrew; snack is distributed in Hebrew; the spaces and scheduling blocks are referred to by their Hebrew names. However, this Hebrew environment is "incidental, not communicative." To use only Hebrew during *z'man chofshi*, for example, would get in the way of full communication between the teachers and the students. It is only during *z'man Ivrit* that Hebrew is used most of the time.

## The Proficiency Approach

In 1999, under a grant from a national foundation, Kehillah worked with a Hebrew professor at a local university to apply what they call "the proficiency approach" to an after-school setting. Using guidelines of the American Council on the Teaching of Foreign Languages as a framework, they identified seven levels of Hebrew language proficiency. During *z'man Ivrit*, the students are divided, not by age, but by their level of proficiency, from *alef to zayin*.

As it has evolved, the *Ivrit* curriculum delineates what the students should be able to do in each *kitah* (class), in the areas of reading, writing, speaking, listening. For example, the goals for *kitah alef* are as follows:

Reading:

> Learner will be able to recognize and sound all letters sequentially and nonsequentially.

> Learner will be able to recognize and sound all vowels.

> Learner will be able to identify the difference between print and script letters.

> Learner will be able to read memorized words, with cue if necessary.

> Learner will be able to sound out short familiar syllables and some familiar words.

Writing:

> Learner will be able to write their name in print.

> Learner will be comfortable playing/experimenting and writing in print.

Speaking:

> Learner will be able to say memorized words and phrases in the correct context most of the time.

> Learner will be able to construct short and simple sentences from memorized patterns and vocabulary.

> Learner will be able to ask questions from memorized material directly related to immediate needs, e.g., going to the bathroom and food.

Listening:

> Learner will be able to understand the language used by the teacher most of the time.

> Learner will be able to identify familiar words from native speech and song.

In addition, the document notes that learners at the *alef* level will begin to be familiar with the following structural patterns: masculine and feminine, singular and plural. They will be able to use some verbs in the present tense. They will be introduced to some basic forms of Israeli culture (the flag, the map, food, and symbols), and will also know a number of Jewish and Israeli songs.

## *Lesson Planning*

During *z'man Ivrit* the goal is for 85 percent of the teachers' talk to be in Hebrew, with a limited vocabulary and a limited number of grammatical patterns. This creates a cloistered Hebrew environment, limited to a small number of subjects, so that the students can feel successful. For example, the teachers always use the infinitive, as in *B'vakashah lashevet, B'vakashah lakum,* etc., so the students don't need to master grammatical forms early on. Classes begin with formulaic exchanges, such as the teacher asking the students "*Aich atah margish* [or *at margisha*] *hayom?* (How do you feel today?) and each student answering "*Ani margish/a . . .*" (I feel . . .) When students don't know the Hebrew word to describe how they feel, they may ask for it, but are then expected to use it in the sentence.

This method is not easy for teachers. American-born teachers find it difficult to speak in Hebrew most of the time; Israeli-born teachers find it difficult to pare their native language down to a limited number of patterns. But all of the teachers understand the rationale for teaching this way, and are committed to trying. And they have lots of assistance from the curriculum coordinators. In addition to the detailed goals, the teachers are given a "project planner" for each particular unit, a suggested set of activities to achieve the goals. For example, the following activity was suggested for *kitah gimel*'s unit on Israel: Each learner will create a display board entitled '*Ha'chalom sheli al Yisrael*' [my Israeli dream]. It will feature a photograph of the child, with a 'dream bubble' drawn to cover most of the poster. In the bubble will be 4–5 different things they dream of doing in Israel. These can be illustrated with drawings, or photographs and post-cards from Israel. The posters will be displayed at *Erev Ivrit* [Hebrew evening]."

Toward the end of the school year, parents are invited to "*Erev Ivrit*," an opportunity to demonstrate what the students have learned, and to celebrate Hebrew. The planning for *Erev Ivrit* is a good example of how meticulous the curriculum for *Ivrit* is. The project for *kitah alef* was to create magnets with Hebrew letters. For *kitah bet* it was the creation of a DVD showing the children greeting one another and purchasing falafel and ice cream at make-believe stands—all in Hebrew, of course; the DVD was distributed in advance to all families so they could buy snacks at *Erev Ivrit*. *Kitah gimel* students created the posters described above, of their fantasy day in Israel. *Kitah dalet* students wrote postcards from various cities in Israel, describing their activities there in a few sentences.

## How Successful is the Hebrew Program?

Learning a foreign language is difficult, especially in just two hours a week. Though the students eagerly participated, we observed numerous instances in which children in the upper levels didn't remember basic words that had been introduced in lower ones. For example, in a *dalet* class, a student who was asked, "*Aich atah margish hayom* [how are you feeling today]?" needed to ask for the Hebrew of the word "tired." In addition, students often reverted to English in their responses.

Students are held accountable for their learning. Several times a year the teacher sends home an "assessment rubric," highlighting the degree of proficiency the student has achieved in each of the goals for that level. (See "Hebrew Rubric for Kitah Alef" at the end of this chapter.) Those who do not master the basic goals and objectives of a level repeat that level the following year; one student spent three years at the same level. The *tsevet* speaks of this in matter-of-fact terms. Rather than placing the blame on either the child or themselves as teachers, they acknowledge that some have a harder time with languages, and some have a learning style that doesn't fully mesh with the Kehillah program. Repeating a level is often harder for the parents, who see it as failure, than for their children, who seem to understand that there is a range of abilities in language learning. In the words of a ten-year-old girl: "We have different levels, so if you're better in reading, you work on speaking. If better on speaking, work on reading. We work on our weaknesses and get them stronger."

## The Yahadut Curriculum

Unlike the typical supplementary school curriculum, which is organized according to grades, Kehillah's *Yahadut* curriculum, in keeping with its vision of a learning community, is designed so that everyone learns the same content at the same time. There is a three-year cycle, so that students who study one unit when they are in *Shorashim* (K–1) will study the same material when they are in either *Nitzanim* (3–4) or *Anafim* (4–5). The three year-long courses are:

1. Jewish Cycles, which includes holidays and life cycles, the "whys" and "hows" of Jewish rituals and customs. To quote from the curriculum guide: "We focus on ways in which time is made holy and distinct, and on the connections and flow between parts of the cycles."

2. Jewish History and Memory, in which the students meet important figures from history, discuss the notion of the *brit* (covenant) between God and Israel, and learn about the ways in which the *brit* has been lived through changing circumstances. *Shorashim* (K–1) focus primarily on the Torah and then continue to highlight other key periods in Jewish history; *Nitzanim* (grades 2–3) and *Anafim* (grades 4–5) move through early history more quickly and spend more time dealing with later history, such as the Golden Age of Spain, the Enlightenment, and early Zionism. *Anafim* are also introduced to difficult periods in history such as the Inquisition and a brief overview of the Holocaust.[10]

3. Values and Ethics, which is made up of eight units, "each exploring a different set of values, concepts and mitzvot." Among the units are *ometz lev* (courage—taught around the time of Hanukkah), *tzedakah* and *matanot l'evyonim* (gifts to the poor—in connection with Purim).

To quote from the Kehillah website: "Kehillah's philosophy is based on the belief that we each have a place in our Jewish history and that we are each responsible for our Jewish future. We teach in a way that we can all be actively present in our Jewish lives."

## Curricular Planning

Miriam Ben-Peretz, a scholar in the field of curriculum, advocates for materials that provide a richness of resources, but leave room for teachers to find their own voice; she calls this "curriculum potential."[11] Kehillah's curricular materials for *Yahadut* contain a great deal of "curriculum potential." They are not based on textbooks, and do not contain scripted lesson plans. Rather, they offer teachers a grounding in the subject, and some creative ideas for projects. Then, during planning meetings with the curriculum coordinator, teachers have the freedom to create their own lesson plans.

In this section we trace the arc of lesson planning from the curriculum guide through the planning meeting through to the lesson itself. Our visits to Kehillah took place in Year 3 of the curriculum, which focuses on values and ethics. The introduction to *Talmud Torah* (Torah study) unit, the last one of the Ethics and Values year, reads as follows:

> *Talmud Torah* is a mitzvah which gives us a chance to enter into and deepen a number of different relationships:
>
> (a) with the text
> (b) with God
> (c) with our *Chaver* (friend)
> (d) with our Teacher
> (e) with ourselves (with our ideas beliefs and values. Also with our soul or psyche)
> (f) with our tradition, and our ancestors who also entered into these relationships.
>
> This section of the unit gives the students a chance to understand the role of Talmud Torah in developing these relationships.
>
> (a) Learners will know that the mitzvah of *Talmud Torah* comes from the Torah itself, and that we mention it in the *Shema*: '*vedibarta bam*' (Devarim 6:7)
> (b) Learners will consider that we need to acquire certain *midot* (values) in order to learn Torah properly, and that learning Torah strengthens these *midot*. The kids will study some of these 48 *midot*.
> (c) Learners will experience some sort of traditional study, and will consider what the effects of the study itself are.
> (d) Learners will have an opportunity to think about why the Torah contains a mixture of stories and instructions, and how this affects the way that we interact with it and learn from it.
> (e) Learners will understand that we return to study what we have already studied again and again. They will connect this to the value which experience brings to understanding.
> (f) Learners will have an opportunity to think about why God might

choose to communicate through text. What does it mean that God chose to communicate with us in this way?

The teachers wrestle with these concepts as adults, and then devise ways to bring them to the students' level. In the case of the youngest students, this involves making some of the more abstract ideas very concrete.

One afternoon in May, Esti and Shoshana, co-teachers of the youngest group (K–1), at Kehillat Ha'ir, met with Shimon, the coordinator of the *Yahadut* curriculum. Their conversation ranged far and wide, and included the following exchange, which later became the core of the first lesson:

*Esti:* Lesson 1 is *dibarta bam* [you shall teach them]. So it should be something that is about learning in your home and in the community.

*Shimon:* We learn through action. We put the text into action. That could be obtuse for Shorashim.

*Esti:* What happens if during *Yahadut* one student really participates, wants to speak, etc. He listens. He does everything great. But just before that, in *z'man chofshi* he wants to be on the swing and pushes one of the girls away. Perhaps we should talk about the gap—bringing what you study into your life. To simplify it for them. For some of them, the gap is really noticeable.

*Shimon:* He whose action exceeds his Torah, his torah endures. He whose Torah exceeds his action, his torah doesn't endure. Use it or lose it . . . There are three levels: text, the experience in front of the text, the reflection of the teacher back to them. The first two have the most relevance for *Shorashim*. Does it really enhance their understanding of the importance of cooperation because they are learning a text on cooperation?

*Shoshana:* The kids may know it from the *Shema*. Wouldn't it be great if they opened up the Torah and saw it, saw it in the *Humash*?

The conversation swirled on and on, touching on many themes that were fascinating to the teachers, but would have been too big a stretch for the children. In the end, Esti and Shoshana created an age-appropriate lesson that we observed:

*Shoshana:* We've been counting and counting and counting. Counting our way to Shavuot. What's special about Shavuot? What did we get?

*Yonah:* The Torah.

*Esti:* This is very, very exciting. You know, just like the Israelites got the Torah, I got it from my parents who got it from their parents, who got it from their parents. It passes from generation to generation the way we're doing it now. Maybe some day you'll pass it along to your children. It's in your heart and in your minds by now. You can look at it, and feel it and say it.

As Esti spoke, Shoshana brought out a miniature Torah and encouraged the students to pass it around, and then open it.

*Esti:* What's in the Torah?

*Lior:* The thing that is inside it are all the miracles that happened to us, and what the commandments are like, you know.

*Esti:* There are stories in the Torah and rules in the Torah. What language is this?

*Haim:* Hebrew.

*Esti:* So in the Torah we have stories and rules. The more we read it . . . do we read it only once? We read it every year over and over. The more we read it, the more we change and read it again. It's not boring. Do you know why it's not boring to read it over again?

*Gila:* Why?

*Esti:* We grow up and change and have birthdays. And learn different things.

*Naomi:* That's why it's not boring.

*Lior:* The Torah will turn to dust.

*Shoshana:* Shimon said that books that don't get used get dusty . . .

*Noah:* But we didn't use this yesterday.

*Shoshana:* When we celebrate Pesach, when we do things with Torah, if we live a life from the Torah it's like we're keeping the Torah. We show it so much *kavod*. It won't turn to dust.

*Haim:* When there's a bar or bat mitzvah, you have to be a certain age to have one and you have to read a lot of the Torah.

Esti called the students over to the work tables, where there were cardboard boxes made to hold 3″ × 5″ index cards. Each box had a hole on one side, so that the students could peer in and see what was on the other end. Working in pairs, the students were going to draw pictures of something in the Torah, and insert the pictures into the box, to be viewed through the hole.

*Esti* (holding up 3″ × 5″ cards): On these cards we're going to put ideas and stories that we have from the things that we've studied this year from the Torah. Let's brainstorm a bit.

*Students* (calling out): Passover, Shabbat, Purim.

*Esti: Ken* [yes], Esther.

*Students:* Purim, Queen Esther, Haman.

*Shoshana:* Technically Purim isn't in the Torah. Purim happened after the Torah was finished. Hanukkah happened after the Torah was finished.

*Naomi:* The sea splitting.

*Shoshana:* How about *Tzedakah*? How about *hachnasat orchim*?

*Noah:* Something-something-*kamochah* [sic].

*Teachers* (in unison): *V'ahavta l'reiachah kamochah* [love your neighbor as yourself].

*Esti:* It's important that we find a *kavod*-ful way to do this.

The students got to work, and, as they worked, the teachers began singing the song *Torah tzivah lanu Moshe* (Moses gave us the Torah) and the students joined in.

This lesson brought together many of the stories and precepts the students had already studied under the rubric of *talmud torah*, and it linked this value with the concepts of *l'dor va'dor* (generation to generation) and *kavod*. The art project gave the students (many of whom do not yet write with ease) an opportunity to review the stories of the Torah that they had learned all year.

The teachers' enthusiasm for and depth of understanding of the subject was evident, but nothing they said or did was beyond the reach of their students. They were also careful to give out only correct information. When the students said (and Esti confirmed) that the story of Purim (which they had studied about a month before) was not in the Torah, Shoshana did not let this get by, but neither did she make a big deal of it; she corrected the student with a very light touch.

The short exchange about books turning to dust is evidence that Kehillah is indeed a community of learners. When a student said that the Torah will turn to dust, the teachers knew this was a reference to a remark made by Shimon, the *Yahadut* coordinator, that books turn to dust when they are not used. Rather than either ignoring the student or denigrating this remark, the teacher was able to discern the original idea behind the comment, and reassure the student that the Torah would not turn to dust.

## Aiming High

Kehillah's *Yahadut* curriculum aims very high, focusing on big ideas that can engage both the teachers and the students, so that they truly form a learning community. In addition, Kehillah wants to impress upon the students the idea that Judaism deals with important subjects that can be endlessly fascinating, as Ben Bag Bag's saying goes: "Turn it and turn it again, for everything is in it."[12] Despite the fact that the students in Kehillah are relatively young, Kehillah believes in stretching them to their fullest potential. Here is how Shimon explains it: "In order to accommodate the developmental level of your students, it doesn't mean making a complex thing simple. It makes a complex thing apprehendable. But if you do that by stripping out all of the sophistication, all of the complexity, the kids will be left feeling that this is a simple thing that they have mastered and there's nothing else there . . . That's one of the most difficult tight ropes that we walk here, and sometimes we over-reach."

In a number of the lessons we observed at Kehillah the "big ideas" were presented so quickly, and so abstractly, that the students were not able to engage with them. A lesson during that same week in *Nitzanim* made reference (as the curriculum suggests) to the fact that Jews throughout the ages have written commentaries on the Torah. The teacher, Orna, read the story of the Tower of Babel to the students, and gave each of them a piece of paper to "write down your thoughts about the story." After the students finished writing, she added, "Each one of you had your own comment. Now I'm going to read to you what one of the big commentators wrote. This midrash is saying that the reason they did it is they wanted to stop the flood." The teacher showed a photocopy of *Mikraot Gedolot* (a classical commentary), and pointed to one section, but did not explain what *Mikraot Gedolot* was, nor mention the name of the commentator. None of the students said anything. The teacher continued: "I'm going to tell you a story and you will do your own commentary in this format." She then told the Talmudic legend about God bringing Moses to the schoolroom of

Akiva, a Talmudic scholar who lived about a thousand years later. The story was told very quickly, and Orna didn't ask any comprehension questions, so we were left wondering what, exactly, the students were making of all this. One student seemed to get some of it, because he asked: "so did they go to the future?" Then the teacher asked the students to share their own commentaries on the tower of Babel; after a number of students spoke, the teacher announced: "now guys, it's *z'man lenakot* [cleanup time]."

The "big idea" or, to use educational parlance, "enduring understanding"[13] in this lesson is that the Torah has been interpreted differently throughout Jewish history, and that we too are commentators. But it was never actually stated in this way, nor did the students have any opportunity to discuss it. There was no explanation of what *Mikraot Gedolot* is. After telling the story of Moses in Akiva's class, the teacher did not probe for the students' understanding, nor did she help them explore the implications of the story for their own role as commentators.

A more skilled teacher would undoubtedly have been able to help the students explore this big idea more fully. But this lesson illustrates the tension inherent in a curriculum that attempts to transmit both big ideas and the concrete examples that illustrate them, to young children growing up in a largely secular culture. This is a particular challenge for the History and Memory curriculum. For children as young as those in Kehillah, periods of history would have to be taught as people, places, and events, without reference to the context; we wonder about the children's ability to grasp and retain this information. In response to our query, Miriam offered examples in which the children brought up things learned in the history curriculum in subsequent years. For example, during the "cycles" year, they studied the blessing for boys on *Erev Shabbat* that says, "May God make you like Efraim and Menasheh." The students were asked which historical character they would want to be blessed as. Without prompting from the teacher, each student picked a different name from a different era. Miriam was surprised at the diversity—not one name repeated. The children remembered some of what they had learned and brought that forward to the next year.

Shimon argues that aiming high sends a message that Judaism is important: "Typically I don't think we do, but over-reaching is a price that it's okay to pay every now and again, if it ensures that people feel free to take the risks to stretch the kids, to give the kids stuff that is really interesting." Miriam makes the same point: "I don't want them thinking that this is easy or unsophisticated. They go to excellent public schools. They are children of academics, some of them. They are deep, smart, strong thinkers and I don't want them thinking that Judaism is any less rich than what else they're learning. Because I want them to have a sense that there's a lot more that they're going to understand later and they need to keep studying this later. So sometimes we just want them to see that there's more out there for them to do as adults."

We believe that Kehillah is to be applauded for presenting Judaism in a deep and thoughtful way. But elementary school students are still very young, however sophisticated their homes and their schools may be. And not all the teachers seem capable of translating the big ideas into concrete, age-appropriate lessons. We are left with the following questions: Would it be better to aim a bit lower in the hope of having the students retain more of the material? Alternatively, would it be better for Kehillah to provide more focused ideas for each level, reducing some of the "curriculum potential," but increasing the chances of having lessons that delivered the big ideas more coherently?

## Benayim (Middle School) and Tichon (High School)

Sixth, seventh, and eighth graders have a special status at Kehillat Ha'ir.[14] They are given the name *Benayim* (middle), and have a program that gives them greater independence and a sense of the larger Jewish community. During *z'man chofshi* and *z'man bachutz*, they are allowed to go out to a nearby shopping area to buy snacks, though many of them still hang out in the special area designated for their group. They are placed in *Ivrit* classes according to their abilities, and for *Yahadut* they are divided by grade: *Te'enim* (figs, 6th), *Rimmonim* (pomegranates, 7th), and *T'marim* (dates, 8th). The recently updated *Benayim* curriculum is divided into seven units:

1. Holidays and Community

2. Problems of Responsibility, including the Torah stories of Adam and Eve, Cain and Abel, Noah, and the Tower of Babel

3. The *Brit* (Covenant), including the stories of the Patriarchs through the giving of the Torah at Sinai

4. Ritual Life, including the rituals of the Temple, the pull of idolatry, the message of the prophets, and the role of prayer in contemporary Jewish life

5. Memory and Application, in which students select one of three tracks: The 'Text' track provides an opportunity to focus on traditional Jewish

texts; the '*Tikkun*' (Repair) track focuses on social and political activism; and the '*Omanut*' (Art) track incorporates art and music.

6. Israel, which includes: the emergence of Zionism and the establishment of the state (for 6th graders); contemporary Israel (for 7th graders); and the impact of Israel on Diaspora life (8th graders).

Often, at the end of the day, *tefila* (prayer) replaces *shira* (singing), in recognition of the fact that the students are becoming (or have recently become) B'nei Mitzvah. While Kehillah does not devote time to preparing students for their B'nei Mitzvah, it helps set families up with tutors, some of whom are teachers at Kehillah.

## Teaching Pluralism

Once the students have reached *Benayim*, they are considered old enough to discuss Jewish pluralism explicitly. During the earlier grades, Kehillah's commitment is more implicit, with a variety of perspectives presented and the choice left up to students and their families. As Miriam puts it: "When kids are five or six or seven or ten, I don't want them to have to take a stance yet. So . . . [we] give them a chance to try out an idea or an example, or argue a side in a debate, or think about it without saying what do you believe—do you think the Torah is true? Because I want them to be able to change their minds . . . When they're older that makes more sense. Like in *Benayim* it makes more sense for them to start practicing, sort of taking a stance." The curriculum summaries on the website includes phrases like: "the tension as well as synthesis between individual identity and community"; "the diverse nature of leaders"; and, regarding the State of Israel, "the complexities of the conflict in the area," suggesting ways in which pluralism is embedded in the *Benayim* curriculum.

One activity that *Benayim* students have done in the past is to visit different synagogues in the area. Miriam remembers with pleasure a time when she took her *Benayim* students to a local Reform synagogue. At first they were taken aback by the vastness of the sanctuary, the rabbis with guitars, and the timbrels that were handed out during the singing of *Mi Chamocha* (a prayer derived from the Biblical account of the Israelites singing after crossing the Red Sea), which were so unlike the worship services they had experienced with their families and at Kehillah. Once they were acclimated to the change, they enjoyed the experience of being exposed to new things and fitting them into what they knew about Judaism, prayer, and the Torah.

## The Students' Perspective

In our interviews (which were held without the *tsevet* being present), the students in *Benayim* all voiced great enthusiasm for Kehillah. They said typical middle-school things like "I like hanging out with my friends" or "we have a lot of freedom here." But they also made comments that reflected their understanding of and adherence to the values that are central to Kehillah. Here is a sampling of what they said:

"You get to know everyone really well, you stay with them year after year, and the teachers too."

"At Kehillah you can learn about Judaism in really interesting ways."

"*Ivrit* is the most important part of the day."

"*Kavod* is important at Kehillah; it's the biggest word at Kehillah."

"If you do something wrong, the teachers will say 'treat people with *kavod*.' That was one of the first Hebrew words that I learned."

"We even made up a song about *kavod* last year."

"We don't learn a lot about *kavod* in our public school, so it's really important that we learn it here."

"I try to live by *kavod*, but sometimes I make mistakes."

## Tichon (High School)

For many years there was no formal program for high school students, though there were always students who came to Kehillah to hang out. During 2006–07, the year of our visit, the *Tichon* program was begun; it met for two hours one evening a week. Shimon, the incoming director of Kehillat Ha'ir, acknowledges that the curriculum for *Tichon* needs work. What draws the students is the opportunity to see one another, and to be in community together. One girl told how she had not attended *Tichon* during the fall, but she had the same piano teacher as a boy who was attending. Every week this boy would leave a note with the piano teacher begging her to return to Kehillah. Eventually, she did.

During these students' early years at Kehillah, a weekly *kavod* award was given out, a hand-made certificate, made sparkly with glitter glue, with the Hebrew name of the recipient, and a description of how s/he had acted with *kavod*. The awards were announced each day during *z'man shira*. After hanging on the main Kehillah bulletin board for a week, they were sent home. It is telling that during our interview, the *Tichon* students, one after another, first sheepishly and then more exuberantly, admitted that they have saved their *kavod* award.

# What Do Students Gain from Kehillah?

## Student Assessment

Student assessment at Kehillah consists of very elaborate rubrics that are based on the goals for *Ivrit*; for *Yahadut*, written comments are sent home. For example, the following are some of the goals for *Ivrit* in *kitah dalet*:

### Reading

- Learners will be able to decode most words in script and print.
- Learners will be able to read a string of 6–8 sentences that include nouns and present tense singular and plural verbs, and answer content-related questions.

### Writing

- Learners will be able to spell all target material with correct or inventive spelling.
- Learners will be able to answer patterned questions with simple sentences.
- Learners will be able to create a string of 6 sentences.

There are comparable goals for speaking and listening. For each goal, there are three levels of proficiency. Thus, for example, the levels of proficiency for the last goal listed above are:

1. The learner can create a string of 6 sentences independently relying on memory and visual cues. The sentences are fluid and nuanced, displaying a firm knowledge of verb forms, and following a logical narrative.

2. The learner can create a string of 4–6 sentences relying on memory, visual cues, and occasional verbal ones. The sentences are comprehensible, but may be inaccurate in terms of grammar and structure. Less ambitious sentences with limited verb usage are rendered accurately.

3. The learner can create a string of 4 sentences, but operates slowly, and will struggle to maintain coherence beyond this number. Sentences are usually comprehensible, but display a lack of creativity and verb usage, often requiring further analysis. The relation of one sentence to the next may be unclear.

The entire document, including goals and rubrics for reading, writing, speaking, and listening, is two and a half single-spaced pages long. For each student, the teacher highlights the appropriate proficiency level, and then, at the bottom, adds a narrative assessment. The following is an excerpt from one teacher's comment:

> Shula has shown amazing progress this year, proving herself a very strong, creative writer and an extremely accurate decoder. With further practice I am certain that Shula will become more confident—and subsequently more fluid—in her decoding, while her understanding and retention of read information is already top notch . . . I can tell Shula enjoys the opportunity to speak in *Ivrit*, and she comprehends most of my instructions from routine language and context.

The *Yahadut* narrative assessments are much shorter, more informal. The following are two examples:

> Nirit [a student in *Shorashim*] is always so excited and happy to be at Kehillah. She loves it! It has been great getting to know Nirit over the last two years. I've seen her grow into this wonderful leader. She has a wild imagination and loves playing with her friends through the Kehillah day . . . During our Shavuot text study Nirit was really excited about the story and really showed her ability to discuss the story with her partner. As the year has progressed I can see Nirit is ready for more information. She will have such a good time and learn so much in *Nitzanim* next year.

> Yehoshua has been enjoying himself in *Nitzanim*. He clearly has a joy of Judaic learning which is evident by his enthusiastic participation. Occasionally this enthusiasm results in overly loud contributions to the group, and we are trying to help Yehoshua show *kavod* by keeping his voice quieter . . . Whether through dramatization, writing exercise, or some other means, Yehoshua always plays a constructive role in his group.

## What Is Retained in Later Years

Our interviews with students in *Tichon* confirmed what we suspected, that the students hadn't retained all of the Hebrew they had learned in previous years. What they did retain, however, was a strong connection to and enthusiasm for Hebrew, and many pleasant memories. As for *Yahadut*, the students felt they had a good grounding, and could now learn more in college or by themselves. Above all, they have gained the ability to be critical thinkers. As one student put it: "The main program is more teaching yourself in a way. We're not really being presented information that we have to learn. But we explore our Jewish identities . . . Our teachers give us specific things to think about, but it's not like we're just taking in information."

What the students in *Tichon* talked the most about was Kehillah as a community and as a haven:

> Kehillah helped to get you through middle school. We were all so self-conscious and insecure . . . Kehillah always supported you through those days.

> At [public] school a lot of the time, it's a place where teachers are in authority and have a lot more power over the students . . . And the teachers take your respect without giving it. But here it's more mutual respect.

> Kehillah is a diverse community. People are actually truly respected here for their differences. There was never any doubt that parents who were [in same sex relationships] . . . it was never an issue. They don't want us to memorize things. They want us to learn things . . . There is always an undertone of happiness. It's really a happy place.

In our interviews with parents and members of the *tsevet*, we heard many stories about how the students had internalized the value of *kavod*. One teacher told a story of a third grader who came home and offered to set the table, after learning the value of *kibud av v'em* (honoring father and mother). A parent at Kehillat Ha'ir commented on her eight-year-old son's reactions: "He really takes to heart the stuff they talk about here, like *kavod*. He'll come home . . . [after they've had a discussion of] what they can do to be respectful of your parents, to be helpful . . . and he'll start doing them. And he's not doing them because he has to come back in and tell them. It's really kind of cool . . . He's in an environment with his peers where it's OK to talk about that. He comes home from public school asking why all the boys want to talk about is war games . . . [when at Kehillah] they're teaching him to become a mensch."

The following incident took place in one of the area public schools and was written up in the local newspaper: At lunchtime, a child was rebuffed by his classmates, who said, "You can't sit here, your parents are gay." Upon hearing this, another child, who attends Kehillah, invited this child to sit with him. When asked why he did this, the child replied, "I go to Kehillah, and *kavod* is what we do there."

One of the most powerful stories about lessons learned was told to us by Beth Davids:

> When I was teaching *Anafim*, we did a unit around Yom Kippur on *tshuvah* (repentence). It was the beginning of the year, so the lesson had a dual purpose: talking about how we as an *Anafim* community should behave to one another, and also what Yom Kippur means. I put a gigantic target on the wall, and talked about *chet* [sin, literally "missing the mark"] and *tshuvah*, returning, and re-aiming. I had the kids sit in a long column leading up to the target. And I had made up scenarios of instances in which we miss the mark, like a missed arrow, and the kids each got a card that corresponded to a *chet* [and discussed how they could do *tshuvah* for that action]. At the end of the day, I just happened to be in the room, cleaning up. One of the kids, Max, a fifth grader, brought his mother in to show her the target. He said, "Mom, I need to show you what we talked about today." Apparently, he and his mother had been having a lot of tension between them. He saw the exercise we had done in class as a way they could resolve it. There, in front of the target, for fifteen minutes, they had a personal conversation using the language of the lesson. They walked out glowing.

Ben, a parent at Kehillat Ha'ir, reflected on what his older daughter, now in *Tichon*, has learned:

> I think the biggest success has been cultural and spiritual . . . My daughter loves prayer. She leads *tefila* in the evening, a *ma'ariv* (evening) service for the kids in *Tichon*. She's very comfortable in synagogue with the ritual part of it. But she's very thoughtful and well educated in the other dimensions, too. She has gotten a much better Jewish education than I did. In fact I'm now inspired—I'm going to enroll in [a city-wide adult education] program; my kids have left me in the dust from a knowledge standpoint. They can discuss things I don't know what they're talking about, put aside the Hebrew part of it. So I say the pri-

mary success has been the cultural identification, the content, the spirit. I think that's true for both kids.

The second thing, which is less tangible, is, for lack of a better word, community. These kids have very strong friendships that have been built here . . . Both daughters' best friends are Kehillah friends, rather than school friends. That was interesting to me and kind of unexpected. I didn't think of this as a place they would forge these kind of friendships; I thought this would be truly supplemental.

## The Board

Kehillat Ha'ir and Kehillat Haparvar have separate boards. In Kehillat Haparvar two-thirds of the twelve-member board are parents; the others are members of the community who are friends with parents. In Kehillat Ha'ir all but one member of the eight-person board are parents.

The main function of the board is to deal with fiscal matters, including setting tuition and overseeing fundraising efforts. Karen Stein, the parent who is in charge of fundraising at Kehillat Ha'ir, distinguishes between two kinds of activities: pure fundraising efforts, like the annual auction, and fundraising efforts whose primary purpose is actually community building. One example of the latter is Kehillat Haparvar's *mishloach manot* (Purim gift-giving) project, which charges a relatively modest fee to send baskets of Purim treats to members of the community. Students dress in costume to deliver the baskets, which a parent and member of the board describes as "a fabulous fundraising, community-bulding, and education for the kids."

Kehillat Ha'ir is trying to tie even pure fundraising efforts to something that the students are learning. The *Benayim* project of looking at Jewish identity through art inspired the committee to give disposable cameras to local (and national) celebrities, and ask them to "picture what matters"; those who agreed to participate include a local NPR reporter, the author Leslie Epstein, and Jerry Greenfield of Ben and Jerry's.

During 2006–07 most of the meetings of the Kehillat Ha'ir board were devoted to the search for a successor to the director, Melanie Fried, who announced that she would be leaving at the end of the school year. Upcoming issues for the board include looking for a new space. Everyone agrees on the need for a space that has better ventilation and provides more safety for the children; but finding an affordable alternative has proven to be a big challenge.

In general, the board does not get involved in curricular issues; this was a deliberate decision made in the early days of Kehillat Ha'ir. In 2006–07 Kehillat Haparvar's board devoted a meeting to discussing how much *tefillah* (prayer) should be included in the Kehillah curriculum. Their conclusion was that there was no time in the Kehillah day to teach *tefillah*, nor did they wish, in principle, to include specific B'nei Mitzvah preparations. However, they did decide that in the following year, when the school grew to include a cohort of sixth graders, either their curriculum would be changed to include *tefillah*, or extra time would be found for that purpose.

## Parents and Family Education

Parents are an important part of the Kehillah community. The *tsevet* sees parents regularly as they drop off or pick up their children. Miriam estimates that two-thirds of the parents come in for *z'man shira* on some occasion; on any given day about one-third attend.

In addition to these informal connections, there are formal modes of communicating with parents. These include the following:

• an open house in the fall, at which the curriculum is explained
• regular emails from the teachers about what is going on in their classrooms
• monthly updates on their child(ren)'s progress, in the form of the assessment rubrics discussed above

Whenever the *tsevet* has a concern about a child, the director contacts the parents. As Melanie explains, these concerns vary widely:

> It could be about getting along with another student, about getting along with the teacher, or that we're noticing that their letter recognition is not coming along where we thought it would be and we want to talk about how the child is doing in regular education classes. Kehillah has many, many times been the place that a parent finds out long before they find out in their public or private school that their child has some sort of learning issue, because the ratio is smaller here. I may meet with a parent because somebody is sick in their family. I may be meeting with a parent who is unaffiliated, who has no idea what it means to celebrate their child becoming a Bar/Bat Mitzvah.

One form of family education consists of holiday packets that are sent home, containing background information on what the holiday commemorates and how it is observed, special recipes, text study sheets, etc. There are also a number of family "get-togethers," like family *havdalah* cere-monies (about every 6 weeks to 2 months), and Friday night dinners (one a year for each *kvutzah*) held in people's homes. As Ben explains, these events create a sense of community for both students and their families: "Kesher is not only the kids' educational resource, but also their Jewish community . . . My wife [who is not Jewish], for example, is not really all that interested in going to synagogue, but she loves coming here for Shab-bat dinners and for *havdalah* services and other events. I think that for people who are either not Jewish but married into interfaith marriages, or people who are very secular in their orientation, or just ambivalent, who haven't gotten around to joining a synagogue, this is a central focal point for their Jewish life." Kehillat Haparvar is experimenting with infusing adult learning into these events. They have started doing short text studies either with adults alone or with the entire family at their family events.

The biggest family event is *"Erev Ivrit,"* a celebration of the children's Hebrew achievements, which comes toward the end of the year. In antici-pation of *Erev Ivrit* in 2006, Miriam considered offering an adult Hebrew "mini-course." She sent an email out to parents, who responded with great enthusiasm. She tried to make it as accessible as possible, scheduling the sessions forty-five minutes before pick-up, in a room in which younger sib-lings could play. Though three parents signed up in advance, no one made it to the classes.

From this experience, and others like it, Miriam has concluded that what has been traditionally thought of as adult education should not be a centerpiece of family education at Kehillat Haparvar. In a parent survey sent out in the fall of 2006, a little over half of the respondents said that they were interested in education programs for adults; but Miriam believes that this need can easily be met by local congregations and/or a city-wide program sponsored by the Federation.

## What Can We Learn from Kehillah?

If one had to summarize Kehillah's many virtues in a single word, that word would be "intentionality."[15] All Jewish schools espouse the value of seri-ous Jewish learning within a community, but few have translated this be-lief into actual educational practice so effectively. Kehillah's unique sched-ule and staffing patterns combine to create a powerful sense of community among students, teachers and parents. Its small size and the fact that teach-ers, and students spend up to two hours hanging out and playing together create strong bonds and a base of shared experiences. Miriam tells of an ongoing conversation with a mother who doesn't understand the synergy between learning and community, and would like her daughter to skip the free time and come in just for *z'man Ivrit* and *z'man Yahadut*. Whenever the topic comes up Miriam is insistent—the informal part of the day is as critical as the formal.

Given that both dual-career and single-parent Jewish families have a need for after-school childcare, it is surprising that the Kehillah model has not been copied by other supplementary schools. Kehillah has been discussed in a number of publications and websites that promote new approaches to congregational education; to date, however, no congregation has seriously considered adopting this model. While in some parts of the country it might be difficult to find teachers who are able to converse in rudimentary Hebrew and are free to work 24–26 hours a week, it should be possible to find 10–15 qualified teachers in any city with a number of graduate programs in Judaica and/or large pockets of under-employed Jewish adults.

As we were writing this chapter, a national consortium of funders had entered into an agreement that would bring the Kehillah model to two institutions—a large Jewish Community Center and a small grassroots organization—in a nearby city during the fall of 2008. Under the agreement, the two programs would follow Kehillah's schedule, and utilize its curriculum. Melanie, Miriam, and/or Shimon, would spend fifteen hours each month consulting with these sites, helping them adapt the curriculum, and working with teachers. During the second year, that consultation would be reduced to eight hours a month. As part of the agreement, Kehillah delineated the essential elements that would have to be incorporated in order for its name and curriculum to be used. They were:

- "Thoughtful policies that allow diversity of Jewish families, children, and staff to participate, and a stance towards multiple Jewish perspectives."
- An attempt to meet the needs of all learners.
- A minimum of two days per week.
- "Less-structured time" (e.g., free time) built into the schedule.
- "The use of *Ivrit* as a living, communicative language throughout the day."
- "A *tsevet* learning community. From week to week, the staff learns together without the children, and has planning and preparation time."
- "A commitment to *tsevet* professional development. From week to week, staff receive individual support and supervision."

- "A commitment to family engagement . . . time for families to be together for events, education, and celebration."
- "A commitment to both documentation and evaluation."

Over and above the problems inherent in replicating the model in its entirety, we believe that Kehillah's curricula for *Ivrit* and *Yahadut* are worthy of wide dissemination, despite the fact that they are still works in progress, and despite (or maybe precisely because of) the fact that they call for a high level of teacher understanding and skill. The combination of ambitious goals and imaginative, even playful methods, makes these curricula worthy of note and, when possible, replication. The curriculum for *Ivrit* is particularly well developed; its emphasis on modern Hebrew offers an attractive alternative to curricula that focus primarily on decoding skills in preparation for bar or bat mitzvah. Both parents and children find the notion of learning a foreign language very appealing. Kehillah's "sheltered vocabulary" approach enables students to feel successful in attaining a reasonable set of goals. Here again, finding teachers who are willing and able to teach in this way might be difficult; but it would certainly be worth the attempt.

Issues of replication and dissemination aside, Kehillah serves as a valuable "existence proof" that the assumptions and conventions of supplementary Jewish education are not immutable. The formal and the informal can be successfully combined; the curriculum can be both challenging and engaging; it is possible to offer extensive coaching and support to part-time teachers. Most important, an after-school Jewish environment can form the hub of a vibrant learning community.

# Hebrew Rubric for Kitah Alef

| | Advanced | Intermediate | Beginner |
|---|---|---|---|
| *Reading: Letters* | The learner is able to recognize all letters and sounds in print, sequentially and nonsequentially. | The learner is able to recognize many letters and sounds in print, sequentially and nonsequentially | The learner is able to recognize some of the letters and their sounds in print, sequentially and nonsequentially |
| *Reading: Target words* | The learner is able to recognize many memorized words from throughout the year. | The learner is able to recognize some memorized words from throughout the year. | The learner is able to recognize memorized words from the current unit. |
| *Reading: Sounding* | The learner is beginning to sound out familiar and unfamiliar words. | The learner is beginning to sound out only familiar words. | |
| *Writing: name* | The learner is able to write his or her name in print, with no cues, in the correct direction all the time. | The learner is able to write his or her name in print, with some cues, in the correct direction most of the time. | The learner is able to write his or her name in print, with some cues, in the correct direction some of the time. |

| | | | |
|---|---|---|---|
| *Writing:* alef bet | The learner is able to write most of the letters in the correct direction and with the correct format most of the time. | The learner is able to write most of the letters in the correct direction and with the correct format with some prompting. | The learner is able to write most of the letters in the correct direction and with the correct format when copying from the *alef-bet*. |
| *Writing: copying target words* | The learner is able to copy target vocabulary in print in the correct direction all the time. | The learner is able to copy target vocabulary in print. The learner writes in the correct direction some of the time. | The learner is able to copy target vocabulary in print. The learner writes in the correct direction some of the time, or when reminded. |
| *Writing: target words* | The learner is comfortable writing most target words from the year in print. | The learner is comfortable writing many of the target words from the year in print. | The learner is comfortable writing target words from the current unit. |
| *Writing: spelled-out words* | The learner is able to write words when letters are spelled out without cues. | The learner is able to write words when letters are spelled out with some cues. | The learner is able to write words when letters are spelled out with cues. |

## Notes

1. Children at Kehillah are called by their Hebrew names; thus, we have used Hebrew names as pseudonyms.

2. After-school education is a relatively new field, whose growth has been fueled by increased federal and state funding. See Gil Noam, Gina Biancarosa, and Nadine Dechausay, *Afterschool Education: Approaches to an Emerging Field* (Cambridge: Harvard University Press, 2003).

3. *Ir* in Hebrew means "city"; *parvar* means "suburb."

4. Edgar Schein, *Organizational Culture and Leadership* (San Francisco: Jossey Bass, 1992).

5. Citizen Schools is a "national network of after-school education programs for students in the middle grades (6th, 7th and 8th), [whose programs complement classroom learning] by engaging students in hands-on learning projects led by adult volunteers after school and supported by a staff of professional educators." http://www.citizenschools.org/whatwedo/index.cfm

6. There was one exception, Bina Gibson, who was out one day a week because her graduate program required her to take a particular afternoon seminar.

7. Subsidies for family educators have come from a special Federation fund for family education.

8. This use of "incidental" Hebrew throughout the day is discussed more fully in the section on the Hebrew curriculum.

9. The activity of creating a classroom *brit* is an adaptation of an activity described by Ruth Charney in *Teaching Children to Care: Classroom Management for Ethical and Academic Growth* (Turner Falls, Mass.: Northeast Foundation for Children, 2002).

10. The Jewish History and Memory curriculum was revised in 2007–08, This summary is based on the revised version.

11. Miriam Ben-Peretz, *The Teacher-Curriculum Encounter* (Binghamton: SUNY University Press, 1990).

12. *Ethics of the Fathers* 5:25

13. The notion of an "enduring understanding," derives from "Understanding by Design," a sophisticated, contemporary approach to curriculum development. See Grant Wiggins and Jay McTighe, *Understanding by Design*, 2nd edition (Alexandria, Va: Association for Curriculum and Supervision, 2005).

14. Kehillat Haparvar, which was only founded in 2003, had only one student over fifth grade at the time of our visit; in 2007–08 they had their first cohort of sixth graders.

15. For an interesting discussion of intentionality in teaching, see, Robert E. Slavin, *Educational Psychology Theory and Practice*, 7th edition (New York: Allyn and Bacon, 2002), pp. 7–9.

# CHAPTER 2

# The Power of Their Commitments
## Lessons for the Jewish Community from a Small Synagogue School*

SUSAN L. SHEVITZ WITH MARION GRIBETZ

If demographers have it right, increasingly large numbers of American Jews across the continent live in small Jewish communities. Some of these have small congregations or informal Jewish groups. Some urban areas have seen a corresponding decline in their once dense Jewish populations and now also host small congregations. Elsewhere, in cities and towns that never had a large Jewish population, Jews work hard to maintain their congregations and other institutions.

This means that many Jewish children are today being educated in small congregations with limited resources. According to the Union of Reform Judaism, of the 901 affiliated congregations, 509 are considered small (under 250 member units). Of the 792 congregations with schools, 403 are small congregations. The picture in the Conservative movement is similar. Of the 707 Conservative congregations in North America, 37 percent have fewer than 200 member units and 28 percent have between 200 and 399 member units.[1]

Jewish schools in these smaller communities operate in a different universe than large schools in metropolitan areas with booming Jewish pop-

---

*I adapt this title from an influential book about public education published in 1995 by Deborah Meier, *The Power of Their Ideas: Lessons for America from a Small School in Harlem*. While the context of the congregational school we studied is not at all like Meier's public school, the sense of surprise is the same. Looking in a place that is easily dismissed—after all, what can a small school in a small Jewish community possibly achieve?—we found an inspiring example of a school that has much to teach schools in large as well as small settings.

ulations and resources. It is easy to think of them in terms of what their communities cannot provide: They don't have enough children, Jewish educators, Jewishly knowledgeable adults, material resources, or contact with other Jews. Nor can they provide young people with diverse programmatic options or multiple Jewish social networks. But based on our study of one small congregational school, we challenge this perspective. Small congregational schools, when well conceptualized, can put the resources they do have to good use and succeed at creating vibrant and excellent congregational education that is as good if not better than elsewhere. This is what we encountered at Tikvah Synagogue in Lincolnville, a small midwestern city (population about 100,000) with 1,800 Jews, or 850 families.[2] Tikvah Synagogue, with 165 member units, refutes a deficit-based view of Jewish education in small communities and in doing so teaches valuable lessons about Jewish education for other communities both large and small.

## Facing Critical Choices

Fifteen years ago it looked as if Tikvah Synagogue might close its doors. Located in Lincolnville, with a Reform congregation and a growing Orthodox presence, Tikvah Synagogue defined itself as traditional and avoided affiliation with any of the denominational movements. A chain closed its parking lot on Shabbat and holidays, there was separate seating, and most of its members' elementary-age children went to the Orthodox day school and wanted nothing educational from their congregation. Tikvah ran a Sunday school and participated in the community Hebrew School taught mostly by Orthodox rabbis. Day school youngsters were not incorporated in any meaningful way into the life of the congregation, and young families felt that the rabbi was uncomfortable with children. One long-time active member recalls that the rabbi "didn't know what to do with them. You could always see him becoming visibly uncomfortable and agitated around kids because they just, I don't know, talk too fast, move too much, something. He just didn't know what to do with them and he just didn't have a focus on that."

Tikvah's building was deteriorating and the congregation faced fiscal problems. Some members were dissatisfied with the traditional bent of the rabbi, whom they perceived as "willing to accept the fact that it was going to be a dying synagogue," while others appreciated his pastoral skills, especially with the aging population. The stark contrast with the Reform Congregation down the street that was attracting the younger families pained their counterparts at Tikvah Synagogue. Some belonged to both so that their children could be in a place with Jews their own age.

A confluence of events in the mid-1990s might have been the proverbial "nails in the coffin." Some Tikvah members, however, believed that the problems they faced represented new opportunities. Faced with the choices to move, build, or close, the congregants decided to build. Driven mostly by younger families, some with generational ties to the congregation but mostly newcomers, they took the financial risk of renovating the building even though there was no history of significant fundraising. One of the younger lay leaders at the time recalls that they had to tell some of the congregation's long-time members that the amounts they were offering were too small. The young families also pushed themselves to be as generous as possible. While a few members left the congregation, most came along and began to take pride in what was happening. By 1995 the renovated and expanded Tikvah Synagogue had attractive spaces for people young and old to feel at home. This success laid the groundwork for future fundraising efforts to underwrite education at the synagogue.

A small crisis arose when the much admired secretary who also administered the Sunday school resigned. A parent, Jennifer King, became the coordinator of the two-hour-a-week school. She realized that the children weren't learning Hebrew and that Tikvah Synagogue was paying the teachers to work with "a couple of children," since anyone who wanted their children to be at Sunday school with "a critical mass" enrolled them (as she had her own child) at the nearby Reform temple. She believes that its Orthodox teachers were not interested in the students. She recalls seeing the teachers spend the entire session on the Sunday before Passover cleaning out their classrooms while the students played games and watched. Jennifer and others realized they would have to step up to the plate if they were to change the reality: "Living in this area you really have to work on having a Jewish life because it's not like [a big city] where there are so many organizations and there's so many people . . . The program will be there whether you're there or not and it's just not the way it is here. Here if you want something you're going to make it happen. You learn that pretty quick." King and some others wanted something for their children. They were ready to try to make it happen.

When at about the same time members wanted to explore becoming an egalitarian congregation, the rabbi threatened that if they were to go in that direction he would quit. After a year of study the crucial vote was taken. Tikvah Synagogue adopted egalitarian liturgical and ritual practices—and began its search for a new rabbi. In doing so, congregants had to confront the question of its identity. Were they to accept the status quo or risk changing the conditions?

The congregation decided to affiliate with the United Synagogue of America (now United Synagogue of Conservative Judaism). It selected as its next leader a young rabbi whose first pulpit had been in an even smaller Jewish community. Most significantly, David Siegal and his wife, Sarah, valued small town life. They wanted to raise their children in a relaxed environment where parents could be accessible and a sense of community real. Lincolnville had three advantages that many other small communities did not: a day school, a university, and a few hours drive to the large metropolis where they were raised.

When the Siegals arrived in 1996 Shabbat services were mostly lay-led. A handful of children showed up for junior congregation. Rabbi Siegal wanted to attract more families into the building on Shabbat. In the past day school students attended Sunday school. By this time, however, they saw no advantage to attending and stopped enrolling so that they could have Sunday "off." The Sunday school families, for their part, said that Sunday was the day for Jewish education, not Shabbat. This view mobilized Rabbi Siegal and some of Tikvah's younger members, who realized what all the families wanted: a viable community. After a series of meetings with different stakeholders, the congregation determined to make Shabbat the centerpiece of its Jewish life. This was far more than a professional choice for the Siegals; it coincided with their personal priorities. They realized that in order to stay in Lincolnville as their children grew (they then had two small children, now they have four), they would have to create a robust Jewish life for their family. They didn't want their children to be isolated and to spend Shabbat alone. They needed to foster a real community among congregants so that they would all be linked by shared commitments and connections and they sensed that their own Shabbat observant home would need to become an anchor of the community.

These aspirations tapped into the needs of other congregants. In a place where many people live far from their extended families, members wanted to find a larger social unit that would provide caring, acceptance, activities, and warmth, or, as some congregants put it, an intergenerational setting in which they and their children would learn from others at different life stages. Because Lincolnville's population is not transient, people make deep connections. In the words of a family that moved to Lincolnville from Annapolis, Maryland, it "was a sense of community that you get or sense of family that you get from the people who are here. In the synagogue that we were in . . . because of the transient nature of the people, a lot of them worked for the government . . . there was a transient nature. Whereas here, people do spend their whole lives here, some do! . . . And that's the strongest draw. The fact that it really, on a week-to-week basis, it really feels like a community. The people really want to be [here], not just drop the kids off . . . It's really being there and the parents being partners." Parents also recognize the advantage to being in a midwestern "churched" community. Since their children see their non-Jewish friends going to church, going to the Jewish equivalent is seen as normative. Their children appreciate having a place where they can be with their Jewish friends and not have to explain themselves to others.

The congregants and rabbi have created a community that operates like an extended family. It is impossible to separate the strands that link Tikvah members to each other and to Jewish life. Supporting each other in happy and sad times, celebrating Jewish and other holidays together, learning and socializing with each other, working on group projects and using one's talents to help the group—all these are part of the Tikvah experience.[3] The learning, for children as well as adults, doesn't come only from classes. It comes from experiencing how their community operates and then enacting its norms. The content presented in classes has real-life implications. From the youngest to the oldest students, people practice what they learn. What they learn is reinforced by many others—not just by their parents but their friends, their friends' parents, and the other congregants. In a place like this, a parent explains, you "can't have the attitude that we can sit back and wait for big shots to do it!" People have to get involved.

One way to understand what is occurring at Tikvah Synagogue and how this frames the Jewish education it offers is to consider the type of community it has created. Writing toward the end of the nineteenth century, the sociologist Ferdinand Tonnies described the shifting sense of community as society moved from an agricultural to an industrial base. The transformation caused a shift from *gemeinschaft,* an intimate, sacred community, toward *gesellschaft,* a form of community organization that is more impersonal, secular, and dominated by secondary group rather than primary group associations.[4] Tikvah incorporates aspects of a *gemeinschaft* model. Because of its size and location, the ties among the community members are powerful. There is a sense of shared identity, experience, place, and commitment that shapes Tikvah's efforts to further Jewish education and nurture Jewish life.

# Components of the New Educational Program

## Shabbat at the Center

Several people are credited with the decision to replace Sunday school with a dynamic, weekly, intergenerational Shabbat experience. In addition to Friday evening services, there are three components to Shabbat at Tikvah Synagogue: (1) services that are heavily lay lead (including pre- and post–Bar/Bat Mitzvah as regular leaders); (2) a Shabbat educational program called FEAST (the acronym for Family Education at Synagogue Today that also alludes to the role of food in the experience!) for preschool through sixth grade; and (3) a community lunch. In addition, on Sunday evenings the post–Bar/Bat Mitzvah students gather for two an one half hours in a program called TAMID (Torah A Midrash Identity Divrei Hayamim). The assumption driving this approach is that, if services and lunch are inviting and provide a sense of meaning and community, parents who bring their children to FEAST will themselves stay at the synagogue to feast on what Judaism offers to Jews on Shabbat. This will become so important to their lives so that they will remain involved after their children celebrate their Bar or Bat Mitzvahs.

The assumptions have been validated by experience. This is in part because as fewer Tikvah members enrolled in the local day school, which has moved far to the right religiously, the Shabbat program has become essential to more families. In addition, the few children still at day school want to participate on Shabbat because it is socially and educationally engaging. Parents come to support their children's development and stay because they enjoy the experience themselves. Some people come late in the morning, probably motivated by the lunch that is waiting. Members without children at home are as much part of the Shabbat scene as the other families. The casual Shabbat luncheon, cooked beforehand on site by members, looks like an extended family gathering with adolescents, babies, young parents, and seniors enjoying each others' company.

## The Shabbat School

Running a Shabbat school is challenging. Not being able to write, do art, or other activities prohibited on Shabbat limits how teachers can present and reinforce content. This has actually helped Tikvah move from a "school" model where tests, homework, and strict attendance policies structure the experience to one that is less formal and in the spirit of Shabbat. Since FEAST *is* Jewish life rather than a representation of it, it is especially important not to alienate students or their families. The goal, several people told us, is for the children to love being there. Rather than translating into a loose environment with poor behavior and erratic involvement, however, it has spawned norms that are flexible enough to fit individual situations. If a child is having trouble sitting in class, for example, she might spend time with the school coordinator, who helps the child focus and then return to class. Or she might go with one of the teenagers into services or just hang out in the hallway for a while. Because the classes are engaging and are the place where they can be with their Jewish friends, the possibility of leaving class is not an incentive for misbehavior. It is an option for the times when it is needed. The teachers we saw were all very skilled at directing the children's energy. In one case a teacher had to manage her own learning-disabled child at the same time she was working with the group. Her calm and firm actions helped her keep the session moving forward while keeping her son engaged. Of course, a small class size helps. Sitting around a table of six, a teacher can easily keep the students productively engaged. A gentle prod, a well-timed joke, a smile and compliment are effective moves in a small class where people know each other well and on many levels.

This relaxed stance works in other ways. We were surprised to learn that attendance is not a rigid requirement. FEAST and TAMID, it was explained, would accommodate a child who needed to be away for a period of time (because of competing family obligations) or to miss a session or two each Shabbat for several months (e.g., soccer practice in the autumn). The reluctance to take a harsh stand and thereby discourage a family from Jewish connection underlies these policies. But it is also true that families do not abuse the flexibility, perhaps because they enjoy being there. This flexibility doesn't seem to impede learning. Perhaps because things are relatively informal and what children are learning is experienced in services and elsewhere, even those who have been absent seem to pick up the content as they go along.

Some of the FEAST teachers point out another advantage of moving to a Shabbat school: not being able to rely on workbooks and art projects is a curricular boon. It forces teachers to focus on important ideas. While the people at Tikvah Synagogue don't necessarily have a sophisticated educational vocabulary to validate their approach, we can clearly hear its resonance as they move from "giving information" to "making meaning" from the information students are getting:

[In the past in Sunday school] you could have them work in little workbooks and get information to them and color the workbook and this
and that . . . You did a lot of the talking . . . What I like about the FEAST
program and teaching in the FEAST program is you don't have those
pencils and paper and crayons and glitter and glue and all that stuff . . .
My focus is you get them to read something and . . . stop and talk about
something. My focus has always been with the kids to have an opinion
about it . . .What do you think about the story? How do you feel about
what this person did? Is this how you would have taken care of the
problem? Do you think this rule is fair? . . . Give them the same ethical
dilemma where they have to pull out of their little heads what they
would do. You read the information . . . [and get to the question] "what
does it mean? . . . What is the story . . . telling us?" For me, to get them
to talk about something and see how they actually incorporate it in
their thinking is where I've always tried to work with the kids . . . The
whole point of the reading is that there is some kind of ethical message . . . behind it. Something that is going to help you find your way
through the world in these stories . . .

Another important aspect of the decision to structure Tikvah's educational
program around Shabbat is the curricular coherence this provides. They want
their students to become totally comfortable with Shabbat liturgy and practice and to have the interest, skills, and motivation to participate fully. Watching Ellen Kaufman with two about-to-be Bar Mitzvah boys demonstrates
this. She was teaching them the choreography of the *amidah*, beginning
with the few steps forward and back before beginning the prayer. She explained that rabbis likened the movement to what people do when they approach a king. Since the children have been davening the Shabbat morning
*amidah* almost weekly for several years, this was not foreign to them. But
now, with an image and knowledge about why the movement is done, when
they would be on the *bimah* in a few weeks for their Bar Mitzvahs, it would
probably feel more natural to them. By contrast, in settings where teachers
and students don't regularly daven together, the movements associated with
the prayers might very well feel alien. Since the congregation has students
lead the different services and encourages them, when they go on to college,
to continue to do this, it is important that the students have the tools that
will allow them to take this kind of leadership role wherever they end up.

## Parent Teachers and Coordinators

Once FEAST replaced the Sunday school, different mothers volunteered to
coordinate the program. Their professional and Jewish backgrounds and

level of knowledge varied. One parent who coordinated FEAST for several years and remains involved brought her background as a special education teacher to the task and spent hours each week creating educational materials and games that the teachers could use in their classes.

The hardest part of coordinating the school has always been finding teachers. By expecting members to teach, FEAST is signaling the importance of parents in the children's Jewish development. This reinforces the communal aspect of Jewish education at Tikvah since the parents who teach have relationships to the other children in the program, as well. There is a sense that the congregation's adults are responsible for what happens to their youth; the students, for their part, realize they are important to the teachers who are their friends' parents or their parents' friends.

Since few of these avocational teachers have strong Jewish backgrounds, the coordinators guide the curriculum to specific themes and provide teachers with background material to help them prepare. They deal with logistics, including finding substitutes as needed. Some coordinators burned out and others had to give up the role when other parts of their lives became demanding. Over the last decade there have been half a dozen coordinators. The rabbi remains the content specialist, curriculum conceptualizer, and sometimes chef. Whenever one of the coordinators stepped down, Rabbi Siegal had to "move quickly to find a replacement." When asked "How did you do it?" he laughed and said, "I find opportunities." He then says that the day before the prior coordinator decided not to return, he sat next to another Jewish man at a blood drive and learned that his wife, Leora Cohen, had just left another job. "As soon as I realized we had an opening I was on her doorstep ..." Moving quickly, he soon had the board's agreement to hire her on a very part-time basis. At the same time, the board agreed to raise an endowment to underwrite the salary. An Israeli by birth, Leora had thirty years of successful teaching and administrative experience in congregational and day schools in other communities in the United States. Over the years she earned a master's degree in Jewish education. Recognizing the strengths and weaknesses of Tikvah's teachers, she now sees her role as: (1) supporting the teachers by finding appropriate curriculum units and texts as well as background material; (2) dealing with the logistical issues; (3) working with the rabbi and lay leaders to conceptualize and create new programs and approaches; (4) dealing with family and student issues; and (5) representing Judaism and Israel in as engaging, caring, and effective ways as she can. Not surprisingly, she knows each family and conveys a sense of respect and care. So despite the presence of a "paid professional," who is now also paying a "very modest" salary to all the teachers, there is still the sense that Jewish education is the responsibility of the community and not of individuals paid to educate someone else's children.

## The Current Program

### Cross-Grade Groupings⁵

The limited number of children of any age at Tikvah Synagogue means that FEAST classes are organized across grades (see table 2.1). Seventy percent of the post–Bar/Bat Mitzvah students stay in TAMID through the twelfth grade.

The prekindergarten and kindergarten students remain with their teacher, Sarah Siegal, throughout the morning. She uses a variety of games, stories, play-time, snacks, and music to teach about Shabbat and the holidays as well as some prayers. Trained as a social worker, Sarah has gravitated to Jewish education. She also teaches in the day school preschool, where she is regarded as part of the general studies faculty since only Orthodox people teach Jewish studies. As the rabbi's wife and mother of four young children, she is deeply invested in the success of Tikvah's experiment. She is active in all aspects of the community and her home is an extension of it with guests often at her table and many children playing with hers during Shabbat afternoons.

Born of demographic necessity, the cross-grade groupings foster the sense of community that is at the heart of Tikvah Synagogue's education. The children develop close ties with those younger and older than themselves. And since most of the children have siblings, as well, there are connections among students in all the grades. Watching their interactions in class and in the other activities outside the classroom—the special *havdalah* program, the weekly Shabbat lunches, attending services, and just hanging around the building—it was clear to us that, rather than feeling restricting, the small number of children seem like cousins in an affection-

Table 2.1

| Grades | Enrollment |
| --- | --- |
| Pre-K and K | 6 |
| 1 and 2 | 10 |
| 3 and 4 | 6 |
| 5 and 6 | 8 |
| 7 and 8 | 12 |
| 9–12 | 10 |

ate, sometimes quirky, extended family. We saw many instances where the older children were helping the younger ones tie shoes, find their place in the *siddur* (prayer book) get food, and play. And there were times when the younger ones followed the older children—watching, learning, and generally being affectionately accepted. When, for example, a younger boy enters the room during the focus group of TAMID students, several of the students ask him to sit near them. Once he is seated the interviewer welcomes him and playfully asks if he will be quieter than he was "yesterday at *se'udah shli'sheet*" [the late afternoon Shabbat meal] when some of the students were at the rabbi's house and we saw how the children of different age interact. She then asks him to introduce himself: "I'm Michael and in the fourth grade. I'm nine years old. I'm going to be ten in February . . ." The teenagers, including his siblings, gladly incorporate Michael into their circle. It is impossible to quantify the amount of information that gets informally transmitted by being with older children in this way. The power of the older children serving as role models and the younger ones benefiting from the attention was clear.

## The Course of Study

The elementary grades rotate through three 45-minute sessions each Shabbat: literacy (sacred texts, generally the weekly Torah portion), values (*midot*), and what is called *minyan me'at*, in which they learn Shabbat prayers and conduct an abbreviated service. From grades 2 through 7, students also attend the community Hebrew School, which, since the Reform temple pulled out, enrolls only Tikvah students. The total numbers of days per week and weekly contact hours, including Shabbat, are shown in table 2.2. Hebrew skills, taught in the midweek Hebrew School, are reinforced in FEAST through prayers and use of *S'fatai Tiftah—Siddur Mastery and Mean-*

Table 2.2

| Grade | # Hours Per Week | # Days |
|---|---|---|
| 2 | 4.5 | 2 |
| 3 | 4.5 | 2 |
| 4 | 6 | 3 |
| 5 | 6 | 3 |
| 6 | 4.5 | 2 |
| 7 | 4.5* | 2 |

*Plus B/B Mitzvah preparation.

*ing* Hebrew,[6] the same textbook used in weekday classes. Post–Bar and Bat Mitzvah students participate in the TAMID program on Sunday evenings.

## The Curriculum

FEAST's focus on Shabbat provides parameters for the curriculum. The specific content in each of the three weekly sessions is influenced by the knowledge base of each teacher. The content changes each year in order to build a spiraling course of study that is not repetitive. By the end of the sixth grade, students are well equipped to lead the Shabbat prayers and have begun to chant Torah using the *trope* (cantillation). They understand the structure of the service and basic value concepts with their Hebrew terminology. Working knowledge of the holidays and of Jewish history is also accomplished, though the core of the experience is understanding and becoming skilled in the liturgy of Jewish life. We will return to this theme in the section "Teaching and Learning" to discuss students' skills and knowledge.

Special programs augment the FEAST experience. As part of the Shabbat luncheon, Rabbi Siegal is now teaching *zmirot*, Shabbat songs traditionally sung around the table. He enlists support by rushing into FEAST classes at times when others are leading the services or reading Torah and quickly teaching the melodies and words to the youngsters. At lunch people are seated at tables throughout the social hall, socializing and having fun. They pay only partial attention to the teaching and singing. Again, the metaphor of extended family is appropriate. Unfazed and enthusiastic, Rabbi Siegal asks the children who know the song to join him and soon a few of them are singing with him. Others tune in and out but for the most part the music becomes part of the background. Based on the number of songs we heard groups sing over lunch and at other programs, it seems that some tunes and words catch on. But perhaps as important, people come to see group singing as an element of the Shabbat experience in an atmosphere that is fun and caring.

In addition, a grant from the Legacy Heritage Foundation, enables Tikvah Synagogue to organize additional programs that expand the Shabbat experience.[7] A *havdalah* and Hanukkah program took place on a snowy evening. Surprised by how many people could sing the *havdalah* prayer that separates Shabbat from the rest of the week, we heard that a few students learned it at summer camp. Other people learned it at the Siegal house where they play with one or more of the four Siegal children and stay for *havdalah*. A latkes dinner followed. A storyteller/song leader who was brought into Lincolnville for the occasion told a Hanukkah story that was geared to elementary school–aged children and also led holiday songs. TAMID students sat on the edge of the stage often holding one or more of the younger children on their laps. Families were on chairs in a circle at the front of the social hall surrounding the storyteller/song leader. The atmosphere was warm and engaging; no one cared if a baby cried or teenagers whispered. The content was not geared to the TAMID children, but even so they had each other and their role as helpers. The "family" was working together to make sure everyone had a good time.

Several teenagers then led the Israeli dancing—with all ages, from toddlers to grandparents, joining in. Wondering how it was that so many students and parents knew the Israeli dances, we learned that one teenager went to a Jewish summer camp where she loved the dances. Upon returning to Lincolnville she took on the informal responsibility of teaching the dances to others. This, again, is a powerful lesson: in this small community, everyone's skills can make a difference.

On Sunday nights TAMID students are divided into two groups: grades 7 and 8 and grades 9 through 12. From 5:30 to 6:00 students socialize over dinner. This is followed by participation in the congregation's *minyan* and then going to classes with their group. The rabbi teaches the seventh and eighth graders for a 45-minute session followed by a session with the ninth through twelfth graders. While the exact topics vary each year, Rabbi Siegal's class focuses on real-life issues from the perspective of Jewish tradition and texts (e.g., parent-child relationships, truth telling, and peer pressure). The other period is divided into modules, each a trimester long. One of the modules is devoted to a four-year sequence of the literature of the Jews. It was developed and is taught by Linda Rosen, an anthropologist on the faculty of the local university and mother of a TAMID student. Over the four years students learn Israeli, American Jewish, and Yiddish literature as well as literature from the Shoah. By studying a piece of literature students learn about the historical context that gave rise to the literary expression. The module culminates with a student presentation or special activity. This year they studied American Jewish literature and produced a play based on their reading of Potok's *The Chosen*. We heard how in the past they "started with Isaac Bashevis Singer and his stories and then we did *Night*." They also read poems by Yehuda Amichai—in Hebrew as well as English—and memorized and presented them to the congregation.

During the second trimester a young teacher who is a native of Lincolnville and a Jew-by-choice taught a unit on eco-kashrut. The third trimester is a course on Israel taught by the *shlihah* from Israel who is housed at the federation. The modules are structured so that students encounter ideas they can incorporate into their lives. When they share these ideas with the congregation through some creative activity, the content becomes real and the links between learning and doing, classes and community, children and adults are strengthened.

From their talk and actions, it is clear that the teenagers value TAMID. The group is their social network: even though they all "have friends at school, these are my real friends," TAMID students say. They come on Shabbat and Sunday in order to be with each other. One girl talks of coming even when she is exhausted and has homework for public school to complete. Another, whose final TAMID project last year was to document the experience, proudly shared her videotape with me. The young people clearly love hanging out together, talking about the social and educational highlights of the year.

Most of the TAMID students come on Shabbat. It gives them another opportunity to hang out together and to contribute to the community they care about. Viewed with pride as "our kids," the congregants treat them respectfully as competent young adults who have knowledge and skills to share. They regularly assist in the FEAST classes, read Torah, or lead parts of the service. While they are asked in advance to prepare the Torah readings, the rabbi casually calls on different adolescents to lead segments of the service. He knows which young people do not like leading. Almost all the teenagers readily assume these roles and their facility with the liturgy is as good as we have heard anywhere else—even among day school students. In one case a young woman who admittedly is gifted with languages was called on to lead the Friday night *ma'ariv* service, which she did flawlessly and with obvious appreciation of the content. To our amazement, we learned that she had moved to Lincolnville the previous year knowing no Hebrew. But once she expressed her desire to learn, the rabbi and other members of the community became her teachers—and she is now comfortable with much of the liturgy.

## Teaching and Learning

With all the talk about the strength of the community and the closeness among the families, we wondered about the depth of the education being provided by Tikvah Synagogue. One parent, talking about the school, asserted that "content is subordinate to feeling good." Based on our observations of TAMID, FEAST, and the Hebrew School, however, we would restate the premise: *content and feeling good are mutually reinforcing.* They are equal partners in the Jewish education of Tikvah's youth.

## At Hebrew School

While still officially a community school, the Hebrew School is now run by Tikvah Synagogue, since the Reform congregation withdrew its support over a year ago. On a weekday afternoon four boys are sitting around a table in a room used as a library, class, and meeting space. Rabbi Siegal is at its head and behind him is a chalkboard. Copies of two Hebrew texts are on the table. One of the boys attends the Hebrew Day School but comes to Hebrew School to be with his friends and the rabbi, who is his father. After some opening comments, Rabbi Siegal asks the boys to start to read the first text, a Hebrew selection from Bialik and Ravnitsky's classic compilation of rabbinic texts translated into modern Hebrew called *Sefer HaAgadah* or *The Book of Legends*. The section deals with naming animals. Given the task, the angels fail, so God has Adam do it. Rabbi Siegal distributes a vocabulary sheet to help with new words. Each boy accurately decodes even difficult words and together they translate the phrases of the text. It is not done in a word-for-word sequence. Instead Rabbi Siegal concentrates on key words by helping the boys find the *shoresh*, the three-letter root that gives a clue to its meaning, and then to figure out how the different prefix and suffix components affect the meaning. He then focuses on the meaning and asks: "Why don't the angels get it? Why can't they come up with names?" "What kind of intelligence does Adam have that the angels don't?" "What are the sages [who wrote the midrash] saying about humans?"

After teaching a new melody to a section of the Friday evening service, Rabbi Siegal turns to Mishnah Avot 1:3. Again, complex words are figured out. For example they encounter *ka'avadim*. The boys find *eved*, remember from Passover that it means "slave," and recognize that it is here in the plural. They look at the *k* prefix and are told that means "like" so that the word means "like slaves." "Can you think of a prayer we say that has that as part of its beginning?" Rabbi Siegal asks, and they associate to a familiar prayer, *Mi Kamocha*. As the lesson proceeds many other words are explored. Words that are legitimately difficult in Hebrew are for the most part accurately read and their associations to known words found. With the Hebrew come important concepts. By comparing several phrases, the students learn that the word *yirah* can mean either "awe" or "fear" and discuss the differences: "Why is fear a good motivator? Why is it not?" They decide, with some gentle prodding, that in this context "awe" is probably the better understanding. They then look at the whole mishnah: In Rabbi Siegal's words, "If the first part teaches us to observe the *mitzvot* out of love for God and not because we are afraid of punishment, it does not seem to make sense that the second part tells us to observe the *mitzvot* out of fear (of punishment). *Mora,* or *yirah* in this case must mean awe and amazement . . . We should do *mitzvot*" he suggests, "out of love of God and out of amazement and wonder at the world God has given us."

The point of this sophisticated lesson.is not to practice reading or develop their knowledge of how the Hebrew language works, though these are important objectives. Rabbi Siegal intends to explore a question: is it better to serve God out of fear or out of love? He wants the students to think about the world as a wonderful, awesome gift from God and roots the discussion in classical Jewish texts so that the students learn how to study them and to recognize that Judaism doesn't shy away from challenging questions.

With the small number of students, it is not hard to keep them moving forward. If one boy falters, another helps. When energy sags, there is a snack to eat. Could this lesson succeed as is in a larger class with a wider range of abilities? Probably not. It would need more carefully developed visual cues, and the discussion would need to go more slowly and systematically. But the idea of using primary Jewish texts whose vocabulary is similar to the vocabulary of the *siddur* (prayer book) makes sense in a school that focuses so heavily on Shabbat experience and liturgical ability. The Hebrew school, which might have chosen to teach modern Hebrew, reinforces the overarching goals of Tikvah's educational program.

Other teachers do not have the knowledge base to do this kind of teaching. But with the schedule that has been developed, Rabbi Siegal teaches Hebrew one day a week. The other teacher, Ellen Kaufman, is a Jew-by-choice who came to Lincolnville from a smaller town community in the west where she traveled for an hour each way to study with the closest rabbi. She has developed a strong knowledge base and superb liturgical skills and is counted on by the rabbi and Leora for her teaching ability. The rabbi also teaches all the TAMID students each week. Other teachers, whether at FEAST, TAMID, or the Community Hebrew School, also find powerful links to the overall program goals, as the following vignettes from FEAST and TAMID show.

## A Substitute Teacher in FEAST

Between their other commitments and feelings of "burn-out," FEAST teachers are sometimes absent. Leora is reluctant to push her teachers too hard. We observed a number of "substitutes." These are active members who had taught previously in FEAST and were filling in on this particular Shabbat since the regular teachers were away. These adults know the children since they see them regularly on Shabbat. There is no hesitation on the part of the teachers to interact with the students and the students likewise know them well. One teacher, substituting in classes about the weekly Torah portion, brought in a "coffee table" book on archaeology in the Ancient Near East. Although the connection to the portion was a bit of a stretch, here was an adult with some interest and knowledge in the ancient near east bringing the children into this facet of the Torah. She ably engaged a group of elementary school–age children in thinking about what life might have been like for the patriarchs and matriarchs: what kinds of homes they lived in, food they prepared, and relationships they had. The children are respected for the knowledge they bring to the classroom; several were able to connect aspects of the ancient near east being presented in FEAST with what they had learned in public school on the same topic. The adults are also respected and asked to share their own thoughts about Torah with the children.

## TAMID *Classes*

Heather Powell is an unusual member of the congregational community. Thirty years old, she grew up in a Christian family in Lincolnville but realized as early as high school that she was attracted to Judaism. Over the years she explored the religion, became involved at the congregation, and eventually converted and spent a year studying in Israel. A teacher by training, Heather works with disadvantaged children in Lincolnville's public schools and is one of Tikvah Synagogue's mainstay teachers. This year she has the energy and time only to teach a module in TAMID although she is also introducing Jewish yoga as an alternative activity during Shabbat Torah reading. Something of an anomaly, as a young single woman, Heather is admired by young and old throughout the congregation. Her commitment to social change and *tikun olam* is clear from her choice of topic for her TAMID module, eco-*kashrut*.

After some joking about the hot dog dinner that the rabbi cooked for TAMID students that night and how that wrecked an activity using (dairy) M&M's that she had planned, Heather locates eco-*kashrut* within the realms of *kashrut*, the environment, and ethics. The students good-naturedly tease her—"oooh, ethics again!"—as she introduces the module's three goals in a handout:

1. Raise everyone's (students', families', teachers', and large Tikvah community) consciousness about these issues;

2. Critically look at the issues through Jewish lenses;

3. Act on the issues (each student or small group will pick an issue and develop an action-oriented project about it).

Heather stresses that just knowing something is not enough. The students need "to act on what they know" and "help the world change, become a better place. It's not enough to talk the talk, we have to walk the walk. That's what Judaism is all about. That's what I like about Judaism. It's concerned with how you act."

Since all the students know that Heather is a Jew-by-choice, her comments are especially powerful. After a masterful review of *kashrut* (students are able to explain what *hecksher* means), she introduces the concept of eco-*kashrut* and *heksher tzedek* (certification that something is kosher according to traditional standards of *kashrut* and according to the principles of eco-*kashrut*, as well) through the writing of Rabbis Morris Allen and Zalman Schachter-Shlomi. She then again connects the concepts to the students' lives: "You're becoming independent. You can make decisions about the food you are buying and eating." She goes on to explain that "*kashrut* isn't negotiable. Something either is or isn't [kosher]. At this point students challenge her:

*Male 1:* I don't understand why care more about animals than about people!

*Female 1:* Yeah, we treat people as bad as animals.

*Male 1:* People get more upset about animals than people. Judaism doesn't care about animals.

*Heather:* In our tradition we have the concept of *tzaar ba'alei hayyim*, laws about how animals have to be treated. [She elaborates and brings in a quote from Maimonides until she is again interrupted:]

*Female 2:* How about migrant laborers . . . ?

*Female 3:* What about Mad Cow disease . . . ?

This leads to a brief discussion of *glatt kosher*. Heather explains that to be considered *glatt* the lungs of the animal are checked, so "maybe that's how they saw the [mad cow] disease." Boy 2 asks, "Well, are those [slaughterhouses] being run by rabbis or by investors?" Heather pulls the themes together: "These are good questions. You seem interested in the treatment of workers, animals, and how animals are raised and killed. I ask you to look into them, to see how things happen and what they mean . . ." She then helps the students think about how each one will learn about one aspect of the problem. "How do you learn best?" she asks, and then provides many options for the students' ongoing study of the topic. According to her worksheet they need to review the literature of eco-*kashrut* and "educate ourselves on the issues you choose. This can be done in small groups, pairs, whole group, whatever fits you best. I have the materials. You pick how to you want to learn it." After two weeks of educating themselves, each student or small group will then focus on an issue and create a way to teach it to the rest of the congregation. Her ideas include a "podcast, movie, poster, table tents, power point, put up a compost bin, audit Tikvah's food for ethics, and write letters to make changes." She is open to students' ideas, as well. At the end of the module they will organize an open house "to teach their parents about the issue."

Though it is not entirely clear how students will make their choices and start their work, by the end of the session they are beginning to think concretely about the topic. Heather reminds them, "when you get home tonight go to the blog I created just for this class" to see the next steps. As they leave the room, a few of the students are excitedly sharing ideas and saying that this will be a good class.

As we saw in the other classes, here too is a commitment to teaching about things that matter and to infuse teaching with Jewish concepts and texts. The selection of subject—something innovative but rooted in Jewish values and something that has ethical as well as ritual dimensions—is age appropriate for adolescents.

The second class, with about a dozen teenagers spread out at several tables that were arranged as a long rectangle, was more difficult. Rabbi Siegal was introducing a unit on the blessings before and after the *Shema* as a way of deepening students' understanding of the prayer service and of core Jewish beliefs. As in the Hebrew School class, a sheet with quotations from Jewish texts was provided, this time a list of eight Biblical citations found in the morning *Yotzer Or* blessing.

Rabbi Siegal introduces the topic by asking why Jews say the *Shema* at morning and evening services. Reading the text from the *siddur*, students finally get his point: the words *u'veshacbecha u'vekumecha*, "when you lie down and when you rise up." Again he helps them figure out what the Hebrew words mean by looking at the root and the other parts, but without a board it is more difficult. "Each time you say the *Shema* there are blessings before and after it and these teach us about Jewish beliefs about God."

The students read the paragraphs before and after the *Shema* with Rabbi Siegal asking a series of questions that focus on the different kinds of light alluded to in each section. It is a sophisticated and quick-moving tour of the paragraphs with comments about the nature of God, angels, and creation as well as a *midrash* about the kind of light that is stored away. Only a few students are fully engaged. The seating arrangement makes visual contact impossible and the acoustics make it hard to understand what is being said. One student frequently makes impertinent remarks and others whisper among themselves or doodle in between moments of attentiveness. The class finally turns to Isaiah 45:7, a verse about God as creator of light and dark, peace (*shalom*), and evil, whereupon one boy asks, "What is this? God creates evil and wipes us out?" The lesson has moved quickly. It covered too many ideas and many of the students were lost along the way. After class two students tell me that this sometimes happens, but it's okay. They come to be with their friends and most of the time they learn things. Tonight was hard, they agree, but predict that Rabbi Siegal will come back to the themes and they will understand. They feel that they are being treated as adults and are learning important things.

As in any setting, not every class session goes well. Some are poorly conceptualized or planned. Whatever the weaknesses of individual lessons, students are clearly learning, and much of what they learn is important. To use the terminology of a current approach to curriculum, Understanding by Design,[8] at least some of the these students are learning "big ideas" such as the nature of God, the ethical dimension of Jewish life, what prayer entails, and how the Promised Land's geographical placement influenced what happened to the Jewish state and people throughout history. The principal, Leora Cohen, would like all the teachers to know more so that the selection of material to teach is less idiosyncratic. Nonetheless, there is synergy among the classes. Since the school's focus is on Shabbat liturgy and experience, concepts recur and can be readily reinforced. Tikvah does not have a detailed written curriculum; yet enough is understood by the various teachers that the values and goals are shared. And in the center of the system is a rabbi who knows all the players well—not only as a rabbi or teacher but as a friend—and can make necessary adjustments.

In addition, the Tikvah community creates a receptive environment for learning. Students' knowledge is respected. They see that their parents are involved and care. They get to know other adults in the community and learn from them. Young people are taken seriously and are expected to contribute their skills to the community just as they see others doing. This is Jewish education for life—not only the future but for the here and now. And each child matters not only to his or her family but to the other students and to the congregational family, as well. These messages overcome logistical and pedagogical glitches.

## Families' View of FEAST and TAMID

In simultaneously held focus groups of parents and of TAMID participants, we asked participants to use a word that best describes FEAST and TAMID. Their lists are remarkably similar. The teenagers say community, beneficial, surprising, friends; the parents are more detailed: welcoming, *heimish,* home, community, warm. The adults see the strengths of the education at Tikvah as their children's "comfort" with the service and their knowledge of it "in and out." They appreciate that during FEAST students learned about "what we are doing upstairs." They also appreciate the program's flexibility. Parents praise TAMID, especially the close ties it creates among the adolescents. "It's a social thing" because the children "love being together" and the "multi-age grouping really works; they get to know and learn from kids four and five years younger and older." They also feel that their children are learning to be sensitive and responsible community members. One example that we saw was when, in order to include the Siegal children on a Shabbat excursion, the entire group decides to walk the mile and a half to a sports event rather than ignore their needs and ride.

When Michael, one of the teenaged boys, uses the word "surprising" to characterize TAMID in the focus group he explains that he moved to Lincolnville from a large city in another part of the country and expected TAMID to be "really dumb and boring." (His parents tell that they practically had to drag him to the program.) He was surprised to find out that it was neither dumb nor boring. His slightly older sister Miriam concurs; the previous synagogue had 1,600 member units and thirty students at each grade level.[9] Its "Sunday school turned our five-day school week into a six-day school. That's what Sunday school amounted to. It was just two or three hours sitting in a classroom, being taught, taking tests," Michael complains. When the interviewer asks him what he found at Tikvah, he responds:

> It's relaxed. It tries to serve more as a community. It tries to encourage both learning about Judaism but also being a community. That's what our old synagogue never had. It's just that you had two hundred kids

in every grade. Here you have maybe two. Everyone knows everyone else. Everyone is friends. As far as I know no one actually dislikes anyone else. That didn't exist at my old synagogue. There were bullies . . . and people didn't get along as well.

At the concurrent parent focus group Michael and Miriam's parents explained that although the move to Lincolnville was jarring, from a Jewish vantage point it was an improvement. Before, the family attended Friday evening services almost every week in their large, well-regarded temple, and yet when they met with the rabbi to begin to prepare for their daughter's Bat Mitzvah, he had no idea who they were or what their children were experiencing. At the various Friday night dinners at the congregation they felt alone. When they arrived in Lincolnville they heard about Tikvah. The parents insisted that their children, dead-set against attending the school, try it. "By the third week they were totally at home. My daughter almost lives here now."

Another teenager who also had lived in a larger Jewish community talks about the importance of each student at Tikvah:

It's this amazing thing we hadn't had any place else [we lived] . . . When someone is not here, everyone knows. Like if Miriam isn't here yesterday everyone's like "where's Miriam?" . . . If someone gets sick everyone hopes you get better. Everyone is really an important part of community. I think that's why I said "family" [when asked for a word to describe the Tikvah experience]. We all really are a big family here. I mean Josh and Noah [Seigal], we call them our brothers . . . I am so comfortable with everyone . . . We all read Torah and lead services all the time and its part of the small community . . . There isn't one rabbi who does everything.

Another teenager explains that the rabbi "gives a list like every month and a half and we're all on there [with liturgical responsibilities]. Oh, you're doing that, and you're doing the *haftorah* and you have *maftir.* We all help out." Others are quick to point out that if anyone doesn't like a particular responsibility, they do something else: "Like Lauren, she doesn't lead services or have an *aliyah* . . . so she is asked to usher." Other students help FEAST teachers or organize materials. Individuals' unique gifts and interests are nurtured. The students value the skills they are developing. Two students point out benefits beyond belonging to the Tikvah community: the type of knowledge they are getting builds character and their skills provide easy access to the Jewish world outside Lincolnville:

. . . everything we do here is beneficial because it helps us build character. And we always are like such good friends and we always can rely
on each other for pretty much everything . . . and we learn a lot of interesting things . . . that can help us out in so many different situations.

. . . we've learned all the prayers and the *tropes* and everything. That's
really helpful . . . My sister goes to . . . college now and she's read two
Torah portions there at the Hillel already.

The Tikvah education is not only about community and usable Jewish
skills. It is also about "intellectual stimulation." They aren't "forced to
learn" and sometimes don't even realize how much they are learning. As
an example, Michael talks about the course the rabbi gave about the
*Golem.*[10] He explains, "it's not just that here's a story . . . that relates to
Frankenstein." What excites him is the bigger question: what makes a person human? "It's about computers [and the question] what if someone created a computer that were as intelligent as a human being . . . ? It's made
intellectually stimulating. You want to think about it because it's interesting and it relates to the modern world. It's not just a well-read story."

These same adolescents think about meaning when they substitute or
help in FEAST. They realize it is "for real" and not just "babysitting at
schul." One boy proudly explains how he made a scale to help younger
children at Rosh HaShanah think about the good and bad things they did
in the year and that "you want to do more good than bad. We teach [the
younger students] important lessons at the same time . . ." This is yet another example of the tightly woven threads of Tikvah Synagogue's approach. Content and community, caring about others, and engaging in
Jewish life are tightly intertwined.

## Challenges Faced

The impressive accomplishments of Tikvah Synagogue can easily obscure
potential problems. Even with its successes, there are issues that are of concern to the congregation and that have implications for the future of its
programs.

### *What Can Be Asked of Volunteer Teachers?*

The teachers, even if they draw very modest salaries from the congregation, are essentially volunteers. Rabbi Siegal, Leora Cohen, and others are
reluctant to supervise or evaluate them or ask them for additional things

because they are worried that they might quit. When, for example, two teachers are funded by the congregation to attend a workshop to learn how to use bibliodrama, there is a reluctance about observing their lessons or asking them to share what they have learned with others. Faculty meetings are rare and formal feedback even rarer. On the other hand, the teachers deeply care about the enterprise and want to succeed. We wonder if there aren't ways to work with the teachers so that there will be ongoing improvement to the program, in general, and individual teachers, in particular, without alienating them. Since several are skilled teachers, can they help support other teachers? How could useful feedback be given? Are there perks (online courses, books, attendance at conferences) that would benefit and delight teachers? It would seem that in the context of their community, people at Tikvah Synagogue could develop ways to surface teaching dilemmas, whether in terms of content, knowledge, or pedagogy, and support teacher growth.

## Burn-out

Burn-out is a constant concern at Tikvah Synagogue. The women who prepare Shabbat lunches, FEAST and TAMID teachers, parents who organize the special activities all experience burn-out. As more women work outside the home, those who are available during the days are called on to do more of the ongoing work. Feelings of being overused and underappreciated occasionally bubble up. The educator and rabbi are always worried that one or another teacher will step down because they are fatigued or burnt out. The congregation is challenged to find ways to deal with these pressures and to create ways that will move people in and out of responsibilities in order to deal proactively with this inevitable problem.

## Isolation

Rabbi Siegal and several of the lay leaders explain that they feel overlooked by the larger Jewish community, even within their own movement. "They come when they want something . . . usually that is recruiting for camp or something like that." In an email from Rabbi Siegal we learn that only once in his sixteen years in small pulpits was he visited by personnel from the United Synagogue "who did not preach to us if we were 'pathetic little people' but actually came to listen and learn and give advice based on what they saw." The two USCJ consultants were trying to understand how Jewish education happens in small congregations. From what we heard about the importance of that one visit, we assumed it stretched over a few days. Instead, we learned, it was less than a full day in length.

There are other grievances. They are quick to point out how most national surveys are worded in ways that make sense only for large congregations with several professionals and that when they turn to other regional and national Jewish education groups for guidance in developing the Shabbat programs, they are given models that could only work in large congregations.

The leaders are also annoyed that the arms of the movement and other national Jewish organizations are not flexible in terms of their work with the smaller communities, where getting even a few young people to Jewish summer camps, or families to Israel, has enormous impact. In an email to the director of this research project, Rabbi Siegal puts it bluntly. "These [small] communities have limited resources for Jewish education, limited human resources, the rabbi is often the only learned Jew let alone the only Jewish educator . . ."After describing how they regularly have "over a hundred people on Shabbat because people see a living synagogue with Shabbat as the focus," he makes his case.

> Many, many [of the small congregation's educational programs] are pathetically bad. But many are creative. The bad ones need support and help and ideas and money. And so little is being done with the internet to increase the level of education in small communities . . . There is no reason why the most isolated community can't have the best Jewish educators whisked in via telecommunications. There are just too many kids in these communities . . . to write off while they try to get Jewish education 'right' for the kids in Chicago, Boston, and D.C.

## Demographic Trends

The most worrisome aspect of the community is the question of young blood. Without a steady stream, however small, of families with young children, the powerful educational model that Tikvah Synagogue has created is in jeopardy. Members are always on the lookout for Jews new to the area, most frequently to join a medical practice or the university faculty or staff. Once people arrive in Lincolnville members can showcase the synagogue's programs and sense of community. Not every family wants this. Ideological or practical concerns lead some families to the Reform temple or Orthodox community.

The benefits of Tikvah Synagogue to those who want a certain kind of religious and educational experience are clear. We wonder if there aren't

Jewish families throughout North America who might appreciate living in the Lincolnvilles of the country—if only they knew they existed.

## What We Learn from Tikvah Synagogue

While the experiences of Tikvah Synagogue have obvious salience for other small supplementary schools, it has much to teach schools in larger Jewish communities, as well. The powerful lessons that we learned at Tikvah Synagogue are:

### Small as an Asset

In *The Power of Their Ideas,* Deborah Meier shows the educational and developmental benefits of small schools where the students are known by all the adults. She advocates that schools should be small enough for their faculties to sit around one table and that all students should be known by many of the teachers and staff. This return to smaller schools, in some sense a manifestation of *gemeinschaft* community in what have become *gesellschaft* settings, is championed by powerful foundations and influential scholars.[11] Tikvah Synagogue demonstrates the benefits of being small once a perceptual shift is accomplished and people see their size as a potential asset. While their specific situations vary, small congregations and schools can exploit their size so that:

• People, both young and old, are known to others and a sense of caring pervades the environment;
• Everyone matters and people feel a sense of personal responsibility;
• Individuals' knowledge and talents are used to teach others; and
• Everyone feels a stake in the community.

Large congregations and schools are challenged to create such conditions. Like the "school within a school" and small school movement in public education, in the Jewish context havurot, minyanim, and Jewish family education can be considered institutional antidotes to settings that having grown large and want to foster a powerful sense of community.[12]

### Purpose Matters

The decision to become a "Shabbat community" is grounded in both pragmatism and religious idealism. It serves the community's educational needs and the rabbi's family needs while, at the same time, demonstrating the centrality of prayer, learning, and community in Jewish life. Tikvah Synagogue conveys that whatever the community does together has implications for families' religious development and commitment.

Congregations, for good reason, feel pressured to provide as much as possible. But by limiting what it tries to accomplish in terms of its educational and communal agendas, Tikvah enables its success. Members explain that with their limited resources "we need to focus" and "we can't do everything well." The focus also makes some things predictable; congregants— old and young—know what to expect and can count on having a joyful, intergenerational Shabbat experience and come away well nourished.

## Coherence Counts

The temptation to teach "everything" is strong in Jewish schools. Communities want to impart the many rich and complex aspects of Jewish tradition and texts as well as show their relevance to contemporary conditions. History, prayers, Bible, spoken Hebrew, customs and ceremonies, prayer, value concepts, Israel, ethnicity, and more vie for attention. By concentrating on Shabbat, Tikvah Synagogue created a curricular focus that determines what is taught—and how. Most of the pieces cohere, especially since Shabbat is neither theoretical nor occasional to the students. They have many occasions to use and to expand their knowledge and skills through the informal contacts, programs, and opportunities that the community provides—whether it is doing *havdalah* at the rabbi's house, helping another family, reading a story to tots, or talking to adults who freely share what they know.

## Educational Commitments

There are several educational commitments that seem to pervade Tikvah's work with its youth that are not dependent on its small size but are nonetheless keys to its success, including the following:

- *It values sophisticated knowledge, usable skills, and enduring understandings.*
  Teachers are encouraged to develop areas in which they have some expertise or interest. Whether, as in Heather Powell's class, it is through social justice/*tikkun olam* or Linda Rosen's literature sequence, teachers deepen their own understanding. In addition, students' intelligence is

taken seriously. If anything, teachers might sometimes push students' beyond age-appropriate levels, though the intimate classroom settings and the contacts teachers and students have outside of school support learning that has been difficult. Asked about this tendency, Rabbi Siegal quotes one of his intellectual heroes, Abraham Joshua Heschel:[13]

> When I was a small boy of seven or eight, my father engaged a tutor for me. He was a great scholar and a great kabbalist. And this was his pedagogic method: he would take long walks with me in Warsaw and while we were walking he would teach me Kabbalah. He would teach and every five or ten minutes I would interrupt and say, "Rebbe, I don't understand." He would say, "Don't worry. If you don't understand what I am saying now, listen carefully anyway, and when you get older you will understand." In retrospect, Heschel continues, I think it was a good pedagogic method. It may not be an American method but it is a traditional Jewish method, and I would suggest that you consider adopting it. Don't be afraid to speak on a high level that means to be authentic in Jewish life. Not all Torah has to be reduced to the level of infants. We all understand the need to go down to the level of the people, but we also need to be aware of the importance of bringing them up. So don't be frightened to speak at a very high level.

Students are repeatedly introduced to important Jewish concepts that can form a solid foundation for Jewish knowledge. The nature of human beings, the relationship of Jews to the society in which they live (whether the ancient near east or modern America), fair treatment of animals, attitudes toward prayer, or looking at the world as a place of wonder and awe—these are a few of the concepts that were at the heart of some of the sessions we observed. It demonstrates not only that Judaism has something to say about life's important issues, but it is done in a way that shows that Jewish tradition values both the questions and the different interpretations.

• *Education for today as well as for the future*
What students learn has immediate application, especially in terms of the rituals and practices of Jewish life. They are given ample opportunity in a supportive environment to use the skills and knowledge they master. This reinforces their interest and their sense that the understandings and skills are important for today and for tomorrow. And this in turn reinforces their interest in learning.

• *Jewish living and learning valued by others*
Seeing their parents and other adults actively involved in all aspects of

their education makes it clear to students that Jewish life and Jewish education are important. These are not relegated to the professionals in the congregation. Instead, young people see that the Tikvah "extended family" cares about them and about Jewish learning and living.

## A Challenge to the National Jewish Community

Congregations and schools like Tikvah, spread across North America, need more support from the larger Jewish community in order to help them develop and sustain their unique identities and approaches. According to people at Tikvah, other than when they are being solicited, they are rarely approached by any national or regional entity. They are left to their own devices and feel unserved and invisible. We recommend several interrelated approaches that might be offered through a transdenominational group dedicated to working with small communities.[14]

### Advocate for Careers in Small Jewish Communities and Prepare Rabbi/Educators to Work in Them

Tikvah Synagogue shows that serving small Jewish communities has special advantages as well as challenges. Small congregations are generally seen as entry-level or second-rate pulpits. If more young rabbis could see the kind of life that is possible, other talented rabbis might decide to do this kind of work. The lifestyle can work well for families who want less pressure, more together time, and a special kind of bond with the congregants. David Siegal enjoys the different roles he plays, is glad to work a few minutes from home and be accessible to his family much of the time. There are fewer night meetings, pastoral demands, and political distractions than in large congregations. And the potential to influence people deeply is easily accessed. It is in the Jewish community's best interest for a group to advocate for these small settings.

To prepare to work in small communities, interested students would benefit from guided internships[15] with successful rabbis who are committed to this work. Since much of their work will be involved in Jewish education, additional training in Jewish education is essential.

### Support Small Congregations and Schools

What we saw at Tikvah Synagogue suggests that there are several ways small congregations and schools could be supported, including:

- Create a network of rabbis and lay leaders from small communities who share ideas and materials and provide support and assistance to each other.
- Organize retreats and/or other events for rabbinic families from small communities to gather for support and nurturance.
- Develop a fund to support innovation in small communities, including access to experts, materials, mentors, evaluators, and others who can help the ideas take shape and flourish.
- Subvent the costs of conferences and events such as *Limmud*, CAJE, biennials, and other relevant gatherings for people from small communities.
- Experiment with ways to encourage and support some forms of Jewish home schooling.
- Create a corps of college students with strong Jewish backgrounds (perhaps alumni of the various summer camps) who would go into the smaller, more remote communities to run *shabbatonim* and other programs.[16]
- Create a fund to subvent salaries of rabbis in small communities so that they are able to stay at the positions over longer periods of time.
- Use the internet to build community and educate people.

## Conclusion

Is Tikvah Synagogue an anomaly? While we have no way of knowing, we suspect that other small congregations have also developed innovative ways to effectively educate their youth. Indeed, several of the members of Tikvah Synagogue whom we met were themselves reared in even smaller Jewish communities where they, too, developed a sense of belonging and commitment. Tikvah demonstrates that small communities that imaginatively and studiously confront their limitations and recognize their potential can find ways to build powerful educational experiences. Tikvah Synagogue is committed to community and education, caring and content, Jewish living and Jewish learning. Its educational approach depends on a strong web of relationships. It maintains clear values and goals that provide the framework for its educational offerings. The Tikvah experience demonstrates that feeling part of a group that shares meaningful experiences both supports and extends serious learning—even when that learning feels like fun.

## *Acknowledgments*

We are indebted to team member Serene Victor for her insistence that we include a small, more isolated school in the sample. I also want to acknowledge the valuable contributions of Marion Gribetz, a partner in the field research in autumn 2007. We discussed and analyzed the data together in order to convey to the best of our ability Tikvah Synagogue's educational program. We are both grateful to the members of the community who opened their homes to us and generously shared their memories and experiences of the Sinai community and its impact on their Jewish lives.

## Notes

1. Data were provided by the educational staff at the Union for Reform Judaism and United Synagogue for Conservative Judaism.

2. Figures provided by Rabbi Siegel. The local federation serves a very large area that extends into neighboring states and claims there are about 3,000 Jews in 1,960 family units spread throughout the region.

3. This is not to say that each member unit is equally involved. All the families with children become part of the school community and take responsibility for something, whether that is teaching a course or preparing the food for some event. According to Rabbi Siegel, once they get used to coming, many continue to participate after their children's Bar and Bat Mitzvahs. When the changes were being made, there were some disgruntled members who did not support the changes. Others were thrilled. To paraphrase two couples who remain involved: We were thrilled. Instead of looking at a dying congregation each week we now look at young, involved, beautiful faces. While the financial costs are higher than they might otherwise have been they believe they have made the best possible investment.

4. F. Tonnies, *Community and Society (Gemeinschaft und Gesselschaft)*, ed. and trans. C. P. Loomis (New York: HarperCollins, 1957).

5. The groupings change as the number of students at any grade level change. For example, if a few new families enroll their children the configuration might very well change.

6. J. Grishaver and J. Golub, *S'fatai Tiftah: Siddur Mastery and Meaning* (Los Angeles: Torah Aura, 2001).

7. The grant is also used to bring a musician/music teacher to town and to fund individual teachers to go to a conference to learn specific skills.

8. G. Wiggins and J. McTighe, *Understanding by Design* (UbD), Association for Supervision and Curriculum Development (ASCD). http://www.ascd.org/portal/site/ascd/index.jsp/, 1998, 2005.

9. This is a well-regarded synagogue whose school has a fine reputation. The family lived about 45 minutes from the congregation, in an area without other members. This made its integration into the congregation more difficult.

10. An animated being created entirely from inanimate matter that is referred to in Jewish mystical and folklore.

11. See, for example, "Rethinking High School: Inaugural Graduations at New York City's New High Schools," WestEd Report to the Bill and Melinda Gates Foundation, January 2007; the Coalition for Essential Schools' Small School Project, http://www.essentialschools.org/pub/ces_docs/ssp/ssp.html; A. Powell, E. Farrar, and D. Cohen,

*The Shopping Mall High School: Winners and Losers in the Educational Market- place* (Washington D.C.: National Association of Secondary School Principals, 1985); L. Darling-Hammond, J. Ancess, and S. W. Ort, "Reinventing High School: Outcomes of the Coalition Campus Schools Project," *American Educational Re- search Journal*, 39:3 2002; T. Sizer, *Horace's Hope: What Works for the American High School* (New York: Houghton Mifflin, 1995); D. Meier, *The Power of Their Ideas: Lessons for America from a Small School in Harlem* (Boston: Beacon Press, 2002); and D. Meier, T. Sizer, and N. F. Sizer, *Keeping School: Letters to Families from Principals of Two Small Schools* (Boston: Beacon Press, 2004).

12. Another example of this is the megachurches that create small "life commu- nity" groups for their participants.

13. From Jack Reimer, *World of the High Holidays*, as cited by Rabbi Siegel.

14. There are three reasons that we believe that a group dedicated to small com- munities is needed, rather than using the services of existing organizations such as United Synagogue for Conservative Judaism or the Union of Reform Judaism. (1) The needs of the smaller sites are too easily obscured by those of the large and influential congregations. (2) It is hard to avoid a deficit model unless a group is specifically committed to small groups. (3) The kinds of services we think might be needed transcend denominational divisions, i.e., small sites share specific character- istics regardless of their theological commitments.

15. Tikvah Synagogue has had six summer interns from the Jewish Theological Seminary over the last eight years.

16. Consider the numbers of college students in places that have access to entire regions. Students from University of Illinois and Indiana could serve the upper Mid- west, Emory, University of Florida, parts of the south, and so on. Depending on the context, these might be organized as credit bearing internships or be incorporated into a course. Jewish summer camps might extend their influence and use their ex- pertise by spearheading such an effort.

# CHAPTER 3

# Between Entrepreneurship and Jewish Mission
## The Making of a Chabad Hebrew School

JACK WERTHEIMER WITH SERENE VICTOR

A half century ago, at the height of the great expansion in the number of congregational schools across the United States, Arthur Hertzberg, a prominent Conservative rabbi, mordantly pronounced the membership of most synagogues to be little more than "the parent teacher association of the religious school."[1] Hertzberg recognized the extent to which Jews were joining congregations largely in order to provide a Jewish education for their children. Their own involvement with the synagogue seemed at best secondary. Congregations, in turn, came to understand the critical role of the school for recruiting members. They also were convinced that children would lead their elders back into the synagogue. The school thus became a barometer of success for the congregation at large: by definition, when a synagogue closed its Hebrew school, it was failing; a congregation with a growing religious school was a thriving synagogue.

The leaders of the Chabad Hebrew school under study in this chapter have taken this lesson to heart, building their Jewish center around the life of the school. The school, declares the Chabad rabbi[2] forthrightly, is the "anchor" of his Jewish center. As the school has grown to some 118 students,[3] it has drawn families to the Center. In this regard, the school functions much like other congregational schools. Where it differs is in the extent to which the Center is a wholly owned, family enterprise; if the Center fails, an extended family will lose its income. Moreover, as one Chabad rabbi has put it to me, these centers operate on "a different business model" than the typical American synagogue. They ask people to pay for services they use, such as the Hebrew School, and then engage in fundraising for the rest. Both elements add a powerful entrepreneurial edge to the work of those who staff the Chabad school under study.

But the business side of the enterprise alone does not explain the drive propelling the school's teaching personnel. The school's primary teachers serve as *shluchim* and *shluchos*,[4] emissaries sent by the late Lubavitcher Rebbe and his outreach-oriented movement into the hinterlands of American Jewish society. As the school's director has stated directly, she and her husband could have gone into business and remained in Crown Heights, Brooklyn, the international capital of their movement, where their ability to observe Judaism would have been far easier. Instead, they were driven by a mission to create an outpost of Jewish life, a center to win Jews back to authentic Judaism, a goal, they believe, no one else other than Chabad can attain. These twin motives—a strong sense of Jewish mission coupled with a keen entrepreneurial disposition—drive the educators who have dedicated their lives to the Chabad school, producing a noteworthy experiment in supplementary Jewish education.

## Setting the Tone

### School Ambience

The Hebrew School under study is integral to the work of a particular Chabad Jewish Center located on the West Coast, one of nearly 110 such Centers in states bordering the Pacific Ocean alone.[5] The school itself was ten years old when studied and therefore among the oldest of roughly 375 Hebrew Schools sponsored by Chabad Centers around the country, the vast majority of which were founded over the past decade.[6] Housed in a former bank on a strip mall, and cater-corner to a Blockbuster video rental store, the Center was established in 1996. Its first home had formerly been a private school. This enabled the Chabad Center to signal its intention to create the right atmosphere for the Hebrew School and thereby underscored the centrality of the school to the Center's operations. Now in its third home, the Center consists of a large all-purpose room used as a synagogue, meeting hall, activity center, and reception hall. From this three other rooms radiate, separated by folding partitions. In addition, the building houses a kitchen, often used for school activities, especially in preparation for upcoming holidays, and a modest office used by the rabbi.

The open design matches the tone set by the Chabad rabbi and his wife, the school head. No sooner do students enter the building than they must pass the school director's desk, festooned with photographs of smiling member families at a Purim celebration, strategically placed just a few feet from the only doors leading into the building. There they are warmly greeted by the director, unfailingly with a personal message of welcome (each child is recognized by name), usually also with a gentle physical touch, a high five, a hug, a handshake. Students are never reprimanded for coming late or leaving early to attend a sports or family event that overlaps with school hours. Instead, the school explicitly invites children to attend classes for an hour or two before they go off to another program, such as soccer. The message is one of informal welcome, and "I'm glad you came even for part of the time." Both at the beginning and the end of school hours, parents tend to congregate in the entryway, and also are greeted with warmth and smiles by the Chabad rabbi and his wife.

The school deliberately cultivates a mood of friendliness and encouragement, repeatedly rewarding children with words of praise and small trinkets. The school director greets arriving children with positive reinforcement: "So happy to see you." When children correctly answer questions, staff members make a point of figuratively patting them on the back. Teachers publicly commend students who remembered an assignment. Here is a small sampling of random remarks by teachers commending students: "Thank you so much; you're helping each other"; "I'm so proud of you"; "Aubrey did a mitzvah; he helped a friend. Hooray!"; "What you said is good"; "Excellent. I'm very proud of you"; "Couldn't have said it better myself." No one is more effusive in praising the children than the school director, but every teacher overtly offers praise and positive messages.

Beyond the words of encouragement, children also are rewarded in tangible ways. Throughout the lower grades, one through six, teachers distribute plastic coins each time a student correctly answers a question. The school gives all the children small satchels to collect their earnings and has set up an elaborate system of multicolored plastic coins representing different currencies. Several times a year, the school sets up a "shop" where students can cash in their earnings to "buy" prizes, much as one does at a carnival or game emporium. Despite the modest nature of these rewards, the children eagerly look forward to the opportunity. The director claims the school does not need the coins, but that "as a whole, we need some kind of motivational system. It's an easy way to make [the students'] experience more enjoyable . . . It just keeps the positive atmosphere that we want. It's really like a side thing. We want our lessons to be so interesting that it doesn't matter." Quite deliberately, the school recruits parents to staff the "store" where plastic coins can be redeemed for gifts, thereby drawing them into the fun, and not coincidentally involving parents in the life of the school and sharing the excitement of their children.

The plastic money is an omnipresent feature of school life, exemplifying the calculated effort to offer immediate gratification for every lesson learned. Younger children also get chocolate and candies; older ones other kinds of prizes and trips. The school even holds special raffles to reward students who did homework, such as listen to a cd of the Passover Seder melodies in anticipation of the holiday. Imagine: *each time* a student speaks up with a correct answer or otherwise cooperates, that child is rewarded with praise *and* a reward!

The informal, welcoming, reward-oriented ambience of the school operates in tandem with the fast pace of activity during the school day. A high school student who serves as teacher's aid describes the "hectic atmosphere" of the school, while the director freely acknowledges that teachers "leave drained" after three hours of nonstop interactions on Sunday mornings.

From the moment they arrive, children are whisked from one class to the next, from one activity to another, with little time to catch their breath. The pace of class discussions is brisk; and the movement from one setting to another is tightly orchestrated. The school director proclaims: "I don't believe in frontal teaching." Instead, classes are highly interactive. At times, the class reviews material by reciting a rhythmic "rap" covering the key points of the day's lessons, adding yet another upbeat tempo to lessons; students also complete "take away" sheets to help them commit to memory what they have learned. But mainly, the style of teaching is Socratic, with questions posed by the teacher, while students try to fill in the blanks coupled with many hands-on exercises, cooking, baking, decorating—engaging in movement. The purpose seems to be to draw the students into active learning at every turn.

"We are very careful about how we use our time," says the school director. "It's amazing what we accomplish. For what we have going, we should have fifteen full-time people. Maybe we can do this because we don't have to spend time cutting through so many meetings, extra boards, and so on." The school does not have a board, a point to which we will return, but something more is at work here: the staff members are acutely conscious of the limited number of hours they have each week with the students. Children participate in classes only once each week—either for three hours on Sunday mornings or two hours on a weekday afternoon, with the large majority attending Sunday school. (A high percentage of students also attend extracurricular programs allied to the school.) To make the best possible use of the minimal class time available, teachers are prompted by the director to come fully prepared, and not even waste a moment going into another classroom in search of chalk or an eraser. In classes too, the emphasis is on quick responses and acting with alacrity.

This approach to time seems to be part of a wider Chabad inclination to emphasize speed and quick action. As one teacher put it to her young charges: [You should act with] "*zerizus*, working very fast. Your mom is holding this heavy bag, and you're just playing. Are you going to be quick to help her? . . . Every minute is precious." The head of the national network of Chabad Hebrew schools, as they are called, even claims some schools have a large poster hanging in the teacher's area with information about the time remaining in the school year; each week another page is torn off to dramatize the limited number of *minutes* teachers will have to instruct their students! The message is clear: we must maximize the use of every valuable moment. Because they are imbued with a high sense of mission to draw young people back to Jewish life, the teachers' "regret when the kids leave the school is real," claims Devora Krasnianski of the national Chabad office. Perhaps, this sense of responsibility more than anything else accounts for the fast pace of activity in the Chabad school.

Children, in turn, are deliberately guided to move between activities without delay. "We spend the first couple of weeks training them," the school director claims. This approach points to a larger orientation of the school: it sets forth clear expectations about the kind of community it seeks to create. Little, in this regard, is left to chance.

## Defining the Mission — In Theory and Practice

Observers of the Chabad school cannot but note the strong "mission driven" quality of the enterprise. And what is that mission? The five principal teachers each offer slightly different, but not incompatible, versions of what they aim to achieve and how: According to the Chabad rabbi, the mission is to teach children so that they enjoy coming to the school. This, he believes, will ultimately lead them to live as Jews when they grow older. Accordingly, the school program is driven by a belief that the students' enjoyment of school time, shared communal experiences, and cultivation of Jewish friends will, over time, draw young people into the orbit of Jewish living.

What flows from this is an unabashed preoccupation with meeting learners where they are. The rabbi speaks openly about appealing to "multiple intelligences." Even more noteworthy is his blunt embrace of what he calls "consumer Judaism." "People can choose," he says, "and we need to motivate them to be Jewish . . . Our perspective is very consumer driven—as long as it doesn't break *halacha* [Jewish religious law]." Over the years, he has pushed himself to learn "what children need and what they want." Even more remarkably, he speaks openly about how he learned "to teach in a feminine way, rather than a masculine way. Masculine teaching is frontal; the feminine way is to get the kids to participate in the learning."

The Chabad rabbi is acutely conscious of the criticism leveled against schools such as his own as "Bar/Bat Mitzvah mills," mainly interested in delivering a minimal and palatable Jewish education on terms set by parents and children unwilling to adhere to the rules set by most denominational congregations. Because his school requires students to attend only once a week, teachers have far less time to work with students and to build their skills and Judaic knowledge base. Chabad schools also appear to have far lower expectations, potentially creating a Gresham's Law effect at surrounding schools by legitimizing a shortening of school hours and meekly accepting minimal communal and religious standards.

> Are we cheapening Judaism and making it easier for people [he asks rhetorically]? My principle goal is that people should be more involved in their Judaism. Will that benefit everybody? Absolutely. I feel we are influencing others by our success. By our being successful, it's making them [other schools and synagogues] better . . . This is the question: as a result of making Hebrew school once a week, are families getting more involved or less? If this [school] is just a Bar Mitzvah machine and is not connected [to other Jewish activities], then [critics] have a valid complaint. But if as a result of this, our young people are more involved in college and when they get married . . . ?

The rabbi's voice trails off. "The overarching issue," he declares, "is that it is more important for children to identify and connect, [to understand] that this is their identity, than the significant or insignificant increase in knowledge. [With more days of schooling], they would know so much more but it would become a burden to them. In our view of things, we feel like we are gaining more in the long run. In the short run there is a lot more lost [because of the limited school hours students attend]. Not in comparison to their schools, but to our own school. But the long term effects [of more school hours] would be detrimental."

Considering the strong disposition of Orthodox Jews to regard day school education as the only form of Jewish schooling capable of shaping young Jews properly, it is noteworthy that the rabbi appears to believe in the power of his kind of supplementary school to accomplish good things.[7]

At the least, he is convinced it is possible to salvage the supplementary school model. Noting that children often regard Judaism "as a pain in the neck," and that their parents who went to Hebrew school recall their experiences as filled with "boredom and meanness," the rabbi is convinced his school can alter such perceptions so that children will be happy to come on Sunday mornings. He certainly believes his school will produce far better results than the supplementary schools attended by the parents of his students. Not surprisingly, he is hypersensitive to the resistance children feel toward supplementary schools. By appealing to children's interests and curiosity, while simultaneously offering them rewards and a "fun" environment, he aims to win them over. Indeed, he claims his school already has.

His wife, the school director, describes the school's mission as follows: "We're not trying to fill a bucket with water. I don't want to fill kids with information. I want to ignite a life. I want kids to realize the relevance of Torah, and not only to be proud Jews, but to see the Torah as humorous, joyous, and Judaism as a happy religion. The Torah is sophisticated and intellectual." When pressed about the ideal outcome she envisions for graduates of her school, she spoke of "confident Jews" who can read and write Hebrew fluently and "go to any synagogue in the world, even if it is not exactly their synagogue." And then she added:

> I want them to be proud but to take it to the next level, to bring it into their lives as a way of living. [When pressed further she added:] Our job is to ignite their souls, teach the Torah as relevant, sophisticated. We are here to inspire the children. God helps us with this. It's not my job to finish it. I have them a few hours a week. I try to make every minute as rich as possible, be practical about who they are, what kind of families they come from. We're trying to understand who our clientele is . . . Everybody is at a different place, some people are open, some are not open yet. I don't push them to kosher their home. My husband will make a five-year plan, a two-year plan, a one-year plan. They know who to turn to when they are ready to take their next step. Everybody in their own time and when they are ready. It has to be the right time. We feel that Hashem [God] is a part of this. We do what we can.

Underlying her approach is a deep conviction in the message of the Torah for everyday life: "I love Judaism . . . the Torah's way. [Growing up, I] didn't see it as rigid and law-oriented; I saw it as very natural. A high school teacher of mine once said: when a washing machine breaks, go to Maytag. God created us. He knows us; He knows us best. So it's all in the Torah. Torah understands us better than we can understand ourselves.

I see Torah as very understanding, and very relevant to our daily life. It's not about matzah and wine on Pesach; it's deeper. We're taking the holiday and making it relevant to them [the students]." This theme runs through the conversation with every teacher. Each is convinced of the direct "relevance" of Judaism to the lives of the families in the Center. And accordingly, as we shall see, the teachers do not shy away from incorporating practical life lessons into their class discussions, at times flouting the cultural assumptions of the world in which their young charges live.

The director's sister, one of the teachers, emphasized the interpersonal dimension of her work as crucial to the success of her teaching: "It's not just teaching the actual subject; it's getting to know them as people. It's very important that they go home with the education they are learning, but they need to grow to be a mensch. You want them to remember not just the subject, but you want to build up a relationship. Teachers need to be great role models, great people."

Another teacher, a rabbi and the brother-in-law of the school director, defines the objectives of the school in more conventional Chabad categories: "One goal," he says, "is to move people along to the best of our ability to increased observance. Even a person doing one mitzvah is not an end goal, but it is a great accomplishment. Every mitzvah does contribute. Rabbis can be accessible. Maybe not hip, but accessible. The hope is [the students] will want to connect with Chabad when they are on campus, seeking deeper connections." As to the Hebrew school itself, it aims to make Jewish life "accessible." "Judaism should be easy, not onerous, not difficult, not uncomfortable. Kids actually enjoy coming. I'm not saying that every kid would come on their own if parents didn't bring them, but they enjoy. It's not how much material a person walks away with but how they are addressing, viewing the material."

Still another teacher, the wife of a Chabad rabbi in a neighboring Center (who is unrelated to the others), defines her goals for the children as teaching what is "real and meaningful to them." She does not regard her task as relating "outdated information from the past," but to "give them information to process what it means to them today." The specific example she cites (perhaps because she was interviewed in the weeks leading up to Passover) is the Exodus account and its relevance to the present.

Taken together, the teachers all reflect the prevailing goal set forth by the Chabad rabbi and his wife, the school director: to create a setting for children to have "positive Jewish experiences." Through enjoyable interactions within the school, children, it is hoped, will internalize the notion that "Judaism has what to offer and is timeless."

## The Culture of Planning and Experimentation

The staff tries to meet the school's goals through an interesting mixture of ongoing advance planning and self-assessment coupled with experimentation. "My head is always thinking a year ahead," says the school director; "I get contact information and put it into my computer. When I'm planning in May, June, April, I plan all the events for the coming year, for families, teens, youth club, Shabbat dinners. It just makes a full calendar. I pull out my stash of ideas." All this sounds highly organized. But the director is also open to new ideas. "We were sitting at a dinner for the local Jewish day school, just having a friendly conversation with someone who has a farm. It's her passion . . . And as I was planning the year, I thought of [a day devoted to a] visit to Israel. Turn the place into Israel. Jerusalem, Beer Sheva . . . a full learning day. I wanted it to feel like Israel. The farm was put in the Kibbutz. It came with goats and turtles." The initial impetus is improvisational, but then details are planned in advance to create a "learning day."

At least for the moment, the spirit of experimentation continues unabated. "Every year," the director claims, "I try to make it better. Every year I try to revamp. We can't get complacent. We have to go the next step. I'm constantly trying to reinvent ourselves. We need to be cutting edge, have new ideas. We should always look fresh . . . We have them [the children] for so short a time. I don't want them going home bored. I tell the kids, now you are in the fifth grade, but we will be telling the story from a different angle [when you are older]. So the kids don't feel like they are repeating. The Torah has so many levels. It's fascinating stuff." If nothing else, these words capture the undertone of experimentation and the driven nature of the enterprise. "Every year we give something new. Maybe after five years we'll repeat," the director muses. Whether she can sustain such a pace for another five years is anyone's guess, but for the moment, she is driven to try.

One cannot help wondering whether the unusual time horizon of the school's leadership plays a critical role in how planning occurs. Unlike the personnel in many synagogue schools who are at the mercy of school committees, professional and lay leaders, and boards, the Chabad school is operated by its owners. The school director speaks in terms of multiyear plans, as she reflects back on the decade in which she has experimented with a school of her own creation, and as she looks forward to a long-term future. Her husband, she notes, has five and ten year plans for programs, families, individuals. Does this ownership model play a role in spurring the educators to experiment and change? This school, this center, is theirs to make or break, a realization that has prompted hard-headed decisions to supervise new personnel very closely and let go of those who do not meet the standards of good teaching to which the school aspires. For members of the family running the operation, their ownership of the school provides a certain measure of security that they still will be running the school a decade hence—and a strong incentive to assess and revise programs.

As they continually rethink how they do Hebrew school, the educators are fairly eclectic in adopting approaches and programs developed by others. To begin with, Chabad offers a network of similarly engaged educators who freely share ideas with one another. Much of this is now done via list-serves and other internet tools, and through personal relationships built up by the school director with her counterparts across the globe. In addition, the *shluchos* (female emissaries) gather at an annual retreat at which they exchange new ideas. Up to a thousand women attend the annual meeting each February for the purpose of sharing tips and offering pointers. For her part, the school director is a frequent presenter at the convention of *shluchos*. Chabad educators also pay close attention to program ideas and other educational approaches developed by the denominations. The national point person for Chabad Hebrew schools is conversant with the latest curricula developed by the Reform and Conservative movements and participates at national educator conferences such as the annual retreat of CAJE, the Coalition for Advancing Jewish Education. The work of the Chabad school, in short, intersects with thinking about supplementary schooling across the Jewish community. Chabad educators are neither naïve about the competition—and they call it competition—nor are they unschooled in the latest in technology and what can be found on the internet. In truth, they are more savvy than most supplementary school educators in these areas.

Behind the scenes, the educators engage in ongoing self-assessment and planning. When the school was observed, its director was working on a ten-year strategic plan, from a series of Friday night family service at set intervals, to longer-term initiatives. The educators work together, develop curriculum, reflect, plan, network with other Chabad teachers, read, listen, and evaluate what is going on in the greater Jewish community. They claim to be thinking always about the school—and there is little reason to doubt their intensity or dedication.

## Running a Franchise Operation

The Chabad rabbi also is self-conscious about the nature of his operation and how it must compete in the Jewish marketplace. The following self-reflections offer a sense of how the rabbi easily mixes charming idealism with hard-headed entrepreneurship as he characterizes his work:

> We have been taught in Chabad dedication to the cause. This is not a job for me. I tell people I am retired. If I had all the money in the world, what would I do? It starts there. If you come at it from that perspective, things become possible. You think possible, rather than impossible. We started a camp five or six years ago. Another group tried to start the camp in the same location, and only eighteen kids signed up, and they realized it wasn't going to be viable; they pulled the plug. So we came in and made a camp . . . same place. It didn't matter if we only had eighteen kids. The first year we had seventy or eighty. Now we have over two hundred. If we were to look at this from the perspective of how do we do our work: we back our way into it.

Reading this account, one should not be surprised to learn that the Chabad rabbi diligently reads popular books on marketing strategy and "how to" books on running a business, or that he speaks intently about the 70 percent rate of success of franchise businesses, compared to the 80 percent failure rate of other small businesses. He is quite aware of the business-dimension of his operation and the role the school plays in the Center he operates.

The school, in fact, is a part of a franchise business model, the Chabad Jewish centers. Its director consults frequently with her counterparts at other Chabad schools to learn about the best buys. She also purchases items in bulk and finds other Chabad schools to share the costs. Yet even as she keeps to a budget, she does not stint on services that add a touch of class to her school. She hires carpenters, artists, and painters to construct sets that will be used in various kinds of school gatherings; she brings in real animals to her Israel day fair. One of the basic courses of her school is about the Jewish home, and the school has various mock-ups to suggest rooms in a house. And then there is the use of graphic design and desktop publishing for everything from the school calendar to spiral texts and laminated handouts. Much of the material is eye-catching and a cut above what one normally finds in supplementary schools. Needless to say, the school also does not stint on its website, which is colorful, inviting, and *au courant*. All are investments designed to appeal to students and parents.

The fiscal base of this operation is a system of donations collected from participants in the community. The school itself charges a fairly modest annual tuition—$600 for registration and fees in the lowest grades and $800 for grades 3–6. Other fees are then levied for participation in programs leading up to a Bar or Bat Mitzvah celebration. In general, the Center and school subsist primarily on donations and secondarily on fees for services, rather than blanket dues. This system seems to work to the benefit of the Center. As the Chabad rabbi explains: "We are not focused on our membership, but on the larger community and therefore our activities reflect that. We are program based, we just did kosher pickle making, with Jews and non-Jews. The goal was to get Jews to associate with Judaism. Also, it's more enfranchising . . . We open the doors; it's free, but pay as you go. Some things have a charge, some don't. It is much more risky, because we're at their mercy. We have an orderly plan; ultimately it is done." Indeed, as quite a few parents have attested, they give more generously to Chabad precisely because there are no compulsory dues. Note, too, the clarity of the rabbi as to the nature of his operation: it is "program based," not membership based. This, in turn, spurs the Center's leaders, including its school personnel, to develop programs that will draw people to the Center. The incentive to innovate, in short, is far greater when the operation subsists on successful programming rather than fixed dues paid regardless of whether members avail themselves of services.[8]

None of this, of course, guarantees that every program and initiative succeeds. In fact, the educators are forthright about failed efforts and sober about the trial-and-error nature of their work. The school director speaks candidly about her failure in the early years to grasp that some Israeli-born parents only wanted their children to learn the Hebrew language and about Jewish culture, but chaffed at the thought their children would be expected to develop synagogue skills. Only after some disappointment did she learn to insist on a registration interview with both parents every time a new child is enrolled. During those interviews, she can learn about parental expectations and also speak directly about the school's requirements. More recently, the school added a high school program on Wednesday evenings, which failed to attract a significant number of students because a weekday evening was impractical for overextended teens. The next year, a Sunday morning option was made available for high school students. Reflecting on failed experiments, the director acknowledges that there are times when the school cannot meet all expectations, bringing into sharper relief the tension between the exaggerated attunement of the school to its consumer-oriented clientele and the limits to which the school will go to satisfy the customer.

## The Structure of the School

### Personnel

The Chabad school offers a remarkable student/teacher ratio, considering that on Sunday mornings up to ten teachers and aids work with under one hundred students. All of the primary teachers are Chabad insiders—the rabbi, his wife, the wife's sister, and her husband, the sister of the rabbi, and the wife of a Chabad rabbi from a neighboring community. With the exception of the latter, the connections make vivid just how much of a family operation the school is. For part of the year, a young Chabad woman from out-of-town taught in the school, perhaps as part of her teacher seminary training. Additionally, two adult Hebrew teachers— non-Chabad—are employed to work solely on Hebrew language, as are four teenagers who went through the school and are now high school or college students in the area.

There is a clear gender difference in the training of staff members. With the exception of the language instructors, the women all attended a Chabad teacher seminary where they gained teaching experience under direct supervision, albeit mainly in day schools, not supplementary schools, and where the language of instruction was Yiddish. To hear them describe those seminaries, one in Brooklyn, another in Michigan, it appears they were exposed to a demanding program and weekly review sessions with a supervisor. Some of the women also had attended Touro College, a traditional Orthodox university setting, where they presumably took some advanced courses in Jewish education. As is customary among Lubavitchers, the women also spent their summers and other free time gaining teaching experience in different parts of the world, beginning already during their teens. They were, in short, prepared to assume a teaching role. Indeed, the school director relates that when she met her future husband she explicitly probed whether he intended to serve as a *shalich* because she was intent already then to open a Hebrew school at some Chabad outpost!

The men, by contrast, came to education with less formal training. True, they studied for *semicha* (ordination), but pedagogy was not part of the curriculum They describe how they worked on a teaching style that would be accessible to children. One of the male educators concedes he still teaches in a more frontal fashion. He learned teaching techniques by observing and through experience: "I was learning and already giving. Going around every Friday afternoon with an older student or someone my own age; we went around to Jewish businesses in our neighborhood. We'd go around and bring them a nice story, sometimes stop in more often to answer a question. Then I became a camp counselor. Always had to have games on your mind, in case you're stuck for a half hour. As you grow up in the system . . . sometimes you get tips from professionals. There is a lot of practice that takes place. I also get tips from my wife."

The primary Chabad rabbi is even more explicit about his intensive, deliberate, autodidactic efforts over many years to learn how to teach young people. He describes a recent interdenominational forum at which a number or rabbis spoke. "I saw the rabbis speaking *at* the kids. It was clear to me I was speaking *to* the children, talking like in a conversation ... I haven't perfected the other parts—hands on is not my specialty. I noticed that when I brought in new teachers, that was me many years ago." He also describes bringing in new Chabad teachers and working with them, insisting they learn how to reach young people. "We tell them up front: we hire you [but] we aren't going to take any chances. This is an internship ... We've learned on the job and learned by mistakes," implying they will be expected to be good teachers as defined by the director. This is not pedagogy as developed in a formal school of education, but it is a pedagogy that is a deadly serious priority. Put bluntly: poor teaching undermines everything the school aims to achieve for the children and for the Center—and is bad for business.

## Curricular Goals

What does the school hope to accomplish with its young charges? The school website sets forth a clear set of goals, and while there is no claim as to the priorities within this listing, an observer comes away with the distinct impression that the goals are ranked in order of importance. The Chabad Hebrew School wants its children to:

• Attain a strong sense of love of Judaism and pride in being Jewish.
• Discover & explore the Torah (Bible), the incredible history of the Jewish people & see its relevance in today's day & age.
• Gain an understanding of the practices & traditions of Judaism.
• Know the morals, values & ethical behavior mandated by the Torah.
• Have hands-on experience & appreciation for all Jewish holidays.
• Master Hebrew skills of reading & writing.
• Understand basic Hebrew words.
• Learn basic prayers so that the students will feel comfortable when attending services.
• Identify with the land of Israel & its inhabitants.
• Express their opinions and questions about G-d, Torah & religion.

Perhaps most noteworthy in this enumeration, which appears to capture the gist of what is addressed in classes, is the high ranking given to the affective (love and pride) and the correspondingly low priority assigned to synagogue skills, identification with Israel, and theological questions. The question is whether the nine last points are understood to be the way to achieve the first goal or whether the first goal trumps the others.

## Sunday Mornings

Sunday morning, as we have noted, is the prime teaching time for children grades 2–8. The time from 9:30 to 12:30 is divided between four class sessions. First, come twenty minutes of *tefillah* (prayer) actively led by the teaching staff and some college students. The prayer book employed is a compilation produced by the school, in which every prayer is transliterated. All the prayers are read aloud; mainly they are sung or recited in a sing-song fashion. It is clear that many children are reading from the transliteration, despite the school's heavy emphasis on decoding Hebrew words. By walking around the room and maintaining eye contact with the children, the teachers succeed in eliciting a high degree of participation.

Older boys also have special time with the rabbi to practice putting on *talis* and *tefillin* (a prayer shawl and phylacteries). True to the school's emphasis on speed, the rabbi puts the boys through their paces: "Wrap it like a tractor . . . a, 2, 3, 4, 5, 6, 7. [He wraps his *tefillin* quickly and kisses them.] Pull it on top here; tuck it underneath; then you go, 1, 2, 3. When I was bar mitzvahed, we all got our *tefillin* at the same time, we used to race, who could wrap faster." It's hard to know what sense the children make of the rapid prayer activities.

The children then divide into grades, with the largest classes numbering no more than twenty-two pupils. Depending on their grade level, students are exposed to a mix of classes and activities. The constant for grades 3–6 is a Hebrew language reading program.

## Aleph Champ

The Chabad School serves as a pilot program for the ongoing development of the Aleph Champ curriculum, an approach to teaching Hebrew language reading now employed, its founder claims, by over 370 schools, including some day schools.[9] Developed by a Chabad educator, the program combines speed of letter and word recognition with the levels of mastery and self-motivation employed by karate. This is how the Aleph Champ manual describes the origins of the program:

A long, long time ago (back in the year 2003), a young and energetic Chabad Hebrew School Director decided to expand her recreational activities by joining a . . . karate class . . . One fine morning it dawned upon her that learning karate was quite similar to learning to read at the Hebrew School she was running . . . Both systems ran once a week . . . few parents were clued in to what the child was learning . . . There were students of all levels in class at the same time.

With all these similarities, there was just one major difference. In karate, students were motivated to progress, practicing for test dates with friends and graduated from level to level quite quickly. Hebrew reading at the Hebrew School, however, was looking quite different.

So what was being done in karate that could be applied to reading Hebrew? . . . If there was some way to divide Hebrew reading into a clear color coded system with levels easily defined and attainable . . . And so the Aleph Champ program was born.

Just as students who master successive levels of karate earn a different color belt as they progress, so too do students in the Aleph Champ program optimally ascend from level one to ten and achieve mastery over sublevels as they advance. The lowest levels (white and red) teach students to recognize each Hebrew letter; later levels move to vowels, then exceptions, and finally speed reading, so that by the time students reach the purple level, they can read sixty words per minute from the Siddur, and then at the brown level they must attain a speed of seventy words per minute. (The top black level has not yet been developed but requires reading at a pace of one hundred words per minute. One student at the Chabad school in fact attained that level and was awarded the black belt, even though the formal curriculum is still in preparation.) Students are monitored and tested regularly and are measured for their accuracy and speed in recognizing letters and words on flashcards, still another example of the school's emphasis on rapid activity.

Consistent with the school's overall quick pace, Aleph Champ involves movement from one station to the next, all staffed by a teacher, within a short period. There is a workbook station with a facilitator/teacher, a timing center where cards are flashed, a reading center, and a game center. Two more are in the planning stages: a computer station and a listening center.

Also consistent with other aspects of the school, Aleph Champ offers numerous opportunities for recognition and rewards. Three award ceremonies are held annually to acknowledge progress over the course of the year. Students are also rewarded with the badges and bracelets matching the color level they have attained. And then the staff takes many opportunities to offer public praise, asking all the other students to applaud and salute a peer who has excelled. Parents, needless to say, are thrilled to see their children progress and wax enthusiastic about Hebrew language acquisition, not a common occurrence in most schools.

The Aleph Champ program has some remarkable strengths.

- Students compete against themselves and can move along at their own pace. Particularly at the lower levels, motivated students make rapid progress and this sense of tangible accomplishment clearly spurs some students to forge ahead.
- The program accommodates children no matter where they are in the hierarchy of colors. This means that students entering the school program in midyear or at a high grade level, can propel themselves forward if they have the initiative.
- Highly motivated students work on their Hebrew at home in order to advance. They are explicitly told that if they practice at home, they can reach the next level quickly. Hebrew school is generally not known as a place where children bother with homework. Here some do—and in Hebrew language skills, no less.
- The program understands the constraints under which teachers must work when engaging in language instruction. Serene Victor, an experienced educator who has studied the method, offers the following observations: "The Aleph Champ materials were designed by someone knowing the real stumbling blocks that face teachers around organizing a room, keeping track of student progress, and obtaining materials. It is often designing and obtaining these administrative and logistical items that inhibit a teacher from using centers in a room." Recently, the Aleph Champ curriculum has expanded to include home review kits, a teacher resource closet, clear instructions to teachers, testing tips, materials and standards, clear instructions on creating celebratory experiences, and other suggestions, rendering the program even more user-friendly for teachers.
- The system allows for parent participation. A parent can serve as a coach and instructor for any level, provided the parent has attained that level of proficiency through testing. Here again, the school can engage parents in the process of their children's education in a constructive fashion.
- Most important, the chase to advance to the next color level seems to excite students. Language acquisition is generally not regarded as a fun activity in schools. Most children at the Chabad school appear to genuinely enjoy Aleph Champ, and are rising to the challenges it creates to master rapid Hebrew reading.

There are negative features too. For one thing, the program is labor intensive. Precisely because students are at different levels, a class quickly divides into numerous groups meeting with two Israeli Hebrew teachers, American-born high school and college teaching aides, and other staff members. Sometimes students work in groups of three and four; other times, a single student meets individually with a teacher. This system requires a large staff. To its credit, the Chabad school invests in personnel, but not all schools can or will spend money on an ample number of teachers. For another, the program emphasizes letter and word recognition and rapid reading; it does not place great weight on comprehending the meaning of a word or stringing words together in a sentence. At advanced levels, students are tested on selections from the *siddur,* but they appear not to understand what they are reading. Whether students in other supplementary programs comprehend the *siddur* any better is a subject worth studying. And then there is the question of whether rapid learning also translates into rapid forgetting as soon as the school year ends. The director claims this is addressed at the beginning of each school year by devoting the first three to four weeks of classes to review, by which time the children are back to the level they had attained the previous year.

Still, an observer cannot help noticing how eager young people are to test themselves and move ahead. According to the director, children in fact prefer the Aleph Champ sessions over all other classes. The close attention paid to each individual—every single child is tracked and charted with appropriate remediation and enrichment provided —cannot but serve as another form of positive reinforcement. Each pupil is getting attention, which surely encourages children to come to Hebrew school. As for the larger picture, it appears that bright and motivated students develop Hebrew reading skills that are rarely attained in the average Sunday school program. It is exciting to see just how rapidly children can advance their Hebrew reading skills in a minimal amount of time when they are properly motivated, taught with carefully designed materials and individually supervised. The breakthrough of the Aleph Champ method is that it fosters motivation. Little wonder the program has been adopted by a growing number of schools, including some non-Chabad ones.

## Content Classes

Not surprisingly, many of the content classes at the Chabad school parallel what may be found in other supplementary schools: classes on the Biblical narrative, lessons on upcoming Jewish holidays, discussions of Jewish history and heroes, mixed with frequent opportunities to engage in artistic and musical expression related to class topics. The more unusual offering is a year-long class devoted to Jewish values and ethics in which each grade addresses a different theme: Grade 3 learns about "Marvelous *Midos* and Manners," exploring a selection of twelve *Mitzvot* involving interpersonal behavior, including respect, gratitude, and *tzedakah*; in grade 4 students learn about "My Jewish Home," a virtual tour of religious observances connected to a home, including *mezuza*, Shabbat, Kosher laws, and cleanliness; grade 5 studies "Thorahpedia," a kind of encyclopedia of commandments including some on the environment, appreciation, humility, the proper treatment of animals, *kiddush*, and happiness; in grade 6, in anticipation of the Bar/Bat Mitzvah, students review the life cycle from cradle to grave. And in the combined 7th and 8th grades, students learn about diverse Jewish communities and Jewish history.

Whenever possible, the school strives to engage students in activities. The teacher of the class on the Jewish home reports, for example: "When I do the *mezuza*, I make a whole bunch of doors, so when the kids do this, they learn how to affix. Get a tape measure and learn exactly how to measure it. You're the carpenter right now. You're good at math. Let's figure this out. Give the kids a feather; you're a scribe. See if you can write the *shema*. It's not so easy to be a *sofer*. It's unique. We learn the laws about the *mezuza*. It's not so simple." In the higher classes, such as the combined seventh and eighth grades, students bake and make jewelry with Jewish themes. The school aims for hands-on opportunities.

The culture of the school, as already noted, is to encourage quick transitions from one exercise to the next. Within classes, teachers shift from questioning to elicit response to question sheets and then to prepared "raps" designed to encourage memorization. In one class, the students recite a rap, outlining the genealogy and marriages of the patriarchs and matriarchs; in another the plagues and Exodus account are subjects of raps.

It is striking how little the school relies upon textbooks or even texts. At least until grade 4, Bible is taught through stories narrated by the teacher, rather than through a direct reading of the text, even in English translation. Beginning in the fifth grade, children work from the Stone *Chumash (Pentateuch)*, published by Artscroll, a highly traditional publisher of Orthodox texts. By the sixth grade, students are put through paces so that they can negotiate their way around the Pentateuch. In addition to working through specific narratives, the class emphasizes the differences between the books of the Torah, chapters, pages, and verses, a set of skills that will stand the children in good stead during synagogue religious services, too. As for hand-outs, the school eschews materials prepared by the standard publishers of Jewish curriculum and generates its own notebooks, hand-out sheets and other written materials.

Perhaps, the most dramatic feature distinguishing classes at the Chabad school is their emphasis on teaching Jewish values as lived experiences. Teachers strive to teach life lessons to their young charges. They do so, moreover, by including Chabad or traditionalist perspectives that fly in the face of contemporary American culture. The Chabad teachers are relatively uninhibited about flouting conventional wisdom.

To begin with the latter point: Teachers are unabashed in defining gender roles. They speak explicitly about the roles of women as mothers and homemakers. From their perspective, this is a serious responsibility for women, at least as serious as the roles assigned, in their view, by the Torah to men. The Chabad educators are also not shy about taking positions on other controversial matters. Note the following exchange in a seventh and eighth grade class led by the rabbi on Maimonides' principles of Jewish belief, the last of which is belief in the physical resurrection of the dead:

*Rabbi:* Aging is unholy . . . It's only in an imperfect world that we age. Adam didn't age; Moshe didn't age. Being healthy is natural. When *Moshiach* [the Messiah] comes we will be natural and healthy. What's going to happen in the "world to come?" It's a place where you are in your body; we are going to be here and in heaven. Those of you who like going to Disneyland, eating hotdogs, cotton candy, . . . there's nothing to look forward to because that won't happen.

*Student:* What about those people who were cremated? How will they be resurrected?

*Rabbi:* It's a sad story. The only people who won't be resurrected are those who don't believe in resurrection, or those cremated. It's a serious sin. According to the Talmud, even if you cremate someone, DNA can't be destroyed. If people were cremated in the Holocaust, it doesn't count.

*Student:* 50 percent of Californians are cremated [at death].

*Rabbi:* I offered to pay $1,000 so this person will get a proper Jewish burial. I only stopped one cremation so far. It turns out that she wasn't even Jewish.

*Student:* Resurrection is only for Jews?

*Rabbi:* For gentiles, too. Have no fear: your best friends will come back, too.

Despite the unconventional nature of his remarks on cremation in a state where, as one student noted, cremation is widely popular, the rabbi expounded upon his understanding of resurrection without flinching. What sense his young charges make of this exchange is hard to know, but the Chabad educators seem unconcerned about expressing unpopular views.

They also appear to relish exposing children to traditional Jewish practices far removed from anything they experience at home. Despite the fact that, as they freely admit, hardly any children come from homes observing Jewish dietary laws, the school insists on teaching fourth graders a course entitled, "My Jewish Home." Over the year, the children move from one room of a mock house to the next to learn about Jewish practices. Unsurprisingly, they spend the most time in the kitchen where they learn not only about the separation of dairy and meat foods and dishes, a practice few member families observe, but also about some of the minute practices of the Jewish dietary laws. In one class session, for example, they are asked to drizzle salt on half an eggplant to dramatize the salting and soaking of meat for the purposes of draining all blood; in another, they learn about *shechita*, kosher slaughtering practices, so that they will learn "the differences between kosher and nonkosher chickens." When asked about these classes, the director calmly explains that the children love the course and parents are unconcerned about children coming away with demands that their families adopt kosher dietary laws. Teachers, she adds, are under clear orders not to "dictate to the kids what they must do at home . . . We don't want the kids to make turmoil at home." But the school does insist on exposing children to traditional Jewish dietary laws. Apparently, this distinction seems to work for everyone.

The school's countercultural orientation is perhaps most dramatically displayed at Bat Mitzvah ceremonies. Whereas boys read from the Torah and Haftorah at their Bar Mitzvah celebrations and offer a sermon during the Sabbath services on the Torah portion of the week, girls celebrate their Bas Mitzvah (as the school calls it) on a Sunday afternoon by reading from *Eshet Hayil*, a paean to women's domestic roles excerpted from the Book of Proverbs, and giving a sermon based on that text. Not only are the roles of boys and girls reaching the same milestone completely different, but the subtext of the entire Bas Mitzvah program is explicitly focused on the separate gender roles of males and females. At one such ceremony, the Bat Mitzvah girl read from *Eshet Hayil* and spoke of the separate sphere of women: "A woman's main business is her family, even if she is a businesswoman," she declared. "Her actions and dress must be aimed at setting a model for her children."

Another subtext also emerged from the ceremony. This one stressed the self-confidence and competence of women. The Bat Mitzvah, for example, served as the master of ceremonies, calling upon her father and grandparents to speak. Moreover, while two Chabad rabbis spoke briefly, the main speaker in addition to the celebrant herself was the school director, who served as a model of a self-confident woman in charge of the school and more than capable of giving the charge to the Bat Mitzvah girl, urging her to leave her "comfort zone" in order to live as a responsible woman because God is with her, the way he was with Jacob when he left his home and traveled to work for his uncle Laban.

Why, one may wonder, would a modern, West Coast family agree to participate in such a nonegalitarian ceremony? And what sense did the family's guests make of this? The mother of the Bat Mitzvah girl was quite forthright in answering these questions. For her the overwhelming import of her daughter's experience was "spiritual." Rather than regard the emphasis on *Eshet Hayil* as undermining of her daughter, she claimed it "gives purpose for what girls do. It makes her proud to be a girl." It also has made this particular Bat Mitzvah an engaged Jew: she prevailed on her parents to send her and her two sisters to a day school. They now attend the day school during the week and the Chabad Hebrew School on Sundays, the former for work, the latter for fun. As to the guests: according to the mother of the celebrant, Jewish relatives and Gentile friends alike were moved by the ceremony and felt just fine about the separate seating of men and women. At least for this family, the nonegalitarian approach of the school is not problematic, especially in light of all the positive experiences in Jewish living and "spirituality" their children enjoy in the Chabad setting.

As to other families, according to the school personnel, the nonegalitarian nature of the Bat Mitzvah does lead some to pull their daughters from the school in the year or two before a Bat Mitzvah and to enroll them in a Conservative or Reform religious school so that they can celebrate their Bat Mitzvah no differently than boys. The Chabad school is prepared to pay this price, especially because some of the girls then return right after their Bat Mitzvah celebration. More interestingly, some girls stick with the Chabad school and forgo the more elaborate and egalitarian Bat Mitzvah celebration. In fact, it is striking to an observer that the school attracts more girls than boys: in the sixth grade, the year before Bar/Bat Mitzvah, girls outnumbered boys, ten to seven; and in the combined seventh and eighth grades, the imbalance is even more pronounced. During the year under study, the school maintained a 90 percent retention rate after the celebration of the Bar/Bat Mitzvah.

## The Extracurricular Programs

Given its integral role in the life and viability of the Center, the school strives to attract children to a range of other activities sponsored by the Center. Not surprisingly in light of its reward culture, the school offers "a system based on in-class and out-of-class participation [which] will allow students to reach different award levels." Over the course of the year, six Friday evening dinners are sponsored to expose children and their families to a Shabbat meal. Then there is an assortment of special events run for all comers, but particularly aimed at students; these range from a Purim carnival to a one-day kosher pickle-making fair.[10] The school also sponsors frequent trips to amusements (e.g., movies, amusement parks), Jewish sites in a neighboring city, and Jewish and nonsectarian facilities where the children can engage in social action activities—always accompanied by the rabbi and his wife, so that they continue to deepen their relationship with the Chabad leadership. And then, the school offers a voluntary six-month "discovery course" for young people approaching Bar/Bat Mitzvah in order to explore the particular meaning of the milestone, the rituals associated with the day, and the values and religious principles to which Jews subscribe. It is hard to know how many children attend these extracurricular programs, but the director speaks of fifty attendees as standard. From the school's perspective, in any event, all these ancillary programs augment what happens in the classroom and draw students closer to the Center and its religious ambience. It is clear from the views expressed by parents that quite a few families partake of these extracurricular opportunities; some even relish them.

## Parents and Children

To the outsider, one of the more controversial and also fascinating questions is why parents send their children to the Chabad school. The conventional wisdom ascribes fairly base motives: parents enroll their children because they want a short-cut to the Bar/Bat Mitzvah; they want to avoid high membership dues common at most Conservative and Reform synagogues; they want a minimal program and nothing is more minimal than Chabad. Parents at this school present a more complex set of answers that are frankly highly critical of the experiences they and their children had at neighboring supplementary schools and remarkably in sync with the self-presentation of the Chabad school. In presenting their views (often in their own words), the following discussion does not suggest their perceptions should be taken at face value, but it does give voice to parental concerns and hopes, views that often are overlooked in discussions of Jewish education. At the least, these views offer some insight into how parents make sense of the disparity between the religious culture of the school and of their own homes.

## The Families

Children at the Chabad school are drawn from a range of families, including parents raised and educated in Conservative and Reform synagogues, Israelis, Russian-born parents, and non-Jews married to Jews. Some are also brought by grandparents who are involved in raising the children of single parents. Many parents concede they approached the Center with trepidation, fearing it was "cult-like," coercive, or highly judgmental. Those who remained—and undoubtedly some families chose to leave—seem remarkably at ease with the environment and wax enthusiastic about the effects of the school on their children.

Certainly, one common refrain is that their children are happy coming to school, whereas the youngsters had felt high levels of stress at other supplementary schools. Large percentages of families had in fact tried neighboring Jewish supplementary schools and had given up because the programs were too demanding in the time and number of days they expected children to attend, and, they claimed, also assigned too much homework. Parents at the Chabad school emphasized the battles they faced in trying to get their children to attend other schools, and the calmness with which their children now prepare for a morning at the Chabad school. "Kids love to come here" was a frequent refrain of parents tired of the battles when their children were enrolled elsewhere. Still, parents contended that their children were receiving a better Jewish education at the school than they would elsewhere. "If you want the best education in the area for your Jewish child, you will send your child here," contended one father. Children here "get the best immersion of Jewish identity and feeling good about being Jewish. If you want rigid Hebrew and structure, you will send your kids elsewhere."

Parents also expressed pleasure at what their children were learning. They felt their children were absorbing far more once a week at the Chabad school than what they took in two or three times a week at other schools. Here they could also move at their own pace. And the hands-on activities were viewed in particularly positive ways.

Parents reserved their warmest and most emotional comments for the impact the school was having on their children's Jewish identity. They delighted in the friendships they had made at the school. They spoke about the pride children were evincing in their Jewishness. Some spoke of how their children now invite non-Jewish friends for Shabbat meals, and others spoke of their children's eagerness to participate in other activities run by the Center.

Parents also spoke of the school's impact on the entire family. A woman of Israeli secular background claimed the Hebrew School had brought the family to Judaism. "We have tears in our eyes," she averred, when watching her children partake in Jewish rituals. A father describes how every week when he drops off his children, one of the rabbis invites him to lay *tefilin* (phylacteries). "I make the time because I want to do it," he says, noting that his brother, a secular Israeli laughs at him. The fact that a rabbi takes the time to offer him the opportunity makes a great difference, as does the nonjudgmental quality of interactions. A lifelong Reform Jew who has found his way to the Center through his children approvingly quotes the rabbi as saying, "I don't look at what you don't do. I look at what you do." In the main, parents concede they have no intention of changing the way they live to observe more of Judaism, though a few spoke of keeping Kosher under the influence of a child.

A large part of the allure of the school, parents made clear, is the couple who runs it. Parents speak glowingly of the family environment, inspiration, and love conveyed by the educators. "If you do it with your heart," one parent remarked, "it can be seen." Another spoke of the difference between rabbis and teachers at neighboring schools, who treat the work as a job, and the personnel at this school, who regard it as "a calling." The fact that the Chabad couple was available at all times impressed parents because it was indicative of their high sense of mission.

And then there is the pragmatic side. Parents chafe at the dues structure imposed by other synagogue schools. "Ten minutes into the Reform service," reports one parent, they played the harp, dimmed the lights, and passed the plate, figuratively . . . Here you give what you want to give." More than one parent conceded he "gives way more to the Center than I had to my previous place," precisely because of the voluntary nature of the Chabad Center.

It would be hard to generalize in explaining why these particular families found their way to the school, while others did not. Undoubtedly, they were moved by a mixture of motives. Most had tried schools sponsored by Reform, Reconstructionist, or Conservative synagogues and struggled with children who disliked their supplementary school experiences. But once they arrived at the Chabad Center, the children and then their parents were won over by the ambience. What is noteworthy is the extent to which parents themselves admitted to wondering why this school works for their family. The answers are hardly conventional: One parent describes how he was so repulsed by his own supplementary education that he enrolled his daughter in a Christian preschool. Only when she asked at age 9 about her Hebrew name did he venture to call the Chabad rabbi. His children began the school at grades 6 and 4, respectively, and were rapidly embraced by other children. At the time of the interview, he expressed an intention of enrolling his children in a Jewish day high school.

Another father, a lifelong Reform Jew who had pictured Chabad as a cult, claims he discovered just how badly misplaced his fears were. His wife, also a lifelong Reform Jew, expected the family would pull their daughter from the school in anticipation of her Bat Mitzvah. To her amazement, when the school director explained the distinctive roles assigned to women by traditional Judaism that would make it impossible for the school to sanction an egalitarian ceremony, the mother concluded "it makes sense," and the daughter celebrated her milestone at the Chabad Center. All this stands in stunning contrast to the assumption of the head of the Reform movement, who seems convinced that Chabad "offers a brand of Judaism that has very limited appeal. The equality of women is a foundational belief for Reform Jews. If we are losing people who don't believe in that, they don't belong here."[11] But is it that this family with deep roots in Reform Judaism is unconcerned about egalitarianism or has this particular family encountered in the Chabad school a quality of inspiration that outweighs for them the relatively narrow issue of egalitarianism? All of this requires far more study, but given the massive expansion of Chabad, the vast sums of money its shluchim raise, and the many tens of thousands of Jews its personnel touch, it is hard to avoid the conclusion that many Jews are receptive to Chabad's complex message, mixing frank countercultural ideas with equally blunt efforts to woo its consumers.

## Studying

As their children are attending classes, small groups of parents engage in study with one of the rabbis. In one such class, a group of women focus on the text of *Eshet Hayil*, the same selection from the Book of Proverbs prepared by girls for their Bat Mitzvah celebrations. The rabbi explains that women are more talkative than men, which is both a virtue and a vice: the virtue is that they can help one another; the vice is that they can be hurtful and sharp with their speech. The lesson ends with the suggestion that women must be kind. After the class, the women linger. Some are somewhat bemused by the discussion; but the overall tone is positive. None of the women protest.

Parents apparently also respond well to the couples club sponsored by the Center. These sessions seem to merge study with marriage encounter therapy. One woman speaks about the help she and her husband received during a difficult period in their marriage when the Chabad people helped them focus on what was really important to them. It is certainly evident that the Chabad educators do not shy away from tough issues. In their work with children and adults, they try to offer lessons applicable to everyday life. Their approach seems to appeal to people searching for ways to find meaning in their lives and aspiring to uphold higher values.

Given the large number of children coming from intermarried homes, the Chabad school has had to clarify its policies about the contentious issue of intermarriage. The school accepts children with one Jewish parent but also makes clear that it cannot accept the child of a non-Jewish mother as Jewish. Such children are free to study in the school, but their parents are told during the registration interview that their child will not be able to celebrate a Bar or Bat Mitzvah in the Chabad Center unless that child converts. To further complicate matters, Chabad centers on the West Coast are forbidden by Lubavitch policies to engage in conversion at all. And in any event, the standards of Jewish ritual observance set by the movement would be far too high for most converts. Still, according to the Chabad rabbi and the director, children with Gentile mothers are enrolled in the school and then go elsewhere to celebrate their Bar/Bat Mitzvah milestones, and families accept the ground rules, particularly because they were made clear from day one. "We offer no judgment," the rabbi declares; "that's just the way it is."

Children raised in intermarried families where the mother but not father is Jewish conform with traditional conceptions of who is a Jew, and therefore Chabad personnel can integrate them into the full range of programs far more easily. A Jewish woman married to a non-Jew related that she had considered withdrawing her son from the school during the year before his Bar Mitzvah in order to have the celebration at a Reform temple. "Let's talk about this before you decide," the director urged; "we'll make this the most beautiful thing for you, so you will be satisfied." Doing her best imitation of a caterer, the director illustrates how the school works to satisfy the consumer—insofar as Jewish law continues to be observed. The family in this instance was apparently convinced, and responded warmly to the celebration at the Chabad Center.

## Assessment

It would take a study beyond the present one to assess just what the children take away from their years at the Chabad school: What do they learn and retain? What sense do they make of the material? How have their experiences at the school shaped their lives as Jews? And what is the long-term impact of the education they received at the school? At best, an observer can comment on the surprising level of Hebraic reading ability in a program that meets only one day a week, the willingness of students to participate actively in class sessions and activities, and the engaged demeanor of the children.

Certainly, no signs of serious behavior problems or even ongoing sullenness are readily apparent. For the most part, children participated energetically and were responsive to teachers. They appeared comfortable sharing their excitement with the staff, and especially celebrated their Aleph Champ progress by rushing excitedly to the director for the praise they knew she would offer. According to the testimony of their parents, the children feel the warmth and hospitality exuded by the educational staff. After observing children and interviewing their parents, one has little reason to doubt the matter-of-fact assertion of the director when she claimed: "The Rebbe gave us a love for every Jew, whatever their observances." Families seem to feel accepted and embraced by the school.

For the larger community of supplementary schools, the effort of the Chabad school to nurture a warm atmosphere, with frequent positive reinforcement, merits attention. No doubt the strong sense of mission coupled with a realistic appreciation of how families must be treated as consumers gives the Chabad school an edge in developing its particular ambience. If they consciously seek to uphold the voluntary nature of their enterprise, other supplementary schools will also strive to create such an atmosphere. The smiles, warm praise, and acceptance Chabad educators shower on their young charges certainly are replicable. Undoubtedly other schools do work at creating an inviting atmosphere. More should.

They also might consider taking a leaf from the Chabad playbook as they move parents and children to embrace Jewish rituals. Note the way the school addressed a question of religious policy during its first year of operation. When the school initially opened its doors, it seemed impossible to insist upon boys wearing a head covering, as is the custom in schools with a traditionalist outlook. Indeed, a yarmulke seemed alien to parents and children alike. Rather than lay down the law, the school leaders decided to treat a head covering for boys as optional. They made yarmulkes available at the front door, sought opportunities to get the boys to invest themselves in a *kippa* by organizing sessions to decorate them, and most important, they praised boys who covered their heads, emphasizing how proud they were of the *kippa*-wearers. They did not, however, say anything negative to the boys who remained bareheaded. By the end of the school year, every boy had decided to wear a yarmulke, even though the school never made such garb compulsory. The positive reinforcement alone seems to have done the job, a lesson not lost on the school director who tells this story.

This early incident in the history of the school can be read in a number of ways: It attests to the flexibility of the educators and their willingness to be patient; it dramatizes how the school works to make Jewish living fun; it also underscores the noncoercive environment the educators try to foster. Were the school to refuse to set clear guidelines in every area, one might be more concerned about its willingness to bend to the wishes of the consumer. But in fact, the school does draw some lines in the sand, particularly when it comes to children it does not consider Jewish according to *halacha*. But on some issues, it uses the carrot rather than the stick, to great effect, a lesson with broader importance.

Two larger cultural trends within the Chabad school also may have broader applicability. One is the matter of pace: as noted frequently, the Chabad personnel like to keep the children moving physically, fill up class time with multiple activities, and place a premium on rapid responses, whether the subject matter is Hebrew reading or exploring a Biblical narrative. It is hard to know how pedagogically sound such an approach is for different types of learners. But what the school does convey is a sense of urgency about making every moment count. The implicit message is that time is precious.

The second broader tendency of the school is toward the unapologetic explanation of traditional Jewish beliefs and behaviors. It is refreshing to hear Jewish educators strive to speak about Judaism without soft-pedaling religious teachings that seem out-of-step with current modes of thinking. True, the educators all allude to movies and other cultural signposts familiar to the students. One rabbi began a discussion of the Biblical tabernacle with a reference to the movie *Raiders of the Lost Ark;* others employ sports metaphors. But when they discuss their understanding of Judaism, they forthrightly promote concepts that may seem alien to the students. They then explain how Jewish practices offer a better way of living than do current mores. At every opportunity, teachers strive to offer life lessons. Not surprisingly, they tend to connect with children who are struggling with larger questions of morality, interpersonal relationships, fairness, decency—and they win over parents who are grateful to the Chabad educators for teaching their children good values that are not necessarily reinforced by the larger culture.

This, in turn, raises the question of accountability: To whom are the educators responsible? The short answer is, to the Chabad rabbi and his wife. These two leaders have proven themselves tough-minded in choosing and mentoring teachers, and when necessary firing those who did not engage the students well enough. But to whom are the Chabad personnel responsible? Who monitors what they teach and choose to emphasize? The answer is no one. Like so much of Jewish educational programming in this country, there is no accreditation system or board of supervisors that scrutinizes how and what is taught in Jewish supplementary schools (or for that matter in other Jewish educational settings). Many congregational schools have school committees and other governance structures to oversee the school. The Chabad school lacks such mechanisms; the top educators police themselves.

The only checks, in fact, are the marketplace and their religious commitments. The educators know that if they fail to deliver an enjoyable, compelling program, children will opt to leave and take their parents away from the Chabad Center. This market reality, perhaps more acutely felt in a small Chabad school than in a larger denominational structure that may have more of a monopoly over services by virtue of its name and scope, spurs the Chabad educators to work harder, experiment, and continually refine their program. The school director put this directly when she exclaimed: "I gotta keep moving, keep fresh and alive, [maintain] movement and [stay] vibrant." Here is yet another larger lesson we can extract from the experience of this school: when a synagogue embraces a program model, as opposed to a membership model, it must constantly spur itself to improve in order to attract participants. Unlike congregational schools that levy a blanket membership fee that entitles families to select or ignore programs the synagogue offers, the Chabad Center's model forces its religious and educational leaders to assess their offerings at every turn because they cannot afford to become complacent lest they lose participants whose fees support its individual program. In this sense, the Chabad model goes well beyond the theory on which many congregations rely. Not only does it expect that the need to enroll children in a congregational school will serve as the largest motivation for getting parents to take out a synagogue membership, the Chabad school does not require such synagogue membership and therefore must insure that children will enjoy coming to the school program.

This business model potentially could lead the school to offer little more than fun and games in order to keep children happy. But here the countervailing values of Chabad play a large role. Educators in the school are deeply committed to helping Jews connect intensively with Judaism and teaching them how to take on increasing numbers of Jewish observances. From this flows their sense of urgency and their resolve to foster a love of Judaism in their young charges. One can only conclude after observing this Chabad Hebrew school that its personnel are driven by a potent coupling of a strong business sense with a powerful mission to "ignite Jewish souls."

## Notes

1. Cited in Carolyn L. Wiener, "A Merger of Synagogues in San Francisco," *Jewish Journal of Sociology* 14 (Dec. 1972), p. 189.

2. Two Chabad rabbis, brothers-in-law, work at the school. But only the head of the Center, whose wife is the school director, is referred to as "the rabbi." Accordingly, this report, too, refers to him as "the rabbi."

3. Educators at the school refer to an enrollment of 130 students, but this number includes children participating in "Mommy and Me" and other early childhood programs through kindergarten.

4. This report transliterates Hebrew terms as they are spoken by Chabad personnel, who tend to pronounce their words in Ashkenazi Hebrew.

5. For a listing of Chabad Centers by state, see http://www.chabad.org/centers/.

6. Perhaps because the schools only emerged in recent years, they are only given glancing mention in Sue Fishkoff's *The Rebbe's Army: Inside the World of Chabad-Lubavitch* (New York: Schocken, 2003). Notwithstanding the recent emergence of a Hebrew school network under Chabad auspices, the Lubavitch movement was involved in supplementary Jewish education already 65 years ago. In fact, the movement played a leading role in the battle for and sustaining of Release Time in New York public schools, lobbying for bills allowing children an hour per week of religious study and staffing classes that served tens of thousands of children. See *Shiurei Limud Hados: Historical Review of the Released Time Program of the National Committee for the Furtherance of Jewish Education* (Brooklyn: Merkos L'Inyonei Chinuch, 2006).

7. It is quite clear, though, that in the view of the Chabad rabbi, supplementary education is still inferior to day school study. When talking about conversion, a process he does not personally supervise, he sets as minimal standards that families must live in walking distance of a synagogue and send their children to a day school (presumably an Orthodox one, such as the school where he sends his own children).

8. For a broader discussion of fund-raising in the Chabad movement, see Fishkoff, chapter 9, "Show Me the Money." Surprisingly, given the title of this chapter, the author pays virtually no attention to questions of fiscal oversight and accountability within Chabad.

9. Information on the system and curriculum are available at http://www.aleph champ.com/.

10. The pickle-making fair was deemed a complete success because it attracted quite a few non-Jews. In the view of the rabbi, the more attractive the Center is for non-Jews, the more effective it will be for Jews. For this reason, he runs an interfaith study group devoted to Jewish theology and prides himself on its attractiveness to neighboring Christian clergy and lay people—who then bring their Jewish friends!

11. Rabbi Eric Yoffie quoted in Fishkoff, p. 128.

# II. *Re-Thinking Large Suburban Congregational Schools*

# CHAPTER 4

# Belonging Before Belief

HAROLD WECHSLER WITH CYD BETH WEISSMAN

> How good it is for friends to sit together!
> —Song sung by pre-K students sitting in a circle.
>
> Behold, how good and how pleasant it is
> For brethren to dwell together in unity!
> —Psalm 133[1]

If this Reconstructionist synagogue ever adopted an anthem, it would be *Henai Matov*. The song emanates from boom boxes in classrooms; the cantor and the congregation sing it in services; congregation members hum it in the halls. Psalm 133 represents the synagogue's credo *and* the essential value of Reconstructionist Judaism: Belonging to a community comes before all beliefs save for a belief in belonging. Belonging comes before behavior. Reconstructionists eschew supernaturalism and reject the possibility of divine intervention in the laws of the physical sciences. Teachers and students in this naturalistic movement frequently discuss the nature of God. But belief in God is neither necessary nor sufficient to belong to this branch of Judaism.

Enter the synagogue office. On the counter is an advertisement for Camp JRF, the Reconstructionist summer camp founded in 2002. The ad shows a man rowing a canoe. Look closely and it's Mordecai Kaplan's head superimposed on the rower. "Kappy" is more than superimposed at this synagogue; he is ever-present. And so are some of his key precepts: belonging before belief; the past gets a vote, not a veto; and democratize the Jewish community. A meaningful Jewish life in a rapidly changing America requires a communal form of Judaism; it may entail "reconstructing" traditions and practices inherited from different times and cultural conditions—even from Kaplan's formulations—to meet changed living conditions.

We're only two generations from the beginning of Reconstruction, but as one would suspect in a religious movement that attempts to balance tradition and innovation, the current leaders are not dogmatic followers of Kaplan. "We have long passed the time when the writings of the charismatic founder and the early disciples were considered definitive," writes one of Reconstruction's current leaders.[2] Policies and practices vary considerably among Reconstructionist rabbis, and movement leaders see these variations as inevitable, even desirable. "Our liberal predilection towards being nonjudgmental coupled with our principled preference for pluralism," one leader writes, "suggests we are unlikely to coerce compliance."[3]

But Reconstructionist thinkers, then and now, promote "community"— a word with special meaning. "A community implies sharing of ideas, purposes, thoughts, and emotions," wrote Gratz College professor and cultural Zionist William Chomsky in the 1930s. But what should the community share? The community, he continued, "must be based on common memories, common experiences, common beliefs and practices, common aims and aspirations; as well as common means of sharing all these, such as language, art, and music." Fraternal defense and charitable goals did not make a community. Neither did "worshipping together under the guidance of a minister or rabbi, who is charged with dispensing sacred knowledge and divine grace." Community, Chomsky concluded, involved sharing, resulting in enriched lives for all members.[4]

Staff members understand the key role of the school and the synagogue in the Reconstructionist movement, though they also understand that the world of their members differs greatly from the time when many Jews suburbanized after World War II. The synagogue is about to celebrate its fiftieth anniversary. One of the movement's founders—a close relative of Kaplan's—was a rabbi here. The synagogue has no written history, but the rabbis and key laity know the congregation's important historical moments. During the 1980s, the synagogue was located in a neighboring suburb, and members celebrated the High Holy Days in a nearby Unitarian church. The congregation, already thinking about a move, accepted an offer to purchase the church building at a cheap price when the Unitarians relocated to larger quarters. Membership could and did increase from 150 to 350 families after that move. Key staff members are part of this history, sharing personal as well as professional ties to the school and congregation. One oft-cited example: Rabbi Abby, the school's director, celebrated her Bat Mitzvah here; she graduated from the school as a member of a class of six. Her young children now attend many school programs, and she participates as a parent in Gan Shalom, the synagogue's cooperative nursery school.

Staff members also know the histories of many families in the congregation, and are often involved in the lives of those families. They give their cell phone numbers to students in the school. Rabbi Tom, the senior rabbi, interrupts a discussion twice to answer his cell phone, explaining that it might be a call from a student. Knowing who attends services and programs allows staff members to identify potential lay leaders, school assistants, and even teachers—Rabbi Abby recently recruited a technologically savvy parent to teach in the school's media center. Knowing whose attendance stops might help to identify a family in need.

Belonging and a sense of history—personal and institutional—define this synagogue's educational endeavors. Rabbi Abby's goal: create a safe Jewish environment with opportunities for all students, parents, and siblings to become one community. Strengthening nuclear and extended families in Jewish directions, she adds, is a prerequisite to and concomitant with communal involvement. And communal involvement is prerequisite for creating a vital, normative Judaism that sustains Kaplan's key tenets while permitting local answers to religious questions in an era of experimentation.

The synagogue and its school largely succeed in eliciting communal involvement. Intense demands on the time of suburban families increase the need and the challenge to create a community built on shared experiences, memories, and beliefs. Community at this school is not a platitude or aspiration; it is available for all. Building community begins with the staff. Rabbi Abby, along with Rabbi Tom and Cantor Sam, who also have lengthy tenures, see themselves as a family of professionals. Their mutual comfort level helps to account for the casual atmosphere pervading school and synagogue. All are on a first name basis. Staff dress is informal during the week. Today Rabbi Tom wears an old sweatshirt and new jeans with the tags still on, while several teachers wear tee shirts. Congregants dress informally on Shabbat, while staff attire is more professional.

This familial attitude among staff members translates into a collaborative ethos. "We all do it all," says Rabbi Abby. "I know how to delegate," she adds, "but we're also resources for each other. Together we deal with what has to be done without duplicating efforts." The staff members teach and conduct services together, and act as a team at weekly staff meetings that include laity and senior faculty. Cantor Sam is not solely responsible for Bar Mitzvah preparation. He helps the students learn to chant Torah—students chant their *parsha* (Torah reading portion) before other students in the Tuesday night pre–Bar/Bat Mitzvah class—but they work with Rabbi Abby on their *D'var Torah* (described later in this chapter), and with Rabbi Tom on the English reading supplements. The teachers share this attitude. "[Rabbi Abby] came here with an aura of change about her," says one teacher. "She's not afraid to throw stuff out the window. Now, we never teach the same thing in the same way twice. We have permission to experiment."

❖

Space is at a premium at this school; storage areas include much of Rabbi Abby's office. The library triples as a classroom and meeting room. Sometimes the nimble staff must quickly convert space from one use to another. On weekdays, the large, multipurpose Blue Room changes from a venue for *Tefilla Breira* (also described later in this chapter) to a classroom to a staging area for the school's car pool dismissal. On weekends, this room accommodates Bar/Bat Mitzvah meals and receptions, family Shabbat services, and adult study groups. The preschool program director takes pride in finding money in a tight budget and space in overcrowded classrooms and constricted hall corridors for state-mandated cubbies for each child. The small rabbinical offices are all off a narrow corridor that also accommodates several floor-to-ceiling bookshelves, a sofa, and miscellaneous cartons. The synagogue courtyard is also small. The classrooms have the high pointed ceilings common in church architecture. Higher ceilings, suggest two educational researchers, may help to prime the concept of freedom over confinement.[5] Reconstructionists would agree.

It's easy to bump into others here; actually it's unavoidable. Consequently, students and congregants know a lot about each other. The staff sees such intimacy as essential to community. The synagogue's new Project Kehillah, which randomly divides the congregation into ten subunits, exemplifies this priority. The synagogue balances community and financial stability by holding membership to around 375 families. But the collectivity comes first when the staff must choose between communal intimacy and financial comfort. Teachers can earn more elsewhere, but the school avoids dependence on contingent labor—it employs one or two new teachers per year—by hiring full-time teachers for nursery *and* supplementary school assignments, and by awarding desirable dedicated classrooms to these faculty members.[6] Focusing on community while remaining within a tight budget enables the school to compete with the educational programming offered by fourteen other synagogues and a Jewish community center in the immediate area. The synagogue's reputation for building a warm community even attracts some non-Jews to its preschool program.

# The School

> The Seder is essentially a lesson in education. It is a kind of model lesson to the Jewish people. It is intended to point to the spirit in which a people must learn to educate its young. If we study the Seder from that standpoint we note that it is intended to serve as a token of three important principles. Those principles are (1) Education can and should constitute a religious experience, (2) The parental responsibility for the education of the child should be prior to that of the state, and (3) the most important training which any education should afford should be a training in freedom . . .
>
> The minds of the participants in the Seder are focused on the liberation of the Israelites from Egyptian bondage. The main theme of the Pesach festival is freedom. The alternative designation for the Pesach festival is *"zeman herutenu,"* the season of our freedom. All this should serve as token of the principle that the ideal education is that in which the child is trained effectively to be free to cherish freedom and to know how to use it.
>
> —Mordecai Kaplan[7]

This school wears its values on its sleeve. These values, derived from the Jewish and the American experiences, include community, caring, democracy, and freedom. These values are lived, not just espoused; they guide decisions large and small. Going green, for example, means *going green*. Today the staff discusses the large amounts of recyclable flatware used at school and synagogue events. They evaluate the quality of the eco-friendly eating utensils as substitutes for plastic silverware. The cups are all right; so is the flatware, made from potatoes. But the soup bowls leak. The congregation upholds a Jewish value—*bal tashchit* (do not waste)—while promoting the values of the secular community. Connecting word and deed enables students and congregants to understand the community's values and their sources.

If Jewish life, as Reconstructionists believe, is best lived in a free, democratic environment, the school must take its American locale seriously. Being Jewish and American may not often be at odds, but being Jewish, at least in the traditional sense, does not always win out in the atypical instances when conflicts arise. Here's an example. The synagogue offers its facilities as a polling center on Election Day—the American Yom Kippur, as Rabbi Tom calls it. The staff and lay leaders view this offer as a sign of the synagogue's commitment to the American polity. But that commitment requires the nursery school to close on Election Day since strangers will enter the building to vote during school hours.

The complication: the state mandates a 180-day per year minimum for nursery schools. Meeting that mandate requires the school to stay open on the eighth day of Sukkot. Reconstructionist schools, including this one, are amenable to staying open: American Jews, school leaders say, need not celebrate Jewish holidays for two days. But perhaps the school should close, since several nursery school teachers belong to synagogues that observe second days. The school depends on faculty from other denominations since Reconstructionist faculty members are scarce, and since competing local synagogues are eager to entice good teachers away. The school's decision: close on Election Day and find substitutes for teachers who observe the eighth day of Sukkot. The staff views this decision as reaffirming Reconstruction's commitment to American society; it also reflects a pragmatism often deemed a quintessential American value. Fortunately, such dilemmas are exceptional; value congruence is more common.

The school takes seriously the primacy of the family as Jewish educator. "The values of our Reconstructionist community are best transmitted," says Rabbi Abby, "when children see their parents living Jewishly, whether it be in the synagogue, in the larger community, or at home." "I'm able to talk to my children about the Torah portion at home because I'm here studying it," says a father whose family attends the synagogue's Shabbat school. "I don't get a chance to think large thoughts during the week," he adds, "like where did the Torah come from or what's God's role. But this study group lets me do that and then I can talk to my daughter about it." Family members, ideally, educate each other. The staff works to assure that no one is embarrassed by a lack of Jewish knowledge lest such embarrassment harm *shalom bayit*—peace at home—where belonging, valuing, and doing come first.

The school opened in 1959, with one teacher and about a dozen children from ten families. The children met twice a week in a mixed-age group. A strong education committee, transient school leaders, and a lack of organization characterized its first twenty years. The school went through cycles of "trial, experimentation, and failure," despite the efforts of concerned parents. Enrollments remained stable at about 35 to 40 students until about 1985, doubling by 1990, and growing to 140 students by 1995. Enrollments increased slightly over the next decade as the synagogue capped membership.

"The place was disorganized when I first came here [in 1999]," says Rabbi Abby. "Whatever anyone did was OK; there was a camp-like atmosphere. The teachers felt they couldn't get anything done." After observing the teachers, conducting regular staff meetings, and otherwise assessing the lay of the land, she focused on implementing structural change.

Concluding that the existing "no homework" policy couldn't change, she strengthened the attendance policy instead. If the goal is to create community, Rabbi Abby insisted, there must be a physical presence. Students must feel part of a community, not by doing homework, but by belonging. "You can't play on a soccer team with part-time attendance," she added. "Ditto for this school."

The synagogue adopted a firm, though some add generous, attendance policy: students with more than fifteen absences (about 25 percent of all sessions) do not advance to the next grade, and therefore forfeit their assigned Bar/Bat Mitzvah date.[8] Nonmember families may test the waters by enrolling their children in the Gan Shalom early childhood program or the K-*Aleph* grade. Both programs require parental participation. A cooperative arrangement, staff believes, allows parents to make an affirmative decision to play an active role in their children's Jewish education. K-*Aleph* parents are asked to interact with the class, bring a Jewish ritual object or family heirloom to stimulate student discussion, and prepare dinner for the entire class. But parents must join the synagogue when their children enroll in *Bet*.[9] The leaders of this school may not believe Woody Allen's aphorism that "Eighty percent of success is *just* showing up." But neither would they argue that the school could succeed with the sporadic attendance typical of the past.

All children interact here, even if they're in different public school cliques. The staff discourages children from wearing personalized clothing received as Bar/Bat Mitzvah favors since noninvitees may feel excluded. The staff may enlist parents to help deal with reported instances of meanness. All classrooms contain computers, but they're not often used. They're not conducive to group work, says a staff member; anyway, the children use computers too much at home.

The casual classroom atmosphere reflects Rabbi Abby's mantra, "It is more important to make personal connections than to learn the facts." A *Bet* class sits in a circle to hear a story about a boy who hugged his mother and caused a chain of good deeds throughout the day. "We are learning about g'*milut chasadim* [acts of loving-kindness]," the teacher says before and after the story. This concept is a cornerstone of the recently adopted Chai curriculum, designed by the Union for Reform Judaism.[10] It is also fundamental to the Reconstructionist emphasis on caring within a community. But informality has a price. The extent of planning for one observed lesson may have been, "I'll read them this story." A child's comment sparks a discussion about skiing. The teacher gently returns to reading the story and maintaining enthusiasm, which have priority over understanding *g'milut chasadim*. Two other lessons on the week's *parsha* also went off topic and did not return.

Some teaching may be less than stellar, but education extends beyond the classroom. The classroom, says Rabbi Abby, is not enough to influence a child's learning or belonging to Judaism. The educators pay attention to improving the classroom experience. They pay at least equal attention to creating concentric circles of influence extending from the classroom to the hallway, the sanctuary, and the community. The school's cross-grade curricular, extracurricular, intergenerational, and interfamilial programs—there's a family social action curriculum for each grade, for example—are aimed at developing a Jewish outlook to be realized over a lifetime. The school does not settle for avoiding bad memories about Hebrew school.

The staff does not see the synagogue or its school, despite their Reconstructionist pedigrees, as the movement's educational innovators. Willing to accept failure, staff members borrow as often as they export ideas, and they do not confine borrowing to Reconstructionist curricula. Dissatisfied with the existing Hebrew curriculum, Rabbi Abby and several teachers piloted, and then adopted, Mitkadem—a five-year Hebrew curriculum designed by the Union for Reform Judaism.[11] But the staff also makes use of Rabbi Abby's willingness to experiment. Bar Mitzvah projects replaced the traditional Bar/Bat Mitzvah speech several years ago. The uneven results led in turn to replacing the project model with the family *D'var Torah*.

Similarly, Rabbi Abby recently ended the family education program. "One year Rabbi Abby paid a lot of money to have a curriculum written for the teachers," says a teacher. "In a short while we threw it in the trash; it just didn't work." No community bats 100 percent in everything it tries, notes Cantor Sam, a baseball fan. But their lengthy tenures allow staff members time to get things right. The school evaluates each program by asking whether it helps to lay the groundwork for a lifelong commitment to the Jewish community and to Judaism.

The consummate insider, herself exposed to a community-involvement model as a congregation member, Rabbi Abby works within the system to gain acceptance of proposed changes. Though she and her colleagues usually play lead roles at first, they encourage the laity to assume leadership.[12] Giving priority to creating effective lay governance and school structures before curricular reform, she recruited enthusiastic congregants onto the synagogue's education committee. Perceptions differ, though, on the degree to which the staff has turned policy making over to this committee. "I'd have no concern if I left tomorrow," says Rabbi Abby, "since a strong education committee is in place." She adds: "We also have key teachers who are also part of the congregation." But one person wondered aloud, "What would happen to the school if we lost Rabbi Abby?" It is difficult to separate the school's programming from the quality and personalities of staff who run the programs; Rabbi Abby is at the center of many circles of influence for children and adults.

A strengthened education committee in place, the staff proposed three key reforms: the more strict attendance policy, a weekend alternative school, and an improved curriculum. Rabbi Abby did not impose any of these reforms. Once convinced of the need for compulsory attendance, she stated her case to the education committee: "Regular attendance helps create the kind of community we hope to build for our kids. When kids routinely miss school for appointments and events they lose a sense of continuity with their peers and it is harder for teachers to teach."[13] The proposal had two key components: a 75 percent attendance record during the school year, and a six-year residency requirement. A student would enroll no later than the second grade and would continue through seventh grade—the Bar/Bat Mitzvah year for most students. This policy, though not anticipated at adoption, also permitted students to complete all twenty-three *ramot* (levels) of the Mitkadem curriculum.

Both components of the attendance policy permitted few exceptions, and violations meant the loss of the assigned Bar/Bat Mitzvah date. Open meetings, conducted by the committee, focused on the desirability of "community." Rabbi Abby took the foreseen heat directly; using the revived committee as a cover would have impeded further changes. Most synagogue members eventually concurred with the changes. Having survived this controversial decision, Rabbi Abby and the education committee felt ready to participate in a national project for re-envisioning religious education. Their involvement focused on designing a weekend school option. Shabbat schools had become more common among liberal congregations, so the group could examine the results of similar adoptions elsewhere. Once convinced of the viability of the alternative, Rabbi Abby and the lay participants gained a gradual acceptance for a decision having fewer consequences than the change in the attendance policy. Ten families agreed to be *Nachshons*—in Exodus, Nachshon literally "tested the waters" by walking into the Red Sea before God parted it—by participating in the Shabbat school model in the first year. The success of this experiment helped lower resistance to opening a new possibility for learning.

The third significant change—adopting the *Chai* and Mitkadem curricula—occurred after the education committee asked parents and teachers to rank curricular options in order of desirability. Most respondents did not consider mastery of Modern Hebrew essential; a "homework required" notation on the questionnaire may have influenced the vote. Staff and laity then opted for Mitkadem, a prayer-based Hebrew curriculum that allowed students to learn at their own pace. By opting for prayer-based over Modern Hebrew, the school freed up staff time for other experiments, such as Project Kehillah.

Rabbi Abby followed the same strategy when implementing the reforms: introduce large changes in acceptable ways and bring congregants on board gradually. She moved one class at a time when the school adopted the Shabbat school model and the Mitkadem curriculum. Save for the compulsory attendance policy, she and the education committee allowed parents to stay the course, if they so desired. The school now offers four pre-K–grade 7 options, including Gan Shalom, a cooperative early childhood program, B'Yachad, the Shabbat preschool program, a two-weekday Hebrew school, and the new family-oriented Shabbat school.

Keeping in mind the desire of the synagogue community to generate Jewish experiences beyond the classroom, let's examine its key educational programs. We'll begin with programs aimed at younger children, which is where the staff started. Deciding those programs would not by themselves achieve the desired myriad of experiences, the school's leaders moved to innovations aimed at older children and families. This portrait is a snapshot; the staff says that more experiments and changes are to come.

## Gan Shalom and Bagels on the *Bimah*

Gan Shalom, the weekday early childhood school with its own director, expects parents to partner in the work of educating Jewish children. All parents must help out, bring a meal, or lead several activities for four to six full school days each year in this "co-op" school for two-, three-, and four-year olds. The cooperative component attracts some parents. In turn, parents who derive fulfillment from their involvement may become synagogue members even if they had not contemplated membership in a Reconstructionist synagogue.

Located in a competitive environment—fourteen area synagogues and the local Jewish community center offer early childhood programs—the school constantly balances its philosophy against the competition's enticements. Gan Shalom, for example, extended the length of a school day for a class of toddlers to meet local competition. The holiday-based curriculum resembles Conservative and Reform programs; its distinctiveness derives from its strong emphasis on gender neutrality.

The school also remains neutral in its admissions policy: along with non-Reconstructionist tots, the school accepts children of intermarried couples and of non-Jews. Some families enroll their children because they live in the neighborhood; others say that the school just "feels right." Competition dictates a broad admissions policy; so does the director's belief that participation in this "warm and cozy" environment forestalls the loss of the growing number of intermarried families to Judaism. All parents, she adds, ask if they and their children will be comfortable in the Gan Shalom cooperative; the question is especially salient to intermarried couples.

Gan Shalom, like the rest of the school, but unlike some competing schools, de-emphasizes computers. "Click on the square, pass the mouse" holds no weight here. Nor does the use of easels, seen as another hindrance to community formation. The school's focus on play, suggests the director, develops the ability to work in small groups—a desirable skill for children soon to begin their elementary education and to participate in a Reconstructionist community. Launching a meaningful lifelong Jewish journey, notes the director, cannot begin too soon.

❖

Once a month on Shabbat morning at 11:00 a.m. Rabbi Abby and a teacher lead Bagels on the *Bimah*—where over twenty parents and their toddlers sit in a circle for a Shabbat service that includes story time, body movement, and prayer. *Elohai Neshama* is sung here, just as at Friday night services and during the *B'Yachad* service. Connecting threads among all the prayer services are the same easily remembered melodies and one-line prayers. After a forty-minute service, the toddlers stay in a classroom for snack and play while the parents go to an adjoining room for adult study with Rabbi Abby. The parents are still discussing their conception of God when someone knocks on the door and says that the session was supposed to end and it's time to go home. Bagels on the *Bimah,* says Rabbi Abby, prepares parents to participate in the *B'Yachad* program. "It's not a stretch for the children because they have already made friendships and get used to coming at an early age."

## Shabbat School and *B'Yachad* (Together)

Several years ago, synagogue staff and lay leaders participated in an intensive eighteen-month visioning process led by a national organization. The exercise resulted in a commitment to strengthening intergenerational learning and relationships. "The visioning process made us take a hard look at what we were doing," one parent said, "and led us to begin to think differently about education." Here's the vision statement produced by the group:

> Jewish education occurs in partnership among the generations and between the Reconstructionist Synagogue and Community and members. Our religious school is integrated into our larger community and draws on the resources of the entire congregation. We place a strong emphasis on intergenerational community and lifelong Jewish learning among all members.

The *B'Yachad* program resulted from the work of this group. Until recently, this synagogue offered only a Tuesday-Thursday afternoon program; it did not (and still does not) have a Sunday school. When Rabbi Abby proposed a Shabbat alternative for grades two through six, she did not contemplate a Sunday alternative. "If we expand, it must be Shabbat," she insisted. "That's our focus: Shabbat is too central to the mission of our synagogue."[14] In Kaplan's formulation: making education a religious experience is a more easily attainable goal on Shabbat.

The Shabbat program began by combining students in two consecutive grades; it grew from 12 students in one class to 28 in two classes, and then to 38 students in three classes, divided by age—a single *Bet* class, and combined *Gimel/Dalet* and *Hey/Vov* classes. Splitting grades into weekday and Shabbat programs came at the cost of grade-wide communities. But the school staff and laity believe the Shabbat program is worth the cost. Joint programming still occurs, they note, since Shabbat program students also attend school on Tuesday afternoons.

The Shabbat school runs from 9:00 a.m. to 11:00 a.m., leaving time for children to participate in sports or other secular activities later in the day. The school's expectation for regular parental participation is balanced with a keen awareness of the rhythm of the secular calendar. "This program actually helps my schedule," notes one mother. "It is one less day during the week I don't have to leave work early to pick up my children. The children go one weekday and then once a week on *Shabbas*. It's a better fit." A father chimes in, "We signed up for this so we come. It gives us structured family time." The father described the need for structure in their busy lives: Without structure, "time just gets away from us."

Parents who sign up for the *B'Yachad* program agree to participate twice a month on Shabbat with their children. Once a month, on Friday night, they join their children for services after the children attend class and have dinner. Parents can opt to join their children for the dinner. The second monthly commitment requires parents to attend with their children on a Shabbat morning. Participating children attend school without their parents on two additional Shabbat mornings each month. They also attend weekly classes on Tuesdays.

Families who do not participate in the *B'Yachad* program sign their children up for the more traditional Tuesday-Thursday program. Children in the weekday only program may participate in *B'Yachad* once a month. Class is skipped on the Thursday preceding the family Shabbat experience. Keeping track of these options can be challenging to families and staff. But the school is committed to serving families who balance a multitude of responsibilities and interests.

During *B'Yachad* on Shabbat morning, children and parents separate for the first hour. Parents leave their school-age children (grades two through six) in age-appropriate classrooms down the hall, and drop off their tots at an adjacent room to paint with teen assistants. They then attend an adult Torah study session, taught in alternate sessions by Rabbi Abby and Cantor Sam. Parents and their school-age children join up in the Blue Room (where else?) at 10:00 a.m. for their own service, apart from the main congregation.

"Passover is the holiday most often celebrated today by Jews," Rabbi Abby begins the adult Torah study class. "Why do you think that's the case?" The parents' answers move quickly from social science platitudes to eagerly shared personal stories. "We celebrated Passover in our house because we knew the Four Questions. It was something we actually knew how to do," says a mom in her early thirties. "I loved Passover because one night we'd go to one set of grandparents and the next night to the other," says another parent. "It meant a lot to see my grandfathers at the head of the table." Rabbi Abby calls on everyone by name, explaining later that she has known most of the families since their children were in nursery school. "We celebrated two Jewish holidays when I was a kid," confesses one dad, "Hanukkah and Passover. And we only celebrated Passover because we were invited out." These adults hold loving childhood memories of Passover, but many possess only basic factual knowledge.

Meaningful Jewish connections for these moderately affiliated Jews— defined as having some involvement in Jewish life but not assuming leadership positions—primarily occurred in family holiday celebrations at home, not from synagogue experiences.[15] "I belonged to the fancy Reform synagogue, where the rabbi was way up high in a black robe," says one father. "I never knew what was going on and it really meant nothing to me." He adds: "I had an old Israeli woman for my Hebrew schoolteacher. She used the drills she learned in the army to teach us. I'm expecting my children will remember something very different." This father chose membership at a synagogue whose school emphasizes active participation and affective growth over deference to authority, familial or rabbinical.

Many other parents in this congregation also hope their children will have markedly different stories to recall when they reach adulthood. They may remember little from their own drop-off days of learning, but they are committed to this program because they don't want, as many parents said, their own children "to hate Hebrew school." These children may (or may not) recall sharing prayers, chats, chants, study, and food with their parents on Shabbat mornings; but *B'Yachad* activities and ambience emulate the intimate, relaxed, and personal encounter with Judaism that more closely characterizes a fondly remembered Seder than the religious school tribulations of their parents. The staff validates all contributions, including unexpected or almost silly answers, with "That's a good question" or "That's a good comment." "We strive to create a climate of acceptance and security," relates the school's mission statement, "where all questions are honored and each child is appreciated."

The *amidah*, Rabbi Abby explains, "says we stand where we are today because of our ancestors." "Who are the ancestors who you think about before you say the *amidah*?" she asks. "George Washington," says one child; "Harry Houdini," says another. Parents enter the conversation, so there's no chance that the few giggles will get out of control. "I think of my relatives lost in the Holocaust." "This is the fifth anniversary of my father's death. I'm thinking about him," says another parent. This elementary personalization of prayer is as much for the parents as for their children. A child might not articulate, "My parent takes this prayer Torah thing very seriously." But parents using prayer to connect to personal feelings and ideas illustrates reconstructed Judaism to their offspring.

Down the hall, the *Bet* students begin class by meditating; then they tell about their week. Their teacher asks them to look at "*Borchu et Adonai . . .*" —the prayer chanted before reading from the Torah—in their *siddurim*. Cantor Sam stops by; he likens the prayer to a signal. "A signal is important; the *borchu* is a call for the congregation to pray together." The children know the prayer: they read it in its entirety in Hebrew and English, and know it's chanted when someone reads from the Torah. Someone notices the absence of vowels in "*Adonai*"—an opportunity for the teacher to discuss why the Torah has no vowels as the now-engaged children crowd around a mini-Torah. We've come a bit far from *borchu*, but the children have experienced lots of mini-lessons along the way. "My 25-year-old son and my 18-year-old daughter were Bar/Bat Mitzvah here," the teacher comments after class.

The *Gimel-Dalet* (middle) group re-enacts the Joseph story. Everyone wants to be Joseph; some kids opt for Judah. The eleven children are assigned to roles as the twelve brothers; they settle down after a few minutes and go to the "stage." All are players; there is no audience. One girl, seeing how the others are clowning around, shakes her head. Judah pleads for food for Jacob. When the brothers recognize Joseph, they exclaim, "Oh boy, oh boy!" "We're in trouble!" Of course, the classmates would like to toss their "brother" into the pit . . . there's lots of giggling.

The oldest group also discusses *borchu*, but the lesson shifts to examining Orthodox practices, especially candle lighting. Why do Orthodox Jews finish their prayers before candles are lit? The answer—they stay focused this way—leads to a mini-lesson on staying focused. Jews remain silent during the time between washing hands and saying the *motzie*, for example. This discussion prompts a child to ask why we do things differently here. Your parents define their own customs, the teacher explains. All practices are OK. The students stand up and stretch before *tefilla*. "You'll be sitting for a while," they're told.

At ten o'clock, the children from all three classes rejoin their parents in the Blue Room for the hour-long *B'Yachad* service. Only the rabbis come to this service in dress clothes. In contrast, most moms and dads—forty attended one week; one hundred another—show up in blue jeans and sneakers. The men wear sweatshirts, sweaters, or sports shirts. Only five parents wear the *kippot* displayed prominently on a table at the entrance to the Blue Room, next to the *siddurim* and a laminated sheet with transliterations of key prayers.[16] The parents sit with coffee mugs in one hand, a Bible in the other, and a child or two in their laps or at their sides.

Cantor Sam's drumbeat greets all with "*Modeh ani Lefanecha*" (the prayer said upon waking up). Rabbi Abby demonstrates how to do the prayer over the *talit*: she likens the words on the *talit* to a cheat sheet. Some parents put the *talit* over their heads, she says, taking a moment of sacred time for themselves in the midst of community. Cantor Sam quotes *High School Musical*: "It's time to get your head in the game," and there's lots of laughter. Rabbi Abby holds her child on her lap; Cantor Sam's children also participate. A settled atmosphere replaces the frequent comings and goings of the first minutes.

No one is embarrassed to rely on the transliterations during the ensuing prayers. All congregants are offered the opportunity to say individual blessings out loud:

Blessed is the world that gives us snow.
Blessed is the One who gives me strength to struggle.
Blessed is the One who keeps us healthy.
Blessed is the One who teaches us things.
Blessed is the One who made next Friday Jillian's birthday.

The *hallelujah* follows, with drum beating, hand clapping, and all standing; Cantor Sam then calms the congregation by calling for all to stretch (he says it's the third inning). After reinforcing the classroom lessons about *borchu*, he discusses the *Shema*. This prayer, he explains, is a communal act. Few wear *talit* and therefore cannot bring the *tzitzit* together, so Cantor Sam suggests that congregants clasp hands and hold the words as long as possible. "That's so that all of you can hear each other as part of the community." "Close your eyes," he instructs at the same point in the service on another Shabbat, "We're making the rain forest rush. Snap your fingers. Clap. Now say shhh." Children and adults follow directions. "That's the sound of the wind. We're hearing the wind inside of each of us." Parents and children sing *"Elohai Neshama Shenatatbi T'horah hi"* (My God, the soul you place in me is pure).

Prayer is soul work, indicate the professionals, who attempt to strike, as one parent said, a "just right balance between traditional prayers—they [the prayers in *Siddur Kol HaNoa*] are not watered down—and ways to feel connected." Body movement accompanies morning blessings; meditative breathing goes with *Shema*. Sharing personal stories is a constant as the professionals convey the ABCs of a Jewish prayer experience to adults and children. "I wish my prayer experience was like that when I was a kid," says one parent. "On the other hand maybe no one was into drum banging and slow breathing in those days."

## Tefilla Breira

It's about 5:00 on a weekday school session; it's been a long day and everyone needs a break after an hour of Jewish studies. So let's daven and then run around the outside of the building with Rabbi Abby! An accomplished distance runner in college and a former Maccabi Games participant, Rabbi Abby gathers children from all grades for a brief prayer, followed by three circumnavigations of the synagogue. But why stop there? Let's give the children plenty of ways to express their Judaism. The result: *Tefilla Breira*.

Rabbi Abby inherited the break in the school day from the previous school director, but she decided to impose a structure on these twenty minutes. She broke the *Bet* through *Vov* classes into mixed-grade teams in her first attempt at filling the void. The teams competed in quizzes, sang, and raced on occasion. But the competition risked getting out of hand, and Rabbi Abby looked for an alternative. Learning about *Tefilla Breira* at Camp JRF, she brought the program back to the synagogue school. Conducted on Tuesday afternoons, when all children attend the school, it attempted to fulfill Kaplan's vision of education as a religious experience, while promoting mixed-grade and grade-wide interaction.

The school offered seven simultaneous activities one Tuesday, including meditating with Cantor Sam and physical activity (running) with Rabbi Abby. Teachers led five other groups: social action (the children are collecting a year's worth of towels to be donated to a local women's shelter), playing an instrument, knitting, Friday *nigunim* (traditional melodies, usually hummed), and songs associated with Reconstruction. Cantor Sam explains *Tefilla Breira* by invoking Abraham Joshua Heschel's recollection of his participation in the Selma, Alabama. civil rights march: "It felt like my feet were praying." Prayer, he says, should be directed to a cause, and for the strength to achieve the goal. *Tefilla Breira* asks students to explore Jewish spirituality in a new language or way to connect.

## Connections: The Pre–Bar/Bat Mitzvah Class

It's Tuesday at 6:30. The students in this seventh grade class have just devoured several large pizzas; there's leftover salad. The co-taught class meets in a large room. All stand. The lead teacher, with years of experience here, asks the students, "Please walk to me if this applies to you: 'I express my opinion freely.'" Everyone walks to her. "I stand up for my friend if someone disrespects him." Some students weren't sure. Some say, "My friend may be wrong." Others add, "Avoid a conflict." Some students say they will stand up for their friends, no matter what.

The teacher continues, "I will stand up for a stranger if they're being disrespected." Almost no one walks to the teacher. "Is it the teacher's responsibility to stand up for her students when they're disrespected?" The students tell stories about teacher interventions or lack thereof. The teacher responds: "A classroom should be safe for everyone. Everyone should feel valued." "What if a student is harassed for being Jewish?" The students confidently express their problems with the public schools in this environment. They must defend themselves in middle schools, and learn to solve their own problems, unless they turn violent, they conclude. "I speak up when someone disrespects my religion," the teacher continues. Only one "No." The students discuss their reactions to the "swastika incident": someone defaced this synagogue at the beginning of the academic year. "Does talking about it make it worse?" A student answers: "My grandparents died in the Holocaust. I can't disrespect them" by ignoring the incident.

Antisemitism occurs in the lives of some students, though eliciting their disclosures required the two teachers to share their own stories first. "I lived in a dorm triple, and one of my roommates thought Jews have horns, and are cheap and mean," said one teacher. She tried to explain, but her roommate was unmoved, and the third roommate was not helpful. So she decided to leave the suite. The lead teacher mentions an incident when she spent time in Florence. Her friends included two Palestinians whom she got to know well. These friends denounced Ariel Sharon when he became ill: "He stole our land." "I felt singled out and nervous," the teacher discloses.

The students begin to respond. Eight Catholic boys on a school bus, one student says, used a barrage of antisemitic epithets, unaware that a Jewish student was listening. She felt intimidated. Another student, overhearing students tell antisemitic jokes, got her teacher and the principal involved. About half the class reported similar incidents. "Be proud of your religion," one student declares. "Stand up for my religion and my friends," another adds.

The lead teacher connects the lesson to major Jewish and American themes and to the students' future. Hanukkah, the lead teacher notes, was a fight for freedom of religion. The Zeus statue in the Temple was a taunt that required force to address. We have freedom of religion now, but not then. But with freedom comes responsibility, including the responsibility to defend that freedom. "People in history are still people; they must make decisions involving their responsibility for others, then and now," concludes the lead teacher. "I'm proud of being Jewish," she adds. "But I also like other kinds of people."

The lesson ends. The teachers bring the kids down to earth with a game of Jewish trivia, centered on Hanukkah. The students form random teams of five; such random groups, the staff believes, create unity within the school and the congregation. Students are asked to sing Jewish songs or to recite *Alef Bet*, or to answer questions such as "When do you say *sheheheyanu*?" "Where is the Book of Maccabis found?" One team wins, a student devours a last slice of cold pizza, and everyone leaves knowing that freedom comes with responsibility.

Not all classes are as intense. Another week, students working in *chevrut* learned to distinguish between two concepts: *kevah* (fixed) and *kavanah* (intentional or changeable). Mastering the distinction led to a discussion of Reconstructionism, as *the* denomination that addresses *kevah* and *kavanah* in today's context. The lesson's conclusion: a reiteration of the vote/veto maxim.

## The Family *D'var Torah*

It's Shabbat morning, and a student at this school is about to be Bar Mitzvah. Prior to the Torah reading, a long table appears on the *bimah*, along with enough kitchen stools for the members of the student's nuclear family. The Torah procession comes first; it's seen as the most important communal act. After the procession resumes its position on the *bimah*, Rabbi Tom says, "We were at the moment at Sinai. We all have something to say about Torah." "A *D'var Torah*," he adds, "literally means 'a word of Torah.' We take it to mean a brief discourse on the weekly *parsha*." Those comments introduce the family *D'var Torah*, a continuation of the synagogue's expectation of parental involvement in the education of their children.

Two parents and four children, including the Bar Mitzvah, sit behind the table on the stools and discuss *Vigigah*—"And he approached them"—in Genesis. The theme is family reconciliation. The explication alternates among family members. "Judah approaches Joseph." "The setting: the Nile." "The time: 1800–1700 BCE." "Jacob's sons entered Egypt." "Joseph is happy inside, but accuses his brothers of being spies." "Joseph learns about Benjamin, and asks for him." "He places silver in a satchel." "Judah vouches for Benjamin, and offers himself in slavery." "Joseph begins to cry." "He reveals his true identity, and asks about Jacob." "My fate was to be sent to Egypt . . . to save my brothers." "He tells his brothers to come to Egypt and to live in Goshen (the best land in Egypt)." "The brothers are upset about the favored treatment of Benjamin, but he had the same mother as Joseph (Rebecca) and was not involved in Joseph's sale into slavery." "Joseph and Judah embrace." "Tell Pharaoh that they breed livestock . . . and won't cause trouble."

From the story the family proceeds to the moral: "What about living in a different country?" "It's worth it to survive famine." "Joseph feels compelled to help his family." "Different siblings have different strengths." "Complementary skills strengthen a family." "When you're arguing with siblings, forgive and forget [one or two furtive looks among the siblings on the *bimah*]." "We are our brothers' and our sisters' keepers."

Why did the staff provide a table and kitchen stools for the family to sit on when delivering the *D'var Torah*? Why does the nuclear family, not just the Bar/Bat Mitzvah, deliver a *D'var Torah*? David Teutsch, former leader of the Reconstructionist Rabbinical College, answered the first question in the movement's *machzor*: "Jews have long considered the table where they eat as an altar, and the food they eat as a link to the sacred," he wrote. "Many of our most vivid experiences and powerful memories involve what happens at the table. This focus allows the Jewish spirit to light our homes."[17] The maxim, "From our kitchen to the congregation's 'kitchen table,'" defined the practice.

The family *D'var Torah* addressed a problem constantly confronting the school and congregational staff: the complexity of the Jewish and American family structure. Not immune to the problems created by intermarriage, divorce, and remarriage, the synagogue searched for a meaningful way of having member families address these problems as part of exploring their Judaism. The synagogue previously replaced the traditional "canned" Bar Mitzvah speech with a Bar Mitzvah–related project. The results, noted Rabbi Tom, ranged from fine to "pathetic." Contemplating their options, the staff members noted that families already worked together to find a location, disc jockey, and caterer for a reception. Why not, they asked, also involve the family in study of the child's Torah portion?

Rabbi Abby, who by this time knows each child well, guides this part of the Bar/Bat Mitzvah preparation. She has dinner at the home of the Bar/Bat Mitzvah family, goes over the week's *parsha*, and suggests topics for discussion. Together, the family studies related texts and writes a script (15 minute maximum). It first delivers the *D'var Torah* at a required Tuesday evening rehearsal. That gives the staff a last chance to offer comments and suggestions—changing "Old Testament" to "Hebrew Bible" and inserting gender neutral language, for example—before the family faces the congregation on Shabbat.

Anyone in the nuclear family may participate. Five brothers shared the *bimah* one Shabbat. But no grandparents, uncles, aunts may take part— no exceptions. Well, only one: one week, understanding a technicality in the *parsha* required a medical explanation. The child's grandfather was a doctor who could explain the point. "I wish your grandfather would call on the cell phone to help us with this medical point," said the father. "The cell phone then rings, the grandfather explained the technicality, and the family got around the stricture," Rabbi Tom laughs. The synagogue does not require the family to offer a *D'var Torah*, but it must accept Rabbi Abby's visit even if it has already decided not to participate. Only one family declined the opportunity over the last two years; most families, notes Rabbi Abby, are more excited about the *D'var Torah* than about anything else. Parents participate because it's the norm of the congregation, and because of peer and child pressure.

The synagogue sets expectations that Rabbi Abby reiterates and reinforces at key moments during the run up to the big day, but it also respects the gifts each family brings to the *bimah*. "A 'serious family,'" recalled Rabbi Tom, "delivered the first *D'var Torah*; on Jacob's dream. They showed off a Hopi ladder obtained on a family trip to the southwest. Their talk compared similar Jewish and Indian legends." The second family, less academically oriented, "were good, generous, and *panicked* people." "What do we know?" they objected. "We already have so much to do. I have to buy a dress, etc." The wife used part of the *D'var Torah* to recount the writing process. She discussed family dynamics, Bar Mitzvah preparations, and her personal fixation on fashion and appearance. The turning point: a trip to Barnes and Noble to buy Jewish books. She quickly got hooked on the project. "We filled the bedroom with books. No sex; we got so involved. And this is what we found out about Hanukkah . . ." And at the end of the talk, she came around to the front of the table and showed her shoes; she had become too involved with the *D'var Torah* to find the time to buy special shoes for the occasion.

Writing a family *D'var Torah* was not always easy, especially for families with mixed marriages or with a separation or divorce. One week, a parent began, "As a practicing Catholic, my view is different . . ." Another week found the child's biological and adoptive fathers together on the *bimah*. Another week: families with same-sex parents. Rarely, Rabbi Tom concludes, does the *D'var Torah* devolve into a trite *Fiddler on the Roof* conclusion that we are all part of the same family. "It's a moving experience." He personally found it so after his own divorce. "It was not so easy to get together," he noted, "but it was cathartic in a different way." And if the study process might be tense; so might the mode of delivery. One week, the rabbi saw a child kick his interfering mother under the table during their presentation.

Judaism would be sterile if confined to Shabbat, Reconstructionists note. A successful community requires meaningful links between synagogue, school, and home. That insight leads to a preliminary answer to our second question: why family participation? In the social scientific terminology frequently invoked by Reconstructionists—a former rabbi at this synagogue became a prominent sociologist—the family *D'var Torah* symbolizes the coming together of the nuclear family, other primary groups (the extended family, friends, and colleagues), and a quasi-secondary group (the congregation) in a common effort to socialize the child to communal norms and to educate that child to key tenets of Judaism.

Tension abounded at one (required) Tuesday evening *D'var Torah* rehearsal. This week's family had difficulty discussing family fissures and semi-intimate problems. Asked about this tension, Rabbi Abby, who oversees the program, argues that the family *D'var Torah* lays the groundwork for future family relations, while reducing the focus on externalities. Sometimes, she adds, today's kids are left behind. "Why should a kid repeat the sacrifice of Isaac? Strap the kids into SUVs; then take them out of the car and into Hebrew school instead of onto the mountain." "When a child here asks: 'Where are you?' the parent must answer '*Henani* [Here I am].'" The *D'var Torah*, she concludes, "does not allow the parent to stay back and watch the child chant. We [the temple staff] can't make this meaningful. You must make the commitment."

The results, concludes Rabbi Tom: "Absolutely fantastic."

## Teen Experiences

Forty percent of teens continue to participate in the congregation past the Bar/Bat Mitzvah. Only five teens continued ten years ago, Cantor Sam noted, now it's thirty. "Teens have choices here," he explains. "They can work as assistants, participate in the choir, and participate in our teen program that combines some learning and lots of informal education. Girls can participate in Rosh Chodesh and now they have the Kehillah program." More than twenty teens will soon go to New Orleans to do community service. A new generation of students, who began in the preschool, stayed through religious school, and are now in eleventh and twelfth grades, he adds, are at the core of the committed group.

The Rosh Chodesh group is another piece of the school's montage of experiences. Almost twenty eighth to twelfth grade girls participate in Rosh Chodesh (held as close to Rosh Chodesh as possible); most will go with Cantor Sam on a social action trip to New Orleans. A few girls also work in the school as teen aides. "It used to be mandatory that if you worked in the school you also had to attend their youth education program," explains Cantor Sam. "Now we just realize every teen needs something different and we let them choose what works for them."

After a sushi dinner, the girls sit on the floor, ready for their monthly gathering with Rabbi Abby, who has an easygoing and affectionate rapport with the girls. Rabbi Abby bases the gathering on material produced by a national project but adapts it to fit their needs. A candle is lit and each girl says her first name and adds the word *bat* (daughter) and names as many grandmothers and great grandmothers as she can.

Tonight, the girls discuss listening. The conversation moves easily from a prepared text on the *Shema* to a discussion of the proper etiquette for text messaging. "Is it appropriate to text when talking to a friend? Is it okay when you are in services?" The girls, says Rabbi Abby, are a mix of the "popular" and "not so popular" girls. At the end of each Rosh Chodesh gathering two girls make a scrapbook page based on the evening's discussion. "Rosh Chodesh—it's more than just the head of the month," one excerpt reads: "It's a sisterhood, a bond we all share. A place and time to be you. It's the friends that I make. The advice that I give and get and a time just to be. It's a place where you feel safe and at home where everyone is honest and true. A place that teaches, a place where you learn. But most importantly a place where you laugh."

## Chai and Mitkadem

The *Chai: Learning for Jewish Life* curriculum, the third innovation at this school, focuses on the three pillars of Judaism identified in *Avot* 1:2: *Torah* (study), *avodah* (worship), and *g'milut chasadim* (acts of loving-kindness). Chai is based on *Understanding by Design*, a popular book on curricular design that advocated instilling "Enduring Understandings": the "big ideas" that "have lasting value to our students long after they have left the classroom."[18] Teachers discuss implementing the curriculum and classroom-related issues at bimonthly meetings; they can also discuss the curricula at their twice-yearly individual meetings with Rabbi Abby.

Many of Chai's lessons encourage critical thinking. Questions like "What do you think?" or "What would you do?" were asked repeatedly. A class of fifth graders participated in a multimedia session. Her purpose, the teacher explained, was to have the students question and see things that may not be readily apparent. "I want them to think, not just know," said the teacher. "What do you know about Abraham?" she asked. The students offered factual answers, including: "He tried to kill his son"; "He spoke to angels"; and "He was the first Jew." "Why wasn't the first Jew a girl?" asked a girl.

The teacher had no response, but she guided the students toward "higher order" questions and answers after praising the students for their answers. Showing four paintings depicting Abraham at different moments described in the Bible, she asked: "What do you see? What do you think is happening? What do you think he is feeling? What would you have done at this time? Who agrees or disagrees with what he is doing?" The students knew the story portrayed in the vibrant, frightening picture of Abraham raising a knife to his son.[19] But the teacher had moved the class from a lesson in facts to personalization and critical thinking: discernment, analysis, and evaluation. Teacher longevity and training and attention to curriculum produced many lessons with clear goals, interesting activities, and some Jewish content. We observed generally well-behaved students and mostly fair to good classroom learning.

To accompany Chai, the school offers prayer-based Hebrew. "People are not sending kids to Hebrew school to learn to read Modern Hebrew," says Rabbi Abby. "If they do, they're not sending their kids here." Recall that the results of a recent parental survey, noting that homework would accompany Modern Hebrew if offered, attested to the parents' lack of enthusiasm. Interviewed teachers seconded this stance. Colleges and universities offer many Jewish studies courses, including Modern Hebrew, noted one teacher. "Most of these kids are going to college; let's ground them in the Jewish community and Jewish life here, and aim them towards serious study during their college years."

The school recently adopted the five-year Mitkadem curriculum for learning prayer book Hebrew. Mitkadem encourages self-paced *chevruta*—pairings are also used in other classes and programs, such as Connections—to master four to six *ramot* (levels) per year, depending on time on task.[20] Such pairings permit asymmetrical tutorial relations that utilize a well-known research finding: tutors may learn more than their pupils.[21] "I've heard from parent after parent who did not go to this synagogue," wrote a parent, "that they were taught words in Hebrew school, but not taught the meaning." Nor, this parent added, do their children learn the meanings. Seeing a friend's child completing her Hebrew homework, she asked the meaning of a word. "I don't know; they haven't told us," the child replied. "My son, on the other hand, comes home and says 'I learned the word *Chag*, and *Yom*, and this is what they mean . . .' I love it and hope it stays!"[22]

## Project Kehillah

With the revised supplementary school curriculum in place, the staff turned to implementing a long-desired Project Kehillah. The project resulted from the same desire for intergenerational education that motivated *B'Yachad*, as well as from a long-standing wish of Rabbi Tom. "We're trying to replicate the serendipity of relationships that happened when we were a congregation of a hundred families," he says. The staff wanted children in the religious school to have a Jewish "neighborhood" experience that no longer exists where they actually live—and bumping into each other in the synagogue's narrow halls was not enough.

Project Kehillah, launched this year, expands the circle of people who know and care about children. Congregants of mixed ages living in diverse areas meet six times during the year for Shabbat celebrations, *tikun olam* activities, and holiday celebrations. Called a form of "in-reach" by Rabbi Tom, the project aims to retain current congregants by deepening their connections, not to recruit new members. Project Kehillah may also acquaint staff members with the new families in the congregation, while helping to identify potential lay leaders.

The staff randomly divided the congregation into ten units of approximately thirty-six households. "This is not about affinity grouping. There already are plenty of groups of people of like mind and interests. We believe being in relationships with people across generations is important." The rabbis talk about the strong push back they got from many congregants who wanted smaller groups based on people they already knew. The staff stood its ground and launched the mixed groups. So far, they report between 30 and 40 percent participation in most of the *kehillot*.

To launch ten *kehillot*, the congregation unsuccessfully applied for a number of grants. Not losing hope, the congregation tried another strategy. It ended all their traditional family education programs such as episodic holiday learning for each grade in the school. "Intergenerational learning is more important than grade-based family education," explains Rabbi Abby. "We saw our family education schedule making it harder for parents' calendars. A parent gets stuck saying, 'How am I supposed to be in two places at one time when I have more than one child in the school?'" So to build "meaningful connections" the congregation used the money designated for a family educator to launch the Kehillah program. Two angels in the congregation contributed additional funds. All activities are therefore free of charge.

During the year, each *kehillah* participates in a Friday evening Shabbat dinner in the synagogue, a Saturday evening *havdalah* service, an oral history project, a social action activity, and a Pesach workshop. Staff members and their families participate, at least until reliable lay leadership emerges. Attaining these goals, staff members believe, is worth the considerable time and effort they've invested in the project—so much so that they place personal calls to all absentees.

On one Saturday evening, twenty-five adults and children in Kehillah Moses (each *kehillah* has a name) sit around a table and trace their hands on butcher-block paper. "In each finger," Rabbi Tom instructs, "write one thing that connects you to Jewish life." Young children, helped by their parents, and a few teens and seniors follow the directions. "Now get up and draw a line from your hand to someone else's who has written the same thing as you did. Make the connections." Colored lines connect one hand, one finger to another. The web of connections across ages is soon established. The staff chose activities that would not "aggravate people," and could keep learners of all ages busy and not under each other's feet. "The first year is just to get people to come and like it."

Kehillah Moses then celebrates *havdalah*. The members hold hands and sing, "Our voices are different, some quiet, some strong. Our voices are lovely, some old, some young." There's food and socializing. "I used to be active in the synagogue and then stopped," says an older woman, who came alone. "This has been a chance to get to know some new people." "We don't have family in the area," adds a father. "So this is a great way for my children to feel part of a family." A month earlier, this *kehillah* bagged up sandwiches, dessert, and beverages for a shelter. Next on the agenda: a communal dinner.

One problem remains: the effects of existing educational and affinity programs on Project Kehillah. Some groups had more children than others, an unintended consequence of random selection and voluntary participation. The staff wanted to include children, but wondered if the school's compulsory attendance policy would affect voluntary attendance at Project Kehillah activities. The staff could not generalize from the early results. The children formed a circle in one group and were uninvolved in another. A third group that participated in *B'Yachad* the same day stayed away entirely. The staff also identified two related secondary problems. The more children in attendance, the staff observed, the less time for parents to connect. Staff leadership might lessen this effect, but such intervention might inhibit the development of lay leadership. The staff is thinking about changes that address these issues. "I think we'll have seven *kehillot* instead of ten," notes Rabbi Tom. "Not all of them are equally strong, so we might need to blend some. And next year we'll try to get lay people to lead more of the planning." Lay members shop for food and do some communication-related work, but the professional team plans and attends most programs to help assure a quality experience.

In the long term, the synagogue board may become a parliament of *kehillot*, a forum for social action work, or the desired leadership crucible. "People want connection," notes Rabbi Tom. Some congregants consider the synagogue their "home" and wish to attend everything. And there's plenty to attend at a "program-rich" synagogue, which Cantor Sam calls a "modified cineplex by default."[23] "But," adds Rabbi Tom, "people also resist change." That's where the staff invokes the insights of Mordecai Kaplan: "Judaism cannot be perpetuated merely by nostalgia for the past," Kaplan wrote. "The conditions that enabled Judaism to flourish in the past are irrevocably gone with the wind." "Nothing less than original and creative thinking in terms of present day realities and future possibilities," he concluded, "can create anew the conditions which are indispensable to Jewish survival."[24]

## Conclusion: A Whole That's More Than the Sum of the Parts

> It devolves upon the Jewish school to revitalize the Jewish community by providing training in intelligent community living, and to stimulate and foster a growing sense of communal responsibility. This can be accomplished most efficiently in and by the process of participation.
>
> —William Chomsky[25]

It's hard to miss John Dewey's influence over this school. There is less concern with "chalk and talk" than with "active learning." There is also less concern with "covering the material" than with "big ideas"—a legacy of *Understanding by Design*—and less concern with assessment than with exploring how to "make meaning." And perhaps most important, there's less concern with the relationship between the learner and the material to be learned than with "learning as a social activity." That's half of why the school favors guided group discussions that promote higher-order reasoning.

The other half is Kaplan's influence. In a world of choice, where social or religious strictures do not greatly limit intermarriage and divorce, Reconstruction says that Jews should not have to tackle difficult sectarian and secular problems on their own. Community membership is liberating, not constricting, as long as the community has a common *raison d'étre*. Participation is everything. "This process begins in a small area, but grows, expands, and deepens with the maturity and progress of the learner."[26] The staff, well versed in Reconstructionist thinking about community, have clear goals in mind and draw on school and synagogue resources—it's difficult to say where one ends and the other begins—to achieve their ends.

Learning is a social activity, agreed the two Morningside Heights neighbors: Kaplan, the Reconstructionist, and Dewey, the constructivist. Developing personal Judaism in adults and children is far from neglected here. But the staff feels that spirituality is best nurtured when the environment engenders a sense of belonging. It takes a community divided at various times into twos, tens, thirty-sixes, and hundreds to teach children how to question, how to turn experience into education, and how to make Judaism their own. And it takes experimentation.

Public school fourth through eighth grade standardized tests are about none of this. Reconstructionists may espouse both Jewish and American folkways, mores, and laws, but the staff views Jewish education as an alternative to the accountability and high stakes testing movements in public education. These movements, staff members believe, in effect cede affective development to religious education. There's no teaching to the test in this school. The goal is to create "innovative ways to provide connections of Jewish culture and ideas to secular life" as a foundation for a lifetime of Jewish learning, not to maximize what children know in the here and now.[27] That foundation, the staff believes, is most solid when built on cherished memories . . . and the memories generated here must compete with those generated on other weekends, when the children are elsewhere. The school, the staff understands, cannot create those memories and connections by itself. In return for providing quality educational experiences—no one is bored here—the school expects a parental commitment to nurturing Judaism in their children's lives and to forming a vibrant community.

How does the school encourage students to experience belonging that produces cherished memories? Let's recap.

Visioning isn't a one-time formal exercise. Staff and lay leaders repeat, like a mantra, their commitment to building community "among the generations and between the Reconstructionist synagogue and community and members." A concrete vision inspires and directs action, especially in allocating scarce dollars, space, and time to the best advantage. It permits the staff to say "yes" to congruent activities and "no" to others—saying no to family education, for example, while saying yes to the Kehillah program and intergenerational learning. Congregational schools are more prone to accommodate than to "just say no," but "doing it all" diffuses efforts and results. This school gets results by staying focused and guiding those who veer off course.

Congregational leaders can say no because they are mutually supportive and possess a shared vision of what it takes to make a difference in students' lives. School leaders don't ask individual educators to make it all happen and to take the fall when success is illusory. They work to generate a committed teaching staff that can withstand expected resistance to change.

Shared conviction, passion, energy, and trust encourage leaders to take risks, make hard decisions, and remain focused on achieving worthy goals.

Vision can be daunting as well as inspiring, especially when the future appears dramatically different from the present. Congregational leadership moved from a "pick up and drop off" school model with sporadic family attendance at best to an intergenerational learning community. One strategy: balance immediate actions and bolder, long-term steps. Rabbi Abby's short-term steps included requiring regular school attendance and banning personalized clothing from Bar/Bat Mitzvah celebrations. She holds bimonthly learning sessions for teachers and meets with each teacher twice a year. She privately tutors a special needs child in her office. These steps promote the desired quality of learning and encourage a communal vision, while keeping the school on an even course.

Rabbi Abby and her team also launched major educational models, including cooperative education, *B'Yachad*, and Kehillah. Knowing it takes years to build the envisioned community, they experiment continually. Rabbi Abby escorts children safely through the carpool line and Rabbi Tom sits on the floor with his sixth graders waiting for dismissal. But they also research community-organizing techniques that a governance committee might apply to the next iteration of the Kehillah program. Taking immediate small steps *and* undertaking bold long-term initiatives might appear akin to tying your shoes while running a marathon. But the dexterity to do both in a school and congregation seems necessary. And after all, Rabbi Abby has been a distance runner since college.

This school generates multiple images of the group experience. Children, teens, parents, and seniors pack peanut butter and jelly sandwiches for the homeless. Teenagers board a plane during spring break to mend the aftermath of Katrina. Everyone from 4 to 74 sings *Elohai Nishama*. This school and congregation design learning and experiences that bring people together in common activity; they also design opportunities to acknowledge, honor, and develop the individual.

This school begins to acknowledge the individual by *seeing the child*. "Among the tribes of northern Natal in South Africa," writes Peter Senge, "the most common greeting, equivalent to 'hello' in English, is the expression: '*Sawu bona*.' It literally means, 'I see you.'" Senge continues: "If you are a member of the tribe, you might reply by saying '*Sikhona*,' 'I am here.' The order of the exchange is important: until you see me, I do not exist. It's as if, when you see me you bring me into existence."[28] Adults and other children who pause long enough to call a child by name offer recognition that is in short supply.

But acknowledgment does not end with recognition. The school knows the personal stories behind the names. "I had Robyn in preschool," says a teacher. "I also had her brother and sister. I've seen them grow up." "How did your recital go last week?" a *B'Yachad* parent, munching on bagels and cream cheese, asks a child. Staff longevity and program design provide opportunities for individuality to emerge within the larger communal setting. If you grow up with the sense that "[a] person is a person because of other people," Senge notes, then "your identity is based on the fact that you are seen—that the people around you respect and acknowledge you as a person."[29]

The school attends, within limits, to individual needs. But it also provides multiple gateways to a common purpose. *Tefillah Breira*'s message— "We all pray" and "We honor the way you pray"—shows how Jews can choose while participating in the larger group. Expressing spirituality and connectedness through yoga and through meditative chanting or traditional words of prayer are equally valid. The school provides multiple educational models, recognizing that common purpose does not always require everyone to do the same thing, at the same time, and in the same way. But "does not always" and "never" are not synonyms; members sometimes do stand and act together.

The family prayer service and the parental Torah study reveal another way the school balances the development of the community and the individual. Rabbi Abby weaves the questions, stories, and experiences of individuals into these activities. She asks parents to share their experiences of Passover. She asks children and adults whom they think about during the *amidah*. Teachers routinely connect individual stories to the narrative of the Jewish people. The seventh grade teacher, for example, artfully connected students' experiences of antisemitism with the history and values of Hanukkah. Students can explore the "Who am I?" "Where do I belong?" and "How do I make sense of my world?" questions through communal Jewish learning and ritual. At its best, the school provides communal experiences in which individuals can connect to their sense of self. Conversely, it supports individuals' search for meaning as a way to be part of a greater whole.

This school, in short, provides a context and model for what is learned. But not everyone who attends experiences the power of the model. Some parents and children participate peripherally or find the education lacks potency. Saying the school has fully achieved its vision goes too far. At its best, this part-time Jewish experience achieves a meaningful community for children (and their parents) by being resolute in its purpose, simultaneously employing short- and long-term strategies, and nurturing the individual while building the community.

The school and the synagogue staff continue to evolve and innovate under Kaplan's (and Dewey's) influence, while taking time out here and there to catch their collective breath and to deepen the quality of their programming. Perhaps the Camp JRF advertisement on the office desk depicts the inlet near the synagogue: close enough for Kaplan to keep an eye on the school, far enough to let it grow on its own.

## Notes

1. *The Holy Scriptures According to the Masoretic Text: A New Translation*, Max Leopold Margolis, ed. (Philadelphia, Pa.: Jewish Publication Society, 1917), 872.

2. Richard Hirsh, "Paradigms for Contemporary Reconstructionism," *The Reconstructionist* 70 (2) (Spring 2006), 5–17, quotation from 9.

3. Ibid.

4. William Chomsky, "The School and the Community in Jewish Education," *The Reconstructionist* 10 (2) (March 3, 1933), 16–17.

5. Joan Meyers-Levy and Rui (Juliet) Zhu, "The Influence of Ceiling Height: The Effect of Priming on the Type of Processing People Use," *Journal of Consumer Research* 34 (August 2007), 174–86 (http://www.csom.umn.edu/assets/71190.pdf).

6. Rabbi Abby saves some other dedicated classrooms for teachers whom she knows will add distinctive touches to the rooms.

7. Mordecai Kaplan, "Democracy and Passover," *Mordecai Kaplan Diary*, April 1943. Reprinted in *Reconstructionism Today* 7 (3) (Spring 2000). Accessed at: http://www.jrf.org/showrt&rid=541.

8. Excused and nonexcused absences count toward the 15.

9. The synagogue membership committee gives preferential treatment to parents with children in the nursery school and K-*Alef*.

10. "The world rests upon three things, Torah, *avodah*, and *g'milut chasadim*." *Pirkei Avot* 1:2. See the discussion of Chai and Mitkadem, below.

11. Chai is intended to "facilitate lifelong Jewish learning within Reform congregations," but Conservative, Reconstructionist, combined, and unaffiliated congregations have also adopted the curriculum. See Jewish Education Service of North America, "Synagogue/School Change Initiatives," p. 4 (http://www.jesna.org/j/pdfs/coaches/Synagogue_Change.pdf).

12. The staff follows the same model in nurturing Project Kehillah.

13. School Handbook, 2007–2008, 5.

14. Sundays are occasionally devoted to some Kehillah-related social action projects.

15. Steven M. Cohen and Arnold M. Eisen, *The Jew Within: Self, Family, and Community in America* (Bloomington, Ind.: Indiana University Press, 2000).

16. Sandy Eisenberg Sasso and Jeffrey Schein, eds., *Siddur Kol Hano'ar: The Voice*

*of Children—A Siddur for Shabbat* (Jenkintown, Pa.: Reconstructionist Press, 2005). This *siddur* is aimed at children aged five to nine; the synagogue uses the version containing transliterations.

17. David A. Teutsch, ed., *Kol Haneshamah: Shirum Uvrahot* (Wyncote, Pa.: Reconstructionist Press, 1991), xiv.

18. Barbara Binder Kadden, *Chai, Learning for Jewish Life: Level 5 Curriculum Core* (New York: Union for Reform Judaism Press, 2004), vii–viii; Grant P. Wiggins and Jay McTighe, *Understanding by Design* (Alexandria, Va.: Association for Supervision and Curriculum Development, 2005).

19. The teacher cleared the picture with Rabbi Abby before showing it.

20. Mitkadem cites educational research that appeared to reinforce this Reconstructionist tenet: "Students learn best when they are actively involved in the process," notes Barbara Gross Davis, a University of California, Berkeley, professor. "Researchers report that, regardless of the subject matter, students working in small groups tend to learn more of what is taught and retain it longer than when the same content is presented in other instructional formats. Students who work in collaborative groups also appear more satisfied with their classes." Barbara Gross Davis, "Collaborative Learning: Group Work and Study Teams," in *Tools for Teaching* (San Francisco, Calif.: Jossey-Bass, 1993), http://teaching.berkeley.edu/bgd/collaborative .html. See also, Phillip Michael (Uri) Treisman, "A Study of the Mathematics Performance of Black Students at the University of California, Berkeley" (unpublished doctoral dissertation: University of California, Berkeley, 1985), and Robert E. Slavin, "Research on Cooperative Learning and Achievement: What We Know, What We Need to Know," *Contemporary Educational Psychology* 21 (1) (January 1996), 43–69.

21. Peter A. Cohen, James A. Kulik, and Chen-Lin C. Kulik, "Educational Outcomes of Tutoring: A Meta-Analysis of Findings," *American Educational Research Journal* 19 (2) (Summer 1982), 237–48. "One who teaches a neighbor's child Torah is understood to have created or fashioned the child; created or fashioned the words of Torah; and created or fashioned her or his own self" (Talmud-Sanhedrin 99b).

22. The parent added a P.S.: "I am curious though if they will learn to write these words."

23. Or perhaps the homonym, "Synaplex," Shabbat programming that combines the *Beit Tefilla* (house of worship) with *Beit Midrash* (house of learning), and *Beit Knesset* (house of gathering). See http://www.synaplex.org.

24. These sentences appear on the congregational calendar.

25. William Chomsky, "The School and the Community in Jewish Education," 16–17.

26. Ibid.

27. "History of Our Synagogue School," 4.

28. Peter Senge, *Schools That Learn, A Currency Book* (New York: Doubleday, 2000), 11.

29. Ibid.

# CHAPTER 5

# Adath Shalom Religious School
## Strengths, Challenges, and Transitions

RANDAL F. SCHNOOR WITH BILLY MENCOW

*Monday, October 29, 2007*
*It is an unseasonably warm evening in late October 2007. Rachel Waxman*
*makes her way from her car to the main entrance of Lyndon Johnson Pub-*
*lic School in this suburb adjacent to a major northeastern city. While Con-*
*gregation Adath Shalom is undergoing major renovations, this local pub-*
*lic school serves as one of the temporary locations for the synagogue's*
*religious school classes. Hebrew school class materials are stored in ap-*
*proximately twenty suitcases (donated by congregants) to keep them out*
*of the way of the regular public school classrooms. As usual, Rachel has*
*arrived forty-five minutes before classes begin. Alone, she physically moves*
*each suitcase of class material to the appropriate classroom and sets up the*
Parshat HaShavuah *question table at the front entrance of the school. She*
*offers a personalized greeting to each arriving teacher and student. Three*
*teenage congregants arrive to staff the table. The table has two easels, one*
*with today's new questions, and one with last week's questions and an-*
*swers, and the names of every student who had answered correctly. Stu-*
*dents enthusiastically check in to the* Parsha *exercise before they make*
*their way to class.*

*Wednesday, October 31, 2007*
*Two days later we again visit Adath Shalom's religious school. This time*
*classes are taking place in makeshift portable trailers located on the prop-*
*erty of a used car dealership owned by a congregant. Four large portable*
*buildings house the temporary synagogue offices, a nursery, and two multi-*

*purpose classrooms. A wooden "boardwalk" sits in the center connecting all the buildings. A few small groups of children arrive, some wearing costumes. They have smiles on their faces and are greeted warmly by Rachel, who walks along the boardwalk. It is Halloween night, traditionally a challenging day for congregational schools in America. Adath Shalom is no exception. The attendance is very low at approximately 25 percent capacity. As the fifth grade students make their way to class, Rachel turns to us and tells us how happy she is that these kids decided to come to school on Halloween, and she will be sending a letter home to their families to thank them.*

## Adath Shalom Synagogue

In order to set the context for the make-up and flavor of the religious school, it is useful first to gain a picture of the synagogue in which it is housed. Adath Shalom is a large Conservative synagogue in an upper-middle-class suburb approximately one hour away from a major northeastern city to which many commute for work. The synagogue was founded in 1920 and saw significant growth and expansion through the 1950s and '60s. This growth was accompanied by a liberal turn allowing women to vote and hold synagogue office. In the late 1970s Rabbi Rubenstein retired after forty years. He was succeeded by Rabbi Barry Posen, who still holds the post today. Rabbi Posen has established himself as a well-known and well-respected clergyman, who has taken a leadership role in the Conservative movement, on the national and as well as international stage. Shortly after Rabbi Posen's appointment, a cantor was hired, followed by Rachel Waxman. These three experienced professionals form a strong core of leadership at the synagogue. The early 1990s saw a major renovation and expansion of the facilities.

Today the synagogue is made up of approximately 900 families. Like a number of other large Conservative synagogues, membership numbers have dropped somewhat in the last several years and this is cause for concern. Adding to the challenge, and as we have seen, the synagogue is involved in another major building project, which involves tearing down most of their synagogue structure and building anew. This has left the congregation displaced for two years, holding their services, meetings, classes, etc. in various public schools, town halls, churches, colleges, and other makeshift locations.

Congregants of Adath Shalom tend to be highly educated, of high family incomes, and politically conservative. "Traditional" families predominate. There are relatively few single congregants, and gay and lesbian congregants are either not present or unknown. Teenagers aspire to and succeed in attending high quality colleges. Many of the congregants grew up in the area, although the synagogue professional leaders are proud to point out that they have successfully recruited a number of *shomer shabbos* families to join the community. These religiously observant make up a minority of total congregants. Nonetheless, Adath Shalom prides itself on its high Shabbat attendance, with 350–500 families participating each week in a variety of different services. These Shabbat services also form part of the religious school curriculum, as we shall see.

The synagogue is egalitarian in terms of the division of gender roles. It has also developed support groups and outreach programs to help its "interfaith couples in their relationship to the synagogue and the Jewish community."

## Religious School

In the 2007–08 school year Adath Shalom's religious school had an enrollment of 220 children in the kindergarten to *kitah hay* (seventh grade) level, and 160 youth in the various high school programs. While the high school enrollments have remained constant or increased over the last several years, the elementary enrollments have seen for the most part a consistent decline. In order for a child to be eligible for B'nei Mitzvah s/he must attend religious school for the five years from *kitah aleph* (third grade) to *kitah hay* (seventh grade). Attending religious school in kindergarten and first and second grades is optional and many families opt out, choosing to send their children for only the minimum requirement. Once a child is in the religious school the retention rates until the *hay* level are very high. One of the strengths of the religious school, to be discussed later, is the retention rates (this includes formal and nonformal programming) into the high school years. This has been reported to be approximately two-thirds for the last several years.[1] A nursery school at the synagogue serves to fuel the school. The day school population of the synagogue is quite high at approximately 200. This naturally works to reduce the congregational school population.

Kindergarten through second grade children meet once a week on Sunday mornings for three hours. Third grade to seventh grade students meet two weekday afternoons a week (for a total of four hours), plus every other Shabbat when they are required to attend specially designed services (for a total of sixteen *shabbatot* over the school year). On any given Shab-

bat there are 200–300 children and youth participating in various programs. High school students are involved in a wide variety of programming that takes place at various times throughout the week. The school
has placed considerable emphasis on the blending of formal and nonformal learning since the time of Rachel Waxman's hiring in 1990 (a time
when such blending was not yet widespread), and also strives to blend
children's education with family education.

The 2007–08 fees for the kindergarten through second grade Sunday
school are $440 per child for synagogue members and double the cost for
nonmembers. The fees for third to seventh grade are $770 for members
and approximately three times the cost for nonmembers. Fees for high
school programs vary and tend to fall around $200–400 per program. The
synagogue has historically maintained a strong financial position and has
generously supported its religious school. This is obviously to the advantage of the school which has not suffered for lack of resources or materials. Rachel was proud to tell us that: "The lay leadership trust us; it's never
a money issue here. It's never like you can't do it because we don't have
enough money. Even [the youth leadership program]; we ran this through
the Star Foundation, we were in Synaplex Synagogue and we were able to
start [the youth program] because of Synaplex. And for three years it was
funded through Synaplex. Well this is year four, so year four the synagogue
has to step up to the plate and the synagogue is stepping up to the plate.
So I think that's part of it; they allow us to bring in these few things and
they get excited with us and they are a part of it." In the case of the rich
getting richer, as this demonstrates, Adath Shalom has also benefited from
a number of grants from external agencies. These include the STAR Foundation and Synagogue 2000, among others.

## Educational Vision

The educational vision of the school flows directly from the larger vision
of the synagogue. Rabbi Posen promotes an atmosphere in his synagogue
that emphasizes a personalized approach to Jewish commitment. He speaks
of a "ladder of commitment" with different entry points. Each individual
can enter the ladder at what ever point they are comfortable and aspire to
climb small steps toward increased commitment. The rabbi insists that it
is not an "all or nothing" proposition, but rather the synagogue is an "enabling institution" that seeks to accept congregants wherever they are and
help them grow. No one is judged by their place on the ladder.

When Rabbi Posen assumed his pulpit over twenty-five years ago he articulated the idea of "three pillars" to help describe the various paths of Jewish commitment: the head, the hand, and the heart. "Head" Jews are those who are most connected to Jewish life through educational initiatives, such as classes, lectures, and workshops. "Hand" Jews are those who feel their closest connection through acts of kindness, social action, and the like. "Heart" Jews are those who best find their place through spiritual means such as prayer and other Jewish ritual.

The religious school philosophy reflects this idea by striving to create an environment comfortable for all children, youth, and families at whatever their level or style of Jewish commitment. Blending the formal and nonformal allows for students to find Jewish connections in traditional classroom learning, social action "mitzvah projects," as well as prayer services.

The congregation's religious school handbook demonstrates that the educational vision of the school is tied very closely to the overall educational vision of the synagogue. Some of the key features include:

- to create a foundation of Jewish learning, encompassing Hebrew, prayer, holidays, Shabbat, values, life-cycle events, Bible, history, synagogue, Israel and God to be built upon through life;
- to provide head (intellect), hand (social action), and heart (ritual) Jewish opportunities to lead to discovery of one's relationship to the community;
- to create life-long learning role models so that children come to see that Jewish education goes beyond the childhood years;
- to create a community of learners so that the students do not see themselves as individuals but as part of a *Kehillah*;
- to communicate with parents so that they are given the opportunity to become part of the community of learners.

In terms of Hebrew Language the school strives to:

- educate our students in the mechanics of the Hebrew language; letter/vowel recognition and reading;
- understand a basic Hebrew vocabulary that is based on prayer and holidays;
- provide an appreciation of the sacredness of Hebrew as a language that connects us to God and to the Jewish people;
- begin a desire to pursue a life-long relationship with Hebrew that could lead to *Ulpan*, fluency, Torah reading and/or being a *Shaliach Tzibor*.

As mentioned, Adath Shalom has a large day school population of about 200 students in the local Conservative and Modern Orthodox day school.

Rabbi Posen and Rachel strongly encourage their congregants to send their children to day school and even offer financial assistance to do so. This part of their educational philosophy does call into some question how synagogue leaders perceive the role of their own congregational school in their total educational vision.

## Staff

As mentioned, Rachel Waxman has been the educational director of the synagogue since 1990, when she was personally recruited by Rabbi Posen. She came with very strong training in Judaica (not always the case in supplementary schools) and has developed a considerable reputation within the educational community. She holds a master's degree in Jewish Education. She serves as a board member on her local central agency for Jewish education, is past chairperson of this agency's Principal's Forum, and has served as scholar in residence for her local Federation. She has played a leadership role in Coalition for the Advancement of Jewish Education and has garnered a number of community awards for her innovative curriculum development and professional excellence in Jewish communal service. She serves as a mentor for a professional institute for educational leadership as well for a university graduate school of education. She has co-authored and published articles on the Bar/Bat Mitzvah experience and family education and she teaches in the local Melton Adult Mini School. Previous to her work at Adath Shalom, she was an award-winning educator at a prominent Jewish camp. Rachel is admired and very well liked and appreciated by her congregation. She has been honored on more than one occasion by Adath Shalom for her years of service.

When she was first hired, Rachel's main responsibility was to direct the religious school. By her second year the synagogue was undergoing a transition to a Shabbat-focused, rather than Sunday-focused, educational system for the elementary grade students where multiple Shabbat programs, including those of the day school children, were taking place simultaneously. Rachel was excited about this new vision and embraced it. Her role thus shifted from religious school principal to educational director of the whole synagogue. This included all adult and family education. The religious school was reduced to one-third of her time commitment. An additional staff member was hired on a part-time basis to direct the high school programming. To date, there is no other staff member to help administer the elementary grades.

In the 2007–08 school year the school had eighteen staff members in the kindergarten to seventh grade classes, and an additional nine staff directing the various high school programs. Each elementary grade has a lead teacher who helps to supervise and guide the other teachers. All staff members except one are synagogue congregants. A number of teachers also teach at one of the local day schools. Teaching loads range from one to thirteen hours per week. Teachers are paid approximately $1,000 per year for every weekly hour they teach. Salary rates for lead teachers and more experienced teachers are higher.

Many new teachers took advantage of a mentored training program at the local central agency. In-service professional development primarily takes the form of Judaic content training through the Melton Mini School and other adult education that takes place at the synagogue. There is little in terms of professional development dealing with pedagogic issues.

## Governance

The synagogue has a lay board of trustees who administer to the various functions of the synagogue. As will be discussed in more detail, those that appear to have the most influence in the policy decisions and day-to-day operations of the synagogue are the professionals rather than the lay leaders. Rabbi Posen, Rachel Waxman, and the cantor, who have all been working for the synagogue for more than fifteen years, are casually referred to as the "triad." This triad yields considerable power and influence in the synagogue. There is an attempt now in the synagogue to move to a model that is more collaborative between concerned lay leaders and staff.

There is a "board of education" at the synagogue made up of lay leaders, but, as will be discussed, this board is somewhat independent of the board of trustees and does not appear to have the power to set policy. As we spent time with this board of education we observed that there is some lack of clarity as to its mandate in terms of whether the board should focus its energies only on the religious school or on the larger educational initiatives of the synagogue as well.

## Curriculum

### Elementary Grades

There are three main components to the Adath Shalom religious school elementary grades curriculum: *Ivrit, Yahadut,* and *Tefillah.* Approximately 1–1.5 hours a week is spent on Hebrew for the elementary age students.

In addition to the regular Hebrew program, which focuses on proficiency in *siddur* reading, the school also offers an optional intensive Hebrew program with more hours devoted to the language and more emphasis on conversation.

The curriculum is designed around the Melton model, Behrman House, and other resources. Tables 5.1 and 5.2 give a taste of the stated curricular goals for the most common entry level, *kitah aleph* (third grade) and the final grade before Bar/Bat Mitzvah, *kitah hay* (seventh grade). In keeping with the synagogue philosophy, formal classroom learning is combined with the nonformal. One of the popular nonformal dimensions of the school curriculum is "mitzvah projects," which are out of the classroom social action initiatives for school credit that involve students' families. Examples include:

**Table 5.1**
*Kitah Alef*

| | |
|---|---|
| Overall goal: To familiarize students with the rhythm of the Jewish calendar year | |
| *Hebrew Reading* | Mechanics of Hebrew reading (phonetics) are taught. Textbooks used are *The Hebrew Primer* and the *Siddur*. |
| *Prayers* | Students begin to investigate the *Siddur*, beginning with rote learning and progressing to reading mastery of selected prayers. |
| *Hebrew Language* | Students acquire a basic Hebrew vocabulary of 60 to 75 words based on terms associated with the holidays and classroom and synagogue objects. Simple stories are introduced to facilitate comprehension, reading, and some Hebrew conversation. |
| *Holiday and* Mitzvot | Holidays, *mitzvot*, and values are studied. Students are evaluated on classroom participation and discussion, plus completion of worksheets. Dramatics, music and arts and crafts are also integrated into the lessons. |
| *Bible* | The Bible is studied during the Shabbat program using Ktav's textbook *Torah and You*, Part 1. The entire book is covered by the end of the year. |
| Mitzvah *Projects* | By learning how to do mitzvot, students put into practice important Jewish values that should be reinforced in the home. Alef classes will focus on the ***mitzvot*** "*Kibud Av V'em*" (honouring parents) and "*Lashon Hora*" (not gossiping) and observing Shabbat. The mitzvah project will be a Passover food drive. |

- *Family trip to the Community Food Bank*. Poverty and Hunger exist here at home. Share the vision of feeding the hungry and come help the food bank fulfil their mission to distribute food and grocery products to over 1500 charities. Learn about and act on the Jewish value of feeding the hungry—*ma'achil re'evim*.
- *A Package from Home*. Participate in Adath Shalom's Annual Walk for Israel and prepare letters of support which will be sent to Israeli soldiers. Bring mini-toiletries, warm socks and hats to be sent to our Israeli soldiers through the organization, "A Package from Home." Learn about the Jewish value—All of Israel is responsible for one another—*Kol Yisrael Areivim Zeh B'Zeh*.

While these initiatives include written curricular expectations for specific grade levels, Rachel concedes that in practice the curriculum is "fluid," not

Table 5.2
*Kitah Hay*

| | |
|---|---|
| Overall goal: To engage in in-depth study and practice of mitzvot | |
| *Power Hebrew Reading and Prayer* | Individually designed assignments are developed for students to stimulate involvement in the prayer service. Students also review and reinforce prayers studied in earlier grades to ensure complete mastery |
| *Holocaust* | Through this eight-week unit, students learn about the Holocaust. Materials used include videos, biographies, and posters. Speakers are also invited to address the classes. |
| Mitzvot / *Jewish Values* | Students learn about *mitzvot* and practice them through hands-on projects. |
| *Life Cycle* | Students complete the life cycle curriculum started in *Dalet* class. In addition to the Bar/Bat Mitzvah unit, the Jewish wedding and the Jewish approach to death will be the major units. |
| *Additional Classes* | Other courses offered will cover Jewish law, aspects of God, and Israel. |
| *Bar/Bat Mitzvah Class* | Students use the text Coming of Age as a Bar/Bat Mitzvah. The students focus on becoming a Bar/Bat Mitzvah and what it means in the home, in the community, and among peers. A Bar/Bat Mitzvah three-week program is coordinated for parents and students, during which they discuss "Why Be Jewish?" |

standardized, not compiled in a master binder, and dependent on the skills and styles of individual teachers. As in many schools, quick discussions in the hall often serve as key moments of communication between teachers, rather than sustained discussion in scheduled staff meetings. This means that curricular coordination between teachers is sometimes lacking.

In keeping with the synagogue's philosophy of multiple paths to Jewish connection, Rachel tries to offer a personalized approach to her curriculum. She strives to provide the right combination and style of classes for everyone. When a group of parents expressed concern about the level of Hebrew instruction for their children, Rachel developed the intensive Hebrew program. Those parents who show strong conviction that one weekday a week rather than two would suit their children better do not meet active resistance. When Rachel observed that a handful of children had left the day school system for a variety of reasons, she created a customized class for these eight to ten ex–day school students.

How are students evaluated in the elementary grades?

The religious school does not have a standardized system for evaluating their students on the content of the curriculum. Individual teachers use their own discretion in deciding if and how they will evaluate students. A *kitah aleph* and b*et* teacher told us she uses the book, *Zman Likro*, by Ariel Lechner and finds the exercises at the end of the book on Hebrew letters and vocabulary to be helpful in gauging her students' progress. Some teachers in older grades told us they design and hold random quizzes in *Ivrit*, covering vocabulary and grammar. Based on the exams that Harry Potter and his friends took called OWLS, one teacher designed a series of tests on the students' basic knowledge of Jewish holidays called *Yanshoofs*. Fig. 5.1 shows a section of the *Yanshoof* test on Passover for *kitah dalet*. In our conversation with Miriam, the lead teacher for *kitah dalet*, we learned her expectations for Hebrew Language proficiency:

*Miriam:* In *dalet* we have about 47–48 children. The *Ivrit* is the divider. The students are divided according to their ability based on their previous teacher's recommendation.

*Researcher:* Is that a test?

*Miriam:* Recommendation.

*Researcher:* What's that recommendation based on?

## PESACH YANSHOOF

1. What is the date for *Pesach*?_____

   How many days?_____

2. What does *Pesach* mean?

3. *Pesach* is called the "season of _____," because . . .

4. Is *Pesach* mentioned in the Torah?

5. Is *Pesach* one of the *Shalosh Regalim*?

6. Describe the following people and terms and how they relate to *Pesach*:

   Moshe _____

   Pharaoh _____

   *Mitzrayim* _____

   Plagues _____

   Angel of death _____

   Red Sea _____

*Mitzvot & Customs of Pesach*

1. Seder means _____. The most important part of the seder is:

2. a. What is *Chametz*?

   b. What can we NOT do with it during *Pesach*?

   c. What is *Bedikat Chametz* and when is it done?

3. According to the Torah, on *Pesach* we are required to eat

   _____, in order to remember . . .

**Figure 5.1**

*Miriam:* A recommendation could be based on the teacher's opinion of how that student did all year in her class the previous year and dependent upon who that teacher is and how they teach and what they test or don't test.

*Researcher:* How would you assess a student who has finished kitah gimel?

*Miriam:* At the end of *gimel*, coming in, I would assess a high student—an A student—as knowing all of the vowels, all of the letters, and being able to read . . . different syllables in the word correctly. That would be my A student. The next level student would be someone who knows most of the letters, 97 percent of the letters, gets confused with a couple, a *shin* and a *sin*. They know most of the vowels but still forget that the "oh" is here and "oo" is here and that kind of thing, so that would be like the middle person.

*Researcher:* What do you expect after kitah dalet?

*Miriam:* I hope that every student finishing *dalet* will be able to know the entire alphabet, will be able to know all of the vowels, will be able to read simple common *siddur* words. I do not care if they cannot write a Hebrew letter, which is very different than in the past [this year's *dalet* students were more challenging to work with than usual], but I do care that if they open up the *siddur* and they see the word *baruch* versus *barchu* they're going to recognize that that's what the word is.

As assistant to the cantor, Miriam also works with students on preliminary B'nei Mitzvah preparations before they begin their lessons with the cantor. This allows her to gauge *Ivrit* competency of students over time. She told us the levels of competency she sees are quite mixed.

Miriam was also helpful in identifying her expectations for the *yahadut* content of her curriculum. On the subject of Passover we observed her developmental perspective:

*Miriam:* By the end of *gimel* at Pesach we would expect a student to know the difference between *hametz* and *matzah*.

*Researcher:* What does this mean?

*Miriam:* They would know what product is unleavened from a Judaic standpoint. And from an Ivrit standpoint we would expect them to know the *Ma'nishtanah* by then.

*Researcher:* To be able to read *Ma'nishtanah*?

*Miriam:* Absolutely!

*Researcher:* By the end of *gimel* are the students learning about the *Hagaddah*?

*Miriam:* Oh yeah, and absolutely they would also be able to go down the steps of the Seder and read *kadesh, urchatz,* etc. and they should be able to tell you what most of them are. In *dalet* they should do all of that and they would also learn how Pesach is one of the *shalosh regalim,* but they would also get into what does freedom mean, when did the Jewish people become a people, that's the next level. What is peoplehood? When did we become a nation? When did we become Jewish? What is *Nisan*? What is the first month of the calendar? Is it *Tishrei*? I always thought it was *Tishrei,* September—new school, new year, new everything. It's the new year, happy new year. This is the year they learn it's *Nisan.* It's the first month, and all of these aspects of the Jewish people becoming a nation, having a leader—*moshe rabeinu.* What does it mean to be a leader? What do you have to deal with? So more from a—not from a religious but a historical—more from them understanding . . . even comparing how we live in this country, so it's just a larger perspective—a higher level perspective.

## High School

One of the strengths of the Adath Shalom religious school is the vibrancy of the high school educational offerings (both formal and nonformal). As mentioned, in the last several years, approximately 160 teenagers per year are involved at some level in Adath Shalom sponsored activities. Approximately half these youth are involved in formal classroom learning and half in a variety of nonformal programs. One parent we spoke to made an illuminating comparison to a nearby synagogue. She said, "I'm from Springfield, which is the next town over. And I can 100 percent tell you that once the kids are Bar-Mitzvah'ed they want absolutely nothing, *nothing* to do with the synagogue whatsoever."

In keeping with the synagogue philosophy, a large variety of programs is offered to teen congregants to try to provide something appealing to everyone. Table 5.3 shows the program listings for the 2007–08 school year. Some of these programs are scheduled together, so that Wednesday evenings, for example, offer a full slate of youth programming with the *Prozdor* text class (1 hour), followed by free pizza (important to keep teens energized), the current events class (1 hour), *ma'ariv* services (thus integrating teens into wider synagogue life), and a USY social event (every other week).

Table 5.3
*Adath Shalom Teen Programming*

| | |
|---|---|
| *Current Events from a Jewish Perspective* | Weekly one-hour class over 18 weeks on current events as seen through a Jewish lens. The objective of this program is to develop one's Jewish identity through media, discussion, and community building. |
| Prozdor *Program* | Weekly one-hour class over 18 weeks on Jewish text taught by a Rabbinic intern. |
| SHINE | Weekly visit to a home for the elderly. The program gives teens an opportunity to learn from elderly people and be an important part of someone's life. The mission is to inspire an ongoing commitment to community service as part of an expression of Jewish identity. |
| *Student Mentoring Project* | A community service project in conjunction with a local Protestant church tutoring and mentoring children from the local public schools. Honor roll high school students with leadership skills are encouraged to volunteer. |
| *Rosh Chodesh: It's a Girl Thing* | Based on the Jewish tradition of women's New Moon celebrations, this program aims to build the self-esteem, Jewish identity, leadership skills, and friendship networks of ninth grade girls. Now in its fourth year nationally. The small groups are designed to provide a celebratory, empowering setting in which girls can support each other in growing and learning while having lots of fun. |
| Kadima *(8th grade) /* USY *(9th–12th grade)* | United Synagogue Youth is a national organization that provides nonformal activities for our teens to meet other Jewish teens in a fun, relaxed social setting. *Kadima* is part of the synagogue's USY program. |
| *Israel Leadership Training Program* | An international peer-led youth movement centered in Israel. It is a place where children and teens gather Shabbat afternoons to play, learn, meet new people, and grow as individuals. Ninth to eleventh grade counselors develop the skills to create nonformal Jewish activities for youngsters. |
| *HaZamir* | Lead by Adath Shalom's cantor, *HaZamir* is the area's Jewish High School Choir. It includes over 60 teen singers and performs 7–12 times a year. The choir has traveled around the United States, to Israel, England, and Spain. |

Several of the programs, such as SHINE, the student mentoring, and the leadership training, offer community service certification, which is desired by teens to help bolster their college applications. In addition, the synagogue's youth director, who is also the current events teacher, has begun a process of exploring a partnership with a local university whereby he would become an adjunct professor and his twelfth grade current events courses would offer college credit through this particular university.

Other programs include a teen *ulpan* program for those who want to continue improving their conversational Hebrew. If a teenager who is enrolled in one of the synagogue programs desires individualized tutoring on some aspect of *yahadut*, this can be arranged at no extra cost. Rachel also enjoys hiring teenage congregants to serve as teachers' aides in the classrooms of younger grades. This keeps them involved in the synagogue's school and, similar to the leadership training program, allows them to serve as positive role models for the younger students.

Rounding out the high school programming is the "Rap with the Rabbi" where students have the opportunity to join Rabbi Posen for pizza and to discuss important issues facing Jewish teenagers and the Jewish community at large.

## A Closer Look at Teachers and Teaching

### Actualizing Vision

As discussed earlier, the philosophy of the synagogue, as initiated through Rabbi Posen, dictates that no one will be judged for his or her level of commitment to Judaism. The synagogue sees itself as an "enabling institution" that seeks to accept a congregant wherever s/he is and, through a variety of different Jewish paths, help them grow in ways that are personally comfortable and meaningful.

Though it took her some time to move away from what she called the somewhat "elitist" mindset of her Jewish camp background, Rachel, as educational director of Adath Shalom, many years ago bought into the nonjudgmental, welcoming approach of the synagogue. We suggest that this is one of the reasons why she is so liked and people speak so glowingly about the sense of community they feel within the school and synagogue environment.

We noticed the same shift in attitude in Miriam, the lead teacher for *kitah dalet* and assistant to the synagogue cantor. Miriam, who was educated in an Orthodox day school, told us, "when I came here I had no experience with Conservative Judaism. I didn't even know what it was. So when this [philosophy] came down from the Rabbi it [provided] so many more opportunities, so many different ways of being Jewish, so that now when I speak to the kids and when I teach, and even when I work with their families who come now for Bar and Bat Mitzvah stuff, they are all coming from different places. They're all coming from different needs and goals for their kids . . . I can so much better internalize what I'm hearing."

## Staff Camaraderie and Support

In our general conversations with teachers we were struck by the high level of satisfaction they felt with Rachel. They spoke of great communication and openness with their supervisor and the support they get from her in terms of Judaic content. The sense of camaraderie and teamwork permeated through the whole faculty. What contributes to this strong sense of community among the staff is the fact that virtually all of them are synagogue congregants. This provides a sense of ideological consistency in that, for the most part, the school has strongly affiliated Conservative Jews teaching in a Conservative religious school. Having congregants as teachers also allows for teachers to take part easily in the synagogue's adult education programs, many of them taught by Rachel. As mentioned, this serves as a key part of staff professional development.

One of the challenges, however, of having congregants as your teachers is that Rachel finds it politically sensitive to fire a teacher. Rachel admitted that some of her teachers are weak, not highly qualified and do not show high enough levels of commitment (for example not arriving early to school to greet the students when they arrive). She conceded that "right now I would like to shake up the staff a little bit. I want to get a younger staff. I do have one or two teachers that I need to kind of retire out."

## Parents' Impressions of Teaching

Most parents did not choose the Adath Shalom religious school for their children because of the school itself, but rather they chose the synagogue first and this was simply the school connected with it. This is not an unusual pattern, as confirmed by the research of Kress (2007).[2] Nonetheless we had the opportunity to speak to a group of parents devoted to the school who were happy to share their opinions of the teachers and the quality of teaching.

Despite Rachel's private admission that some of her teachers are weak, the teachers, in general, made a strong impression on one parent in terms of their level of training. One mother told us: "The teachers take being Jewish educated seriously. Its not just an extra couple of hours for an extra couple of dollars or it's not just because somebody twisted their arm. I think they take it seriously. It just speaks highly of our teacher training program. Three teachers are graduates just this year from that program . . . many of our teachers have been matched with mentors [through the central agency's mentoring program]. That says something about how they see themselves and their roles and how seriously they're taking being a Jewish teacher in this school."

In terms of what their children are learning in school, parents provided mixed reports. One parent was very impressed with the Holocaust curriculum. She told us that when she was a child, "we saw that movie *Four Hundred Blows*. Do you remember that movie? I still have nightmares about the whole thing. I think maybe I'll let David watch that when he's like 40. It's so devastating, not that the Holocaust is anything but, but the way that my kids learned about the Holocaust, it was poetic. It was beautiful! [speaks softly] Low and easy and personal, you know little pieces about real people that went through it. It starts to sink in around third or fourth grade that this is a really horrible thing, but it was amazing. That was probably what impressed [me the most]. Everything else I knew . . . they would learn Hebrew. I knew they do Bar Mitzvah, but the Holocaust curriculum is really like my heart. I'm just really impressed with that."

While the sense we got was that most parents with children in the elementary grades are not particularly knowledgeable about what the school teaches and do not have particular curricular expectations for their children, there was a small group of highly (Jewishly) educated, committed parents (these are the ones more likely to speak to researchers) who were not satisfied with all aspects of the curriculum. One had concerns about the teaching of Jewish thought:

*Parent:* Do they discuss the rabbinic age? No. I don't think there's much discussion beyond Biblical times. They touch on Maimonides but there's no real depth in learning beyond the Biblical stuff.

*Researcher:* Do you have expectations that way?

*Parent:* Why not? My feeling is why not.

Another was concerned about the Israel curriculum. She told us, "I felt my children had little connection to Israel because that was not being communicated in an effective way." A third parent felt there was too much repetition: "My kids who happen to be very bright will come home and go, "can you believe that we did the blessing over the *challah* in fourth grade?" There is too much repetition. Unless you, God forbid, have an IQ of 30 you know the blessing over the *challah* by the time you are four."

## Researchers' Impressions of Teaching

In terms of our own impression of the quality of teaching, we were impressed, for example, with the seriousness with which Miriam takes her work. Besides having clear curricular expectations of her students, which we have seen, we observed the effort that she puts into finding stimulating age-appropriate material for her students.

*Researcher:* Where do you go for your information or for materials that will challenge your kids? Where do you have that kind of process, or not?

*Miriam:* I first see what's available. So I will go into my own library and I will go into books that I have like a Michael Strassfeld. He's written some wonderful material and I will go and I would look. I'll pick it up and I'll go in and look. And I'll go online and I'll look into whatever site it might be, and I'll teach myself. I enjoy looking for the information and then I might even open up the *chumash* and I'll say okay, we were talking about the birth cycle, let me go see what it said in the Torah there. I want to see the actual words. And I can do that because I can read it in the Hebrew and get the *ta'am*. And I can even go in and look at the commentaries and get an idea, so I will really do it myself.

We observed that as lead teacher Miriam recognizes her role as a resource person for other teachers. She readily shares her ideas with her colleagues. Teachers take their own initiative as well. A *kitah bet* teacher told us: "I love hanging out at the local Jewish agency resource center to get more ideas. A group of us go regularly."

We were also struck by Miriam's dedication and ambitiousness in setting up a blog to try to further engage students: "You can just go to the site and you will see exactly what I'm doing. You will see that the goal for this was for the kids to go on the site, read whatever is on the blog, ask questions related to that information or answer questions that I may have put in the blog or ask any questions that they might want—anything that was Jewish, Judaic related. And I'm the head honcho. If you ask an appropriate question you get ten points. If we collect X amount of points we do something."

As Kress (2007) points out, one important strategy for improving the supplementary school experience is to find ways to better involve and engage parents in the educational process. As is clearly reflected in her work, Miriam is working on this as well:

> I send an email to the parents, "check the new information on the blog and see what Johnny did." They'll go on, they can ask a question. They can see what their kids are interested in. I want them to know what's happening in Hebrew school because a kid comes home, he doesn't talk about Hebrew school. So the idea is to engage the parent in what the kid is doing. If I sent home a thing on birth that said what is your Hebrew name and where did you get it, I want to let the parent know the kid is bringing it home and I want them to engage together and have these sweet memories of your experience of birthing your child. And all of a sudden I have a parent letting me know that Johnny is not coming out to Hebrew School because he is playing saxophone, *what can I do to keep him up?* . . . I'm happy! I'm happy! . . . So take a look . . . it's just the beginning but I think we're heading in the right direction . . .

In terms of the school classrooms, the classes in Lyndon Johnson Public School were lively and engaging with colorful posters on the wall thanks to the efforts of the public school teachers. Furniture was flexible allowing for multiple layouts. As mentioned, the religious school was resourceful in storing their materials in suitcases, but this, and the fact that they are sharing rooms with an active public school, limits the amount of Jewish content items that can displayed on the walls, etc.

The temporary classrooms in the portable trailers were lacking somewhat in appeal. They were set up in a frontal design with all the desks facing the teacher and a standard blackboard. One of the two rooms was lacking bright colors, some leather chairs were ripped, and there was a mess of papers on the teacher's desk when we walked in. The calendar on the wall displayed the month of October, rather than *Tishrei/Chesvan*. The Israel posters (likely received free from a travel agency) on the wall had very small Hebrew writing which was not effective. The other classroom was brighter and cheerier with a large colorful chart of Hebrew letters and vowels and attractive pictures of objects starting with each Hebrew letter; *shin* had a picture of a *shulchan* (desk), *shemesh* (the sun), and *shinaim* (teeth).

Our observations of classes also gave us a mixed impression. A fifth grade class was somewhat chaotic with kids not paying attention and the teacher reading aloud to the class with a large Jewish history picture book which was not age-appropriate (we also learned that the *ulpan* class for teenagers uses the same Hebrew textbook as the second grade Hebrew class). Other classes we attended saw the kids attentive and intellectually engaged.

The fourth to sixth grade students enjoyed the cantor's music class. They enthusiastically ran into the public school auditorium with smiles on their faces. The cantor knew all the kids by name. "Quick, quick to the front," he told them as he started to engage them right away in a "who can sing *ashrei* louder and clearer" contest. He called in Rachel to serve as judge. Multiple winners were chosen. The cantor led them in a round of *al kol eileh* on his handmade overhead transparencies with transliterated Hebrew.

Barry Goodman, the director of the Adath Shalom high school programs, led a current events class of five ninth graders on issues around drug and alcohol use and abuse. Opening with a video clip of contemporary rappers talking about "saying no to drugs," he related well to the students and sensitively facilitated a mature discussion. He kept the class moving at a quick pace to keep the attention of his students. Half way through the class he introduced the Jewish concept of not damaging one's body. We wondered whether the Jewish angle could have played a more central role from the outset of the class.

## Some Challenges Facing the School

### *"Classic" Religious School Challenges*

Adath Shalom faces the same challenges as many other Jewish congregational schools in the country. One parent summed it up this way: "They come out of six hours of secular studies; you are now putting them back in a classroom for two hours. It's a tough battle; so market that!" While students generally enjoy class once they are there, the synagogue cantor described it as an "uphill struggle" to keep attendance at a high level: "The atmosphere is one of 'we like being Jewish, we like doing Jewish things,' and there's enough stuff that's fun to keep interest and to keep that going. It doesn't mean that religious school is necessarily the highest priority for our families. 'Not going to be there today, we've got a swim meet, we've got a skiing match, we've got a boxing match, we've got . . . heavens exactly knows what.'" Rachel described the situation as "classic religious school issues. You know, the wrong time of day, other commitments, people being picked up early, teacher frustration . . ."

As mentioned, the majority of parents choose to start their children in religious school only when mandatory to do so (third grade) to be eligible for b'nei mitzvah at the synagogue. This lack of motivation from parents may be related to their own less than favorable memories of their own religious school experiences as children (Kress, 2007). Rachel described her synagogue's families this way: "We do have a small population of *shabbos* regulars, cream of the crop religious school families, committed families, we do have that. But we don't have a big amount because [most of] that group is in day school. So then we have a huge group of people who are doing it because they need a Bar Mitzvah . . ."

## Too Much Flexibility?

As we have seen, Rachel is a tremendous source of strength for the religious school and the synagogue as a whole. She can be credited for fostering a warm, accepting, and caring educational environment where meaningful relationships and community are forged. We have also seen Rachel's adaptable approach, where she strives to develop personalized programs for students based on parents' requests. One particularly committed parent of a first grader explained her delight in Rachel's accommodating style: "[At a nearby congregational school] I had asked to explore the idea of supplementing that Sunday with one other day [of instruction]; with anything. I didn't care. I just wanted her to understand that this was a priority [for me] and it met with much resistance [from the principal]—much, much resistance. And someone suggested I go to Adath Shalom. I met with Rachel. I wasn't even a member and she said what day of the week would you like to have? So how can you not be here . . . ?" Another parent confirmed, "I think that really is one of the strengths of [our religious school]. Rachel does whatever it takes. She will make it work for you."

On the issue of Hebrew instruction, Rachel told us she does not want to push some students too hard or burden them with too many standardized examinations for fear of alienating the student (and thus possibly alienating the family from the synagogue). She explained that "[t]here is going always be a population that would do perfectly well and learn the *tefillah* and be Torah readers and love Hebrew language. And there will be a population in the middle that will feel comfortable enough and then there's always going to be the non-Hebrew speaker. There is always going to be the child who feels stupid in the Hebrew class. They could look at

Judaism that way completely, if they're rejected in Hebrew they could look at their entire Jewish life as being rejected. I hate it!"

As discussed earlier, Rachel works in a culture where parents feel they have the autonomy to develop personalized plans for their children. This could mean, for example, attending school one day a week instead of two or not attending the Shabbat programs as often as required. Rachel allows this. "That's my problem," Rachel told us. "I am an easy touch. I don't *tzit-tzit* check. I don't close the door on anyone."

We wonder if this flexibility and inclusiveness might at times compromise the ability of the school to meet its curricular goals. Some parents as well as Rabbi Posen told us at different times that the school is not currently reaching its goals in Hebrew language instruction and that weak Hebrew students are sometimes falling between the cracks. Rachel herself admitted the difficult challenges in this area: "Hebrew language is a huge issue for me because I believe that you can't do Hebrew language twice a week properly."

In general, it was not easy to find any critical comments about Rachel from the parents, but in this area of her leniency some concerns did surface. One parent stated: "She is the queen of positive reinforcement. Your kid could miss four times and come the fifth, and she will embrace them and be so excited, and listen to why they didn't come and praise them for how they did in the soccer game . . ." Another parent reiterated this concern: "My complaint was my son goes to Shabbat school every week and none of his friends are there. You have a minimum requirement and these people aren't making it. It's a long day and I don't pretend that it isn't, but it's something he needs to do. He has a commitment . . . I do think if I were to criticize Rachel she is too nice to the parents. She is too tolerant."

## Overprofessionalization

We observed at Adath Shalom a certain culture where the synagogue professionals (meaning the "triad" of Rabbi Posen, Rachel, and the cantor), rather than the lay leaders, hold the majority of power and influence in questions of synagogue planning and policy. Lay leaders seem to have grown accustomed to following the vision of their professional employees, particularly Rabbi Posen, rather than generating their own agenda for the synagogue. We were a little surprised to learn that Adath Shalom employs only one rabbi for a synagogue of this size (900 families). We were also struck by the fact that there is almost no mention of a lay board of trustees on the synagogue's website, while the three main professional staff are well recognized. In general, we wonder if there is too much power and responsibility in the hands of too few people, without sufficient checks and balances built in.

In the case of the educational arm of the synagogue, including the religious school, we noticed that Rachel (in consultation with Rabbi Posen) has almost total control of the design and implementation of the educational programming, with little accountability for her work. Interestingly, Rachel is quick to praise the lay leaders of her synagogue: "We have an amazing lay leadership. I didn't say this before but I should say it now, that the lay leadership allows us to do whatever we want to, you know what I'm saying? Like the lay leadership trust us and they are willing to experiment with us and put their money into this experimentation."

Trusting your professionals is clearly a positive thing, however we also sense a lack of leadership and initiative from a lay board that "allows us to do whatever we want to." Rachel herself recognizes and laments the fact that within her realm of synagogue educational programming she sees little active leadership from lay people: "Karen leads a book club. And you know what, she is my only example that I could give you right now in the synagogue of a lay leader who is not being paid. Isn't that interesting? If there's no professional attached to a program it doesn't happen. And that is the state of Adath Shalom world. So what I worry about is, if I leave the synagogue, who is going to pick up the pieces of it? Another educator will come and do [the work], but they've never evaluated me. Some synagogues evaluate their professional staff; we never got evaluated and it's not healthy for the institution."

This lack of lay influence on the direction of the religious school is seen clearly in the structure of the synagogue's "board of education." In our conversations with the seven members of board of the education we heard frustration that they serve merely as a support system for Rachel without any real power to affect school policy. One example given was the board of education's recommendation not to increase religious school tuition in the last year. The recommendation was ignored by the synagogue's board of trustees, which, in close consultation with the Rabbi, raised the school fees. In order to reflect on their mission, the members of the board of education discussed some questions relating to their role in the school. In terms of the expectations they had of their position, many thought the Board of Education would be more formal, with actual job specifications such as curriculum, budget, staffing, problem solving, fundraising, etc. As it functions now, the board members considered their group as mostly a "sounding board" for Rachel without any "clout."

One of the results of this lack of true sharing of responsibilities between Rachel and her board of education is that Rachel takes on much of the work herself and certainly works, as she states, "more than full time." Being a single woman helps her to be able to log extremely long hours. The synagogue has created and perpetuated a culture where Rachel is in charge of everything concerned with education, with few other professionals or lay leaders to share the load. One member of the board of education told us, "One thing the group has felt is [that we need to try] to help protect Rachel from herself, from saying yes to too many things. That's an issue."

Rachel seems to thrive in this level of control. One of the teachers enthusiastically told us, "I am a Rachel Waxman groupie." We observed many other groupies. As we have seen, as educational director of the whole synagogue only one-third of her time is designated to the K–12 religious school. Rachel told us, "I'm at [community meetings and workshops] where people only have to focus in on the religious school and nothing else and I'm jealous because if they're only focussing on the religious school . . . but yet I would be so bored. I would never have stayed here all these years if it was just the religious school."

With the amount of responsibility that Rachel has taken on she could benefit from an assistant director of education or a principal of the religious school who would work under her. And although she is clearly in a senior educational position, she could also benefit from someone who serves as a mentor of sorts to offer her guidance in her work.

## Transitions for the School

Our research at Adath Shalom was well timed. Starting a few years previous to our visits, Adath Shalom received grants from some prominent Jewish organizations that helped the synagogue enter a new mode of reflection about its operations, including its religious school. This, combined with its current large construction project, precipitated a long-range planning process with some key strategies for moving forward. This period of transition for Adath Shalom is particularly instructive for our purposes. It provides a clear example of how a synagogue school attempts to addresses its challenges.

The first step to addressing some of the challenges described above is to acknowledge that there is indeed room for change and improvement. In this regard, when we asked Rabbi Posen about the process of formal evaluation of the synagogue professional staff by the Board of Trustees, he answered honestly that this area ". . . is in need of a lot more fine tuning. That has been an area of weakness. Partly it's because of the admiration and comfort level with the staff that we have." As part of the synagogue transition, lay leaders and other congregants for the first time facilitated focus groups for themselves to have a chance to explore their collective views and ensure that their perspectives play an important role in long-range planning. Rabbi Posen spoke of "igniting more enthusiasm throughout the institution" to encourage more congregants to voice their concerns and take on leadership roles in the synagogue.

Rachel also recognizes that there is room for change in the top-down structure of Adath Shalom where the synagogue vision is developed by the professionals. She told us, "We have always been like this. We're very strong . . . we're very, very professional staff–driven. And now we're such that we don't have lay leadership to volunteer." She admitted that "we have been ignoring our lay leadership" and that she "needs to let everyone [else] grow." In terms of how she directs the religious school, she committed herself to some changes. She told us, "I have [always] spoon-fed the staff the curriculum. [Today] is the first time in the history of the religious school where I'm asking staff to be part of curriculum development. And they're excited about it. It's not that they don't want to do it but they don't even know what I'm asking them to do because I have always said, "Let's do [this]." So it is a powerful time in the Adath Shalom world."

## Establishing New Positions

One strategy of the new long-term planning process is to appoint and hire more people to share the load of responsibility for the religious school. During the course of our research a new position was created within the synagogue's board of trustees called VP of Education. Unlike the previous independent body called the "board of education" it is hoped that this position will yield more influence and have the power to effect policy decisions. The long-range plan is to have this new committee on education oversee all aspects of synagogue education from nursery to adult education. Each dimension of synagogue education (religious school, family education, adult education, etc.) will be overseen by an education subcommittee.

A congregant named Jill Kaplan has been appointed to this new VP of Education position. Jill has an MBA and eight years experience in business. She grew up in the congregation and sends one of her children to the religious school. She appears very talented and capable in this position. Jill has observed the top-down structure of her synagogue and through her position will endeavor to help transform this culture. Time will be the judge, but it appears reasonable to suggest that this shift can bring more accountability to the work that Rachel does in the religious school, be it curriculum, hiring, or otherwise. Jill strongly supports the hiring of an assistant for Rachel to serve as principal of the religious school. This idea is supported by Rabbi Posen and Rachel herself. It would clearly be a significant change for Adath Shalom that could bring about additional accountability for the quality of the instruction at the school.

## Youth Commission and Teen Council

As discussed previously, one of the strengths of Adath Shalom's religious school is its range of high school programming. In order to continue to improve this aspect of their programming one of the subcommittees within the education committee will be a Youth Commission that will oversee all the formal and nonformal programming available to teenagers. In addition to this new facet of lay leadership, the synagogue has just established a Teen Council, run by the youth themselves. Representatives from each of the varied teen programs meet once a week to share their experiences so that those who are involved in formal learning in the classroom (head), those in social action (hand), and those involved in the choir or religious ritual (heart) have a chance to gain exposure to other aspects of Jewish life. As Rabbi Posen explained, the strategy is to have "[those] who are involved in pillar X integrating with others and radiating their interest . . . kids who are *shul* goers but aren't involved in acts of *chesed* can be more inspired by what they see from the [social action] kids and the like. There are a lot of pieces of this puzzle that the new mission will help us to explore." Plans are already in place to develop an annual Israel leadership trip for members of the Teen Council.

## Broadening the Vision

Another part of the long-range planning is to broaden the vision of the synagogue by including two new pillars. In addition to the current three pillars of head, hand, and heart, the synagogue has added one pillar called *chevreh* or community connections, and another called *k'lal Israel* dealing with linkages to outside Jewish communities. The idea is that the curriculum of the religious school will reflect this broader synagogue vision.

Rabbi Posen explained that these two new pillars bring a new dimension of nonformal education to the synagogue and school that complements the formal educational components. He told us that his synagogue has not focused enough on friendship building in the elementary years. The plan is to create *chavurahs* of families (parents and children) of similar interest for educational and social activities:

> So the idea is that part of your experience of education and school as a child is that your family is part of a *chavurah*. That would lead to a natural effort to maintain *chavurot* of the various age appropriate children of families . . . the best people we've always found to market and sustain *chavurot* are not staff. It's lay people who are motivated to do so. We'll staff it. We'll provide it, but we need people who are willing to get their buddies or people they like to be buddies with, people they would like to meet. That would be an example [of implementing this pillar into the educational lives of our students].

The fifth pillar of *k'lal Israel* is intended to help students and other congregants forge connections with Jewish communities both in other parts of the United States and around the world. We see here Rabbi Posen's preliminary thoughts for how this will play out:

> Under that pillar we're going to have not just the Israel Committee but a world Jewry Committee. So with those committees as they evolve, that should play itself out in terms of the educational structure in all kinds of conscious ways to connect the ages K through 12 and their families. The Walk for Israel has been one way, but there are a lot of other ways. We're creating a pen pal twinning with Bar and Bat Mitzvah kids [in Buenos Aires]. We should establish much stronger ties with those children and the same in terms of stuff in the U.S., both for people in terms of needs, like Katrina in New Orleans. But it's not only in terms of needs. I think we've learned from this that the Jews are on the move. They perceive in their own lifetime they're going to be moving around a lot. Their family members locate to all kinds of places. Students routinely spend time abroad for a semester or more. Jobs will often take you at least for a period of time [to other] places, so the world is getting smaller. So I think both of those major pillars are going to conceptually make their way measurably into the whole educational plan, that's what I believe.

## Conclusion

There are many strengths to be found in the Adath Shalom religious school. The school is housed in a synagogue with strong, experienced, professional leadership who are proud Conservative Jewish role models.

There is a large critical mass of congregants that form a school of significant size. The synagogue is financially stable and is committed to providing the school whatever resources they deem necessary.

The school is administered by an educational director who is well trained and accomplished in Jewish education. Her teachers admire her and enjoy working under her supervision. She is well respected and liked within her congregation. With her broad educational mandate, Rachel is able to place her stamp on many facets of the synagogue. The overlapping relationships between her different duties enrich her ability to create a better and more integrated religious school. Her warm and welcoming style fosters a strong feeling of community between teachers, students, and parents.

The personalized, nonjudgmental approach of the synagogue is actualized in the attitudes of Rachel and her teachers in their relations to students and parents, many of which are not overly religiously observant. The school excels at offering a large range of educational offerings (both formal and nonformal), particularly in the high school (which has a reported two-thirds retention rate in the last few years). The strategy of offering multiple paths to Jewish engagement (head, hand, heart, etc.) is in keeping with the latest successful trends in supplementary education. The school also places considerable emphasis on integrating children's education with family education. Some examples include the "*mitzvah* projects," a teacher's new blog initiative, and the new synagogue pillar that aims to forge *chavurot* between families.

In keeping with their wider educational philosophy, the synagogue nursery school is participating with a regional central agency program also concerned with connecting children's education and family education. One congregant who works in the local central agency spoke with pride about the commitment of Adath Shalom to consistently working toward improving their educational offerings: "So they are one of the eight schools that wanted to be part of it, wrote that they want to be part of it, applied to be part of it and is actively working on it. So that's just one example of how they are a very professional, coordinated, dedicated team that sees that's something that will benefit their community, the teachers, the family, the children, them as a whole—and they do it and they do it right. There are other synagogues who are also doing this and other temples who are also doing this and doing it right, but you can always count on Adath Shalom." Other strengths include experienced and talented lead teachers who help supervise newer teachers in the elementary grades, and the popular practice of offering community service certificates to high school students to help bolster college applications.

As we have seen, Adath Shalom encounters some of the same classic challenges as many other congregational school in America. Perhaps because of their own negative experiences as children in religious school, we know that a sizable portion of Adath Shalom parents make only a small emotional investment in their children's Jewish education and thus some children learn that religious school is not a high priority. The high Shabbat service attendance of which the synagogue is proud likely comes primarily from the families who have chosen day school for their children. To risk some oversimplification, we see here two different streams of families at Adath Shalom: the more Jewishly active and engaged day school families and the less motivated religious school families who primarily seek the Bar/Bat Mitzvah for their child. While the school does value the idea of family education, we recommend that it continue to find ways to involve religious school parents in the educational enterprise. An educationally engaged and empowered parent helps to promote an engaged child, who will then likely have higher attendance and interest in school.

Adath Shalom is a place that has been highly professionalized for many years. There are clear benefits of this, but we have also uncovered the challenges lurking underneath the surface. A culture has developed where lay leaders stand by and allow the professionals to develop vision and implement it. This takes away an opportunity for concerned lay leaders to have real influence on the direction of the synagogue and school and also overworks a small cadre of professionals. We know from previous research on supplementary schools (Holtz, 1995) that one important feature of a strong school is a clear vision that is developed and shared by all stakeholders.[3]

We were pleased to see new levels of reflection about this situation of overprofessionalization and new strategies put into place. A new Vice President of Education and a recontoured education committee within the board of trustees is a first step. Starting the process of involving teachers in curricular development is another important step. While we recognize it is not easy to change a structure that has been in place for a long time, the lesson we can learn from this case is the importance of developing a culture in a synagogue that fosters collaboration between lay leaders and professionals and implements mechanisms for accountability of the employees for the work they perform. While also recognizing that the synagogue's financial position is not as comfortable as it was before embarking on the major renovation, on the issue of the level of Rachel's responsibility, we strongly recommend that the synagogue follow through with the idea of hiring an additional staff person to serve as principal of the religious school.

Although the curricular expectations for each grade are identified on paper, the delivery of the formal education component of the curriculum is uneven and inconsistent, dependent on the skills and abilities of the teacher. Rachel and others concede their Hebrew language instruction is not meeting their own goals. More attention to professional learning in content and pedagogy can help teachers be more effective. As we know from the work of Stodolosky et al. (2006: 97–98), the fact that teachers enjoy their jobs and speak well of their workplace in terms of genuine camaraderie with their supervisor and colleagues "is certainly a necessary, but not sufficient, condition . . . for the development of effective professional culture."[4]

Rachel explained to us that she spent much of her energy in her early years on the job developing and expanding the high school programming. Because she is only one person, she was unable to devote the same energy to the elementary grades religious school. In general, we may be seeing a slightly unusual case where the high school program of a congregational school is thriving more than the elementary school. Rachel told us that "the success of the high school years has been because I've been able to figure out that they have other needs and pull their Judaism into their other interests. I have to say the religious school needs more love and attention. It probably deserves and needs a little bit more nurturing—some fresh eyes and so forth."

We see here a situation where not all formal curricular goals are consistently met in the elementary grades, but the majority of the parents appear relatively satisfied. Because many do not come in with high curricular expectations, they are pleased that the school (particularly in its flexible and accommodating approach) helps them meet their basic goal of instilling Jewish values in their children or, as one parent put it, allowing their children to "get the menschy-ness of being Jewish." This parent went on to explain, "maybe what Adath Shalom did was inspire them to want more. There are limits to what an after school can do. And obviously I love Rachel and I'm very protective, but really there are limits. It's not fair to say that they fail because you want your kids to do more Jewish education. I think that that shows a great success in inspiring that much yearning for more knowledge. That's the way that I look at it."

Jewish supplementary schools today are becoming more comfortable recognizing that, more than high levels of Jewish literacy, one of their main achievements is Jewish enculturation (instilling a strong sense of Jewish community, values, and identity). One possibility is that Adath Shalom may move more in this direction and alter their expectations accordingly.

Rachel hinted at this possibility when she told us that, similar to her design of the high school, she has thought that she might bring more of the "camp-like" nonformal structures into the religious school and "not look at the religious school through the classic eyes of four to six pm."

Another direction is to bring more academic rigor and accountability to the formal curriculum component of the religious school, which could become possible with the fresh eyes of a new education committee and a new principal. Future research could monitor these interesting developments. Whichever direction the school goes, we recommend that it continually strive for consistency and intentionality between theory and practice.

## Notes

1. One must be cautious in interpreting these "retention rates." When comparing the numbers of students in high school programs (formal and nonformal) to the numbers in the elementary school, we must be aware that some of the high school students may not ever have attended the synagogue's elementary grades of the religious school. For example, they may be day school students or general USY participants coming from elsewhere.

2. See Jeffrey Kress, "Expectations, Perceptions and Preconceptions: How Jewish Parents Talk about 'Supplementary' Religious School Education," in *Family Matters: Jewish Education in an Age of Choice,* ed. Jack Wertheimer (University Press of New England, 2007).

3. See Barry W. Holtz, ed., *Supplementary School Education* (Mandel Foundation, 1995).

4. See Susan Stodolsky, Gail Zaiman Dorph, and Sharon Feiman Nemser, "Professional Culture and Professional Development in Jewish Schools: Teachers' Perceptions and Experiences." *Journal of Jewish Education* 72:2 (2006).

CHAPTER 6

# Innovating Inside the Box
## An Ongoing Process to Improve a Congregational School

SUSAN L. SHEVITZ WITH MARION GRIBETZ

## An Overview of Temple Reyim and Its School

One of the first things that catches the eye in the foyer between the sanctuary and school wing when you enter Temple Reyim is a large portrait of
its emeritus rabbi with three young children at his side. It is a warm and
peaceful picture and quite possibly unusual. How many rabbis choose to
include children in the formal portrait by which they will be remembered?
How should we understand this choice? To what extent do young people
feel as comfortable in the congregation and with its staff as the portrait
suggests? And, if they do, what does it mean in terms of the Jewish education that is provided by the congregation? These questions, it turns out,
provide a window through which Temple Reyim can be understood.

Temple Reyim is a Reform congregation of just over 1,000 member units
situated in a wealthy suburb of a large city. Founded after the Second World
War, it has expanded beyond its original building several times and another addition is being constructed. Originally classically Reform, under
the leadership its current rabbi, Peter Hirsh, Temple Reyim has embraced
more traditional practices. Hebrew is visible throughout the building and
incorporated into services; Israel is important; *kippot* and *tallitot* are worn
by clergy and others. Had we not known the denominational affiliation we
would not have been able to tell easily whether Reyim is a member of the
Conservative, Reconstructionist, or Reform movement. As one person
quipped, "We're the Reform congregation anyone can eat in."

The services also have a more traditional feel. One very active member
who grew up in a classical Reform temple put it this way: "I'm uncomfort-

able with some stuff. I won't turn to the door for "*Lecha Dodi*"[1] . . . There's lots of bowing, shaking, and going on and on . . ." She shares that she uses that "on and on" time to meditate. Deeply devoted to the congregation, she served as its first female president. She values the staff and appreciates the stability that comes with staff members who are committed to the congregation and its congregants.

The executive director, Ellen Rosenberg, estimates that 10 percent of the 1,030 member units are either interfaith families or those where one of the parents converted to Judaism. The explanation given for this surprisingly low number is that local congregations with less Hebrew and fewer traditional customs suit them better. If this estimate is accurate, the school has less religious diversity than many.

Temple Reyim recently merged with a smaller nearby Reform congregation, Temple Torah, that brought its well-regarded nursery school to Reyim. Several people from Temple Torah mention the friendliness they encounter at their new congregation and specifically mention Rabbi Hirsch's approachability. "Friendliness," "warmth," "caring," inclusiveness" are the words most often used to characterize Temple Reyim and its school by many of its new and long-term members and staff.

We arrived at Temple Reyim on a snowy Sunday morning. The path to the school door had not yet been shoveled following the Saturday night nor'easter that dumped many inches of snow (and slowed our arrival); parents and children were entering in the front and going through very narrow corridors to the school wing. On a typical Sunday there are morning classes for kindergarten through seventh grade, adult Bar/Bat Mitzvah class, and other activities. Stopped almost immediately by a smiling woman, we are asked in a friendly way if we will support her son's confirmation class by buying a ticket for the raffle to be held that evening at the annual dinner for the class and their families. As we walked with the mother and son to the school wing, we noted that the walls of the narrow corridors were artfully covered with children's work, posters, and photographs. Each room was in full use, and students and others were in the hall, yet there was a calm, purposeful feeling. Lilly Cohen Jones, the middle-aged director of education, was greeting students, parents, teachers by name as they went by, frequently adding a personal comment: "You were great at *ma'ariv* last week"; "I'll see you after class to go over that assignment"; "How are the Bat Mitzvah preparations going?"; "glad you're feeling better . . ."

Jones is the switchboard, command-central, and creative director of Temple Reyim's school. Middle-aged and high energy, Jones grew up as a "poster child for the Conservative movement," spending almost all her free time at her congregation's youth groups and school. Needing money to help pay for her first trip to Israel, she approached an educator at the synagogue who helped to arrange a paid job for her. This got Jones hooked both on the trip and on Jewish education. She has been working in Jewish education in one capacity or another most of her adult life and has a Masters degree in Jewish Educational Administration. Lilly came to Temple Reyim thirteen years ago, having led a small Conservative congregational school. She "quickly felt at home at Reyim" and believes its vision matches her own. Characteristics of the school, based on 2006–07, are summarized in Table 6.1.

When Lilly Cohen Jones first began at Temple Reyim she was part time; the school enrolled 325 students and was "just school." Once she began to offer family education programs, the congregation increased her to full time. She pushed for things she believed in, including more lay involvement in terms "of logistics, back support such as calling parents." About five years ago a series of problems came to a head and her relationship with some lay leaders deteriorated. Within these last five years, many of the problems have been addressed and there is widespread agreement within the congregation and community that the school is in much better shape than it was then. We see Temple Reyim as a school that is improving incrementally by trying to confront its weaknesses and to capitalize on its strengths. How this has been happening—and with what effects—are the central questions that we address.

The convergence of two things stimulated this effort to improve. The realization that the emerging crisis had to be addressed came at a time when external resources were becoming available to schools seeking to advance. This put Temple Reyim in a position to move from discord and "business-as-usual" (even when the business might be going too well) to one that people on the inside characterize as "tremendously improved." The enthusiastic senior rabbi says of the school that they "achieved a metamorphosis, a transformation that was nothing short of . . . 180 degrees."

Temple Reyim is in many ways typical of other Reform and Conservative congregational schools: weekday and Sunday programs, part-time teachers with widely varying backgrounds, ambitious aspirations and severe time constraints, and dedicated and talented leadership. On their own, it is unlikely that the staff and lay leaders would have come as far as they have. They benefited from the additional expertise and time that outsiders could bring in terms of governance, curriculum, and pedagogy. There is much to be learned from this work-in-progress. Its story raises questions that are of critical importance to supplementary education.

**Table 6.1**
*School Characteristics*

| School Staff | |
|---|---|
| *Director of Education* | Twenty years of experience in Jewish educational administration; also taught, did informal Jewish education; BA in music therapy and MA in Jewish Educational Administration; sees self as "the one who knows everything that is going on" and "sees the whole"; supervises two very part-time youth group advisors and full-time director of preschool as well as all the teachers. |
| *Director of Preschool* | Came with merger; experienced; not involved in other aspects of education at Reyim; preschool has excellent reputation. |
| *Teachers* | 35 and 4 special needs |
| *Congregation's Senior Staff* | • Senior rabbi in 18th year at congregation. <br> • Associate rabbi in final year (will be replaced with an assistant rabbi). <br> • Cantor in 22nd year. <br> • Administrator in 3rd year; previously involved in congregation for 20+ years including 2 as its president. |

| Educational Program | | |
|---|---|---|
| *Schedule* | K–3: | Sunday for 2½ hours |
| | 4–6: | Sunday for 2½ hours; Tuesday for 2 hours |
| | 7: | hours at different times |
| | 8–10: | Tuesday night for 2 hours |
| | 11–12: | In community-sponsored program and work as trained classroom aides and SPED "wrap-arounds" in the school. |
| *Enrollment (2007–08)* | K–3: | 140 |
| | 4–6: | 185 |
| | 7: | 55 |
| | 8: | 31 |
| | 9: | 20 |
| | 10: | 27 |
| | 11–12: | 25 (see "Special Population Traits" below) |
| *Teachers' Professional Development* | Twenty or more hours per year of paid professional development working with other teachers in the school | |

*(continued)*

Table 6.1 — *Continued*

| | *Educational Program* — Continued |
|---|---|
| *Informal Education* | • Youth groups for grades 2/3, 4/5/6, 7/8 and 9–12<br>• Junior congregation monthly<br>• Tot Shabbat monthly<br>• Family Shabbat service monthly |
| *Jewish Family Education* | • Rabbis and educational director share the responsibility<br>• Primarily single sessions organized by grade<br>• Shabbat service organized by grade |
| *Special Program Traits* | • Comprehensive special ed program with capacity for severely disabled and hearing impaired<br>• Student led *ma'ariv* service every other week for grades 4–6<br>• Popular Junior Choir |
| *Special Population Traits* | • Many third generation temple members<br>• Many families from Conservative backgrounds<br>• Some students go to an intensive regional Hebrew high school and are also trained to be aides in the religious school and special ed specialists |

# The Ambience at the Temple Reyim School

Consider three snapshots of the congregation and its school.

## *Vignette One: The Deserter*

The hallway is crowded with children changing classes. A mother and boy about ten or eleven years old are near the door to the parking lot. Lilly, rushing by, notices, stops, and engages the boy with a warm and open attitude. "Paul," she says, "I know you're leaving and going to a different school." Lilly hears that he visited another congregational school where he has a few friends and had decided to go there. He was not happy at Temple Reyim. In turn, Lilly tells him that she was so glad he was at her school and the Temple will miss him. "You know, sometimes in situations like this, people can feel uncomfortable with each other. There is no reason to. You will always be welcome here—to visit or if you find you don't like the new school to return. And if you see me in a store or somewhere, you don't have to feel strange and ignore me. Come over and tell me how you're doing." After a few more encouraging remarks, the mother and son leave with smiles on their faces.

## Vignette Two: Casa de Samantha

We are interviewing mothers of children in the elementary grades. One grew up in the congregation, the second came from Temple Torah, and the third "married-in." The first mother actually met her husband in the temple and could show us where they first kissed. The second had a shaky relationship with Judaism during her teen years. She feels that there is "openness even though her husband is not Jewish" and she enjoys the adult classes that she takes. It is important to her that her children see that their family is accepted and that she, too, is studying. The third described what it means to her that Rabbi Hirsch visited her ailing mother even though her mother was not a congregant. It is very important to all of them that their children are comfortable in the building. As the first mother said, "Yeah, my kid thinks it's 'casa de Samantha.' She is so comfortable here."

## Vignette Three: Students Becoming Teachers

Thirteen percent of Temple Reyim's teachers were themselves students in the school. For some, returning as teachers is a homecoming; they enjoyed their experiences at Temple Reyim and want to give back. Others were actively recruited by Lilly. One summer, for example, she bumped into a graduate who was close to finishing college and talked with her about teaching at Temple Reyim. The student decided to try it for a year or two and is still there; she can't imagine working any place else. Talking to involved twelfth graders, Lilly teases them that before long she'll be hiring them to teach. Seen through the eyes of a veteran lay leader: "[I]t's good . . . [We] have a bunch of kids that went to college and then approached Lilly about wanting to teach here. We have a lot of alumni that teach here. In fact our youth groups this year were led by three college kids who were alumni. Next year it will be two of them. It was kind of an experiment this year, 'cause we did have a professional who left, so we thought we'd try—we have two who are really outstanding. Really, really good, and really committed, and they're still in college. But they came back . . . [to] be involved."

These snapshots capture much of what seems distinctive about Temple Reyim. There is a palpable sense of belonging and being cared about. The professional staff is friendly. As the executive director puts it, "we have to prove ourselves every day," since people have so many other options and places to be involved. Lilly epitomizes this; she is frequently in the hallway greeting people personally, remembering a teacher's concerns, a child's upcoming role, or a parent's new job. "She's everywhere; she knows everyone; she talks to everyone!" marveled a lay leader. An active lay leader's impression of the synagogue:

*Lay Leader:* . . . I have to remind myself how many families we really have. Because it doesn't feel like a synagogue of that size.

*Interviewer:* You mean because it feels larger?

*Lay Leader:* No, it feels smaller. It feels more intimate . . . That's why our professionals get so pulled. Because, I think in a larger synagogue, people don't think they own a piece of the rabbi. In this synagogue they do. 'Cause everybody knows everybody. So he gets pulled in a lot of directions. Lilly gets pulled in a lot of directions.

While we do not know how less involved members experience the congregation, the ambience in the building is of warmth, access, and acceptance. When we asked the parents, teachers, lay leaders, faculty and high school students we met to state the first words that come to mind when they think about the school, the lists made by different constituencies were remarkably similar. In addition to "friendliness," "warmth," "caring," and inclusiveness," the respondents added "*haimishe*," "responsive," "listening," "improving," "comfortable," "open," and "Lilly."

We saw these qualities throughout our visits. As two outside educators who assessed Temple Reyim's progress in 2005–06 wrote, "*Kehillah* [sense of community] is evident from the moment one enters the synagogue. There are clusters of people talking, including some in sign language . . . Visitors are greeted by everyone they encounter. The halls are full of positive energy—tutoring, study groups, conversations." Students are respectful and cooperative and even in overcrowded spaces there is a sense of calm engagement.

Parents also commented on the rabbi's accessibility to them and their children. At the twice monthly *ma'ariv* service there is the "rabbi's rap" so that students can ask their questions and engage in discussions with them. We heard from many of the students who went on through confirmation that getting to know Rabbi Hirsch was very important to them and they think that students should have more exposure to him.

The *hazzan* is also part of the team. She conducts a popular Junior Choir, teaches Torah trope to the sixth graders and helps the older students prepare for their Bar and Bat Mitzvah services. She also attends *ma'ariv* along with the song leader who, with students, leads the service. Families are encouraged to participate in *ma'ariv* and the monthly Saturday morning Shabbat *B'Yachad*. This is a learning service that "is a great way to enjoy Shabbat services and learn and have fun at the same time." The temple also advertises a family service "geared towards our school-age children and their families to enjoy a relaxed, music filled Shabbat evening service with our Rabbi, Cantor, and Junior Choir" [composed of fourth to sixth graders].

Temple Reyim's ambience seems to be an extension of Lilly's warm, seemingly unflappable nature. One lesson she derived from her own experiences in Jewish camps, youth groups, and schools is that students' relationship to the educator matters. She recalls times when people gave her opportunities that opened her eyes to Jewish life and helped her develop usable skills at the same time. She values the caring and warmth that she experienced. Echoes of these experiences are visible in the school—from trying to know all the students to giving significant responsibility to the teenaged aides. Lilly sees them as "her students" no less than the youngsters enrolled in the school. In one unusually painful case, the father of a child in one of the elementary classrooms accused a teenaged aide of incompetence and demanded that he be fired. Lilly refused to back down since the high school student was learning (and had not done anything worthy of being fired). She adroitly used the conflict to teach both her student—and the parent, as well—ways to resolve it.

Concern for individuals' feelings is also seen at events in which students have responsibilities that might otherwise be seen as performances. All the Shabbat activities we observed—class service, Shabbat *B'Yachad*, and a double Bat Mitzvah—conveyed a sense that these were not just for show. Even at the Bat Mitzvah, where the rabbi and cantor sounded more formal, the children were praised and respected for their contributions to the service. There is an authenticity and consistency between the accomplishments of the children and what they have learned and practiced during their time in the school.

## Accessing Available Resources

Organizations facing problems sometimes "hunker down," avoid outsiders who might see their weaknesses and go it alone. Temple Reyim, on the other hand, used available help. It avails itself of as many Jewish educational "loops" as possible and, according to other educators, "Lilly uses all the resources . . . [She's ready] to try everything." Lilly, Rabbi Hirsch, the school committee chair, and many others acknowledge that without the help of these outside resources not much would have changed. They needed the expertise and guidance.

The work began by strengthening the lay-professional relationship and the school committee. With tensions between lay and professional leaders and their limited understanding of the legitimate roles and boundaries for each side of that partnership, the school was not yet ready to look at substantive issues. The committee was unclear about its mandate. Terms of office for school committee members were unspecified, note taking and record keeping nearly nonexistent. School committee members did not necessarily care deeply about Jewish education. A consultant worked with the school to sort out the committee's mandate and to strengthen relationships among the lay leaders and with Lilly. The consultant found that influential lay leaders held assumptions about management and change that derived from the for-profit sector; they expected (or perhaps wanted to believe) that things in the school could change by fiat. The professionals were unclear about the role of lay leaders in setting overall policy and the need to keep them informed of developments in the school. In addition, policies and patterns that might be considered standard operating procedures in organizations were mostly missing from the committee's practice. The move from meetings where topics flowed into each other and people spent time reacting to different congregants' complaints, to meetings with a set agenda was accomplished, and more attention was given to follow-up after the meetings, as well. Looking back on it, an involved lay leader says, "It's so much more professional [today than it was]. And the people who are on [the education committee], even from her committee down to the subcommittees, [are] very committed people. And it's not one person comes this week 'cause they have a gripe, then you don't see 'em for three months. I know on the Religious School committee, we don't have any of that. And what you heard today, one of the members of my committee, "whenever you need me, I'll be there." And that's the way it's been since they restructured." Another concurs but recognizes the ongoing challenge of attracting lay leaders who are sufficiently committed to Jewish life to insist that their own children go beyond Bar or Bat Mitzvah:

> Well, we underwent a very major change . . . So it led to huge restructuring and it definitely got the school more respect from lay leadership. And it changed the way lay leadership interacted with the school and with Lilly. But I still think, for example, I would like it to be almost a

requirement that if you're gonna be in lay leadership, if you're gonna be on the general board or the executive board, you make a commitment to keep your kid in school, no matter how much they whine, through seventh grade. . . . The way we've restructured . . . our education committee, is really supposed to be a model for the congregation. It takes a while for things to catch up, for things to change. But, we've really just done a 180.

"Today," explains another school committee member, "we've very organized meetings. We have [agendas] . . . and clearly defined roles and responsibilities for committee members and subcommittee members."

The changes came about through several mechanisms. The consultant worked behind the scenes as a coach to the school committee chair and the director of education in order to untangle misunderstandings and to foster mutual respect and ways of working together effectively. They learned to discuss issues as they arose and to collaborate on developing meeting agendas. Lilly became more adept at sharing information and problems and the school committee focused on policy and overall direction rather than on the day-to-day management. Giving credit to the coach's interventions, Lilly is proud that the once antagonistic chair became an ally of the school. While "it may take a little time for lingering bad feelings to disappear," there is agreement that things are "working" much better and there is a sense of mutual respect among the different leaders.

Together the consultant, Lilly, and the committee developed an organizational chart for both the professional and lay structures. While these helped to clarify roles and responses, they reveal another interesting problem which we will address later: the extent of the educational director's role.

The group then began to tackle the school's priorities. Temple Reyim had to confront the difficult questions of Jewish edicational vision and purpose: What did they want the graduates of the school to be? What skills, knowledge, and attitudes should they develop? What educational experiences would lead to such results? What would teachers have to know in order to teach such a curriculum effectively?

The mission statement that the group adopted is now posted in every classroom:

The religious school of Temple Reyim inspires Jewish learning through study, worship and acts of lovingkindness. The school provides educational resources and develops a personal relationship with God in an environment where students of all ages and abilities can understand

and practice a lifelong commitment to Jewish heritage, Jewish family values, the State of Israel and the Jewish Community at large.

Several aspects of this mission statement ring true to us based on our visits:

1. Learning is for the sake of doing; the school expects its graduates to understand and practice;

2. The school helps people access resources;

3. God and *tefillah* are at the core. It is through a student's relationship to God that a Jew's commitments are hewn;

4. Graduates are expected to enact their commitments to the wider Jewish community here, in Israel, and in other diasporas; and

5. Jewish family values are important to know and to practice.

The statement makes no mention of Reform Judaism and it leaves open the door to any Jewish practice or belief. Points 3, 4, and 5 suggest curricular foci to be developed while points 1 and 2 are about overall approaches to the educational process.

Moving from crafting a mission statement to actually using it to guide educational choices, however, is a big jump. Mission is not vision; it doesn't provide direction about how to teach toward the goals it espouses. In his book about the place of a guiding vision in Jewish education, Pekarsky makes the point that schools need two types of vision. There is an "existential vision . . . of the kind of person and community it's hoping to cultivate" as well as an "educational vision" that will shape an environment in which it can achieve the existential vision.[2] The educational vision is based on an integrated set of ideas that is the result of a profound understanding of current conditions, the nature of learning, human development, and human nature. Together these form a coherent and comprehensive approach that guides all aspects of the school. Temple Reyim is beginning to organize education around the vision implied in the mission statement: the prominence of prayer and Hebrew are two such examples though the educational vision is not yet articulated in a coherent and detailed enough way to guide practice.

An external assessment of the school extols the changes to its leadership and governance: "[The change is] remarkable . . . [in how] lay leaders work together and with the rabbis and education director. There is a real systems approach to the school as part of the synagogue with sub-committees . . . doing substantive work, and with all the sub-committees working together with common language and goals, reinforced by the mission statement."

In addition to using external resources to guide its improvement efforts, Temple Reyim accesses them in other ways. True to its goal of "providing resources," it actively supports a range of other Jewish activities and programs throughout the area. Hallway brochures advertise many activities sponsored elsewhere and we frequently heard staff members encouraging people to go to an area-wide event. The school participates in Passport to Israel[3] and gets federation-generated funds for some of its activities, most notably the sign language interpreter who makes many of the programs and services accessible to hearing-impaired members of the community. The implicit message is that Temple Reyim is the hub for its members' Jewish lives but many worthwhile things go on outside its doors. It tries to connect people to them.

Temple Reyim also participates in a regional Reform-sponsored program for its post-confirmands. Its goal is to train future religious school teachers and leaders for the Reform movement according to the following objectives:

- Acquire knowledge of the history of Reform Judaism;
- Show proficiency in the reading of Hebrew and understanding of basic Hebrew prayers;
- Demonstrate basic knowledge of Bible through a Reform Jewish lens;
- Demonstrate basic teaching skills by student teaching weekly under the aegis of the student's home congregation;
- Demonstrate knowledge of educational theory as covered in the education curriculum.

This program is fully integrated into Temple Reyim. Each Sunday class has a classroom aide who participates in this program. The aide helps the teacher, works with individual students, or functions as a "wrap-around" for a special needs child who requires that level of assistance. They take the responsibilities seriously and are paid for their work. Visible throughout the school, they forge relationships with the younger students and become positive role models. An additional advantage that is not insignificant is that the adolescents are developing skills that can help support them through college since their training, experience, and supervision means they are employable in congregational schools and youth groups elsewhere. Lilly often receives calls to be a reference for her alumni college students seeking employment in other communities. Participation keeps these high school students connected to Judaism, the synagogue, and each other.

## Teaching and Learning: The Educational Core

While the mission statement that Temple Reyim crafted provides the "big picture," the quality of the educational experience depends on specifics. What are the goals? What content and experiences will help students reach these goals? The question of what students learn from the lessons—or, to use today's terminology, what are their "enduring understandings"—is of central importance.

When Temple Reyim embarked on the path of improvement, its curriculum was mostly a list of topics and textbooks by grade. With the limited hours available, teachers felt the pressure to cover "everything" because each one felt that it may be the only opportunity for any particular child to learn the basics. Teachers had considerable discretion over what was taught.

In order to address "big picture" questions, the consultants based their work on an approach to curriculum development from general education, "Understanding by Design" (UbD). Characterized by "backward design," curriculum writers and teachers begin with the end in sight. The first step is to identify desired results, then determine acceptable evidence of achieving these results. This then leads to the planning of learning experiences and instruction. UbD presupposes that the teacher has deep and sophisticated understanding of the content, so that desired results are meaningful and support "enduring understandings."[4]

As part of the twenty hours of professional development that are part of teachers' compensated, contractual obligations, they are developing rubrics for the prayer and Hebrew curricula. They have identified the "enduring understandings" around which the prayer and Hebrew curricula are organized although the "essential questions" for each grade have yet to be developed. This understanding is, "The study of prayer provides relevance and meaning in our lives through which we develop a spiritual relationship with God and a link to Jews worldwide."

This is a clear expression of something important to Temple Reyim: the sense of connection to God and to other Jews through *tefillah*. Six agreed upon goals for the curriculum are considered for each grade. These are shown in the charts that emerged from the teachers' discussions (table 6.2). Performance assessment rubrics are then elaborated for each grade, as shown in tables 6.3 and 6.4.

A close reading of the rubrics raises questions about the appropriateness of some of them. Recognizing that a curriculum foisted on uninvolved teachers is likely to go unused, Lilly made the decision to engage the fac-

Table 6.2

*Prayer and* Tefillah *Rubrics by Grade (as of 2/4/07)*

|  | Grade | | | | | | |
|---|---|---|---|---|---|---|---|
|  | K | 1 | 2 | 3 | 4 | 5 | 6 |
| Did the student read* the prayer fluently in Hebrew? | X | X | X | X | X | X | X |
| Is the student able to translate the meaning of the words from Hebrew to English? |  |  | X | X | X | X | X |
| Did the student explain the meaning of the prayer in his own words? | X | X | X | X | X | X | X |
| Did the student explain or demonstrate how the prayer helps develop a spiritual relationship with God? |  |  |  |  | X | X | X |
| Did the student explain or demonstrate how the prayer serves as a link to Jews throughout the world? | X | X |  | X | X |  |  |
| Did the student make a personal connection to the prayer? |  |  |  |  | X | X | X |

*Subsequent documents for grades K, 1, 2 say "recite" the prayers rather than "read" them.

ulty in developing the rubrics. She recognized the downside—that the work might not be as thoughtful as needed—but believes that inconsistent and vague thinking can be remedied by reworking the rubrics at subsequent meetings or over the summer. This point was conveyed in the *D'var Torah* with which Lilly began the professional development meeting we observed. The Israelites were "deliberate, goal-centered and concrete" when they built the *mishkan* (tabernacle). She suggests that the curriculum is the school's equivalent of the *mishkan* and invites the teachers to "build the school's *mishkan*" together. Between the long time allotted for lunch and the following discussion of several other issues (e.g., what teachers learned from an in-service day they all attended, how their co-planning and attempts at peer supervision were going, among others), work on the rubrics was allotted less than an hour. A few teachers were enthusiastic and engaged. Others were not sure of why they were doing this or what, exactly, they were expected to do. It was not clear which teachers knew the specific prayers and they were not being pushed to think specifically and concretely about particular aims and objectives.

Table 6.3

*Rubrics for Performance Assessment of Prayer/Hebrew, Kindergarten*

| | *Excellent* | *Good* | *Satisfactory* | *Not Yet* |
|---|---|---|---|---|
| *Did the student recite the prayer fluently in Hebrew?* | Consistently recites prayer with 100% fluency and accuracy | Recites prayer using one of the two techniques | Inconsistently recites prayer | Cannot or unwilling to recite prayer |
| *Did the student explain the meaning of the prayer in his own words?* | • Give examples (stories, poem, artwork) <br>• Give a detailed explanation using varied modalities to show understanding | • Some partial connection <br>• Brief explanation, less detail given | • Is able to give one example of meaning of prayer/has made limited connection <br>• Limited explanation | • No examples give[n], "I don't have a clue" <br>• Unable to explain meaning, however limited |

Before the rubrics were distributed, however, an intense conversation about the goals and assessment of the prayer curriculum was stimulated by a teacher who argued that prayer and personal meaning should not be evaluated in the way being discussed. The kindergarten teachers argued that the students were not yet ready to recite prayers and there is not enough time to focus on them. They wondered, "Where are the kids in this?" Other teachers argued that it is not possible or right to assess children's relationship with God. Teachers of older students asked how they can teach this content to sixth and seventh graders who say they don't believe in God?" As the conversation ensued, other questions that are essential to crafting a coherent approach to prayer emerged. One teacher confided that she has trouble teaching prayer because she is unsure of what she believes. Others wondered whether experiential learning and focusing on *kavannah* (intentionality) would be better than the strong emphasis on proficiency.

The animated and honest discussion shows a commendable level of trust within the faculty. Pressured for time, Lilly ended the discussion with an admission and request, "I recognize that I need to rethink the rubric about God . . . and [invite] the teachers who have a sense of Reyim's approach to work with me." Lilly expects that a few teachers will come forward.

Table 6.4

*Rubrics for Performance Assessment of Prayer/Hebrew, Grade Six*

|  | *Excellent* | *Good* | *Satisfactory* | *Not Yet* |
|---|---|---|---|---|
| *Did the student read the prayer fluently in Hebrew?* | Consistently recites prayer with 100% fluency and accuracy | Recites prayer using one of the two techniques (fluency or accuracy) | Inconsistently recites the prayer | Cannot or un-willing to recite the prayer |
| *Is the student able to explain the meaning of key words from Hebrew to English?* | Translate all key words in-dependently | Can translate most key words with minimal assistance | Can translate key words with assistance | No knowledge of key word meanings |
| *Did the student explain the meaning of the prayer in his own words?* | • Give ex-amples (stories, poems, artwork)<br>• Give a de-tailed expla-nation using various mo-dalities to show under-standing | • Partial con-nection<br>• Brief explana-tion given | • Is able to give one example of meaning of prayer/ has made minimal connection<br>• Limited ex-planation | • No examples given, "I don't have a clue"<br>• Unable to ex-plain mean-ing, however limited |
| *Did the student explain or dem-onstrate how the prayer helps to develop a spiritual rela-tionship with God?* | Student identi-fies how prayer relates to God and can iden-tify with God through prayer using examples from daily life | Student can only identify how prayer re-lates to God (using 3 ver-sions—ac-knowledge, praise, petition) | Student can't grasp relation-ship between God and prayer (may not un-derstand mean-ing) | Student can't read or under-stand prayer meanings |
| *Did the student make a per-sonal connec-tion with the prayer?* | Student actively participates during class as-signments, can always share and relate meaningful personal experience | • Student par-ticipates dur-ing class as-signments<br>• Can often share and re-late meaning-ful personal experience | • Student occa-sionally par-ticipates dur-ing class assignments<br>• Can rarely share and re-late meaning-ful personal experience | Student rarely participates during class as-signments, is not able to re-late meaningful personal expe-rience |

The faculty is being asked to institute other innovations, as well: critical colleagueship, co-planning, peer supervision, curriculum design, and more. Temple Reyim, devoting far more time than most supplementary schools ever do to professional development, is struggling to find a balance between all that it wants to do and all that it realistically can do well at any one time.

However difficult the process of developing a coherent curriculum is, the mission statement is bringing some focus to the school (or reaffirming what the school was already trying to do) in terms of developing students' personal relationships with God.

Hebrew and prayer constitute the largest block of the curriculum. From the kindergarten through seventh grade, students learn to chant and understand different prayers. The purpose of learning to decode Hebrew, introduced in the third grade, is to be able to read prayers. Spoken Hebrew is not attempted. Each student's reading progress is assessed at least annually by the school, and to the extent possible teachers or the learning center staff provide remediation. Students are expected to participate in Shabbat services outside the school context.

Each of the two family education programs we observed also had a piece related to Judaism's understanding of God. Several parents enthusiastically described how their young children were given a camera and asked to photograph a place where they see God. They welcomed the opportunity to discuss the photographs together at a family education program.

Commitment to developing students' relationships with God is most clear at the school's *ma'ariv* service. It is held for approximately an hour every other week—a significant chunk in the school schedule—for the third through sixth graders and the few parents who come. Lilly wants students to become comfortable with the prayers, praying, and being part of a community, as she herself experienced in Jewish camps and youth groups.

Each *ma'ariv* is led by a fourth, fifth, or sixth grade class. The service that we observed coincided with *Yom HaShoah*. The most Hebraically advanced sixth grade class was responsible for the service, which also served as the culminating experience of its study of the *Shoah*. Each student presented at least one original piece to express something that he or she learned. These ranged from a musical composition, to "book talks" in which students impersonated a character in the book, to a play. Many were remarkable in content and presentation. They were, by and large, sophisticated and captivating. Surmising from their affect throughout the event, it was a powerful educational experience for the presenters—perhaps even one that will be remembered as a highlight of their years in religious school.

Because of these presentations the service was much longer than usual.

Although the students assembled in the sanctuary were generally well-behaved, except for the sixth graders there wasn't a deep sense of engagement. According to the teachers and other adults present, this decorous but subdued behavior was typical of the *ma'ariv* services and not a result of the longer-than-usual format.[5] One teacher claimed that some students, tired from their long, demanding days, use *ma'ariv* as a time to "fog out." In a sense *ma'ariv* becomes a safe haven for students to unwind or to actively engage.

While *ma'ariv* and the other services clearly connect to the school's mission, this is not necessarily understood by the faculty and students. The structure is in place but the deeper questions of what a spiritual experience entails for children of this age and how *tefila* might engage them in questions about God still needs to be confronted.

The classes also present a variegated picture of the success of Temple Reyim's new approaches, though we again caution that the new curriculum "is a work in progress," developing only over the last three years.[6] Not all the children succeed in reading fluently. When the sixth grade students lead *tefillot*, or the seventh graders become Bar or Bat Mitzvah, some students stumble over the Hebrew. Some of the staff is disappointed that some sixth graders are not really ready to learn *trope*—chanting the Torah portions from the unvocalized text rather than chanting by rote.

While most of the classes we saw were primarily "talk and chalk" events, there were indications of movement, at least on the part of some teachers. Two teachers in nearby rooms sometimes combine their classes and co-teach. The week we were there they showed *Paper Clips*, a documentary dealing with the *Shoah*. Asked about their collaboration, the young teacher said that the two teachers plan together on the telephone. She describes the rationale for this effort: "[We do it] 'cause . . . I get a lot of her kids for my Hebrew class, and they always come in and they're like, 'you did exactly the same thing as us.' So, sometimes it just works out well. And they all have so much to say, and they like being together, and we like being together, so it works out well." In another example of co-teaching, however, the combined classes listened to two teachers dominating the discussion.

Several of the teachers have taken a difficult, new step. They have observed each other teach and provided useful feedback to each other. In at least one case, a teacher asked another for help and says that the other teacher was "another set of eyes" and gave some useful feedback. Lilly sees these and other examples as major accomplishments and, if these efforts continue, they most certainly are.

The area that most frustrates Lilly and many others is the struggle to retain students beyond Bar/Bat Mitzvah. A conversation with two veteran lay leaders quickly turned to this topic:

> And being on Education Committee all those years, an issue that always comes up, it doesn't matter what group of parents are on the Education Committee, the post–Bar and Bat Mitzvah. And I don't wanna say it's horrible, that's not where I'm coming from. But it always seems that age-group [early adolescence] . . . the dynamics of Jewish education at that time in their lives, parent involvement, it's just like a thorn. And I don't know what the answer is—being on the committee all these years, and everything we try, 'cause we do. Every couple of years we do try to change things, to reflect what's going on in secular education, to try to make things better. There's just something with that group!

A second lay leader concurs: "I don't think it's a school issue; I think it's a societal issue, I think it's a family issue, where parents stand on that. But, that's my opinion."

It is not just retaining most students through confirmation that has been elusive, some students don't return to school after their Bar or Bat Mitzvah ceremonies. On the one hand, leaders recognize that some of the changes that have been made over the last several years are just now taking root and the current seventh grade classes have not benefited from the innovations. On the other hand, they worry that the problems engaging young people will not be solved by the school and believe families' attitudes and values must change. The eleventh and twelfth grade students who remain are especially critical of those parents whose children talk at the Bar/Bat Mizvah ceremony about "how meaningful Judaism is to them and how they will continue to be involved but then allow their children to drop out the week after the ceremony." Parents of high school students wondered whether Temple Reyim could do more creative thinking about this—as it did when the seventh grade was completely revamped to respond to student and family needs. Hours were reduced and students given a choice of a wide-range of experiential course options.[7] But most parents believe that the demands on the teenagers and attractiveness of competing activities will continue to curtail Jewish education during the crucial adolescent years.

If retaining adolescents is a frustration, serving special needs students is a source of pride. Temple Reyim's Special Education (SPED) program is considered a great asset. It was started many years ago (before Lilly's tenure) by a very active second-generation temple family. A father very much wanted his own child, who had serious learning and physical disabilities, to participate in the religious community. This family made sure that a fully staffed resource room would be available to all children. It was an up-hill battle, but today Lilly and the congregation are fully committed to it. Many current lay leaders have children who were able to participate in the temple's activities because of the resource room and staff. Parents of grown children remain active. They have spent many years shepherding the SPED program so that their own children could benefit; but possibly they remain active and committed because they care deeply about the program and want to ensure that it remains a focal point for educational activities at Temple Reyim. They pride themselves on the fact that their SPED program provides educational access throughout the community, including the children of nonmembers.

In addition to the resource room staff that works individually with students, the teenage aides play an important role. As "wrap-arounds," they accompany individual children through their classes and provide additional support and structure. Others work with small groups of children within a class. All this means that having people with different developmental and learning disabilities in the building is the norm. Parents and teachers alike think that all the children are learning an important Jewish value: respecting all people, whatever their capacities.

Congregants and staff are also proud of their work with hearing-impaired people. Stories about how this developed abound and are captured in the temple's publicity:

> [We are] unique in many ways . . . one being that we have worship services not only in two languages (Hebrew and English) as most synagogues do, but often in THREE languages.
>
> Quite a few years ago, a long-time member of our congregation . . . brought to our attention the need to include deaf Jews in religious services, life cycle events and religious education. As a child of deaf parents, [she] was painfully aware of the isolation deaf Jews felt when they attended family life cycle events (or even their own) and of their reluctance or outright refusal to attend Erev Shabbat and Shabbat morning services because there was no way to follow what was happening.
>
> [We] decided to invite the members of the [regional] Chapter of the Hebrew Association of the Deaf (HAD) to be our guests at a congregation dinner and interpreted *Erev Shabbat* service . . . The members of HAD thoroughly enjoyed themselves . . . and were finally able to follow a religious service . . . Those who participated in this event were

so moved that [we] decided to make the "HAD Shabbat" a yearly event. While it is not always possible to have the service coincide with a congregation dinner, the tradition has been going on for about 12 years and Temple Reyim's commitment to the Jewish Deaf community has grown exponentially.

Temple Reyim now provides a sign language interpreter for Family *Erev Shabbat* Services on the first Friday of every month, a second *Erev Shabbat* service each month, High Holy Day services, holiday services, parent education classes and other events, such as Family Fun Night, adult Hebrew classes and *ma'ariv*.

The acceptance and promotion of these initiatives is consistent with the welcoming and caring atmosphere central to Temple Reyim's identity. When asked about the aspect of Temple Reyim that they are most proud of, an active member stated, "How inclusive we are," and elaborated:

. . . we left another synagogue because they couldn't provide for my daughter educationally. And we came here, and they said "well, we've never had a kid like her, but why not?"

. . . My daughter's severely disabled. And so not only [was it] okay to take her, it was so far above and beyond that. She was welcomed with open arms, she was loved. She became a Bat Mitzvah at fourteen using a communication device, and we have so many different kinds of kids here and nobody—not only is nobody turned away, but nobody's ever made to feel different or unwelcome. And that's what's really special.

The commitment to these students does not end with the joy of Bar and Bat Mitzvah:

Lilly gets a lot of credit for this 'cause Lilly is very open-minded and very creative. After my daughter's Bat Mitzvah I said, "well what now? 'Cause she loves coming!" So we started a group for post B'ne Mitzvah special needs kids called the *Lamed-Vavniks*,[8] and there was a group of them that were very closely bonded, and they came every Sunday to class, they had a social activity once a month, they went to New York every year, and then they had confirmation.

## Assessing Progress

Temple Reyim regularly seeks and uses information to shape its programs. We already indicated how students' Hebrew reading progress is monitored through school-wide evaluation and have given examples of how openness to criticism, whether by staff or members, has led Lilly to modify programs. A third way that information is gathered and used is in an annual, school-wide evaluation.

For three years the evaluation was conducted by two educators who, though outsiders to the school, are involved in some of the specific interventions that Temple Reyim undertook. Last year they trained ten members of the congregation to take this over so that the evaluation will be integrated into the school's ongoing operation. Lilly is both proud that the school does this and open about the findings, which, for the most part, document the school's improvement and suggest areas for continued effort.

The evaluation tool is based on nine areas that are considered to be the building blocks of a school: leadership, instruction, curriculum, professional development, co-curricular programs, school culture, facilities, human resources, and practices and procedures. Each area has a set of practice-based rubrics that describe the four possible scores (ranging from "exceeds expectations" to "does not meet expectations") and the reason for the particular score. Scoring is based on the evaluators' on-site observations, focus groups, and document analysis. In addition to charting the progress within each area, the evaluation stimulates the discussions that lead to concrete plans for measurable improvement in specific areas. In a school that has a lot going on and a tendency for distractibility, this imposes a helpful focus.

At the time of our visit, data from 2003 through 2006 were available. In general they are consistent with our own observations and analysis.[9] Since Lilly is very aware of what goes on at the school, she has not been surprised by most of the findings; they reaffirm her own observations. Leadership, school culture, teacher engagement are strengths. There is limited evidence that teachers are using the preferred pedagogies and approaches so that most classes are still frontal. Suggestions for improvements include developing a formal, systematic way for Lilly to observe and supervise teachers, to creating a formal assessment process for the educational director, and creating procedures for various kinds of emergencies.

Temple Reyim is guided by many of the recommendations. During the first round of curriculum work the evaluators indicated that Temple Reyim should "provide professional development on curriculum so that all staff can implement it with understanding, depth and enthusiasm." The subsequent year saw a serious commitment to professional development: twenty hours of professional development for which the teachers were compensated.

The evaluation has a powerful symbolic role, as well. It helps people see—and celebrate—their successes. It identifies areas requiring additional attention in a way that empowers people to act; rather than criticizing the area, the evaluation pinpoints the problem and suggests practical steps toward remediation. And, because it looks at many components of the school, it balances the need for improvement with recognition of areas of excellence.

Perhaps the most important point, however, is the context in which the evaluation is conducted. Lilly has created an environment that is open to others' ideas. While some things, because they are deeply embedded in the school's culture and are consistent with its leaders' personalities and values, might be very resistant to change, there is commitment to becoming a more effective school. Lilly models inquiry and reflection, as well as a willingness to consider new approaches. A parent recalls a situation that happened when her son was in the seventh grade class: "And some of those kids were brutal, and things they were saying and doing . . . they were obnoxious to the teacher, they were disruptive to the class, and they were causing discontent in the whole class . . . The interesting thing is that Lilly actually called a meeting of the seventh grade parents [to talk about the situation] and . . . she actually took over that class for a while, because she wanted to see what was going on." Another parent states it more succinctly: "I feel like they're listening. If the kids are not happy, they're listening, and they're trying to do things."

The new, more flexible program gives families a choice of which sessions students will attend and what they will study. It includes ongoing service projects, "where . . . the kids went together, and it was not only a *mitzvah* but it was also a social thing and it was really meaningful." In the face of a problem, Lilly searched for information and opinions and then developed an alternative approach.

If anything, Lilly is restless in her commitment to creating an ever-improving school. This might sometimes lead to taking on more than can be handled in depth at any one time—at least given the school's current resources. But, as a parent who talked about the SPED program noted, Lilly's attitude when confronted with a new challenge is, "why not?" In general, there is a commitment to finding a new way rather than loyalty to the status quo.

## Accepting Limitations on Time and Personnel

While some supplementary schools are trying to reinvent themselves by creating new educational models that break out of the format of schooling, Temple Reyim is committed to improving within that format. It is betting that with improved governance, curriculum, faculty development, and pedagogy the school will be an effective vehicle for producing the kind of Jewish adult that is implied in its mission statement.

Two limitations seem to us to be especially problematic: (1) insufficient professional resources and (2) limited contact time with students and families. Temple Reyim's organizational structure clearly shows potential overload on the director of education. There are the frontline worker staff members—teachers, aides, youth leaders—and Lilly, who is responsible for everything from preschool through adult education, including Bar and Bat Mitzvah preparation and programs for the college students. Except for the preschool director who came with the merger with Temple Torah, there is no middle management. For a school of Temple Reyim's size and aspirations, the lack of other education professionals is surprising. Rather than hiring a Jewish family educator, program director, or youth educator, all of whom would be responsible to the director of education,[10] the programmatic and administrative responsibility for these areas lies with Lilly. According to Lilly, part of "the problem" is her own personality: she likes to see what is happening first hand and is a self-described "control freak." "If I am responsible for something I want to be sure it is done right," she says. She wants everything about education to go through her and, as she points out, hiring, delegating, and supervising other people is often difficult and time-consuming, as well.

With so much going on, however, adding the responsibility for leading and managing the school's change process in addition to all the other tasks means that there is not enough time and attention for each of the components to thrive. The budget for the school is about $500,000. No one is lobbying hard for funds to hire additional personnel who would bring the requisite attention and expertise to the different arenas. In his study of a congregational school that was succeeding, Joseph Reimer argues that a factor associated with success is for the school to be the "favored child" of the congregation.[11] It is possible that at Temple Reyim education is important—but not *that* important. Perhaps the school is sufficiently good so that the status quo is acceptable; perhaps the idea of a larger, differentiated staff fits poorly with Temple Reyim's sense of itself as an intimate, caring family; or perhaps the type of Jewish education offered is what the congregation really wants.

Whatever the reason, the current structure stymies consistent educational excellence. Consider one example: Jewish family education. There is no one with enough time to focus on it by charting an overall direction and being responsible for implementation. This means that Temple Reyim mostly offers individual sessions for the parents of each grade. A session we saw had Lilly substituting for Rabbi Hirsch, who had to perform a funeral. Busy with several other things, she arrived late. The session was rushed and did not engage parents in meaningful activities with their children. The topic, angels and whether Jews believe in them, did not seem to relate to the children's studies or to prior family education programs. Because the paragraph of the prayer traditionally recited before falling asleep refers to the different angels who will stand guard through the night, Lilly related angels to bedtime rituals. Parents had more to say than they could in the large group within the time constraints. Another session taught by the rabbi also started late and left the parents and rabbi less than fifteen minutes to study and converse together. These problems result from Temple Reyim's staffing patterns. Unless someone has the time and expertise to conceptualize, plan, evaluate, and offer more sophisticated forms of family education, this pattern will continue. A similar case can be made for other types of educational activities that Temple Reyim sponsors or might want to develop.

Temple Reyim also seems to accept the limited contact time with students and families. Like most congregational schools, its work is contained to Sunday and one weekday during an ever-shorter school year. Within this structure, there are frequent interruptions to class time—*ma'ariv*, holiday programs, music, junior choir, special events—which some teachers believe hinders learning. To achieve its goals within the available time would require laser-sharp focus so that the extra programs would not be distractions but would be closely related to what specific grades are learning. Contact hours might also be increased with other sorts of ancillary programs that build on what goes on in the classrooms.

## Lessons Learned

The overarching reality of the supplementary school is the limited time it has available to achieve its ambitious and critically important goals of socializing the next generation of Jews into Jewish life while simultaneously imparting the knowledge and experience to understand why living a Jewish life is important. Rarely is there sufficient time or energy to focus on many things and do them well. As such, Temple Reyim's efforts to improve have several lessons to teach:

1. A warm, inclusive, and caring environment is a foundation for effective education;

2. Trusted outsiders who can troubleshoot and help a school sort out problems can reverse negative trends and put a school onto a positive trajectory;

3. External resources providing time, expertise, energy, and a critical eye are needed to stimulate and support comprehensive efforts to improve;

4. Key professionals, capable of collaboration, need to be behind the change efforts;

5. Sources of information, both systematically amassed through evaluation and informally gathered through ongoing communication, need to be cultivated and regularly shared and used;

6. A school needs to concentrate on its priorities and avoid diversions. Trying to do too much at once impedes excellence, while having too limited an agenda prevents deep, systemic change;

7. Focus is crucial in terms of teaching and learning. In light of the limited time available, every part of every lesson is important and can be evaluated by several criteria. Is what is being taught directly related to the mission and the educational goals? Is it the most important content? Is it being taught in the most effective way for each particular group?

8. Despite having limited contact hours, the supplementary school is a complex, multifaceted institution. In order for it to thrive it needs an appropriate staffing plan that puts enough qualified and talented educators in key roles. It is insufficient for schools as large and educationally ambitious as Temple Reyim to rely primarily on one educator, no matter how energetic and talented the educator is. There are different staffing options. There might be directors of the different levels of the school (e.g., primary, elementary, post–Bar/Bat Mitzvah) who report to a director of congregational education. Or there could be functional specialists, such as family educators, adult educators, Hebrew specialists, staff development specialists, informal educators, and so on, that cut across the school. Other models are available.

9. The time-frame for effecting change needs to be long enough to allow in-depth program and professional development. School improvement projects often fail because they underestimate the time it takes for professionals to learn and incorporate new ways of doing things. Ongoing support is needed.[12]

10. Schools such as Temple Reyim have the potential to be communities for their staff, students, and families. This sense of community—*kehillah*—can be systematically nurtured.

## Lingering Questions

We have described many things that Temple Reyim is doing to become an ever-more-effective congregational school, and we have documented its noteworthy improvements. Its experiences raise questions that are basic to supplementary education.

### *Working Within the Current Framework*

*Ladies Home Journal* has for decades run a column, "Can This Marriage Be Saved?" The magazine made the assumption that marriage is the preferred fall-back position and addressed relationship problems from within that framework. Temple Reyim similarly accepts the structure of classes organized by grades, limited contact time, and mostly part-time teachers. If this is the framework, then the strategy of improving many aspects of what goes on in the school is logical. It assumes that the school does not need to be reconceptualized but rather requires serious adjustments. The adjustments, however, cannot be made to any single component; "only" improving governance or "just" creating a robust teacher development program is insufficient in a system comprising interlocking components. This is why there are several things occurring simultaneously at Temple Reyim. But because of the school's spare staffing, it lacks the capacity sufficiently to focus the components so as to ensure excellence. Concentrated attention cannot be sustained. This raises questions that need to be considered by all schools attempting large-scale reform: how many innovations can the system absorb without diluting them or enacting them superficially?

### *Support from Outside Resources*

There is widespread agreement that Temple Reyim could not have moved in its new directions had many outside resources not been available. The task of improving a supplementary school is too big and complex, and many congregational professionals and lay leaders do not have the requisite skills or time to coordinate a multifaceted change effort. This is why so many local, regional, and national school and synagogue change processes have developed scales the last decade.

Temple Reyim makes good use of resources and expertise from a central agency of Jewish education, from academic programs in both general and Jewish education, and from denominational and youth movements. All this is costly in terms of the time and energy devoted by the agencies' staffs and the school's leaders. If Temple Reyim's story is representative of the schools—and we have reasons to think it is better positioned than most when it comes to using the outside resources[13]—the community needs to think creatively about several questions:

- Can adequate expertise be developed and more broadly shared so that many more schools can benefit from the sorts of support that Temple Reyim experienced?
- How much ongoing support is needed after the acute phase is finished?
- Can more economically viable models be developed?
- How can resources be made available to schools in communities that do not have the kinds of organizations and expertise that stimulated and support Temple Reyim's work?
- Temple Reyim's experiences suggest that helpful national, regional, and local resources must remain available if supplementary schools are to improve in significant ways.

## Structural and Substantive Change

One way of understanding Temple Reyim's current reality is that it has created an infrastructure for an effective school. Its governance and administration are now clear; a curriculum is almost complete; and staff development is a regular and serious part of the teachers' responsibility.

Moving from structural to substantive change is complex. This is especially true for the linchpin of any school: what happens in the classroom. With the additional teacher education and curriculum deliberation, and all of Lilly's support for active learning, we saw only limited evidence that Temple Reyim's teachers are teaching differently. Our observations are consistent with the 2005–06 evaluation data. (The active phase of this study ended in spring 2007. It is possible that progress was made during subsequent years, especially since the intensive teacher development work continued through 2008.)

The promise of all the school improvement at Temple Reyim will fade if its changes remain primarily structural. The new approaches need to be understood and incorporated into ongoing practice so that structure and substance are aligned. At this transitional time Temple Reyim needs to have a clear, viable multiyear plan to help its teachers master and incorporate the new approaches.

## Families' Priorities

No one can foresee how Temple Reyim's changes over the past few years—with the improving curriculum and professional development—will affect the children currently going through its elementary school. Currently there is ongoing disappointment with the high post–Bar Mitzvah attrition rate, limited participation in youth group, and uneven participation in Shabbat *B'Yachad* and other special activities, though the students who continue beyond Bar Mitzvah are really devoted to their Jewish education, and some even return to teach in the school.

The explanation for these disappointments offered by many of the congregation's professionals and parents is the family. If a family does not value and encourage Jewish education, it is unreasonable to expect that their children will continue into their teenage years. One parent put it bluntly: "But guess what? . . . It's parents. Those kids stand on the *bimah* at their Bar Mitzvahs] and . . . it's all a bunch of hoo-hah, 'cause half of them have no intention of [continuing their Jewish education] . . . I would never let my kids stand up there and read that speech [if they didn't . . . intend to continue]. So if my son really felt that way then I would say "make a beautiful speech, but don't say that you intend on pursuing blah blah blah blah blah—say that you enjoyed your studies thus far, and you intend to raise your kids Jewish, or something like that."

If Temple Reyim wants to increase high school enrollment, and believes that the family is the key to this increase, it needs to find ways to influence families' value systems.

## Is "Feeling Good" Good Enough?

We have argued that Temple Reyim's most powerful characteristic is its unusually warm and inclusive ambience. While Lilly and the staff care about content, its warmth is the trait most frequently referenced when people talk about the school. It is what we repeatedly saw in action: concern for all those involved in the enterprise.

While warmth and acceptance are essential, and perhaps even preconditions for effective religious education, questions about the relationship between content and ambience need to be considered. It is surprising how few times people associated with Temple Reyim, even with prompting, talked about content areas or knowledge-based goals, despite the fact that the newly developed mission statement and emerging curriculum clearly express commitment to outcomes to be achieved through the successful transmission of content. In the presence of teaching that is erratic, is emotional engagement and a feeling of belonging, of the temple being "casa de Samantha" enough to have staying power? To risk oversimplification we want to ask: Is feeling good a good enough goal for a school?

In a world of radical choice, where any and all religious options are available to people, wanting to be Jewish is the first essential step, or as the current slogan goes, "we are all Jews-by-choice." The school is a symbolic representation of Judaism to families, and if people are attracted and feel that they belong—that is a positive achievement. For so long the talk about religious school has been negative: jokes about Israeli teachers or parents' statement that "I went and hated it, so you'll go and hate it too!" With such a negative legacy, forging an environment of warmth, acceptance, and value is a large step forward and should not be minimized. Perhaps it is a corrective measure for an era of depersonalized institutions and pressured families. If, as they move into adulthood, many of the graduates of Temple Reyim (especially as it continues its journey of improvement) engage in aspects of Jewish life because it "feels right," this is surely an achievement.

We would challenge Temple Reyim and other similar schools to balance the need to *belong* with the need to *understand* in order to provide an enduring foundation from which Jewish identity and identification can develop. Ultimately, Jewish education has to provide answers to the question: why be Jewish today? This requires an educational system that nourishes the mind *and* the spirit. Through its commitments to ongoing improvement over a long period of time, Temple Reyim continues to move in that direction.

We are reminded of a cartoon that shows the bird's-eye view of a large office area where each staff member sits in an identically small, enclosed cubicle—except for one man who has a much larger cubicle to himself. Asked how he got this, he responds, "I moved the walls one-eighth of an inch each day." Temple Reyim is moving its walls. It may very well succeed in creating a stronger, more engaging school by improving the many aspects of Jewish education. Temple Reyim, and others who are working hard to make meaningful incremental changes, are betting that the cubicle, or box, in the middle can offer a compelling model for Jewish education in the twenty-first century.

# Notes

1. A prayer recited in the Friday night service. It is traditional for the congregants to turn to the door and give a slight bow as a way of welcoming the beloved Sabbath bride.

2. D. Pekarsky, *Vision at Work: The Theory and Practice of Beit Rabban* (New York: JTS Press, 2006), p. 10.

3. Passport to Israel is a communal program that encourages families to save money for their children to go to Israel on Jewish educational programs when they become adolescents. The families, federation, and congregation each contribute to each child's Israel savings account.

4. See http://www.sdttl.com/2002/ubd.htm; http://xnet.rrc.mb.ca/glenh/under standing_by_design.htm.

5. We do not mean to belittle what we see as a great strength. At all the group events that we saw—whether when moving between classes or being at *ma'ariv*, the students were consistently cooperative, well behaved, and positive.

6. The consultants who were involved in introducing Understanding by Design to Temple Reyim have determined that it is not realistic for congregational school teachers to be responsible for developing a UbD curriculum and have been modifying their approach.

7. The thinking behind this change is that the pressures of the Bar Mitzvah year as well as the extra learning that goes on to prepare for it justify the reduction in hours, and that a curriculum that presents students with options and is organized around activities will keep their interest.

8. The allusion is to a rabbinic notion that there are thirty-six (*lamed vav*) completely just people alive at any given time and it is because of this that the world is not destroyed because of (or by) the wickedness of so many other people.

9. To avoid biasing ourselves, we did not read the evaluation until near the end of the research.

10. This is sometimes called by "director of lifelong learning" or "director of congregational education." See, for example the essays in this volume by Aron and Wechsler.

11. Joseph Reimer, *Succeeding in Jewish Education: How One Synagogue Made It Work* (Philadelphia: Jewish Publication Society, 1995).

12. See, for example, the analyses of R. Elmore, "Getting to Scale with Good Educational Practice," *Harvard Education Review*, 66:1 (1995); M. Fullan, *Leading in a Culture of Change* (chapter 7) (San Francisco: Jossey Bass); S. Sarason, *Revisiting the Culture of School and the Problem of Change* (New York: Teachers College Press, 1996); P. Wasley, *Stirring the Chalkdust* (New York: Teachers College Press, 1994).

13. The educational director is an experienced educator with academic and professional credentials in Jewish education and was ready to work hard with the different consultants and coaches. There are several other well-trained professionals on the faculty. The professional staff of the congregation had a track record of working well together and they all wanted to see the school improve. These are among the assets that Temple Reyim brought to the table.

# CHAPTER 7

# Promoting a Counterculture

## Harold Wechsler with Cyd Beth Weissman

> A person whose inside is not like his outside cannot
> be a Torah scholar.
>
> —*Yoma* 72b

It's Shabbat. The senior rabbi at this West Coast temple sermonizes today, as on many other occasions, on growing up in the twenty-first century. "It's so easy for our children to be bruised by the world," begins the rabbi. "Life can break their hearts and shatter their deepest beliefs." Just as bad, "It can turn them into cynics and skeptics at a tender age."

So they need *us*, adds the rabbi. "They need the adults in their life, to be solid and dependable and true." We're models for our own children and for the children of our friends and neighbors. "They need to see us stand for something. They need to learn from us that some people can't be corrupted and some principles can't be compromised, no matter what," the sermon continues, "and that doing the right thing always matters." Then the conclusion: "It matters more than a high SAT score. It matters more than making a lot of money. It matters more than anything else."

We are countercultural, declares everything at this temple. We are not a Bar and Bat Mitzvah factory. We are not about material wealth. We are about living, modeling, and promoting Jewish values. Adam, a year shy of his Bar Mitzvah, discloses his ambitions on one Shabbat. "I want to be the Chief Executive Marketing Officer for Microsoft when I grow up." When asked why, Adam replies without noticing his mother's raised eyebrow, "I want to have a very very big house, so I can fill it with lots and lots of stuff." "That's why we belong to this Temple," says the boy's mother.

Adam's mom gladly meets the temple's expectation for regular Shabbat afternoon family attendance for Jewish learning. These *Shabbatons*, she and her husband believe, will help counter the overwhelming odds that their son will grow up to be a CEO, CFO, or some other set of initials, holding in highest regard all things that can fit into a very, very big house.

The glass-walled chapel of the temple is filled with the chatter of a hundred parents and children performing the acts that have become as much of a weekly ritual as dipping the braided candle in wine. Learning is about to begin. A staff member strums his guitar. On some Shabbat afternoons several confirmation students back him up. One *Shabbaton* begins with a Beatles medley, played on guitar. The adults sing—the kids don't know the words. "One more Beatles song," says the staff member, "then we'll get to the boring ones."

Some join in while others continue to talk. The mix of Jewish song and chatter makes for a welcoming melody. Adam's mom sits next to the mother of Adam's good friend. Both women prefer the chat to the songs. Work and family leave little time to share the stories or questions of their week. They learned about *dibuk chaverim*—cleaving to a friend—at a parent study session. The Jewish way of friendship means more than sharing a cup of coffee. For them, Saturday afternoons are holy time.

Adam, too, has a sense of awe about these Saturday afternoons. Attending private school with children from different neighborhoods means few hangout friends. "IM-ing" is great for most days, but he likes kicking around with the boys at the temple. "Got my new guitar," he tells his buddy, while a staff member leads more singing. "Rabbi said I could be in the rock band here. He's gonna show me some more cords." His buddy is going to play the drums in the band. Neither boy is good enough to make his own school band. But showing up is good enough here. "Now," said his mother, "he thinks he is a rock star." Adam shows up because the staff member, parents, and children know and care about him, even if he isn't a CEO.

Children in this community, located at a center of business innovation, grow up outside traditional familial and social influences on Jewish identity. Congregational leaders knew they inherited an ineffective drop-off/pick-up model of Jewish education designed to supplement these influences. The purpose of religious school, they concluded after much experimentation, is not to supplement Jewish home life by focusing on skill and knowledge building. Rather, as the senior rabbi's sermon signals, these leaders provide children a "religious school" experience akin to living in a Jewish neighborhood of past decades. Children are known and cared about in this neighborhood; they experience joy and see adults committed to Jewish learning and living.

Engaging children emotionally is this congregation's priority. Children who feel "connected," they believe, will be better able to contribute to growing a generation that says, "I like being Jewish and want to be Jewish." Kids can learn facts later on, note professional and lay leaders here, but an uninspired heart is hard to open to knowledge or connection afterward. This principle underscores their educational designs. Phrases such as "developing connections," "engaging the heart," and "building identity" are now common in Jewish education. But two elements make this congregation distinctive: the ability to replace an isolated, fact-focused school with a relaxed, caring, and joyful communal experience, and the ability to address individuals' needs by creating multiple gateways to this experience. *Shabbaton*, as experienced by Adam and his family, is its most successful model. The weekly family learning, singing, and ritual ending with *havdalah* recreates a Jewish neighborhood-like experience and regularizes Jewish family living.

But no model stands by itself. The congregation's gestalt forms a context conducive to promoting Jewish caring and commitment. All aspects of congregational life, not just the formal educational program, are focused on becoming a community committed to learning and caring. The campus and its architecture, educational program, governance process, prayer services, and staff dynamics all foster a context for learning. This is a story of how at its best—things fall short at times—a congregation signals that Jewish learning is a worthy and joyful pathway to a life well lived.

## The Surroundings

> How goodly are thy tents, O Jacob,
> Your dwelling places, O Israel!
> And I, with thy great loving-kindness,
> Shall enter thy House.
>
> —*Mah Tovu*

The turnoff onto the campus of this established forty-year old community—designed by an award-winning architect and early member of the congregation—resembles the access to nearby office complexes. But within seconds of entering the campus any comparison to a business-like milieu is replaced with serene images of immaculate grounds featuring abundant trees, grass, shrubs, and blooming purple and pink flowers. Hebrew and English signs welcome and direct guests.

Intended as a respite from the hectic tempo of secular life, this synagogue appears a throwback to an earlier time in the region's history. Originally a summer recreation area for the wealthy, the nearby town has been designated a "residential-agricultural zone," with limited commercialization. Its founders were dedicated to preserving the "rural atmosphere" of its environs and to "orderly and unhurried growth." But the area's economy grew substantially over recent decades, and the temple benefited from a location that continually attracted white, upper-middle-class residents. About 1,500 families belong to this Reform congregation; leaders expect 1,700 in a few years. The temple is located on a ten-acre campus in a community where housing prices average $1.4 million. A $3,000,000 budget reflects the congregation's commitment to education—a large slice of expenditures—and its affluence.

No building exceeds one story in height. Each structure has wood-shingled roofs, natural wood exteriors, and glass walls overlooking the grounds. The parking lot—full-size cars, scattered hybrids, and SUVs predominate—is too small; neighboring property is the subject of a much-discussed expansion. There's always a grease-board announcement of an upcoming service or educational event under the "pick-up here" and "drop-off here" signs. The upper campus—site of most educational activities—surrounds an interior lawn, with a playground featuring a jungle gym and an enclosed pit for "Gaga," a dodge ball variant popular in Israel ("*Ga*" means "hit" in Hebrew). There's easy access to the synagogue and the adjacent social room from the upper campus. Locating classroom buildings around central courtyards permits a free flow of people and promotes communication and connection; students never miss a break time since the staff considers socializing and sharing essential.

*Mah Tovu*, the opening prayer for the Saturday morning prayer service, suggests the rationale for the campus layout. Balaam, a non-Jewish prophet, composed *Mah Tovu* to honor the principles of Israelite communal organization. The Israelites arranged their tents close together, the rabbis said, to demonstrate communal cohesion and loyalty. But what prompted the blessing *mah tovu*, "how good"—the Temple's *siddur* tells us—was that the doorways of their dwelling places did not directly face one another, "thus retaining the integrity of the individual within the framework of the community."

Only one pair of doors faces each other directly on the temple's campus—and even those doors are a bit off line. All congregants—and each of the four full-time staff members—have their own strengths. But the campus design reminds all members that they are parts of a larger community. There's little anonymity here; adults know the children, call them by name, and give them hugs. "Will you bring your guitar?" the guitar-playing professional asks a nine-year-old boy. "I'll see you at the retreat," another staff member calls across the campus.

The education office adjoins the administrative and rabbinic offices. Schools and synagogues are often in separate wings in larger synagogues; their proximity here reflects the strong connections between the two. Doors easily open and close from one office to the next, indicating a flow of people, ideas, and energy. Every Friday afternoon at 3:00 p.m. a bell beckons administrative and professional staff to the main office to say *brachot* over juice and cookies. Some observers would sense a camp-like or neighborhood-like environment. Others might liken the campus with its connecting sidewalks and casual atmosphere to a kibbutz.

"Designed to be like Abraham's tent where everyone is welcome," as a teacher notes, classroom buildings are circular, maximizing window space. *Shalom* is written on every window. Hebrew calendars, alphabets, and phrases, maps of Israel, children's artwork, and photographs of the students cover the classroom walls. Artifacts reinforce the school's values; in this case its commitment to Israel and Hebrew. Teachers can easily rearrange the brightly colored furniture from schoolroom style to layouts enabling small group discussions. In a school and temple striving to harmonize the "inside" and "outside" of its students and congregants, the appearance of the classrooms, school and temple buildings, and campus supports—and agrees with—the inner values of the congregation.

Today, music emanates from several offices; the cantor's office faces the interior lawn, so passers-by often hear her voice and her recordings. Not far away is a rehearsal for *Shabbaton*. A well-trained fourteen-year old student leads a Friday service, backed up by the guitar-playing staff member, and by teens on bongos and on an electric keyboard. The professional leads *Tizmoret*, a five-piece band, once a month at a Friday Shabbat service. Music and singing knit this community together. Here, as elsewhere, the staff involves students and families as they move from familiar secular music to new songs in Hebrew that will soon be familiar.

Fifty yards away is a closed-door, well-carpeted music room, featuring an electric piano with soft-pedal. Today's Mother's Day–related activities include "Thank you to mom" and "My mother loves me," songs alternating English and Hebrew lyrics. Some songs in the music class are coordinated with academic lessons. Other songs are typically heard in Jewish summer camps.

Music, theater, dance—all the arts—are integral to the educational programs here. The staff plans ways to minimize attrition between Friday night services and the *oneg* that immediately follows—which doors to open, what music to play, and when to start playing it—and ways of maximizing participation in the singing and dancing. How should the temple

improve congregational attendance at Saturday morning services dominated by Bat/Bar Mitzvah guests? Cultivate a regular clientele through
music, a strategy that has worked elsewhere in the temple, said a task force
report. Play piano music as worshippers enter the sanctuary; start the service with congregational singing, and use piano and guitar accompani-
ment, not the organ, throughout. "We create multiple points of entry into
active participation in our congregation," notes the temple's values statement, "and encourage our congregants to experience the joy of full participation in Jewish life at home, at synagogue and in the community." Music
is the point of entry for many; it is the glue that rabbis and teachers use to
hold students and congregants together.

The temple uses an outdoor synagogue for services during late spring;
the weather poses few obstacles to people moving in and out, and between
rooms and activities. Some older congregants participate in an alternative,
intimate Friday night service that retains *Gates of Prayer*[1] and the Plautedition Torah;[2] the main service replaced these books with a spiral-bound,
congregation-authored *siddur*.

A Friday night service for children with special needs takes place in a
nearby classroom, as an education staff member gently guides four children—ages 11–14—through the preliminaries. Three of the four children
remain on task for much of the service and activities; the fourth got plenty
of hugs from parents and staff anyway. All four children made pillowcases
featuring the word "*Shema*." The cantor leaves the main service in the
sanctuary to lead the blessings over the *challah* and the wine for these children. "In the face of a secular culture which values outward appearance
and conformity," notes the temple's values statement, "we seek to cultivate
in our children appreciation for the unique gifts inherent in each of us as
well as empathy for the individual challenges that each person faces." Relationships—here, relationships among and across generations—count
for everything, and the surroundings encourage relationships . . . and education.

Education is central to, indeed unites, the temple's myriad activities for
children and adults. Everything at this congregation is educational, says
one staff member. And "teachable moments" can occur at any time. "Multi-
locational learning," notes a staff member, "takes place in the classroom,
the sanctuary, the office . . . the whole campus." Even among formal activities, another staff member adds, "I can't keep track of the entire goings
on." But education here is not just about the classroom, the curriculum,
and formal instruction. Children and adults are immersed in Judaism in all
places and at all times. People and surroundings strongly influence stu-

dents here; the campus, the Hebrew on the walls, the hugs, and the flowers in the garden—contribute to immersion in a Jewish community.

## The Educational Program

> We value lifelong Jewish learning and seek to help our congregants become committed, knowledgeable, participating Reform Jews. We will continuously identify and address obstacles and barriers to learning so that congregants will not be inhibited from participating fully in our education programs.
>
> —The temple's values statement

Here's the schedule for a typical fall Thursday—perhaps a few more classes than on some other weekdays, but not by much:

| | |
|---|---|
| 8:00 A.M. | Thursday morning *minyan* |
| 10:30 A.M. | Intermediate Modern Hebrew |
| 12:00 Noon | Talmud class |
| 1:30 P.M. | Jewish spirituality class |
| 4:00 P.M. | Hebrew program |
| 4:00 P.M. | Prayerbook Hebrew |
| 4:30 P.M. | Hebrew program |
| 6:15 P.M. | Intermediate/Advanced Modern Hebrew |
| 6:30 P.M. | The many faces of Hebrew in film and music |
| 7:00 P.M. | Russian theater group |
| 7:30 P.M. | Advanced Modern Hebrew |
| 7:30 P.M. | Psalms for everyday life |

The temple's "something for everyone" approach to educational activities ranges from countercultural to traditional. Lay governance and staff deem a "full-service" temple a necessity in an age when Jews have other congregational and educational options. Attracting congregants to this temple requires programs targeted to the needs and wants of specific constituencies.

Staff members frequently use the words "inclusion" and "inclusive" to describe a key goal for the educational program as a whole; they also work to maximize inclusion in each specific program. "We strive to provide an environment in which each individual has the opportunity to grow Jewishly in his or her own way while wholly within, and as an integral part of, our community," notes the temple's values statement. "We are open, welcoming, and embracing of all Jews regardless of gender, age, race, sexual orientation, physical ability, financial means, special learning needs, family composition, marital status, interfaith relationships and cultural and religious backgrounds."

Constituencies include children with special needs; members of the local Russian-Jewish community; retired adults who wish to study Talmud, and sizable numbers of Jews by choice and intermarried couples. Once, on the High Holy Days, the senior rabbi invited all non-Jewish spouses and relatives to the *bimah*, offering a blessing and thanks for supporting their spouses and their children in their congregational and educational choices. "You are the moms and dads who drive the children to Hebrew school," she said. "You take classes and read Jewish books to deepen your own understanding, so you can help to make a Jewish home." Just as music at this temple brings people on a journey from the familiar to the new, here, too, the temple meets these spouses and relatives "where they are," but then goes beyond the standard nonjudgmental welcome by offering an affirmative act of inclusion.

Informality is the norm for some educational activities: "We study over lunch, over bagels, over coffee, and over a stove," states the adult learning announcement. "On *Tishah b'Av* and *Yom Kippur* we study without food. But, most of the time we nosh and study." The announcement adds: "We study in pairs, in groups, and in classes. We even study on walks, runs, or hikes with one of our Rabbis."

Yet, other classes look and feel decidedly formal and traditional. Adult men and women, for example, sit on opposite sides of a long table in a noontime Talmud class. The men dominate the discussion. "Where they are," in this group, is likely "where they'll be"; enthusiastic noshing won't change that. All told, at least five hundred adults participate in one or more classes each year, including one hundred in the senior rabbi's Shabbat morning Torah study class.

Adults are a key audience for the temple's educational offerings. "You can always learn a little something," notes the introduction to the adult learning program. "Jews study," the announcement continues. "Through study we honor our past; we learn to deal with our present; and we insure a Jewish future as we pass on our heritage to our children." The staff works to make this statement more than a platitude. But adult education is not always an end unto itself. Parental learning tied to the supplementary education offered to their children is a desideratum at this temple, though not the ultimate goal. "We help people in our community to make connections, form friendships and participate in synagogue life," notes the temple's values statement. Education builds these connections among and between families and communities.

The temple's offering for adult learning is impressive. So are the curricula for children. Keeping them straight is not an easy task. *Beit Midrash* is the umbrella name for all youth and educational programs for children in pre-K to eighth grade. These programs include Hebrew, *Hagigah, Shabbaton*, Sunday and Tuesday Night Programs, and *Tzavta*: Family B'nei Mitzvah Enrichment. There is also a newly created preschool called *Gan Ami* and a confirmation and youth group program.

Other congregations around the country have adapted *Shabbaton*, one of the more innovative programs. *Shabbaton*, for pre-K to fifth graders and their parents, is an alternative to the traditional drop-off Sunday program. Parents and children participate weekly on Saturday afternoons. Established with a dozen families about fifteen years ago, the program quickly grew to seventy families.

*Hagigah* is another alternative to the traditional Sunday school model and is offered for students in second to fifth grades. This program, which meets for two hours on Wednesdays, explores Jewish values through the theater arts. The children put on a play in the fall and a musical in the spring. Learning is focused on the theme of the year—a value that is brought to daily life. Children in grades three through six also attend a two-hour class on Thursdays for Hebrew studies. In seventh grade students can elect to study conversational Hebrew. Hebrew song, letters, and prayer define the program for younger children. All participants are required to attend services throughout the year.

*Tzavta* is a program for all sixth and seventh graders including day school children. Designed to prepare the whole family for Bar/Bat Mitzvah, the program fosters community among participants and aims to develop meaningful understanding of this life-cycle ritual. Parents and students attend seven Shabbat services and regular classes (seventh graders help lead the services).

The traditional Sunday morning program is designed for pre-K to fifth graders. The congregation's website includes carpool safety directions for parents who drop their children off weekly. Occasional traditional family education programs are part of the Sunday curriculum. Instructors in the Sunday program include parents, college students, and professional teachers; specialists move between classes in a round robin. Adults with children in the Sunday program can enroll in *Toledot* and study a parallel curriculum in depth, thereby reinforcing the lessons taught to their children, while serving as role models for voluntary learning (*Toledot* is now open to all congregants). Sixth through eighth graders participate in the weekly two-hour Tuesday night Judaica Program (TNP).

The school's pre-K though eighth grade enrollments increased from 515 to 526 between 2005–06 and 2006–07. Confirmation class enrollments decreased from 35 to 28 for the same years. Lower grades showed year-to-year growth—from 58 to 67 for second graders and from 53 to 69 for fourth grade students. The number of seventh graders, in contrast, declined from 72 to 48.

Changes in enrollments from one grade to the next may be a more revealing indicator of the school's staying power since the number of potentially available children in the local Jewish population could vary from year to year. Enrollments increased between grades among students moving up from pre-K through fifth grade in 2005–06 to K–sixth grade in 2006–07. The school had enrolled only 54 sixth graders in 2005–06; that meant a decline of six students between the sixth grade in 2005–06 and the seventh grade in 2006-2007. Declines were greater between seventh and eighth grades (72 to 55) and from eighth grade to the confirmation class (50 to 28).

These declines suggest the holding power for the Bar/Bat Mitzvah; this school, like most supplementary schools, requires attendance at the *Beit Midrash* prior to the Big Event—four years in this case. Expressing concern about post–Bar Mitzvah enrollment declines, school staff targeted a dropout rate reduction from 50 to 33 percent. One strategy: hiring a youth director with a mandate to increase persistence rates to confirmation. One tactic: moving some Bar Mitzvah instruction to the school, though activities such as writing a *D'var Torah* and learning *trope* remain in the cantor's portfolio.

But after Bar Mitzvah, notes the senior rabbi, it's difficult to keep the kids. Staff members know that congregants and their children live in a primarily non-Jewish environment. Most students, they add, cannot and should not completely shut out the rest of the world when on the temple grounds. The ever-present stiff demands of secular schools and the increasing demands of the college admissions process, they conclude, take a predictable, and near-inevitable toll after age 13. Staff members laughed knowingly when a visitor, who teaches at a selective university, reported that several TNP students asked for tips on getting admitted to that university during a program break.

The school launched a new option for ninth and tenth graders to reduce the dropout rate while responding to the needs of learners. The program gives students credit for participating in community, worship, and education in lieu of attending weekly classes. Many high school students, though not attending formal classes, regularly participated in local Jewish life by volunteering in soup kitchens or belonging to youth groups without receiving "credit." Under the new program, the temple confirms tenth grade students who accumulate 180 hours of active participation in Jewish activities of their choice over two years. Attending Torah study or services, volunteering, and participating in the *madrichim* program all count toward the confirmation requirement.

All K–6 educational choices for children include some parental participation. "A teacher can craft a great lesson," notes a staff member. "But if the kid isn't open to it, it's not going to happen. This is where the parents come in." The available choices balance the belief that parental engagement is essential with the reality that all parents are not equally ready to engage. Some parents spoke of switching between programs because of their own changing interests or the needs of their children. Working to respond to complex and fluid family needs, the staff offers programs with different entry points. But parental choice does not imply parental abdication. When the culture and values of the congregation and the family are conversant, if not congruent, this staff believes, the positive outcomes they seek in learners become possible—even if these values conflict with the secular community.

The temple, says its senior rabbi, offers a critique and a corrective to the region's culture. The critique begins by noting that life here is "intense and stressful;" the demands of secular education and college admission are a subset of a larger problem. The senior rabbi's sermons often use adjectives such as "narcissistic," "materialistic," "intense," and "all consuming" to characterize the region's lifestyle. Chastising "a culture that values what is sleazy and shoddy and cheap," the temple continually urges parents to model good values and behavior for their children.

"All of us, of course, are leaders and teachers of the people around us, who watch us and take note of what we do," stressed one sermon, "and especially of our children and grandchildren, who watch us with eyes especially keen and spirits especially sensitive to hypocrisy." "They'll notice if we tell them that Hebrew school is important but we let them skip it at the slightest pretext," the senior rabbi added. "They pick up the message that these are just words that sound nice but aren't really meant to be taken seriously by grown-ups." Promoting honesty in this temple begins with the senior rabbi's candor.

The temple's professionals attempt to reconcile the desirable and the possible in their pastoral and educational work: have the temple—especially on Shabbat—serve as a refuge from materialism, careerism, and me-ism. An inherently countercultural Judaism that brings a balanced perspective to daily life—the heart of the senior rabbi's vision—is an inheritance all parents must pass on to their children. Rejecting attempts used elsewhere to influence parental behavior by intervening with children, perhaps by instilling guilt, the school focuses on eliciting voluntary commitments from adults, and then on complementing and reinforcing parental messages to their children.

The school adopted this strategy knowing that the temple competes with parents' other obligations. Adult members, according to a recent poll, most frequently cite a lack of free time as the greatest barrier to participating in more learning activities. The senior rabbi, for example, initially encountered resistance to moving Friday evening services from 8:00 to 6:15. "I just can't leave work at 5:45," objected a prominent and influential congregation member. But, the rabbi added, resistance diminished after about six months as congregants reconsidered priorities.

Creating a haven in a heartless world, says the rabbi, is an inescapable prerequisite to successful formal education. Parents, as well as children, may recover here from fatigue and burnout. Learning at this school, therefore, is geared to relevance, ethical behavior, and strengthening relationships and connections. Staff members cite an enculturation model they learned at the school of education at Hebrew Union College, the seminary that educates Reform rabbis, cantors, and teachers. When students learn the norms and values of Judaism, they feel good about feeling Jewish and commit to Jewish values. They value Jewish community and *tikkun olam*, and they devote more time to the study and practice of Judaism.

"We want our kids to feel comfortable in Jewish time and space," says a staff member. "It is a loving place, where they are comfortable in Jewish holidays and culture, know basics and develop enduring understandings." The price: "Some of the content doesn't get covered." "We're using the camp model," said a senior staff member. "We build a community that is vibrant. Content will follow. You can look at the depth of the adult learning that we offer here. The content will be there; they'll take Hebrew and Jewish courses in college."

Creating strong emotional bonds to at least one staff or clergy member facilitates enculturation. Kids should say, another staff member contends, "This is a place where people know my name, invite me to show my stuff, to take risks, to laugh." Beginning in the sixth grade, every child gets a business card with the home and cell phone numbers of all the educational staff and the phone number of a local teen hotline. Call when you need us, says the card.[3] "In high school I know my future is riding on my school work, but here it is not as apparent," says a *madrich*. "Kids here are really good friends with each other. Meeting all their friends here overrides the whole school thing." Constantly creating multiple modes of entry into Jewish education that require parental involvement, the staff aspires to do for all congregants what it already does for many.

## The Curriculum

> We sing together. We study about meaningful Jewish topics together— birth, death, parenting, marriage, bar and bat mitzvah, aging parents, helping the sick. We sing some more. We eat a little (What did you expect?). We celebrate *Havdalah* with candles and sniff spices circulated by little children who thrust fragrant sachets under our noses with big smiles. We sing some more. And if we are lucky, we dance like crazy maniacs while the rabbi plays the guitar. It is fun. It is meaningful. It is the highlight of our Shabbat day as a family—and we miss it deeply when it is not there.
>
> —A temple congregant, writing about *Shabbaton*

Educational goals for the formal curriculum in the *Beit Midrash* include mastering the fundamentals of the life cycle, holidays, Shabbat liturgy, Bible, history, Torah, and Israel. The instructors are asked to move from fact acquisition to applying key concepts to daily life and to helping students derive personal meaning from those concepts. According to the objectives for the sixth grade TNP curriculum, students will:

• Explain the *mitzvot* and *middot* (values and comandments) that they are already performing.
• Integrate the performance of *mitzvot* and *middot* into their daily lives.
• Explain how Jewish texts and values inform the way in which Jews interact with other people.
• Apply *middot* and *mitzvot* to their decision-making.

TNP's "Mitzvot and Middot" curriculum includes four units. All unit titles begin with *Ani* or "Me": students explore their relationships to Judaism, their community, and the world. The unit on Judaism involves decision making that results from "serious reflection on the implications of choices—for self, family, community, and the world." Students focus on specific *middot* or *mitzvot* each week.[4] A class in the unit on community signals the integration of the school and Bar/Bat Mitzvah curricula by exploring the values underlying that ceremony. Students watch and discuss "Keeping Up with the Steins," a comedy in which a Hollywood agent sponsors an ultra-extravagant Bar Mitzvah celebration for his son.

Observers note the parallels between "Mitzvot and Middot" and secular progressive curricula as students move from parental and community relations to reckoning with the larger world. But this curriculum goes further than secular equivalents. Students begin to "wrestle with God" (*Ani Ve'Hashem*) by exploring their "pre-existing definitions" in the fourth unit. "Our tradition not only permits us to question our beliefs," states the curriculum guide, "it demands it." Students, for example, confront *bachar banu* (chosenness) in discussing their attitudes toward other groups.

"It's not important that the students know the three sons of Noah," says one teacher. "It's more important that students confront key ethical dilemmas." This teacher, a thirty-year veteran known as one of the school's best, teaches ethics to the me-generation by rewarding students who answer "morals" and "values" to the question: "If Torah is to be part of your future, what does it mean to you?" The Bible, his peroration notes, is not a fundamentalist document, but is itself filled with ethical dilemmas. He then commends Reform Judaism for its willingness to confront these dilemmas.

The school's curricula reflect the weight Reform Judaism gives to *middot* and *mitzvot*. In explaining *mitzvot*, the curricula note the importance of ethics *and* ritual. The curricula also reflect the congregation's self-definition as a place of alternative values that models and teaches *middot* and *mitzvot*. This temple does not teach a deterministic Judaism: "We value a decision-making process about living our Judaism that is the result of serious reflection on the implication of choices—for self, family, community, and world." The words "choice" or *timshel* ("thou mayest") appear often in curricular materials. The word "Reform," in contrast, appears infrequently, though Reform's focus on ethical behavior pervades most lessons.[5]

Other observed classes raised ethical issues in the context of teaching Jewish history. One teacher, for example, asked students to compare the "I was just following orders" defense in several different settings, including the Holocaust, Iraq, and the prison for enemy combatants at Guantanamo Bay, Cuba. Another teacher showed an episode of *South Park* that posed a dilemma for Jews: is silence or a strong objection the best response to a showing of Mel Gibson's movie on the crucifixion of Christ? Let it go and antisemitism spreads, suggested the teacher, but objecting might also result in antisemitism.

Why the focus on ethics and identity in this sixth grade curriculum? "Middle school is a tough time," notes a staff member. "I want kids to be here and parents to get it." The curriculum includes sensitive topics that parents may not have discussed with their children, acknowledges the staff. But students grow up fast, so they should learn Jewish values before making difficult decisions, and should seek out adults, including empathetic temple staff members, when troubled.

TNP's seventh and eighth grade curricula focus on Torah exploration.[6] These curricula reinforce the school's goal of "feeling connected to one piece of the Torah," to use a staff member's phraseology, as a student approaches Bat or Bar Mitzvah. Stated curricular goals and objectives pick up on themes introduced in sixth grade, including connectedness: "Provide opportunities for students to God-wrestle"; "Recognize that questioning and examining will always be part of our lives"; and "Explain at least two Torah stories that explore issues that are similar to their own issues/ struggles/questions/concerns."

Teachers use individual *parashiot* (portions) and verses to revisit questions raised in the sixth grade curriculum.[7] TNP seeks to gently introduce students—"not overwhelm them," states a curricular guide—to the concept of Biblical criticism. The guides do not explicitly use this term, but they ask why Genesis includes two competing stories in *Bereshit*, how students approach repetitions in a text, and how Reform Judaism views Torah. A dinner of pizza, salad, and drinks—the school recently responded to student and parental lobbying by adding burritos to the menu—allows students to decompress before filling out their evenings with less intense *chugim* (electives).[8]

TNP asks for student self-evaluations that include questions about content: "This semester I learned . . ." and "I want to learn more about . . . ," for example. Other questions ask about attitudes: "I am here to please my parents," and "I am here to learn more about Judaism," for example. A third set of questions examines values: "To me, social action is the most important thing about Judaism." Two of the most important questions: "True or False: 'My parents would be proud of my behavior at TNP,'" and "I do Jewish stuff away from the temple." The school must expect the students to treat the questionnaire honestly: they're asked to sign their names.

The staff also gives primacy to Hebrew. The goal of the Hebrew program is to "plant seeds of excitement and a love for the Hebrew language that we hope will lead to lifelong Hebrew study." Hebrew today is recognized as a "fundamental component of Jewish living and learning," and is therefore integrated into all subjects. Ten years ago, the Hebrew program director had little contact with the other staff educators. Senior staff heard frequent expressions of dissatisfaction from parents and teachers, despite agreement that the students learned how to decode the language. The diagnosis: first, too many missed opportunities to link to the other programs. The Hebrew program director had no confidence that, say, Purim, would be taught in Sunday school, so the Hebrew teachers taught it, even if it resulted in duplication. Second, which Hebrew: Biblical, *siddur*, or modern? Decode, read, or converse?

Getting answers required a painful staff change and reconceptualizing programmatic, staff, and parent relations. When an economic downturn at the beginning of the decade forced further downsizing, the staff asked some parents to lead classes to help make ends meet. This request became a precedent for greater parental participation in the school. "Integration" across educational programs simultaneously became a staff mantra. "We had three good, but independent programs," notes a staff member. Now the temple "integrates its curricula whenever possible."

A few years ago, parents objected to the stress on themselves and their children created by the demands of a three-day-a-week program.[9] In response, temple governance accepted a parent-staff task force recommendation to cut religious education to two days a week.[10] The still-used task force process brings lay and professional leaders together over a twelve to eighteen month period during which questions revolve around shared values and outcomes. The conversation shifts from "How many hours a week?" to "What do we agree is most important for our children to embrace?" Identifying lay leaders who are open to participating in this deliberative process allows the congregation to face questions with no easy answers. A temple priding itself on reducing stress could not ignore complaints that its program had the opposite effect, especially after passage of the No Child Left Behind Act in 2001 increased secular school demands on third and fourth graders. In exchange for this reduction, the school increased instruction on the two remaining days from two to two and a half hours.

Knowing that this reduction came at the cost of Hebrew instruction, the task force also opted to begin language instruction in earlier grades, to focus on Modern Hebrew in the formal curriculum, and to use prayer book Hebrew in *Tefillah*. The school also required home instruction in reading *siddur* in the upper grades—an innovation its leaders hoped parents would view as part of a package, not as a punishment for moving from a three-day schedule. The agreement thus honored a commitment to parental participation in temple and school decision making via the task force. Moving the study of *siddur* Hebrew to the home risked diminished knowledge acquisition and skill building, but it allowed greater focus on school activities that built identity. It also permitted staff members to express their preference for creative homegrown curricula congruent with the needs of an "alternative" congregation and school. Lay leaders and professionals addressed a problem by merging different ideas and giving voice to values instead of blaming the educators or parents or making the staff fix things. The proposals offered by this experimental community are now in the testing phase.

Exposure to the Hebrew language begins with the oversized alphabet letters displayed in the playground, and continues throughout the curriculum. A focus on Modern Hebrew also assuaged several Israeli Hebrew teachers; including some who disagreed with key messages of Reform Judaism. Hebrew language–related goals include learning vocabulary, reading Modern Hebrew texts with vowels, and, most important, understanding that Hebrew is a living language. The new seventh grade learn-with-your-parents-at-home Hebrew curriculum includes help from a CD and other media. "We also have *Tefillah* [reserved for the last 20 minutes of each Sunday]," noted a staff member. "They use the Hebrew, we try to build a prayer life that way."

In addition to the established curriculum, each year has an academic theme that focuses on a value that can be applied to daily life. *Tzedek* (justice) for example, is one year's filter for much of the learning across grades and programs. Each grade has its own prayer during *Tefillah*.[11] The Israel curriculum, taught in fifth grade, provides students with a good dose of history. The semester begins with classes on major Zionist and Israeli political figures, and on the history of the Palestinian mandate and the Israeli nation.[12] The second semester focuses on Israel's geography and demography through a map project, and on its current social, economic, and political status.[13]

*Tefillah* brings together all the children and some parents in the sanctuary. This week, a staff member leads some Hebrew songs in a relaxed manner, mixing in humor. The children cooperate, but don't seem to know the songs. All stand at the end for *Hatikva*; a staff member says that learning *Hatikva* is a goal for next year.

*Shabbaton*'s curriculum assumes that adults will influence children by their example—not vice versa. The staff also contrasts this program to venues in which "Jewish education was something that was done to you, not something you participated in." "Spending time together with friends at this temple on Shabbat is FUN!" says one announcement. "Many people say they hated Hebrew school," says a program coordinator. "So I want kids to say 'I loved it.'" The *Shabbaton* curriculum minimizes repetition from year to year, and permits seamless transfer between the Saturday and Sunday programs. The curriculum focuses on life cycle events, values, and rituals "that give structure to and enrich our lives and homes as being Jewish."[14]

Goals for learning and performing Jewish rituals include awareness of a shared Jewish past, preserving Jewish tradition through family tradition, and enriching family life and community connections. The program seeks to build awareness that "[t]he innovation and cultural adaptation of new ritual has always been a necessary element in the development of life cycle traditions." Seeing life cycle events as an inviting gateway into Jewish tradition, new members of the congregation, Jews-by-choice, and intermarried couples often opt for the program.

Often seen as a lay leadership crucible (including Jews-by-choice) for the congregation and for other educational activities, *Shabbaton* asks parents to study with their children and other families in groups for an hour (*mishpachot*), and to remain for adult study for a second hour while their children receive separate instruction by grade (*kitot*). Group activities often incorporate music and the arts. Sessions typically begin with *shira* (singing) and culminate in *havdalah*, celebrated by entire families in a communal setting. Children share blessings while sitting in a circle or on a parent's lap; this week, one child holds the *bsamim* (spice box) to be used in *havdalah*. In contrast, a Sunday school teacher was heard saying "Zip it" to a misbehaving child the next day.

One *Shabbaton* focused on the theme of *brit* or covenant. During *mishpachot,* families with older children explored the concept of covenant and the reasons for devising a *brit* ceremony for girls. Families with younger children explored elements of the *brit* ceremony before discussing which family member played each role at *brit* ceremonies and why. In *Kitah*, teachers taught the younger children by dividing the group into pairs and by talking about teamwork, building to a discussion of the partnership asked of Jews with God. Older children discussed the *Brit Milah* (circumcision) ceremony, before moving to z'man Ivrit (Hebrew time). One might question the age appropriateness of some concepts taught in *Shabbaton*, but staff members defended the curricular inclusion of controversial subject matter. Some parents lead the adult study sessions; others lead the children's sessions. A teaching institute supports the lay instructors in *Shabbaton* and in other programs; the professionals who develop most sessions offer this guidance.

*Shabbaton* assigns homework projects to families, often based on life cycle events. Families share the results at sessions near the end of the academic year. One family's project showed the life cycle as a series of mountains to be climbed. Another family designed a London Underground subway-like map, with each "tube line" representing a different part of a life—personal, professional, and religious, for example—and the different journeys along these paths, along with the intersections. Creating personalized projects over an extended time period, staff members affirmed, enabled the hundred participating families to become Jewish teams, not just members of a weekly audience. Through *Shabbaton*, Shabbat, they add, becomes part of the rhythm of Jewish family life. Many congregations, staff members conclude, aspire to this goal, but experiencing Jewish family life in real time has a greater impact on a child than a Jewish arts and crafts demonstration in an occasional Shabbat workshop.

*Shabbaton* developed a passionate following. "My daughter cried when she learned that this was the next to last *Shabbaton* of the year," reported one parent. "That's when we knew we were in the right place." Parents, one participant commented, "are so busy, maybe too busy, with little time to schmoose. *Hafsakah*, the break in *Shabbaton*, gives them some time." Several parents in the same temple-based *havurah*, says a member of the temple board, jointly participate in *Shabbaton* and then discuss what they've seen and learned at dinner afterwards.

One student spoke at her confirmation about the impact that *Shabbaton* had on her life. "*Shabbaton Mishpacha* showed me that kids and adults can have important conversations together and both bring something meaningful to the discussion," she began. "In *mishpacha*," she noted, "the adults never took control of a conversation and they rarely sat silent during a discussion aimed at teaching kids things that the adults already knew." Today, she added, "even though nearly all the children in our *mishpacha* have graduated from *Shabbaton,* our families still get together on a regular basis and I am still very good friends with the other kids, even though only one of them is in my grade." "I still come to *Shabbaton* every Saturday, but now as a *madricha*, a teen aide," she concluded. "Watching a new group of families getting the opportunity to discuss and share ideas the same way my *mishpacha* did fills me with an indescribable joy."

There were some dissenters. "I didn't like going to *Shabbaton*," commented another *madrich*. "I didn't like learning with my family. This school is for friends, not to go with your family." But *Shabbaton* mainly elicited enthusiastic testimonials. "*Shabbaton*, week after week, throughout the year, is transformational for families," wrote one congregant. "It weaves them into congregational life, smile by smile, lesson by lesson, song by song, *havdalah* by *havdalah*." "It not only brings depth and meaning to their own Judaism as they practice it as a family," added this member, "it places them, step by step, right into the heart of congregational life." Many lessons imparted during *Shabbaton* reinforce the senior rabbi's candid sermons; conversely, few *Shabbaton* participants are surprised at such candor. The synagogue's direction is congruent with this signature program.

Two key strengths emerge from examining the temple's programs: the emphasis on choice, and the linkages among curricular elements. But, staff members acknowledge, the demands on parents committing to these multiple programs (especially parents with more than one child) may still conflict with the temple's stated mission of offering refuge from professional and social demands. "Three years ago I was the lay coordinator for the *Shabbaton* program," notes a temple board member. "I have a twelve-year-old who is in *Tzavta*. We come ten times during the year on identified Friday nights or Saturday mornings. I have a nine-year-old and a five-year-old in *Shabbaton*," this member adds. "We come Saturday afternoon." Sometimes, she notes, "it is hard to manage the days and the programs. I have to get a babysitter for the younger children when we come to *Tzavta* on Friday night."

A transient teaching force may compromise the ability of the school to translate even well-written curricula into real learning. Linkages that are evident to the curriculum designers may not be apparent to contingent classroom teachers. "We need more teachers," notes a senior staff member. "We've had a lot of turnover this year. At times we are just putting in a warm body." Area colleges and universities and native Hebrew speakers residing in the area provide two pools of teachers—neither consisting exclusively of Reform Jews. Staff members hope that an initial orientation session helps teachers—the "front line" of any program—to see their role as teachers and the content of the curriculum they impart in a larger context. But maintaining curricular coherence and linkages despite reliance on contingent faculty is a problem that goes beyond Jewish education.

Observations ratify the need for educating teachers on effective ways of engaging their students. Two observed teachers demonstrated little control of their third grade Sunday program classes. One teacher gave directions for an activity, but provided little support, purpose, standard, or meaning. Not surprisingly, children spoke out of turn, acted silly, and behaved badly. Only recess saved that teacher from complete loss of control. Another teacher, having distributed a package of (possibly age-inappropriate) materials related to Yom Haazmaut (Israeli Independence Day), spent most of the lesson telling some children to "Sit down" and "Be quiet."

Student engagement and behavior fared better in other classes, but novice teachers need tools for controlling behavior beyond food and glue. Teachers in the Sunday program currently participate in one orientation, three teacher meetings, a special needs training session, and three individual meetings scattered throughout the year; numbers the permanent staff hopes to increase. A teacher development program run by the local Bureau of Jewish Education may help; so would a focused recruitment program. In any case, poor student behavior undercuts the school's stated goal of making people feel good about being there.

Jewish decision making, feeling connected, and applying learning to daily living are high priority outcomes for the *Beit Midrash* curriculum. Achieving their goals is sometimes elusive. But, when successful, the result is seen in a child's action and internal dialogue. The writing of a thirteen-year old offers a window to the inner life of a child who transfers knowledge into a way of living. "I always know that I can come here to ask my fellow congregants, not to mention the staff and clergy, about what I should do," she writes on the occasion of her Bat Mitzvah. "And when all else fails, I know that I can turn directly to my tradition, to this Torah and, ultimately, to God." Sometimes, she adds, "just studying an ancient text, or reading about how my ancestors confronted similar challenges, or by simply saying something out loud in a prayer, I feel like I'm not alone. I feel like I'm not the only person who has ever felt this way." Knowing this, she concludes, "gives me courage and helps me confront whatever challenges that may come my way."

## The Staff

> We rely on each other. We support each other. We work hard to be a good effective team, to help each other out. We do that naturally, for each other, and the lay leaders do it too.
>
> —A staff member

This temple's view of congregational and educational life requires a warm, enthusiastic, mutually respectful and supportive staff. Recruiting such a staff means identifying charismatic colleagues with well-developed interpersonal skills and strong Judaic knowledge. Intense competition for these positions permits selectivity; candidates want to work at the school because of its established reputation. "This is a dream opportunity to work with shared leadership," noted a recent recruit. In turn, said the school's director, recently recruited staff members "have done extraordinary jobs. They're highly professional. They can't be brand new!"

Staff members show their commitment to building community by their own interactions. They interact early and often, value fluidity over rigidity, and find synergies among their own talents and among their programs— music plays a key role here. Meeting regularly, they challenge each other and build off each other's ideas. They also look for ways to incorporate what they learn from each other into their own work lives and lifestyles. Studying together (*Torah Lishmah*, not educational theory and practice) every two weeks enables personal growth and a common Jewish language for thinking about the work at hand. "Good and welfare"—a staple at Jewish committee, board, and staff meetings—*precedes* substantive discussions among the educators.

Each staff member has a school and congregational following. "Our relationship with the kids is really important," notes a staff member. "I remember seeing the kids at a retreat; they are friends with the program director. Kids come up to her and hang on her. The relationships keep the kids happy." But they claim to leave their egos at the door. "We know we have to work together," said one staff member. "We have a culture of how to do things."

One norm for working together is the expectation for change. "We value innovation, experimentation and continuous improvement," notes the temple's values statement. "Experimentation and innovation, when undertaken with care for our tradition and in order to move us toward fulfilling our mission, are consistent with the highest Jewish values." The staff takes pride in its creativity. "We are not afraid of failure," says a staff member. "We are willing to experiment. If it doesn't work, we speak the truth about it, either move on or fine-tune it. We continually are troubleshooting."

Committed to assuring quality, the staff seeks to translate creative designs into successful ongoing programs. Ideas for new programs are encouraged and supported; a new staff member proposed *Hagigah*, a theater program for second through fifth graders, for example. *Hagigah* quickly attracted children who wished to express themselves through the theater arts. A priority goal of providing multiple gateways to this learning community spurs innovation.

Staff collaboration over appropriate curricular and instruction elements enables good ideas to hit the ground running. Three staff members lead the educational professional team. Each educator has a portfolio of primary responsibilities and is expected to work collaboratively across programs. When asked who was in charge, the staff replied that leadership was

shared and depended on the question of the day. An educator leads the Hebrew program and the family *Shabbaton* program. Another professional
directs the theater arts program and the Sunday program. A third educator runs the confirmation program, TNP, and the sixth grade *Tzavta* program for day school and supplementary students. One staff member nom-
inally coordinates the group, but this team is mostly self-managed.

Can spontaneity and continual experimentation, team members wonder, co-exist (or be reconciled) with the need for careful planning? Recruiting a creative staff helps, but the challenge is constant. Innovation can
keep a talented, movable staff engaged, but it can require others to implement educational designs to which they did not contribute and in which
they have less personal investment. The breadth of activities, while exhil-
arating, may imply the sacrifice of depth; care in teacher orientation and
supervision, and concern with program assessment. It can lead to burnout;
staff members often work six and a half days a week. "We are constantly
in a state of change that is exciting," said a staff member. "So much is going
on, we are constantly juggling. It is exhausting."

Staff members, in short, internalized a key characteristic of the dominant culture—the premium placed on innovation—while attempting to
avoid falling victim to another—its intensity. Could this temple offer a critique of the dominant culture without adopting some of its characteristics?
Perhaps not. Flexibility and teamwork were essential, even if also rewarded in the larger world. But selective and intentional adoption, the
staff believed, would not compromise the school's essential goals.

One factor permitting interconnected and overlapping roles among
staff members: similar backgrounds in Jewish education. "We use a lot of
HUC-speak here," noted one staff member, referring to the education program at Hebrew Union College. Most staff members, if forced to, would
choose process over content. "We use reflective practice," said another
staff member. "We are very process oriented; we have task forces to resolve
significant questions; we are said to be an HUC satellite."

That staff members invoke "enculturation," an oft-used term at HUC, as
a one-word summary of their goals is not surprising, given their critical social outlook. But a newer staff member stressed the importance of content.
This staff member asked students in an elementary class to name the Five
Books of Moses. Hearing no correct response, she unhesitatingly provided
the answers herself. The intervention did not appear to embarrass the
teacher, nor were the students nonplussed. Enculturation, to this staff
member, did not preclude content mastery. A successful educational program, the senior rabbi concurred, required the presence of some staff

members who advocate the primacy of process and of others who focus on content. We observed the best of learning when teachers placed content in service of a child's belonging. Enculturation thus includes content; it is not just a feel good experience. But you learn best, the staff believes, in a living, breathing, and practicing community, not in isolation. In turn, a student becomes a part of the community by experiencing the rituals, the laws, and values of the group.

Cultivating relationships requires staff to make time to talk to parents and children, to hear their stories, and to learn their interests. Staff members work first to involve children *and* parents at *Shabbaton*, services, and annual retreats. Each participant, they believe, in turn serves as an ambassador to other family members and temple congregants. Relationships, not just good programs, build a community.

All parties cultivate salutary relations between the governing board and the professional staff. Engaged lay leaders report that their strong commitments and their willingness to volunteer time and energy resulted from staff inspiration and invitation. "Relations between staff and board are healthy and respectful," says one staff member. "Staff and board are on the same page because they jointly created the list of values that guides all decisions. This temple is neither rabbi nor board dominated." "We bring together our talented congregants and staff both to set the direction for our congregation and to implement what we choose to do," notes the temple's values statement. "The benefit of this partnership is self-reinforcing, inspiring further participation and leadership in our congregation." The senior rabbi and a school staff member serve on the board's executive committee. Ironing out differences among staff members in advance allows these colleagues to present a unified position to the board.

Staff and board work to assure that financial priorities reflect the value the congregation places on education. Tuition for pre-K through second grade programs ranges between $475 and $650, depending on the program; the price increases to $1,220 for the sixth grade program (including the pizza), and then declines to $695 for the seventh and eighth grade programs. Tuition fees, here as elsewhere, do not cover the cost of the educational program. But parents of enrolled children are young, and often less able to afford tuition, board members note. The board discussed raising the membership fee when the congregation committed to increasing scholarship money by one-third. Past experience suggested that families paying the full freight would respond favorably. Similarly, the board decided against a tuition increase when deciding to hire a youth director. Instead, it hoped to offset the cost of the position by generating tuition revenue from additional enrollments, and by asking staff members to fill in for the recently resigned *madrichim* coordinator.

Maintaining a high level of creativity requires energy and commitment. Recruiting from the same educational institution and having similar generational experiences promote synergies, while collaborating on primary assignments permits renewal. The temple complements these internal moves by supporting many professional development activities. The senior rabbi annually participates in a program requiring five weeks of study at the Hartman Institute in Jerusalem and a weekly teleconference throughout the year. Another staff member reports about ten professional development activities.[15]

But staff turnover inevitably occurs. Regional and national activities allow staff members to convey their views to others, and being on display may also lead to job offers.[16] But turnover, even of talented staff members, may be advantageous when a school has a choice of replacements who share the temple's values and who can fit in immediately. This year's new staff members quickly improved existing programs and implemented new ones, such as *Hagigah*. The school encourages intergenerational professional exchanges as its own form of *l'dor v'dor*. Teachers, for example, are asked to write their impressions of individual students and of programs for colleagues who will work with these students and in these programs the following year.

This staff is modest, though not self-effacing. No one is content with the status quo. All staff members raise questions about policy and practice. Most important: staff with a passion for Jewish learning and living enjoy their work, because they are in a supportive, goal-directed and innovative environment.

## Conclusion

> We start with the assumption that the people around us have good intentions, that they are seeking something special, better, different here than they have in their life outside of here. Just like Shabbat separates the holy from the ordinary, I believe that when we walk through the door at [the temple], we expect to be in a place that is not ordinary and seeks to be holy. Because of this we assume that we will be treated differently— greeted warmly, listened to, and have community to celebrate our greatest joys and deal with our deepest grief.
>
> —A lay leader

This school, many observers would probably argue, is *sui generis*. The size and wealth of this congregation allow the school degrees of freedom shared by few peer institutions. But the real lessons learned from this school have less to do with the entirety of the enterprise than with the elements making up its success. Five lessons seem especially important for other supplementary schools to consider.

First, congregations should ask how their supplementary schools could serve as effective means of achieving a collective vision. *Shabbaton* at this temple, for example, reinforces the senior rabbi's approach to congregational life. The school, lay leaders and staff believe, is not an entity unto itself. The classroom teacher alone cannot convey the importance of Jewish education. Children, surrounded by secular influences, do not learn how to live a Jewish life if placed in a vacuum. Because laity and staff understand the need to integrate school and congregation—the contiguity of offices symbolizes this understanding—they regularly identify synergies within the school and the temple. Such synergies result from intentional planning to reinforce the goals and values of the congregation and the school.

Second, shared partnership needs to include parents. Education and schooling are not identical, Lawrence Cremin reminds us.[17] Jewish education is most effective when the synagogue, the child's family, and other children's families reinforce the formal lessons. Congregations and schools must do more than pay lip service to the goals of building a shared sense of purpose, and of creating honest, open ways to process challenges. Much of this work occurs in one-on-one parent-educator collaborations. Little things at this temple—the Beatles songs, the signs in the parking lot—and bigger things—adult education classes and *Shabbaton*—reflect the school's constant efforts to place parents and school in conversation about the lives of children. Parental complaints may be inevitable; but ultimately school and parents must partner—so must teachers, staff, and lay governance—to avoid a culture clash. Open, reflective, and inclusive decision making helps to build trust between congregants and staff.

Seventy-five years ago, Cyrus Adler, president of the Jewish Theological Seminary of America, recommended a six-hour norm for supplementary school education as adequate to teach the basics of Judaism to children. But today's parents challenge that norm. The move from three to two days per week at this temple reflects larger changes in American Jewish life, including demands for greater professional productivity and the primacy of secular education for many parents and children. Parents may want fewer hours, but the temple's staff believes that even daily doses of Jewish education would produce few results in families that do not value and practice Judaism. Children need active parents, and a community that models what is being taught. When conflict occurs, the task force process practiced throughout the congregation facilitates productive conversations producing agreed upon goals and strategies. The foundation for that essential partnership is formed when the conversation shifts from "How many hours?" to "What are the hopes the temple and parents share for a child's life?"

Third, innovation is a murky process that happens only when a congregation replaces self-satisfaction or constant criticism with a yearning to realize more fully its mission and vision. Creating countercultural learning that is a respite from the rest of the world is difficult, to say the least. Lay leaders and professionals must take risks while focusing sharply on achieving their shared goals. But such risk-taking requires a clear mandate from lay leadership for innovation. This mandate allows professional staff to concentrate on goals, not only on the unending tasks of running a school. Many staff members studied where the professors wrote books on creating new models of congregational education; so they have training in how to act on that charge. The coupling of permission and an ability to translate ideas to action is a powerful engine for change.

Lay leaders can give more than consent. Innovation requires intimate lay involvement in the creative process. The use of task forces is one way this congregation brings multiple perspectives to a challenge. Once formed, task force members think boldly, modify designs by learning lessons from initial implementation, and discover paths to success from prior failures. The staff knows how to ask busy, but gifted and passionate lay leaders to accomplish targeted and worthy tasks. Some schools are criticized for never doing anything for the first time. This school continually experiments; it is creating new programs as this chapter is being written.

Fourth, successful experimentation requires careful, thorough implementation. The best designs *will* fail without careful execution. The staff members at this temple focus on the broad brush strokes of new programs. But strong programs need to be filled with quality experiences; boldness and imagination are compatible with sweating the details. Teacher weakness, for example, can thwart the best design of an innovative program. Teachers must understand how their activities advance the larger mission of the school. Professional development should provide such understanding by giving teachers a role in strengthening that mission. Not unaware of this insight, this temple offers some professional development and conducts some assessments, but these are not the highest priorities. Additional investments in professional development and program assessment could deepen the Jewish learning of contingent, inexperienced faculty members and facilitate their integration into a community of learners. Nitty-grittys are as important as grand designs when educating children.

Fifth, take to heart this temple's focus on authenticity—in personal relationships and in living a Jewish life. Children can spot hypocrisy in adult thought and behavior that undermines any content coverage. Creating an environment where what is learned is also lived is essential. Teaching *middot* in a community where people are acting with *middot*, saying study is a lifelong endeavor in a place where people of all ages study, and advocating caring in a temple that demonstrates care, makes a significant difference in how children experience Jewish education.

This temple's prescription for securing the health of American Judaism: challenge all that is "sleazy and shoddy and cheap" and immerse children and adults in a community that vividly displays with symbols and deeds that it strives to live what it teaches. Children dwell in this tent, this community, by playing on a *Gaga* court with Jewish friends, singing Jewish songs, practicing making decisions based on Jewish values, smelling *bsamim* with their parents, and feeling valued by staff just for "being." This picture of Jewish education deserves consideration. The remedy offered here for the challenges facing Jewish education may not be the answer for all supplementary schools. But, intentionally creating a palpable Jewish caring and learning culture, a Jewish neighborhood, that values individual choice while privileging community, seems worthy of deliberation by educational leaders making informed, effective choices. "Effective" here means taking action that can lead to a positive, long-lasting impact on learners' lives.

## Notes

1. Chaim Stern, ed., *Gates of Prayer: The New Union of Prayer* (New York: Central Conference of American Rabbis, 1975).

2. W. Gunther Plaut, *The Torah: A Modern Commentary* (New York: Union of American Hebrew Congregations, 1974).

3. The congregation had a suicide several years ago.

4. Examples include *Emet* (truthfulness) and *Lashon Harah* (gossip) during "Me and My Community," *Tzniyut* (modesty) during "Me, Myself, and I," and *Kol Yisrael Aravim Ze Be'Ze* (All Israel is responsible for each other) during "Me and the World."

5. Among the handful of specific mentions: the objectives of the seventh grade Torah curriculum include "Explain the Reform Movement's view of Torah." And, among the reasons offered for Torah study: "Reform Jews are expected to engage in God wrestling."

6. Genesis and Exodus in seventh grade; Leviticus, Numbers, and Deuteronomy the following year.

7. Topics include the role of gossip in the lesson on *Tazria* and *Metzorah* (Leviticus) and peer pressure when studying *Shelach Lecha* (Numbers), for example.

8. The *chugim* include "Jews in Film," "Israeli History," *tikkun olam* (social action), and "Art."

9. On student and parental stress, see Uri Bronfenbrenner, "Ecology of the Family as a Context for Human Development: Research Perspectives," *Developmental Psychology* 22 (1986), 723–42; Mihilay Csikszentmihalyi, "If We Are So Rich, Why Aren't We Happy?" *American Psychologist* 54 (1999), 821–27, and Suniya S. Luthar, "Over-Scheduling vs. Other Stressors: Challenges of High Socio-Economic Status Families," *Social Policy Report* 20 (4) (2006), 16–17. These psychologists downplay the role of overscheduling per se, saying that extracurricular activities are generally salutary. The true culprits, they argue, include stresses on parents—especially pressures toward material success, and work policies that "render it near-impossible for parents to maintain satisfying high-impact careers along with close, connected relationships with their families" (Luthar, 17).

10. Israela Aron, "The Longest Running Social Drama, Now Coming to a Congregation (of Learners) Near You," *Journal of Jewish Education* 73 (1) (2007), 21–49.

11. These prayers focus on the *Amidah*: Kindergarten—Jewish symbols and *Shema*; first grade—Jewish holidays and *Mi Chamochah*; second grade—Torah and *Avot V'Emahot*; third grade—prophecy and *Gevurot* (along with laying groundwork for Hebrew instruction that begins in fourth grade); fourth grade—Jewish life and *Kedushah*; and fifth grade—Israel and *VeAhavtah*.

12. The figures include Theodor Herzl, Henrietta Szold, Golda Meir, and David Ben-Gurion. The events include the Balfour Declaration, the birth of the State of Israel, and the Six-Day and Yom Kippur Wars.

13. One class examines U.S.–Israel relations, while two others consider Israel–Palestinian relations. The themes of these classes: "Neighbors in a crowded house: Israelis and Palestinians," and "One has to make peace with one's enemies—not with one's friends." Guests speak at the two classes on Israeli Army Day—the children participate in a mock basic training lesson—and on Yom Hashoah. Parents attend the Yom Haazmaut celebration.

14. These events and rituals include birth, brit/covenant, adoption, parenting, creating a Jewish home, Bar/Bat Mitzvah, conversion, wedding, divorce, relationships, aging/illness, women's rituals, end of life, and living a righteous life.

15. These activities include participation in the Mandel Teacher Educator Institute, a Legacy Heritage Foundation conference, and the HUC Alumni Seminar in Jerusalem.

16. Staff members assume responsible extramural roles. One professional, for example, is heavily involved in NFTY (the North American Federation of Temple Youth), Reform's national youth group.

17. Lawrence Cremin, *Popular Education and Its Discontents* (New York: Harper Collins, 1991).

CHAPTER 8

# Beit Knesset Hazon
## A Visionary Synagogue

ISA ARON WITH NACHAMA SKOLNIK MOSKOWITZ

Beit Knesset Hazon, a Reform congregation whose modest building is tucked away on a side street of an East Coast suburb, does not look like an educational powerhouse. At 8:15 on a Sunday morning in November it looks quiet, even a bit sleepy. But as the building fills with the voices of teachers, students, and parents, it becomes clear that this is no ordinary congregation. Every available space, including the back of the social hall and the offices of half the professional staff, are used as classrooms for the *Yesod* (elementary) program, which runs on double sessions. Seven adult classes (including beginning and intermediate Hebrew, Talmud, and a course entitled "What Does it Mean to be Israel?") meet in a public school down the road. Groups of middle school students set out for the sites of their "*ma'asim tovim*" (good deeds) social action projects. From 10:45 to 11:15, in between the first and second sessions, fifty members of the *Alef-Bet* choir sit at the front of the *bimah*, singing in harmony, and with hand motions, while their parents sit, beaming, in the audience. At 1:30, fifteen minutes after the second session has ended, the *Mishpacha* Missions social action group prepares for a visit to a senior citizen center; and the teachers sit down to lunch, to be followed by two and a half hours of professional development. The maintenance staff scurries to and fro with tables and chairs, and the social hall is set up for a sixth grade family education program, which runs from 4:30 to 6:30. And, just to round things off, from 7:00 to 8:30 forty adults meet for a class called "Modern Israel: Beyond the Headlines."

On a different Sunday afternoon one might see one or more of the seven high school *havurot* (friendship groups), such as the Jewish Actor's Workshop or *Sherut* (literally "service"—devoted to community service and social justice). One might, in addition, see *Chug HaSefer* (the book club), a family-based alternative to the religious school that is still in the pilot stage, and a number of different adult classes. All this in addition to the Tuesday and Wednesday afternoon classes, weekday adult classes, and the *Shabbatonim*, that are held off-site.

What makes this rich and variegated menu of educational offerings even more impressive is that it is relatively new, and viewed very much as a work in progress. Ten years ago there was only a religious school that was, in the words of one parent, "really a mess"; ten years from now there are likely to be many additional changes. To fully appreciate Beit Knesset Hazon (BKH)[1] one must understand both its recent past and its aspirations for the future.

## Perfect Storm

> You asked about how it all happened and I started thinking . . . [it was] a bit of a perfect storm . . . This is the congregation that disproves the [idea] that it is all about the rabbi . . . [It] was a lay-driven revolution that was happening here. We did not have rabbinic support. Sometimes we had resistance and sometimes we just had neglect, but it was really a lay-driven thing for many, many years.
>
> —Brenda Hecht, former vice president for learning

Founded in 1949, BKH had approximately 350 member units in 1994, the year Irwin Levy became president of the congregation. "I became president, I think, because no one else wanted to be . . . there was just an apathy that existed in the synagogue," Irwin notes. It was not long before people began coming to him to complain. "Everybody had their own problem. So it became clear to me that we had no direction, we were having a lot of problems."

Irwin decided to bring together a small group of potential leaders for a day-long retreat, at which they could dream together about the synagogue's future. He had been active in the local Federation, and sought advice from a key Federation professional. "I said, 'Carl, I'm in way over my head. I have no idea what I'm doing.' And Carl said 'I'll do whatever I can do to help you.' I said, 'Well I'd like you to come to a meeting and help us form a vision.'"

Everyone present remembers Carl Taller's speech, the same speech he had given before, and would continue to give many times over the years. Wendy Stern, one of the participants at the retreat, recalls:

> Basically he embarrassed us into—he embarrassed me into—thinking seriously about what my Jewish identity meant to me. He said, "How is it that Jews in America, who are among the most highly educated in the history of Jewish life, who know Rembrandt from Cezanne, . . . can name five Shakespearean plays, . . . can speak articulately about almost anything, except if I ask them who Maimonides was, they wouldn't know." I didn't know who Maimonides was, so I'm sitting there thinking, "It's true." What's really sad is that we're generally not embarrassed by our Jewish ignorance. I thought that was really fascinating because I really took seriously almost every other aspect of my life. If I sent my kid to nursery school, I researched it. Vacations I researched. I took seriously almost every other choice in my life, but when it came to their Jewish education, like I said, it was by default.

One of the immediate outcomes of the retreat was that Wendy and a friend created a Torah study group that was led by Bruce Victor, a local Reform rabbi, who had already gained a reputation as a dynamic teacher. He recalls: "I think if you had any really good teacher who had walked in the door to BKH, who loved text and was willing to build the bridge from where the people were to the entrée into the text, people would have flocked . . . people were so hungry and so interested."

In 1997 BKH became one of the first sites of a two-year intensive course of study for adults, sponsored by the Federation; so many people signed up that they had to offer two different classes, with a total of 52 participants. Thanks to the Federation, the synagogue continues to offer a new cohort of this program every two years; today it boasts 350 graduates of the program.

In 2000 the board offered the rabbi an attractive early retirement package, and hired Joseph Tepper, who had been an assistant rabbi at a nearby congregation. Under Rabbi Tepper's leadership, the "perfect storm" gathered force, as the synagogue participated in both Synagogue 2000 and a leadership development program offered by the Federation. With adult learning burgeoning, and a transformation underway in worship, the congregation knew that the next step would be children's education. As Brenda Hecht, another participant in the 1994 retreat, notes, the religious school curriculum "was coloring, more coloring and more coloring. "The adult learning that a lot of us were engaged in put pressure on the religious school, because suddenly we had an experience that was positive and phenomenal . . . We realized that what our kids were getting was so old school, . . . and that there was another way to go about this." As another graduate of the Federation program notes: "[It] gives you this really deep understanding of Torah and history, and then you see that your kids are coloring apples for Rosh HaShanah."

Because of the synagogue's proximity to a university offering a master's in Jewish education, Rabbi Tepper had already identified the educators he wanted to bring on—Sarah Isaacs, who created the synagogue's high school program, and, a year later, Beth Lorch, who became the congregational educator. Beth was a lawyer whose experience as chair of the board of her children's day school motivated her to enroll for a master's in Jewish education. She recalls how she had her eyes on the position at BKH two years before the job became available:

> I was looking for a particular kind of culture, one that was excited about experimentation, and that was willing to engage in a process that would bring all of the constituencies together in partnership . . . And BKH was that kind of place, and so I was very excited about working there. I spoke to Joseph almost two years before I took the job, when they were thinking that they might have a director of congregational learning. Then I took another job at the Federation to bide my time, so that I could wait it out until the board at BKH actually created the position and funded it. It's an entrepreneurial congregation. They enjoy experimentation. They were ready.

Upon arrival, Beth formed a year-long task force on congregational learning.[2] "I told them that I was not going to talk to them about one program for a year, that we had to talk process." The task force met six times over the course of a year; the vision they arrived at can be found, in part, on the congregation's website: "At BKH, we know that each person has a story; each person is on a journey. We assist and enrich the lives of our members and our congregation by providing a wide range of learning opportunities, and multiple gateways, enabling individuals to make choices that are the best with our community. Jewish learning is a lifelong endeavor and we seek to engage all learners from preschool through adult, from novice to expert."

In the seven years since Rabbi Tepper's arrival, the congregation has grown to just under 900 member units, and enrolls 630 students, from nursery school through twelfth grade. Having outgrown its facility, the synagogue has begun to plan for a new facility, which will not be completed for a number of years.

Serving this population are seven full-time professionals: the director of congregational learning, the director of *Havayah* (literally "experience"— grades 6–12), the director of *Yesod* (grades K–5), a family educator, a youth educator, a preschool director, and the newest member of the staff, an early childhood family educator. Integral to the "education team," as they call themselves, are two full-time administrative assistants. In addition, there are at least four significant part-time positions of 16 to 20 hours each (these will be discussed below); and the assistant rabbi devotes approximately a quarter of her time to working with school-age children.

The "perfect storm" continues to this day, as BKH has taken advantage of every new program developed by the Federation and many grants available nationally. The Federation's *Mishpacha* (family) program enabled them to hire their family educator; and they applied funds from another Federation program to create a full-time position for the youth director. In coordination with a Federation-sponsored Jewish Camping Initiative they are actively encouraging parents to send their children to a Jewish camp. The synagogue became a pilot site for *Sherut*, a Jewish Community Relations Council program of service learning for high school students. BKH was among the first cohort of synagogues to receive a grant for family education from a national foundation. And when a local Jewish college decided to create a program of professional development for religious schools, they chose BKH as their pilot site.

In our concluding interview, Beth stressed that the program is a continual work-in-progress. What we observed in the fall of 2007 "[is] where we are at this moment . . . it's iterative—it's going to continue to move . . . One of our best practices is that we we're not satisfied ever with exactly how it is. We haven't landed, and I don't think we ever will."

## Goals

The power and coherence of BKH's educational program lies in the high degree of consensus about its overarching goals. The professional staff, teachers, parents, and even high school students describe the school's aims in similar terms: to create a strong sense community; to make Judaism an integral part of people's lives; and to make Jewish learning a lifelong endeavor.

### Creating a Kehillah Kedoshah — Sacred Community

Although many of BKH's members come from the town in which it is located, congregants also reside in any of thirty other townships, each with its own public school system. It is not uncommon for BKH's children to be among the very few (sometimes the only) Jewish children in their public school classes. For this reason, the primary goal, mentioned by nearly everyone we spoke to, is the creation of a *kehillah kedoshah*, a sacred community.[3]

Rabbi Tepper emphasized this goal from the outset: "As soon as I came in I went into the school and I said, 'If your kids know the alef-bet before everyone's name in the class, everyone gets an F. Don't even open the book the first class.'" As Beth puts it: "We work hard to help faculty understand that it's not all about the content. The content is important, but the community building is also really critically important . . . If we're going to have a feeling of warmth and welcoming and family we have to dedicate some serious time to helping kids know each other."

The consensus among the parents and children we interviewed is that this goal is, to a large extent, achieved. One parent we interviewed noted that "the sense of community is super-strong here." Another parent said: "It's been amazing . . . BKH has given my kids that home where they know that there are other people like them around and that they can establish relationships accordingly."

The tenth and eleventh graders we interviewed all agreed that "you really can't find a community like this anywhere else." Another said, "All the people I know who are part of their church youth groups . . . it's not the same. Everyone I know [says], 'I'm so jealous of the kind of community [you have]. I wish I was Jewish.'" And another: "My Temple friends and I will talk about retreats, about Temple, about how much fun we have. And my secular friends are usually like 'wow that sounds really fun. I kind of wish I was Jewish so I could go to your temple and have that much fun.'" One student invited a friend from public school to a BKH youth group activity. The friend liked it so much she persuaded her parents to join the synagogue. "She joined the temple because it was awesome."

## Making Judaism an Integral Part of the Students' Lives

As in most congregations, parents at BKH range from those who lead deeply committed Jewish lives to those whose sole motivation for joining a synagogue is so that their children can "be Bar-Mitzvahed." The challenge facing the education staff (and, indeed, the entire professional staff) is how to deepen the experience of those who want only minimal engagement. The way to accomplish this, Beth believes, is to make as many possible connections between the learning that goes on at BKH and people's lives. "If we're integrating the learning and connecting it with things that are important to these kids in their own lives and connecting these topics with each other, there's a greater probability that they'll retain some of it."

Dr. Kineret Blum, the director of the *Yesod* program, phrased this goal in terms of "building a Jewish life vocabulary." Key terms in this vocabulary are *kehillah kedoshah, tikkun olam* (repair of the world through social justice), and the notion that people are created *b'tzelem elohim* (in the image of God). These concepts are woven into every aspect of the program, from the lessons that are taught in the *Yesod* program, to the songs that are sung on retreats, and, most prominently, in the program for students in the sixth and seventh grades, which is centered on these core concepts.

## Motivating Students to Become Lifelong Jewish Learners

Keenly aware that students are enrolled in the formal part of their program for, at most, 100 hours a year, BKH's staff has a third goal—motivating students to continue learning at a Jewish summer camp, in college, and on into adulthood. As Beth puts it: "We want them to feel like [learning] is going to be part of their lives forever; we want them to want that and to seek it out at different stages of their lives." Ethan Cohn, coordinator of the high school retreats, says of his program, "Obviously you don't have the same amount of time to cover material, so what we're doing is really much more about exposure and passion . . . It's more about getting them excited and passionate about what they're learning, in the hope that they'll go on and do more study about it."

But motivation is only one of the keys to lifelong learning; two other elements are having a firm foundation and having the confidence in one's abilities to continue learning. Thus Hebrew is taught from grades K through 7; and text study, primarily the Torah and *Pirkei Avot*, is infused throughout the curriculum. Rabbi Tepper notes: "The most important thing is giving them the tools to explore Judaism outside of the synagogue, recognizing that we're only a part of the story. They need to have a familiarity with the basic building blocks . . . The other thing is to show them the complexity and not be afraid to access it." He adds, "We're just a part of the puzzle. So our job is to enable other learning environments." Bulletin boards in the synagogue's hallways are covered with flyers advertising the local Reform day school, a nearby URJ summer camp, and a variety of Israel trips. Thanks to the Federation's camping initiative, $1,000 "camper-ships" are available for up to twenty first-time attendees of a Jewish overnight camp. During the summer of 2007 this program attracted fourteen BKH children; in 2008 they expected to enroll twenty new campers.

## Assumptions

In its effort to achieve these goals, BKH has developed an ambitious, carefully articulated program that includes both formal and experiential learning. In this section we will explore the assumptions that underlie their approach.

### *Experiential Learning*

> We know that . . . real learning happens best when it is connected with experience. Consequently our learning programs integrate formal and informal learning, joining academic and experiential approaches.
>
> —The BKH website

John Dewey's dictum that experience is the basis of all true education has been the watchword of progressive education for over a century.[4] In keeping with this principle, BKH attempts to add an experiential component to all its educational offerings. This principle is most evident in the high school program, which is termed *Havayah*, Hebrew for experience. In this program students choose among an array of *havurot* that combine an activity such as acting, cooking, or wilderness exploration with text study; they also attend retreats that teach Jewish history through films, simulations, and informal activities. The *Havayah* program will be discussed in greater detail below.

Experiential learning in the sixth and seventh grades centers on an eighteen-month program of service learning, called *Ma'asim Tovim* (good deeds), which will also be discussed below. And while the K–5 *Yesod* (elementary) program is centered on formal classroom instruction, students are encouraged to participate in a wide range of informal options, including youth groups (which begin in Kindergarten), *shul*-ins, choirs for every age, the drama *chug* (club), family-based social action projects, a Rosh Chodesh program called "It's a Girl Thing," and "Rak Shabbat"[5] (an informal worship service with contemporary Jewish music, held several times a year). Once a year the entire *Yesod* program participates in a large-scale experiential project. In the 2005–06 year it was an archeological dig in a mock tel that contained 500 pottery shards and replicas. This served as the vehicle for learning about life in Ancient Israel; groups at every age level participated in the dig and/or related classes and workshops. In the 2006–07 school year, as the synagogue had begun to plan for its new building, the all-school project was the creation of a replica of the Second Temple, made up of 35,000 Legos. Designed by Dr. Blum's husband, who is an engineer, the replica was 8 feet long and 4 feet wide. Before they began building, the students learned about the Temple, its ceremonies and rituals, and the ways in which its architecture and appurtenances are represented in contemporary Jewish symbols. Then each class received a packet of Legos with instructions for its particular part—the walls, the columns, the menorah, and so on. The experience served as a springboard for discussing how it takes an entire community to create a synagogue.

## Multiple Gateways and Differentiated Instruction

In keeping with its goal of building community, BKH believes in accommodating a range of learning styles and special needs. When Dr. Blum became the director of the *Yesod* program in 2005, she began requiring (and paying teachers to attend) ten hours of orientation at the beginning of the year, followed by ten hours of staff development during the year. Along with classroom management, her highest priority was helping teachers utilize a wide range of teaching methods, in keeping with Howard Gardner's theory of multiple intelligences.[6] Frontal teaching was discouraged, and teachers who were unable or unwilling to change their teaching style either left on their own accord or were let go. Two years later, the newer techniques had taken hold. In most of the classes we observed, students worked in small groups or rotated through learning centers. Hebrew decoding, in particular, was taught through activities that appealed to different intelligences. We observed Kindergarten students forming Hebrew letters with their bodies; students in the first grade forming letters in clay, and drawing them in chalk on miniature slates; students in second grade sounding out letters in different voices, "like a chipmunk," "like a ghost," and so on.

Two special education consultants (one works 15 hours a week, the other 8–10 hours a week) are on hand on both Sundays and weekdays to observe classes and work with students and teachers, to assure that students are on task and that teachers receive the assistance they require; the specialists also lead a support group for parents of children with special needs.

Barbara, one of the consultants, notes that the school deserves credit for its willingness to try a range of techniques with students who are struggling to keep up. And she gives the teachers high marks for their desire to reach each student, however difficult. "They care about the kids individually. Everybody really wants to find the best way they can to learn about them as learners." Teachers, for their part, appreciate the kind of assistance they are receiving in dealing with all manner of challenges. One teacher, Nessa, described a student in her fifth grade class who began the year with a terrible attitude. Having "decided that she hated Hebrew school . . . [s]he was a black hole of despair . . . She sat through two hours of Hebrew school with her arms crossed and . . . a sulk on her face." By the third session, Nessa reported, "she giggled twice in class." "She has moved in the right direction, but I can't say that it is me. It's the special-needs staff who have given me great clues. The youth director, Cory, took her and gave her a great time at Rak Shabbat this past Friday. And we've been together totally under the radar for her to really bring her to a place where she could open up and see, hey, this is fun."

At the opening session of the fall *Havayah* retreat, one eighth grader seemed unable to sit still and pay attention. As he began to distract the boys sitting next to him, the youth educator, Cory, stepped in to calm him down. Later Cory explained that this boy has ADHD and a number of other learning disabilities, and that he (Cory) has been cultivating a relationship with him. Rather than excluding this boy from the program, Cory was determined to help him make it through the weekend, having participated appropriately, without causing undue interruptions. And that is, indeed, how it turned out.

Parents applaud BKH's inclusive and flexible stance: "Any time there has been an issue," one says, "the special-needs coordinators or Kineret have always been more than happy to sit with me. And I know that last year when [my daughter] was struggling a little bit they had [one of the teachers who also does tutoring] come in, and she would take her and maybe another child or two out, and they would have special reading time, so they practiced a little bit extra one-on-one." Another parent reports, "They're always looking at what's going to engage the kids and what's going to work for different families with different schedules. I think they really try to accommodate a lot of different family structures and attitudes."

## People Will Pay for High Quality Education

[When I ask for a higher budget allocation for some program] I get an initial, "I can't believe we're going to spend the money on this!" But then, almost always, the money comes through. If we have a great idea, the funding happens. Sometimes it's because an individual steps up to the plate. Sometimes it's because the board says this is too important for us not to do. So the funding has been there.

—Beth Lorch

BKH is the only congregation we know of that has seven full-time education professionals, not to mention a significant number of well-paid, long-term, part timers. Naturally, we were most curious to find out how they are able to afford this level of staffing. There seem to be three answers to this question: First, some of the money (about 10%) comes from grants. Second, the strong value placed on Jewish learning among lay leaders, between 325 and 350 of whom participate in ongoing study groups of various sorts, translates into steadfast support for children's education. Third, and most surprising, parents pay a great deal, over and above dues, for their children's Jewish education.

In 2007–08, BKH's education budget was a little over $1.25 million. This included the salaries of all education department employees, but not the assistant rabbi, and only part of the salaries of the song leaders. Of this about $300,000 came from the congregation's overall budget. Grants from the Federation and private donors brought in about $150,000. The remaining $800,000 came from tuition. Unlike many congregations that assume that the cost of children's education should be covered by dues and shared equally among all members, regardless of whether or not they have children, BKH charges separately for each program. So, for example, in 2007–08, tuition for one child in the grades 3–5 was $757 (including a discount for early registration); for grade 7 it was $995; and for grades 8–10 it was $625. Thus a family with one child in each of these programs paid an additional $2,377 over membership dues of $2,800. Scholarships and dues abatements are available to those in need. Fifty-nine children received scholarships averaging $700; in addition, 18 percent of congregants paid reduced dues, with an average reduction of $1,510. Adult courses taught by the members of the professional staff are free; in 2007–08 there were thirteen courses and/or programs of this type. There were also eight courses taught by outside instructors, with tuition ranging from $100 to $500; if a minimum number of students does not enroll that class is cancelled.

The fact that membership at BKH continues to increase demonstrates that people are, indeed, willing to pay for quality education programs. Nonetheless, the synagogue's board and finance committee is considering whether dues should be increased, and whether, alongside the capital campaign for a new building, they should be raising money for an endowment.

## *"Hire the Best Possible People and Then Empower Them to Do the Job"*

Job descriptions at BKH are somewhat fluid. For example, in addition to her work with families, Naomi Vogel, the family educator, coordinates the alternative religious school program, *Chug HaSefer*, teaches sixth graders two nights a week, and runs a sixth and seventh grade program for girls called "It's a Girl Thing." Cory Misrky, the youth educator, teaches seventh grade two nights a week and leads *Sherut*, the social justice *havurah*, in addition to directing and/or supervising the youth groups. Cory explains that in 2006–07 he and Naomi each taught only one night apiece, but decided that in 2007–08 they both needed to be there on both nights, so each of them would have an opportunity to get to know all the students. "It's really hard when you don't have continued face time with the majority of your target population, to create those bonds and those connections . . . So we said . . . 'we need to be teaching both nights.' [This year] we're seeing a huge difference." This kind of dedication is typical of all members of the professional staff, who are continually reflecting on the challenges they face and trying out new ways to meet them.

## *Collaboration*

Being "empowered to do the job," does not mean bearing sole responsibility for it. On the contrary, one of BKH's great strengths is the degree of collaboration among members of the professional staff. The major programs that were created since Beth's arrival in 2003 have all been the product of teamwork; the new curriculum for *Yesod* was also written by a team. Though this is not the most efficient way of doing things, Beth sees it as well worth the time: "It takes a lot of time to do program planning in a group, but my personal belief is that that kind of collaboration always results in a better product, and so we make the time to do it."

Over and above the collaboration that takes place in planning and teaching, there is a strong sense of camaraderie and collegiality among members of the professional staff. Dr. Blum offers an example: "Naomi is not involved directly with my program, but she comes in and says, 'What do you need from me?' That's the kind of etiquette people have. And I will never go home before asking her if she needs something because . . . that's the way it is."

This sense of partnership filters down to the teachers as well. Shira, a college student, who teaches second grade, recalls: "I came here just having experience as a *madricha* (teaching assistant) . . . and I basically had no idea what I was doing, and I very much felt supported. When I started out there was a lesson plan system and I really was able to get feedback right away, and that was really great. I had a really challenging class my second year . . . it just worked out that I had a lot of special needs kids in that one class. And within a month I had another teacher co-teaching with me, and they provided the support system that I needed."

This culture of collegiality and support extends to lay people as well, beginning with parents and extending to lay leaders. Sadie, a college student who teaches first grade, says of the parents she has encountered: "I have loved working with the parents at BKH . . . They're always looking for ways to join in; 'how can I help?' 'what can I do at home with my kids?' 'my kid missed class, what work can I do?' And a lot of times it's not me sending homework with them. It's they who jump in . . . They want to make the education the best they can for their kids."

When the local Jewish college approached Dr. Blum, asking if they might pilot a staff development program at BKH, she needed to find funding for ten additional hours of professional development a year for twenty-two teachers (she already had the funds for 20 hours, but the program called for 30 hours), for a total of approximately $10,000. She was able to find some money by trimming the *Yesod* budget, and then she sought advice from the *Yesod* Committee. They decided to write a letter to parents suggesting that they honor their children's teachers by making a contribution to this special fund. In that way they raised $2,500. Kineret was prepared to cut the number of participants in the program, perhaps excluding the college students who would be leaving upon graduation in a year or two. But the Finance Committee decided that this was an important program, and that distinctions should not made between the various teachers; so they allocated the additional funds.

## Continual Experimentation, Reflection, and Assessment

The reflective and experimental spirit of the 1994 lay retreat seems to pervade the entire synagogue. As Beth puts it, "This is a community that really wants us to constantly be thinking about what we were doing and what we can be doing." Explaining that she doesn't believe in making long-range plans, Beth notes, "The plan is an evolving plan and we're constantly looking at what we're doing and how we're doing it and what's the next best way to do it."

As they started to create new programs, the education team realized that it would be helpful to have them evaluated by an outside evaluator, and so they brought in Dr. Denise Quinn. Dr. Quinn, whose background is in the evaluation of community-based healthcare programs, and who, incidentally, is not Jewish, has served as the evaluator of a variety of programs for the Federation and local Jewish agencies. Her approach to evaluation is collaborative. She begins by meeting with the staff two or three times to clarify the goals of the program, and to consider the kind of data that would be needed to determine whether the goals have been met. Then they work out together how these data will be collected; some of the methods they have used are an online survey, interviews, and analyzing samples of student journals. After the data is collected, Dr. Quinn writes a preliminary report, which she then shares with the staff at a group meeting. The willingness of the educators to learn from feedback, she says, is crucial. "I really dislike it when I give feedback, and everybody listens, and you just know nothing is going to be different." In contrast, she finds working BKH very rewarding: "What I like about working here is that they really believe in evaluation. The key variable in predicting the success of congregation-based learning is the willingness to ask for feedback, to collect data, to inform what you do . . . This is a group that asks ahead of time, asks during, asks after, revises, does another iteration, and they do it based on information rather than anecdote and so on, and I admire them for that very much."

## The Educational Programs, in Depth

The distribution of Beit Knesset Hazon's 630 children among its five programs is shown in table 8.1. The next four sections describe the four programs for school-age children: the *Havayah* high school program, the Bar/Bat Mitzvah program entitled Bar Mitzvah Adventure, the alternative *Chug HaSefer*, and the K–5 *Yesod*.

### Havaya: The High School Program

> I learned how to look at different aspects of things; different ways of doing things—like cooking. I've learned about being Jewish and that being Jewish doesn't necessarily mean you have to sit in services for a couple of hours and listen to words and not know what they mean. It can be having fun and learning. Now I understand more about what I'm singing about [when at services]. *You don't have to be bored to be Jewish.*
>
> —From an evaluation of the *Havayah* program (emphasis added)

In 2002, two years after Rabbi Tepper's arrival at BKH, he recruited Sarah Isaacs, who had just received a master's degree in Jewish communal service, to be BKH's congregational educator. Sarah was concerned that that job was not very well defined, and that the congregation might not be ready for such a position; she chose, instead, to be the youth educator. At the time, BKH's retention rate after Bar/Bat Mitzvah was less than 25 per-

Table 8.1

| | |
|---|---|
| *Havayah* (grades 8–12) | 88 |
| Bar Mitzvah Adventure (6–7) | 125 |
| *Yesod* (K–5) | 345 |
| *Chug HaSefer* (a pilot alternative for grades 3–5) | 34 |
| Preschool | 32 |

cent, and attendance for those enrolled was "maybe 50 percent on any given week," so it was clear to both Sarah and Rabbi Tepper that an entirely new approach was needed than the once-a-week classes that were being offered.

Sarah set about researching alternatives, but was disappointed to find that "there wasn't a whole lot going on that was different." Fortunately, as a participant in a leadership seminar at a local university, she was given an assignment to articulate her vision of Jewish education. "I started thinking about how would you create a program that was experiential in nature, that would interest kids, that would get them involved, that would have a flexible enough schedule for them to be able to come with good attendance." She came up with the idea of a program for eighth graders that included interest-based *havurot* and a number of retreats. When she shared this idea with Rabbi Tepper at one of their ongoing meetings, he suggested that the program might be good for the entire high school.

In retrospect, "we probably should have involved more people in the planning process instead of just dreaming it up and saying okay here's our new program." BKH had never had retreats before, and many high school students simply dropped out, rather than going on the retreats. Nonetheless, Sarah persisted, with the complete backing of the rabbi and the board. "We felt really strongly that the retreats were an important part of the program, and that with time people would see that." As the program's brochure explains:

> We believe very strongly in the power of informal Jewish education. In informal settings such as retreats students learn together in the context of authentic Jewish community. Students participate in Shabbat services, engage in community building, and socialize over the course of a weekend. These interactions deepen bonds and comfort with peers, which results in an increased readiness to learn. A retreat format also provides more flexibility in terms of class timing, space, resources and staff than a classroom format, allowing us to provide the highest quality learning program for our students.

The *Havayah* program, as it came to be called, has both a "Confirmation track" and "à la carte" options; those choosing "à la carte" options can be involved in some of the programs, without committing to the entire package. In the Confirmation track, students in grades 8–10 enroll in one of a number of *havurot*, and are required to attend two out of three weekend retreats. The *havurot* meet approximately twice a month for anywhere between one and five hours. Though the themes of the *havurot* vary somewhat from year to year based on students' interest and instructor availability, *havurot* that are offered annually include Jewish Actors' Workshop, Youth Choir, Tastes of Judaism (cooking), *Madrichim* (teaching assistants in the *Yesod* program), and *Sherut* (social action). For post-Confirmation students in eleventh and twelfth grades there is a leadership *havurah*.

All of the *havurot* span grades 8–10, and some go through grade 12. The study of Jewish texts is woven into all of the *havurot*, and a family component is built in as well. For example, students in the Jewish Actors Workshop (called JAWS for short) read and discuss books and/or texts on which the plays they will be performing are based. Some previous productions are: *The Story of Anne Frank, Joseph and the Amazing Technicolor Dreamcoat*, and a Neil Simon play, *God's Favorite* (a contemporary Job story). During the 2007–08 school year they studied Talmudic texts on Rabbi Akiba and wrote a play about his life that incorporated songs from the popular Jewish singer Sam Glaser. Parents and other family members participate in JAWs by helping to build the sets for the production.

*Sherut*, the *havurah* with the most students (28 in all), is part of a project run by the Federation's Jewish Community Relations Council. A flyer describing *Sherut* explains its purpose (and its name) in the following way:

> *Sherut* is an initiative to promote community service and social justice among [our city's] Jewish youth. Say what? Actually, it's simple. Sherut is an *awesome program* . . . It incorporates social action, social justice (yes, these are two different things), *Jewish learning* and a whole lot of fun! This creates a balance between studying text and learning, going out and doing "community service," and *having fun with your friends*. [emphasis in the original]

BKH's students are part of *Sherut's* hunger and homelessness track, volunteering at a shelter for homeless veterans.

*Havayah* retreats are held three times a year, with topics that rotate on a triennial cycle: world Jewish history one year, American Jewish history the next, and Israel the third year. In 2007–08 the theme was American Jewish history, and one of us was present at the first retreat of the year, which covered the period from 1492 through the 1940s. Among the segments of the program were:

- A discussion of the diary entry of a *converso* (secret Jew) who traveled to the New World with Christopher Columbus;
- A debate on whether the Jewish community of 1850 should take a position on slavery;
- A simulation of the arrival of immigrants to Ellis Island, in which each participant was given an identity, and some were welcomed in, while others were denied entry;
- A simulation of a sweatshop, coupled with the reading of a newspaper account of the Triangle Shirt Company fire.

As with all of BKH's programs, staff members were given detailed lesson plans, and each participant was given an attractively produced booklet with all the relevant documents. The quality of the facilitation varied from session to session, and, given the limited time allotted to all the disparate activities, it seems unlikely that participants came away with a coherent narrative about American Jewish history. Certainly, these activities bore little connection to the high level history courses they were taking in their secular schools. But most of the students remained engaged throughout the program, participating appropriately (and sometimes showing great insight) in the discussions.

The retreat program included much more than content delivery. In fact the informal part of the program may have left a deeper impression than the formal part. There were hour-long *tefillot* (prayer services) on both Friday night and Shabbat morning that included a number of short *iyunei tefillah* (prayer discussions). *Tefillot* were led by Nathaniel, a college student who is an experienced songleader, and by Rabbi Tamara Davids, the assistant rabbi.

Perhaps the most memorable moment of the retreat, at least to the staff (who discussed it at their Monday staff meeting) arose spontaneously during the Friday night service, when an eighth grade boy asked: "Why don't we ever clap?" Upon clarification, it turned out that he was asking why they never applauded at the end of a service. Rabbi Davids turned the question back to him, and then to the other participants: "What do *you* think?" Among the answers:

"It disturbs the mood."

"You would be patting yourself on the back."

"Prayer is just a normal part of life, and you don't need to clap for that."

"We show recognition by our silence."

Rabbi Davids asked, "Have you ever been at a service at BKH when people applaud?" Rabbi Tepper tells them, "when someone does well at a *mitzvah*, we say *tizku l'mitzvot*—may you have the privilege of performing more *mitzvot*"

This discussion highlights a characteristic we saw often in our observations—the staff's openness to the questions and comments made by students, and their habit of not giving definitive answers, but turning to the students for answers. As a parent interviewed by Dr. Quinn noted: "The clergy's vision or mission is to create a dialogue and debate within the congregation as a way to create and foster community. There have been times when we have turned to the leadership for an answer but we get the opposite—they think we have the answer if we debate it enough." Thus, rather than answering the question herself, and proceeding with the rest of the service, Rabbi Davids was eager to engage in this discussion because it stemmed from a students' curiosity. In fact, later in the service, Rabbi Davids noted, "I was going to do a teaching, but [what I had planned] was not nearly as good as the conversation we had [about clapping]."

Each night, after the end of the official program, a film was shown—*The Frisco Kid* on Friday night and *The Chosen* on Saturday. And, in keeping with the value he places on community building, Rabbi Tepper came by after the film ended (the retreat was held at a conference center about 45 minutes from the synagogue), to play games and hang out with anyone who was still awake.

All in all, 88 students in grades 8–12 participate in the *Havayah* program. This represents a retention rate of between 65 and 68 percent (up from 23 percent in 2004).[7] The education team is hopeful that as students in the improved *Yesod* and Bar/Bat Mitzvah programs get to eighth grade the retention rate will continue to increase. In addition, they see many improvements that can be made. Esther Fisher, who was, when we visited, brand new in her position as *Havayah* coordinator (Sarah had taken a position in a high school program offered at a nearby university) wonders if the "retreat culture" has sufficiently taken hold so that attendance at all three retreats, rather than simply two, can be required, She was brought in with a mandate to improve the program for eleventh and twelfth graders, and to deepen the program's content throughout. As Rabbi Davids notes: "We need to do more substantive teaching so that the kids come out of *Havayah* not just having had two or three fun retreats and knowing a few basic names and dates from various aspects of Jewish history, but so that they're ready to be Jewish in college and so that they have the tools that they need to make Jewish decisions beyond college, so that they're challenged rather than just entertained. So I think that that's the real overhaul that's going to happen."

## The Bar Mitzvah Adventure (BMA)

In 2005, Beth's second year at BKH, she, Sarah, and Cory created the BMA program for sixth and seventh graders. This complex program includes:

- Weekly sessions that include 45 minutes of Hebrew, 45 minutes of text study, and 30 minutes of *teffilah*;
- An annual retreat;
- Nine family sessions, six in the sixth grade (including one devoted to writing the students' *D'var Torah* (Torah teaching) for their Bar/Bat Mitzvah) and three in the seventh;
- Two meetings with Rabbi Davids devoted to writing a *D'var Torah* to be delivered at the student's Bar/Bat Mitzvah service, and two meetings with Rabbi Tepper devoted to writing a personal prayer.

In addition to this, the program has a *ma'asim tovim* (good deeds) component, described in the parent manual in the following way: "Part of becoming a bar or bat mitzvah is becoming an active and responsible member of the community. Over the course of the BMA experience, students will engage in classroom learning about mitzvot and ethics, social justice training workshops, long-term volunteer service activities, and service learning."

From October through February of the sixth grade, students participate in weekly classes that center on Jewish values, many of them drawn from *Pirkei Avot* (Ethics of the Fathers). Beginning in March and continuing through the seventh grade, the students no longer attend class, but rather spend 1½–3 hours every 2–4 weeks volunteering at one of 8–10 places, such as a food bank or a recycling center. To make the connection between Judaism and their volunteer work, each site visit begins with a 20–30 minute text study; to maximize the personal impact of the work, students keep journals.

In November, we observed a family program that introduced the concept of *Ma'asim Tovim* and began the process of finding an appropriate volunteer opportunity for each student. Approximately 50 families (in most cases one parent and a child, but in some cases both parents) sat around 14 tables in the social hall. On the screen up front was a saying by Rabbi Harold Kushner: "When you are kind to others, it not only changes you, it changes the world." The outline of the program was as follows:

1. Each table had a stack of 26 blue cards, each describing an activity, such as: feeding the hungry, freeing captive Jews, showing hospitality to strangers, and advocating for peace. There were also five white cards, each with a Hebrew term on one side and an explanation of that term on the other. The terms were: *Gemilut Hasadim, Mitzvot, Tzedakah, Ma'asim Tovim*, and *Tikkun Olam*. Participants were asked to work together to put the blue cards into the categories represented by the white cards. The goal of the activity was for participants to familiarize themselves with these different categories, which, it was acknowledged, have overlapping meanings.

2. A clip from the movie *Pay It Forward* was shown, in which a middle school teacher gives his students an assignment to find a way to change the world.

3. Following this, the children (together with their parents) were asked to fill out a worksheet with three questions:
   • What do you want to change in the world?
   • Why do you want to make this change?
   • How can you help make this change?
   Students were then asked to look, once again, at the white cards on the table, to see which of the cards fit most closely to the answers on their worksheet. The faculty circulated in order to help out.

4. At this point, signs that had been posted all around the room were uncovered. Each sign corresponded to one of the 26 blue cards. The students and their parents were asked to sit at the table nearest to the sign that most closely approximated the way in which they wanted to change the world. The most popular activity was planting trees/protecting the environment; other areas that drew a significant number of students were supporting those with disabilities/healing the sick; providing shelter/providing clothing/feeding the hungry; and helping children who are less fortunate.

5. Students were given 16 green cards, each with a short saying from the Bible, Talmud, or a Jewish philosopher, and asked to discuss with oth-

ers at their table the saying that best reflected how they felt about participating in the *Ma'asim Tovim* program.

6. A short music video entitled "If Everyone Cared" was shown; it focused on individuals who made a difference (such as Nelson Mandela and the founder of Amnesty International), and ended with a quotation from Margaret Mead: "Never doubt that a small group of committed people can change the world. Indeed, it is the only thing that ever has."

7. Finally, the logistics of the program were explained. The *Ma'asim Tovim* coordinator (a graduate student who works 20 hours a week) would contact sites that had been part of the project in previous years, and find new sites, if necessary.

This well-crafted program introduced students and their parents to the value concepts that undergird the *Ma'asim Tovim* program; connected these concepts to both Jewish texts and popular American culture; and challenged the students to articulate how a particular social action project might embody these values. Students and their parents were fully engaged throughout the three-hour program. Excitement about the projects was palpable, with many staying on after the official ending of the program to ask questions and discuss arrangements.

We found the BMA classroom sessions more mixed. Given BKH's emphasis on small groups and learning centers, we were surprised to find two classes in which students were decoding Hebrew aloud in front of the whole class; not surprisingly, the students who weren't reciting were tuned out. In one of these classes the teacher launched into a long and inaccurate digression about the difference between two vowels. Another teacher had great difficulty managing his classroom. In another class, students debating whether Jacob acted correctly or incorrectly when he dressed up as Esau in order to receive his father's blessing made broad generalizations, some of them incorrect, without any reference to the text. Midway into the lesson the teacher realized that she should have reviewed the basics of the story, but by that point the students were calling out their answers, and the opportunity for a thoughtful discussion had been lost.

In contrast, when teachers had good content knowledge and asked thought-provoking questions, the students were enticed into conversations that deepened their understandings of Judaism. For instance, we observed a class entitled "Hip Hop Midrash," taught by Cory, the youth educator. Their point of departure was a song entitled "Dear Mr. President," by the band Pink, which includes the following verses:

Dear Mr. President,
Come take a walk with me.
Let's pretend we're just two people and
You're not better than me.
I'd like to ask you some questions if we can speak honestly.

What do you feel when you see all the homeless on the street?
Who do you pray for at night before you go to sleep?
What do you feel when you look in the mirror?
Are you proud?

After discussing the song on its own terms, students considered it within a context of Jewish emphasis on *tikkun olam*. Quite impressively, the students made a number of connections from past learning and experiences. Toward the end of the lesson, the class conversation included:

*Student:* The song is really deep.

*Student:* It has to do with the issues that Bush isn't dealing with now.

*Student:* Maybe a lot of people have these issues and they feel really passionate about this.

*Cory:* You're all on the money with this! Today in my email there was a card of social action blessings from the Union for Reform Judaism. I wondered what this email has to do with me. Then I realized this is stuff that I do in my life!

Cory showed the students the words of the blessing on the card, a photocopy of which was on the handout he had given them. A student looked at the blessing, and asked: "Is this the na-na-na song?" referring to one of the songs sung often at the youth group, which includes the blessing. Cory excitedly gave the boy a "high five":

*Cory:* Yes! 10 points! Why do we have a blessing . . . for giving us the opportunity to mend the world?

*Student:* He or She [referring to God] is giving us the opportunity to make the world a better place if you choose to do it. If everyone cared.

*Student:* What it's saying is that they're thankful that God didn't make the world a perfect place, but gave *us* the opportunity to make it a perfect place.

*Student:* God gave us the supplies and resources, but we need to do it. If He just made the world a perfect place we wouldn't learn from our mistakes. This helps us learn from our mistakes.

*Cory:* That's awesome! That's incredible!

Like most of the teachers at BKH, Cory praised his students effusively for interesting thoughts, for making connections, and for their engagement in the learning. This was the norm, in almost every classroom we visited.

## Chug HaSefer

In rethinking the program for students in grades K–5, Beth worked on two different tracks simultaneously—improving the *Yesod* program, which meets twice a week, and creating an alternate model of the religious school, one that would involve parents more deeply in their children's education. The alternative program, *Chug HaSefer*, began as a pilot in 2005, with grades 4 and 5, and expanded to the third grade in 2007, but was still very small, with a total of 34 students. It has three components:

- Students read Jewish books and complete a series of assignments related to the books. Parents are also asked to read the books, so that they can discuss them with their children. Approximately every six weeks, students come together to discuss their reading, and to study traditional Jewish texts related to the reading.
- Students study Hebrew in a number of possible ways: in small groups, with other *Chug HaSefer* students; through private tutoring; or at the local Reform day school. These options make the program available to students who attend day school, but whose parents want them to be connected to the synagogue community, as well as to students whose learning disabilities prevent them from being in the regular *Yesod* program.
- Families are brought together for Shabbat celebrations and *tzedakah* projects.

*Chug HaSefer* is based on the assumption that time spent reading at home and in discussion with parents is equal to, or better than, time spent in formal classes. Because the program was designed to accommodate students with learning disabilities, parents whose children read at or above grade level are somewhat frustrated that the books they read are not sufficiently challenging, though they understand, and tacitly endorse, the ideal of inclusivity. Beth argues that the level of challenge in the books is beside the point, which is for parents and children to be discussing important Jewish issues together: "If we choose good books and ask [appropriate] trigger questions, it enables families to engage in a really important serious dialogue about being Jewish, that I think really helps to inform these kids' sense of who they are as Jews. And not only that, but they see their parents doing it with them in a way that the kids in a regular religious school don't."

Although *Chug HaSefer* meets much less frequently than *Yesod*, the parents we interviewed found that it gave their children a strong sense of community, perhaps because the sessions are less formal or perhaps because the parents are involved. One mother commented: "For my third grader, who tends to be an introvert, I wanted to sort of force her to develop more bonds with other people. *Chug HaSefer* seems to be working because it's smaller."

We observed the opening session of the pilot for third graders. Ten students, Naomi, the family educator, and a teaching assistant sat on the carpet in a large, open room. The picture book that children had read with their parents was *When Zaydeh Danced on Eldridge Street,* by Elsa Okon Rael. It tells the story of a young girl who visits her grandparents on the eve of *Simchat Torah.* Knowing her grandfather (Zaydeh) as a demanding, stooped over old man, she is amazed to experience a different side of him. Matched with the book, and the focus of the day's lesson, was a verse from *Pirkei Avot* (Ethics of the Fathers)1:6: "Obtain for yourself a teacher, get for yourself a friend, and judge every person favorably."

We arrived too late for the beginning of the session, which tied the book to the Jewish text, but observed a number of different activities. The children engaged in a discussion that examined the text in relation to situations in their own lives. In the discussion below, note the connections that the students make, as well as the addition of the opinion of Rashi, a Jewish commentator from the eleventh century:

*Naomi:* We're going to explore what it means to judge everyone equally.

*Student:* If you're playing a game, don't exclude anyone.

*Naomi:* Very good

*Student:* If you yell at your friend they're going to yell at you.

*Naomi:* So it's like treating someone like you want to be treated? What if you see two people whispering to the side—what are you thinking?

*Several students:* They are talking about you.

*Naomi:* How do you know if it's good or bad? What if they're talking about your birthday present?

*Student:* You'd know if they are very carefully whispering, not talking aloud.

*Naomi:* Could someone read for me the Rashi? *(on a sheet that had been handed out).*

*Student:* "Unless one knows for sure, one should believe that other people's actions are all good."

*Naomi:* How does this go against what we just said?

*Student:* If they're whispering, you don't know if they're talking about something good or bad.

In this discussion, and others that were interspersed throughout the session, we were impressed by questions that challeneged students to think at a high level, and apply the verse from *Pirkei Avot* to their own lives. However, we felt that some of the activities, such as a word search and matching labels with photographs, were pitched at a lower level, and felt a little like busy work. And we, like some of the parents, wondered why a picture book, rather than a novel, had been assigned.[8] While we appreciated the value of including students whose learning disabilities make it difficult for them to read at grade level, we wondered if those students might be read to by their parents.

## Yesod

By all accounts, the program that was in need of the most work when Beth assumed her position was *Yesod*—the K–5 religious school; and, by all accounts, the changes in *Yesod* have been dramatic. It was not entirely clear, at the outset, that the program would remain in existence. Rabbi Tepper fully expected that it would be dismantled and replaced by an alternative model like *Chug HaSefer.* But Beth felt strongly that many parents wanted a traditional religious school, and would not participate in an alternative. Rabbi Tepper recalls: "I would say, 'Beth why are you spending your time on *Yesod*? I brought you here to develop an alternative program and watch [*Yesod*] die.' And she said, 'You can't let it die. We have too many people in the program. It's unfair to them to have their children learning in a program that's not excellent.' I actually think she believed that it's a good model . . . And she would keep explaining and I would sometimes get frustrated . . . And she invested in *Yesod*."

Though Beth's reconstruction of *Yesod* began soon after her arrival, the process was greatly accelerated in the fall of 2005, when Dr. Kineret Blum came on as director. Dr. Blum, who was born in Israel, has a Ph.D. in teaching and curriculum and had worked at the local Bureau of Jewish Education, first as a consultant to religious schools, then in family education, and finally as coordinator of a partnership program with a city in Israel. When funding for that position dried up, she was intrigued by the opening at BKH, because it had already gained the reputation of having a serious commitment to education. In retrospect, she notes, with a wry smile, "It was a good thing I did not know the disarray that the program was in." The curriculum was outdated, the teaching was mostly frontal and formal; not surprisingly, there were serious problems with classroom management.

The change in the two years since Dr. Blum's arrival have been dramatic. As one mother recalls: "When my now third grader was in kindergarten, I was horrified. This is slightly overstating it, but the things that she brought home—the stupidest worksheets. They were so boring . . . And it has gotten better every year since then, as the teachers get more training."

The high school students we interviewed had similar observations:

When we were in elementary school and middle school it was kind of boring. We all hated it. But the religious education program got a major overhaul, and . . . the Temple was starting to do all sorts of great new things and I was jealous. I wanted to be a part of that because all of a sudden I saw kids that were liking Sunday school.

I can totally see the change with the kids' attitude. Not everyone loves to come, but I definitely don't see as much reluctance as I did when I was little . . . I hated Hebrew school . . . And kids are learning. In fact I'm TA-ing [serving as teaching assistant] for a grade—they're learning the stuff that I never got to learn about then.

To achieve these changes, Dr. Blum increased the number of staff development hours from sixteen to twenty, and devoted all of this time to demonstrating and practicing new models of teaching. She worked intensely with the teachers and did not rehire those who were resistant to the new methods. Working with Beth and Rabbi Davids, she began revising the curriculum. She instituted a requirement that teachers send her lesson plans three or four days ahead of time, and still spends considerable time emailing back and forth, refining the plans that need work. She designed a program for the eighth to twelfth grade teaching assistants, arranging for them to participate in parts of the ten-hour staff orientation, so that they would truly understand, and be able to fulfill, their responsibilities.

A father recounts his pleasure at being informed of his children's progress: "Every week we would get, not just emails with a paragraph about what happened in the classroom, but a seven to eight-paragraph email detailing everything that got done—the vocabulary, the prayers. As a parent, it was phenomenal because you felt like you were a participant in the classroom."

In our time at BKH, we observed over fifty discrete *Yesod* classes, staying anywhere between ten and fifty minutes. We saw a range of lessons: from those we perceived as truly outstanding; to those that had ambitious objectives but were missing some steps in the execution; to lessons that simply skimmed the surface of a subject. We did not see any classroom management problems; even in classes that seemed boring, students were respectful and well behaved. In many of the classes homework had been assigned, and, for the most part, completed.

In a number of classes "incidental" Hebrew was used for routines, such as when the teachers took attendance and when students asked to go to the bathroom. We saw whole-group decoding of Hebrew (something that both Beth and Dr. Blum vehemently oppose) only once. And we noted with interest that Torah cantillations are taught in the fifth grade by a specialist, and that the students were fully engaged in learning them.

We observed classes that seemed boring and/or superficial, in which teachers simply asked fairly routine questions about a story the class had read, to take just one example. We saw many more classes that struck us as very engaging, but were more standard religious school fare, such as reviewing the concepts of prayers or practicing Hebrew decoding or writing. In contrast to these lessons, we have chosen to highlight classes in which the goal was to teach a fairly abstract concept. Some of these attempts were more successful than others, but in all cases we applaud the teachers for embracing ambitious goals.

## Second Graders Consider the Meaning of "B'tzelem Elohim"

Grace, an avocational teacher who works as a health-care manager, has been teaching second grade at BKH for many years, and has a "legendary" reputation. To quote one mother: "I think she is magnificent. She just sets the bar really high. You get these emails, and boy, that work had better be done! My daughter thrived and just loved Hebrew, loved her, loved performing for her, loved having the bar set high, loved learning, loved [out-stripping] her hero, her sister, in Hebrew. But not all parents felt that way. Some parents thought she was too tough. I think maybe if your kid has a different learning style it could have been not a good fit . . . But I think that there is an awareness of which kids need to be in [her class]."

On the day we visited her class, the students had just finished reading an account of the sixth day of creation.

*Grace:* Why did God create people last?

*Student:* To take care of the world.

*Grace:* "Let them be a little like me." This is the word we are learning today: *B'tzelem Elohim.*"

*Student:* It's being like God.

*Grace:* Is it the way we look, or the way we act? How many people think *b'tzelem elhoim* is looking like God? (no one raised their hand)

After a brief discussion of this question, Grace continued:

*Grace:* We say that God is real, but how can that be? What are the things that are real, but we can't see?

*Student:* Air.

*Grace:* That's great. Can you put air in my hand?

*Student:* No.

*Grace:* What if we didn't have air?

*Students:* We'd die.

*Grace:* What else?

*Student:* Germs.

*Student:* Wind.

*Grace:* That's great. We can't see wind. We can see the leaves blowing.

*Student:* An imaginary friend.

*Grace:* What else is real, but you can't see? What goes in your ears?

*Student:* Sound.

*Grace:* So what are the qualities you have that I can't see?

The students gave several examples.

*Grace:* What are the kinds of the emotions you can feel? Things you can't see. Maybe how you'd feel if [the local baseball team] wins tonight?

*Student:* Happy.

*Grace:* Yes, you can't put happy in your hand.

Grace divided the class into three groups, and asked them to make a list of the things that are real despite the fact that they can't be seen. After five minutes she had the students read out their lists:

*Grace:* So you get the point. There are a lot of things in life and this list could go on and on—courage, freedom, the thoughts that we have, the feelings that we have. These things are real even though we can't see them. So we can see things that God creates, we can see in each one of us the goodness, the potential and the good qualities that God hopes for all of us.

We wondered whether these second graders truly grasped the rather sophisticated concept that Grace was teaching—that God, like certain emotions and values, doesn't need to be seen to be real. The students seemed to be engaged in the discussion, and Grace worked hard to include a number of learning modalities and to have the children be active learners. But without some kind of learning assessment for each individual child, it is hard to know just what each one took away from the lesson.

## A Fourth Grade Class on the Concept of Kehillah Kedoshah

Terry is another teacher who has been at BKH for many years. She teaches six hours a week at BKH, does tutoring, and teaches in at least one additional religious school as well. This lesson took place on the day of open house for fourth grade parents. Each student had at least one parent with him or her, and two students had two parents present. We arrived about ten minutes late, but could see that the session had begun with a discussion of the terms *kehillah kedoshah* (sacred community). On the left side of the board Terry had written "Kehillah—What is community?" Listed underneath it was a list, "a people, a place, working together, sharing interests, supportive shared goal," which we assumed were the students' answers to that question. The question on the right side was: "Kehillah Kedoshah: What is holy community?" and, underneath it, "respect, working together, a place, 10 people, honesty, love, kindness, cooperation, Torah."

Terry asked the families to work in groups of two or three. She distributed Hebrew and English Bibles. Each group was given two index cards, each with the number of a particular verse. Terry instructed participants to "Find the verse. Is it an example of *Kehillah*, or *Kehillah Kedoshah*? Then write or draw how this verse applies to our lives." The students did not seem to have any difficulty finding the verses. And while the connection between the verse and the concepts of *kehillah* and *kehillah kedoshah* were not always obvious to us, everyone seemed to be on-task and engaged in the conversation. Terry and her TA circulated to help answer questions and engage the groups in discussion.

After about 15 minutes the groups each shared their conclusions.

*Student:* we read the story of Sodom and Gemorrah; we're drawing a picture of two angels protecting Lot.

*Terry:* Three angels. Is this an example of *kadosh* [*sic*] or *kehillah*?

*Student: Kadosh*.

Terry did not follow up by asking why.

*Student:* We had the instructions for building the *mishkan* (the tabernacle). God gives exact measurements. When He says "wood," he doesn't mean any old wood—he tells them exactly what kind of wood.

*Terry: Terumah* (the name of the Torah portion) is a how-to section. One of the main points of the story is that God is telling the people to bring what they can, because some were more able than others. Is this an example of community or *kadosh*, or both?

*Student:* (pauses, and answers thoughtfully): I don't really know.

*Terry:* I thought it was both.

Then the next group reported:

*Student:* We had Abraham and the three strangers; the strangers come to Abraham's house and he shows them hospitality.

Terry summarized the story for the class.

*Student:* Then the three strangers tell him that Sarah is going to have a baby.

*Terry:* That is really secondary; Abraham was sick and the angels express the value of *bikur cholim* (visiting the sick). So we have two very strong Jewish values here: visiting the sick and hospitality.

*Student:* And then Sarah overhears the strangers . . . and she laughs.

Three additional groups reported back in similar fashion, but the distinction between *kehillah* and *kehillah kedoshah* remained, at best, implicit. At the end of the lesson, Terry concluded "Thank you guys, you did wonderful work. I like to look at every Genesis story as a form of creation. If you're doing your best, eventually you get a holy community."

Like the second grade lesson, this lesson had an ambitious goal, in this case to reflect on what is involved in a sacred community. But unlike the second grade class, Terry's lesson was not fully focused. It was not clear to us why some of the examples had been chosen, nor why some qualified as examples of *kedushah* while others did not. We found the level of engagement impressive, along with the fact that the students could all locate the verses easily and seemed to be familiar with the characters and events. But we were troubled by Terry's conflating a story from the *Midrash* (that Abraham was sick) with the Biblical text.

## A Fifth Grade Class on Prophets

In a fifth grade class, Nessa, a young woman who is Modern Orthodox and teaches at a number of area religious schools, was teaching a lesson about the prophets.

*Nessa:* A prophet is . . .

*Student:* Stands up for himself.

*Nessa:* Or herself. What else is a prophet?

*Student:* A prophet is someone who listens to God.

*Nessa:* Does that mean that God is a rock concert? A voice in your ear? A feeling? Could be . . .

*Student:* Someone is filled with God's spirit. It's not just hearing God's voice and broadcasting it. It's being immersed in God.

*Nessa:* For some it might be hearing God's voice, or broadcasting, or being immersed in God.

Nessa helped her students concretize the complex and abstract concept of prophecy through two activities. She structured a role play in which students took one of four roles: a bully, the person being bullied, God, and the prophet. She directed the student playing God to tell the prophet about the bullying incident; and she directed the prophet to intervene to help. In debriefing the role play, Nessa noted that what made the prophet a prophet was that he intervened at God's behest.

*Student:* I know why God doesn't speak to people. It would scare them out of their skin.

Nessa then gave the students butcher paper and asked them to trace the outline of one of their bodies. Their task would be to show how the different prophet's body parts might be used in their calling. Among the answers students gave were: "My eyes are used . . . to see the future" and "My eyes are used . . . to see injustice."

## A Class That Missed the Mark

Not every lesson of Nessa's was planned as carefully. About a month later, at Open House for fifth grade parents, each student had a parent with him or her. The topic for the day was the story of Joshua and the spies. Nessa divided the class in two, with the boys (and their parents) given the scene in which the walls fell down, and the girls (and *their* parents) asked to enact the scene in which Rahab, the Canaanite prostitute, hides the spies. The students were asked to read the story in the book, and were given guiding questions. But it became clear, during the performance, that neither the girls nor their parents had read the story very carefully. They spent most of the allotted time dividing up the parts, and were not clear about which character was on which side. One of the questions Nessa had asked them to consider was what conflict Rahab might have experienced in giving shelter to enemies of her people. But because the students were not clear which side Rahab or the spies were on, this question never got answered.

## Weekday Tefillah

More impressive than even the best of the classes were the *tefillot*—half hour *minchah* (afternoon) services that are held each Tuesday or Wednesday afternoon both for *Yesod* and (separately) for the BMA program. The service is held in the main sanctuary and is led by Rabbi Davids, together with Oren, a young, enthusiastic musician, who instilled a sense of *kavan-nah* (intentionality) with a very light touch.

Because our visits came so early in the school year, we observed what the staff called a "practice *tefillah*," in which the Oren made very explicit his expectations for appropriate behavior. At the edge of the *bimah* was a large screen onto which were projected the words of each prayer as it was sung. Dr. Blum changed the slides as the service moved along; she also kept track of the place in the service with a pointer.

Oren did many things to guide students into the proper mood for prayer. For example, he began the service with a song he had written, that they had all sung before:

Am I awake?
Am I prepared?
Are you listening to my prayer?

He then said, "I want you to pretend that you are really asking yourself these questions. It would be great if you really really meant it, even without acting." Oren mouthed the words silently, so that the voices of the students filled the room. He encouraged them to cover their eyes during the *Shema* and to lower their voices for the second line, and then led them in an English song that served as an introduction to the *Shema*:

Open up our eyes
Teach us how to live
So we will know that you are One.

Hearing some giggling, Oren said, very softly, "I was trying really hard to do my own prayer. But it was hard to concentrate with the giggling. We don't usually do this again, but we're going to do it again today, and I want *you* to hear your own prayer." When they sang the V'ahavta, he asked, "Do you think I have this prayer memorized?" The students nodded "yes." "But if you noticed, when I say it I usually turn my back to you, and I look up at the screen. Even though I have it memorized, I really like to look up at the screen. Each time you pray, you should read the prayer as if it's the first time you do it."

Later the same day, we had the opportunity to observe *tefillah* for the BMA program (sixth and seventh graders). At an age when students can be quite cynical about praying, especially in a public setting, we were impressed by the level of participation and apparent *kavannah*. One never knows really what is in the heart of another, but *all* of the students had their eyes covered at the transition to *Shema*, and it appeared that all were concentrating on the words. The two of us observing looked at each other in awe to see if we both had seen the same thing—preadolescents, in a school setting, engaged in *tefillah*.

And it appeared that we had.

## Challenges That Remain

The most immediate challenge BKH faces is that its growth now far exceeds the capacity of its facility. Scheduling is a complicated problem, at times requiring a forced choice between two programs that the staff would have preferred to run concurrently. Programs like *Shabbatonim* have had to be shortened to make room for other synagogue events, like weddings. As mentioned above, a capital campaign is underway, and the shortage of space should be alleviated in a number of years.

The explosive growth of both the membership and the programming has led some leaders to wonder if the synagogue can continue to grow without losing its character and its impact. In the belief that it would be unwise (and perhaps untenable) to raise tuition even higher, the finance committee has started thinking about raising an endowment. We ourselves wonder if and when this enormously talented staff might burn out, as they continue to dream up creative, but demanding, programs.

Challenges the education staff hopes to tackle in the near future include revising the curriculum of the *Havayah* program and reaching out to parents. Having undertaken significant improvements in the *Yesod* program and created a home-centered alternative for religious school children, BKH is now poised to circle back and revise the *Havayah* program. Esther Fisher, the new director of *Havayah*, was brought in with a mandate to add depth to the curriculum; at a staff meeting she wondered out loud if, now that the retreats were seen as integral to the high school program, it might be possible to require attendance at all three for those on the Confirmation track. Beth remarked, on several occasions, that she would like to add a *havurah* that is more academic. Currently, the few students who are interested in more formal Judaic and Hebrew study attend a community high school program. Beth would like to bring those students back to the synagogue, where they might be joined by others who have similar interests and inclinations.

Another challenging area is that of family education. Beth notes that BKH has "made a very conscious effort to stop doing grade-based family education because it wasn't working. Family education from a grade-based perspective is convenient . . . but I'm not convinced that ultimately it has an impact in the home. If you've got one parent and one kid learning together, they have a nice learning experience; but if your goal through family education is to have an impact on the way that families are Jewish together, then you have to be with the family together."

In 2006–07 the synagogue was awarded a grant from a national foundation to pilot a complex family education program that had four tracks (*Torah, Avodah, Gemilut Hasadim*, and Israel), each of which met three times on Sunday mornings (in place of *Yesod*). Three of the tracks had about twenty families each; the Israel track had twelve families. While feedback on the program was generally good, the grant was only for one year, and the staff was unable to find the funding to continue the program in its entirety (a significant portion of the funding had gone toward the rental of a space large enough to accommodate all the families). The *Gemilut Hasadim* track, which was folded into another program, the *Mishpacha* Missions, was the only track that continued in its entirety during 2007–08; elements of the other programs were incorporated into the existing grade-level family education programs.

The question of how to handle family education is related to a larger concern—how to convey to parents the depth of the experience their children are having, and how to bring these parents "on board." Though there are many exceptions, it seems that BKH is having more of an effect on the children than on families. Sylvia Israel, vice president of education, notes: "What we're finding now is that there's a whole group of kids who are more engaged than their parents, and the challenge is getting the parents to agree to bring them here or sign them off . . . Not all the parents understand what's happening here, and it's a little bit of a struggle, and our responsibility to find ways to communicate that."

## What Can We Learn from Beit Knesset Hazon?

BKH represents a powerful existence proof, demonstrating that it *is* possible to reimagine congregational education and reinvigorate a congregational school within a relatively short period of time. Rabbi Tepper assumed his position in the year 2000; Beth Lorch in 2002; and Dr. Blum in 2005. Though they all acknowledge that there is much left to be done, by 2007 they had accomplished a great deal.

As important as the fact that congregational education can be transformed, are the *conditions* that make such a transformation possible:

## Collaborative Leadership

Contrary to what some have argued,[9] *it doesn't take a charismatic rabbi to revitalize a synagogue.* BKH's success is due to the initiative of lay leaders, who, faced with the dissonance between the ideal and the real, worked behind the scenes to articulate a vision, and recruited a rabbi to help them enact that vision. One of the rabbi's first steps was to hire two creative, capable educators, with whom he worked closely to brainstorm new ideas and new approaches. For her part, Beth Lorch, the congregational educator, began by convening a task force to help her conceptualize the new directions education would take; to this day she continues to work with the lay members of this task force, and, of course, with the senior members of her staff.[10]

## Adult Learning

The visionary lay leaders who got the ball rolling were inspired and energized by their own Jewish learning. Their first-hand experience of transformative Jewish learning made them realize what their children were missing, and helped sustain their interest in pursuing change.[11]

## Focus on a Limited Number of Attainable Goals

Reading BKH's many brochures, observing the teachers in action, and interviewing parents and staff alike, we were struck by the recurrence of certain key terms, such as *kehillah kedoshah, b'tzelem elohim*, and *tikkun olam*, and the repeated mention of the same goals—the creation of community, the acquisition of some basic tools, and the integration of Jewish values into students' lives. This laser-like focus on goals that are attainable is, we believe, essential to BKH's success. BKH doesn't promise more than it can deliver, remaining mindful of the time constraints under which it operates.

## Community Resources

The maxim that "it takes a village to raise a child" might be paraphrased, in this context, as follows: it takes the resources of a community to transform a school. At every turn, BKH has been the beneficiary of the resources of its community. A key Federation professional served as a catalyst for change; a Federation-sponsored program of high-level adult learning inspired, and continues to inspire, those in leadership positions; and Federation grants made it possible for BKH to pay the salaries of several new staff members for the first few years of their tenure. A local college of Jewish studies has provided the funding for the professional development pilot. Last but not least, four out of seven full-time members of the education staff are graduates of a local master's-level program in Jewish educational leadership; their shared language and understanding of Jewish education has surely facilitated their collaboration. While few synagogues in the area have maximized these resources in as significant a way as BKH, without these resources, change would have come much more slowly, if at all.

# *Chug HaSefer* Reading List

## Third Grade
1. *Sofer: The Story of a Torah Scroll*, by Eric Ray*
2. *Rivka's First Thanksgiving*, by Elsa Okon Rael*
3. *When Zaydeh Danced on Eldridge Street*, by Elsa Okon Rael*
4. *Like A Maccabee*, by Barbara Bietz*
5. *Penina Levine is a Hard Boiled Egg*, by Rebecca O'Connell**
6. *A Picture for Marc*, by Eric A. Kimmel**

## Fourth and Fifth Grade

### 2005–06
1. *Confessions of a Closet Catholic*, by Sarah Littman*
2. *The Koufax Dilemma*, by Steven Schnur
3. Unit on Jewish Folklore:
   > *While Standing on One Foot: Hillel The Wise, The Wise Fools of Chelm*
   > *Zlateh The Goat and Other Stories: The Snow in Chelm*
   > *Wise . . . and Not so Wise: Hanina'a Stone, Wise and Wiser*
   > *Stories for Children: Elijah the Slave*
4. *Seymour, the Formerly Fearful*, by Eve B. Feldman

### 2006–07
1. *Joseph's Wardrobe*, by Paul J. Citrin*
2. *Alexandra's Scroll*, by Miriam Chaikin*
3. *The Travels of Benjamin of Tudela: Through Three Continents in the Twelfth Century*, by Uri Shulevitz*
4. *My Guardian Angel*, by Sylvie Weil

### 2007–08
1. *Confessions of a Closet Catholic*, by Sarah Littman*
2. *Stealing Home*, by Ellen Schwartz*
3. *Ice Cream Town*, by Rona Arato**
4. *The Christmas Menorahs*, by Janice Cohn **

### Proposed 2008–09
1. *Joseph's Wardrobe*, by Paul J. Citrin
2. *Alexandra's Scroll*, by Miriam Chaikin
3. *The Travels of Benjamin of Tudela: Through Three Continents in the Twelfth Century*, by Uri Shulevitz
4. *A Shout in the Sunshine*, by Mara W. Cohen Ioannides

---

*Asterisks denote books that were deemed successful enough to be used in subsequent years.

**Items with double asterisks hadn't yet been used as this chapter was being written.

## *Notes*

1. In the remainder of this chapter we will use the acronym BKH, as members of the congregation often do.

2. For a discussion of the uses of a task force as the engine for change in congregational life, see chapter 6 of Isa Aron, *Becoming a Congregation of Learners* (Woodstock, Vt.: Jewish Lights, 2000)

3. For more on the synagogue as a sacred community see Lawrence Hoffman, *Rethinking Synagogues: A New Vocabulary for Congregational Life* (Woodstock, Vt.: Jewish Lights, 2006).

4. John Dewey, *Experience and Education* (New York: Macmillan, 1938). For a discussion of how this idea has been applied over the years, see Tara Fenwick, *Learning Through Experience* (Malabar, Fla.: Krieger, 2003).

5. This is a pun on "Rock Shabbat." *Rak* in Hebrew means "only."

6. Howard Gardner, *Multiple Intelligences: New Horizons* (New York: Basic Books, 2006).

7. Given the dramatic increase in enrollment in recent years, the vast majority of post *b'nei mitzvah* students are in eighth and ninth grade.

8. Novels are assigned in the second half of the school year.

9. For an example, see Sidney Schwarz, *Finding a Spiritual Home: How a New Generation of Jews Can Transform the American Synagogue* (San Francisco: Jossey Bass, 2000), pp. 243–47.

10. For more on collaborative leadership in synagogue life see chapter 4 of Isa Aron, *The Self-Renewing Congregation* (Woodstock, Vt.: Jewish Lights, 2002).

11. For more on the transformative power of adult learning, see Kathleen Taylor, Catharine Marienau, and Morris Fiddler, *Developing Adult Learners* (San Francisco: Jossey Bass, 2000).

# III. *High School Models*

# CHAPTER 9

# Western Hebrew High
## A Place for Social Belonging and Personal Meaning

RANDAL F. SCHNOOR WITH BILLY MENCOW

A̲t the dead end of a long road, tucked at the foot of a major highway, lies a collection of trailer-like structures connected in the shape of a "T." This modest complex serves as the Jewish Community Centre of a small western city, and is the home of the smaller of two campuses of Western Hebrew High. The building consists of an office opposite the front lobby, a boardroom, eight classrooms, and a small gymnasium with an adjacent kitchen. Billboards and posters fill the walls describing Jewish lectures and programming happening in the city and the wider region. It is a Wednesday evening in late April, the last week of the 2006–07 school year. The senior students are anxiously milling around the lobby of the JCC in anticipation of the annual "seniors' dinner." For them it is the culmination of four years together at Western Hebrew High. Soon most will be going off to different colleges around the country and embarking on the next stage of their lives. Within fifteen minutes the seven students, ten parents of these students, the school directors and some teachers assemble in a nearby classroom. Four long rectangular tables form a square on the periphery of the classroom where all are seated. A dinner buffet of kosher deli sandwiches awaits the group at the back of the room. It is a charged atmosphere. The students are excited and nervous to have their parents at the school with them, in many cases the first time this has happened. The parents look equally uneasy. The principal of the campus, Kyra Yermus, welcomes the group and turns the attention to the student presentations.

*Kyra:* Your kids have been here four years now and they want to take this opportunity to share a little bit about what the school has meant to them. They have decided to focus on their senior seminar class that they loved so much.

Anna Jessin, their senior seminar teacher and known as one of the strongest teachers in the school, beams at the group in pride and tells the parents a little about the nature of her seminar in Jewish philosophy. The students take turns sharing their thoughts about the class. Tania Wagman has been accepted to UCLA for next fall. She tells the group how the class has helped her grow as a Jew and as a person.

*Tania:* It was really nice to go every week and have a new topic of Judaism to discuss. You could just speak your mind. Everyone was there to listen. No one was going to shut you down. You could talk about anything. Hearing a lot of other people's views was really important to me because it helps you strengthen yourself as an individual. You can decide what you agree with and what you don't and learn new things and I thought that was really cool. And learning about Judaism—a lot of sides I did not know. And being with people I spent the whole summer with. It's nice to see them every week. We really looked forward to class. We didn't like it when we to missed it.

*Anna:* They always wanted to work right through the break!

*Parent:* Really?! This is a breath of fresh air. You don't have to come here, but you choose to do so. In my day you stopped school at your Bar-Mitzvah!

*Another Parent:* I agree. It is great that you have spent these four years together. I see that the seven of you have formed a tight-knit friendship. How are you going to keep in touch now that you are all going off to different colleges?

*Tania:* Well, actually . . . we have a class at Anna's house next Wednesday night! [laughter]

Anna confirms that, upon the request of her students, she has agreed to continue the class in her home the following week. The formal conversations end as people move to the back of the room to get some dinner. A number of parents approach us eager to talk about how much the school has meant to their child.

"My daughter talks about this senior seminar with me all the time."

"It has been such a good experience for my son, both socially and intellectually."

"The Israel trip was life-changing for my daughter."

This brief vignette gives us a first taste of the strength of Western Hebrew High. It offers a lively and engaging setting for Jewish teenagers to feel comfortable and explore what Judaism and Jewishness mean to them. By employing dynamic teachers that offer "hip" classes that young people can relate to, and ensuring there is ample time for socializing, Western Hebrew High delivers a successful product in the marketplace of Jewish youth programming in this city.

Sociologist Steven Cohen and religious studies scholar Arnold Eisen[1] have put forward a persuasive thesis about the changing nature of Jewish life in America over the last several decades. Rather than conforming to external normative standards of what constitutes a Jew, many of today's Jews have turned inward for their sense of Jewishness. Increasingly, Jewish identities have come to be perceived as freely chosen and individually constructed. As such, many Jews in the North American context and elsewhere now feel free to appropriate only those aspects of Jewishness that they find personally meaningful. The designers of Western Hebrew High have taken this lesson to heart. The school understands that, if any Jewish subsection of the population is going to embrace a personal meaning–based approach to Judaism, its student body of upper-middle class liberal Jewish millennials[2] is more than likely to be among them. An important part of this approach to Jewish identity construction is the realization that a person's experience of Jewishness is a fluid, rather than fixed, aspect of their life. Social psychologist Bethamie Horowitz[3] emphasizes that individuals often go through "Jewish journeys" where identity evolves over the life course, paralleling growth and personal development. Anna Jessin encapsulates this philosophy: "My objective is to get them to really begin the road to figure out who they are and where Judaism is going to fit in their life . . . [Y]ou're born Jewish whether you like it or not, you're sort of in this. So why don't you investigate . . . Something is there—some connection. Why don't you spend the rest of your life, a piece of it, finding that out?"

As the new school handbook explains, "your personal Jewish journey" over the next four years will allow you to "travel through five areas of study as you uncover things you never knew about your Jewish heritage." In order to tap into the meaning-based mindset of its students the school

pays special attention to developing multiple experiential or affective learning experiences that allow for personal engagement with the educational
material. The school believes "it has never been cooler to be Jewish!" It
hopes that its students will come to feel the same way.

Western Hebrew High is a grade 8–12 supplementary school program
in a large western city. A secondary campus of the school, as we have seen,
exists in an adjacent smaller city. Both campuses are run under the auspices of the local central agency of Jewish education. The main campus has
been in continuous operation for approximately three decades. It has been
housed in a number of public schools over the years and is currently operating in the city's new Jewish day school complex. The smaller campus has
been in existence for eleven years. Each independent program operates
two and a half hours a week on a weekday evening.[4]

The host city has a culture of interdenominationalism. It is a place where
it is not unusual for people to have memberships in more than one synagogue. The school reflects this spirit of religious diversity. It is a community
school that "celebrates the beauty and relevance of all Jewish movements."
The majority of students are affiliated with one of the large Conservative or
Reform synagogues in the city. A small number belong to the Reconstructionist synagogue or are unaffiliated. Approximately 30 percent of students
come from intermarried families. A large proportion comes from upper-
middle-class backgrounds.

The enrollment for 2006–07 was approximately 275 at the larger campus, with approximately 100 at the smaller campus. The school offers a
popular six-week Israel and Poland summer trip between the eleventh and
twelfth grades, in which approximately three-quarters of the eligible students participate. The school offers a rich variety of courses that appeal to
teenagers, many of which integrate Judaism with popular culture. Hebrew
language and "classical Judaica" form the minority of the classes.

## Confirmation Program

One ingredient that contributes to the success of Western Hebrew High is
its partnership and close coordination with local synagogues. Both campuses of the school have arrangements with local synagogues where the
eighth to tenth grade confirmation programs of the synagogue are housed
within the larger community high school program. Eighth to tenth grade
students take an elective course together during the first hour of the evening,
and then organize into their respective synagogue confirmation classes dur-

ing the second hour. Synagogue confirmation has thus become a key rite of passage for many Western Hebrew High students.

This strong relationship and synergy with local synagogues offer a number of benefits to the school and the community at large. Synagogues, some of which have been struggling to support a confirmation program within their own institution, have access to a wider infrastructure within which to house and sustain this important educational piece, and also enable their youth to participate in a larger community school. At the same time they are able to deliver their own specific "brand" of Judaism to their congregants (be it specific to a Jewish "denomination" or synagogue). Partnerships with local synagogues also easily facilitate the use of congregational rabbis, some of whom have extensive teaching backgrounds, as educational leaders in the school. Rabbis spoke of their ability to develop courses and, to some extent, shape the curriculum content of the school, thus exerting influence on the total Hebrew High experience.[5] In a school where the majority of the courses are "lighter," often fusing Jewish content with American popular culture, the more tradition-based courses that Rabbis are able to teach, both as part of their confirmation programs and as elective courses, offer a healthy complement.

In total, this arrangement allows the high school to be religiously diverse, serving a wide range of Jews in the community, while still offering specific classes for students with specific synagogue commitments. Of course this relationship with local synagogues also plays the important role of consistently bringing in large numbers of students to the school.

There are some potential cracks in the system, however. As the tuition of Western Hebrew High continues to increase (in the 2006–07 year it increased by more than 25% to $800[6]), the synagogues are finding it more and more difficult to subsidize their congregants to attend the school. The level of subsidy expected from the synagogues was raised to $175 per student in the 2006–07 year. As the lay and professional leadership at the participating synagogues changes, and as the leadership of the school changes, we wonder if the trusting relationship and partnership between these institutions will maintain itself.

## Staff

It's a chilly and drizzly Monday evening in March 2007. Hyundai Santa Fe's and other sport utility vehicles belonging to Jewish teenagers fill the parking lot of the new, modern Jewish day school completed in 2002, which houses the larger central campus of Western Hebrew High. Eighth and ninth graders who do not yet have their driver's licenses are dropped off at the door by their parents. The students are greeted by two members of the school staff upon their arrival. Tara Weinstein, the new, young full-time principal of the school's central campus, makes sure to greet each parent as they drive through the drop-off area. Susan Parsons, the long-time youth programs administrator of the central agency, welcomes the students in the spacious lobby. Most students are dressed in shorts and flip-flops despite the cool weather. They assemble into many circles of animated conversation. It is an important socializing time that the students count on at Western Hebrew High. Several students approach the staff enquiring about specific classroom assignments. Each student is known by name and enthusiastically told where their first period class is being held. Susan rings a hand bell to signal that it is time to go to class. In no particular rush, the students make their way to their classrooms, and another evening of Hebrew High begins.

Tara confides in us that since it is her first year on the job she still seeks recognition from the parent body. This is why she makes sure she personally greets each parent that pulls up in the parking lot. It does not help that Tara herself is in her late twenties and does not look much older than her students. Susan, on the other hand, is a middle-aged woman whom parents recognize as a longtime school staff member.

Tara has a bachelor's degree from an East Coast college in Human Resources and Society with a business emphasis. She does not have formal university training in Judaica or Jewish Education, although she is considering enrolling for a master's in Jewish social service at a local college. Before assuming the role of principal of the central campus of Western Hebrew High, Tara served for several years as a very successful youth director of a synagogue in the city. Here she was closely mentored and nurtured by the synagogue executive director and senior rabbi. At this time she also had the opportunity to attend a number of conferences of the North American Alliance for Jewish Youth and the Jewish Youth Directors Association. When the position opened up at Western Hebrew High the community encouraged her to apply and, if the fit was right, make the transition to this next step in her career.

Kyra Yermus, a middle-aged woman, has served as principal of the smaller campus since its inception eleven years ago. Unlike Tara, she has lived in the region and played a leadership role in the local Jewish Federation for much of her life. Like Tara she does not have formal university training in Jewish education, but she has been active in the Coalition for the Advancement of Education and a professional development program through Brandeis University.

Despite their lack of formal educational credentials, we were struck with the two principals' passion for Jewish education and their sheer energy and dedication to making their schools better. They both emphasized the importance of high quality teaching. When we asked Tara what she was most proud of at the end of her first year, she replied: "that I was able to keep [the teachers] motivated, excited and the [positive] feedback that I've gotten from them. I really do think that it trickles down; that I have re-energized their passion for teaching at Hebrew High; that my enthusiasm and my excitement makes them more enthusiastic and excited every day. And that it made them try to be more successful in the classroom . . . I learned how to be a better teacher because I took advantage of all of the options that were presented to me. I want to inspire more of my teachers to take advantage of those options." Professional leaders in the city spoke glowingly of Tara in terms of her passion for her job and her ability to serve as a role model for the students of her school. A local rabbi reported that "she is passionate about being a Jew and perpetuating positive Jewish consciousness. It's not just a job. It's really something that she feels very close to."

We were also impressed by the level of self-reflection undertaken by the leaders of the schools at both campuses. Principals were comfortable in acknowledging that there are areas where the school needs to improve. Key themes that were mentioned in this regard were bringing more intentionality to the curriculum and more accountability for the quality of the teaching. These issues are discussed further in a subsequent section.

Staff working within the youth programs division of the city's central agency of Jewish education also plays a role in the school. Rhonda Kaplan serves as the immediate supervisor to the two campus principals and thus serves as the conduit between the school and the central agency. As mentioned, Susan Parsons is the youth programs administrator. For many years she has served as the face of the school in the eyes of the parents. She is responsible for public relations and marketing of the school as well as all administrative matters. Her office is command central for the school. Vera Becker is responsible for overseeing the school's summer Israel trip.

There are twenty-three teachers at the school: fourteen at the larger campus and nine at the smaller campus. As is the case in many supplementary schools, the teachers come from a wide variety of backgrounds and age groups and varying levels of experience and teaching skills. Salaries range from $30 to $40 per classroom hour. We will meet some of these teachers in more detail in a subsequent section.

## Governance

The school itself has no formal board of directors. It thus has a vacuum of lay partnership to support and guide its vision. As a community school housed within a central agency, the potential exists for substantial institutional support for the school. Despite the central agency's involvement in curricular restructuring, we are not convinced this support is being maximized. We sense something of a disconnect between the school and central agency. Decisions such as the significant increase in tuition in the 2006–07 year were made by central agency leaders without consulting the school staff. The agency does not maintain close contact with the day to day operations of the school, and school administrators report that they cannot always turn to the agency for nurturing and mentorship when needed. Freedom to make changes in the school is limited by agency bureaucracy. We sense that considerable energy among school administration is expended in negotiating the delicate politics of the relations with the central agency. We wonder if this energy could be better spent.

## The Israel Trip

As mentioned, the school is convinced that experiential learning that allows for personal engagement with the educational material serves as an essential complement to purely cognitive learning. Western Hebrew High thus exerts considerable effort in implementing nonformal learning experiences within their program. We see this as a strength of the school. The annual six-week summer Israel trip, which now includes a Poland component, is the central programmatic piece of the high school. It is one of the largest community-based summer teen trips in the country. Over one hundred eleventh grade students participated in 2000. The number of participants was seriously compromised in 2001 and the trip was cancelled in 2002 because of the *intifada*. A new staff position—Vera Becker, youth programs manager—was subsequently added specifically to restore the popularity of the trip. The numbers had rebounded to approximately one hundred by 2007. As mentioned, approximately 75 percent of eleventh grade students participate in this key high school program. One local rabbi described the Israel trip as "the crown jewel of [this city's] Jewish community."

Clearly the trip, with its long history and positive legacy, is tightly embedded within the fabric of the local Jewish community. As Vera Becker opined, "this trip has a reputation in this community. It's been around since 1971 and we're seeing a lot of parents sending their kids on the trip now. So we are seeing two generations, which is fascinating and thrilling. The rabbis push our programs before they push their movement trips, which is unbelievable. The community reputation is huge in [finding] funding sources. Synagogues really support us; Federation supports us. It is an expensive trip but there are funding sources out there and parents take advantage of that."

A high level of organization is essential for facilitating the smooth running of such a large trip. Our evidence indicated that Western Hebrew High excels in this regard. We had the opportunity to observe the careful attention to detail that the school provides in its private information sessions with families in preparation for the trip. Below is a field note that we made during such a meeting:

## Pre-trip Interview

Each of the 101 Israel trip applicants is interviewed at length. Participants include eleventh grade student and parents. On March 14, 2007, Western Hebrew High staff member, Susan Parsons, interviewed a student's family before the summer Israel trip: This interview included the participant's eighth grade brother, allowing the younger brother to experience the careful interview process of Israel trip participants. He now knows what to expect regarding the serious approach to the program when his own turn comes.

The first part of the interview was about administrative details—medical and financial forms. This interview took place in the public lobby of the school and seemed very comfortable. The second part was private, in an office, around a round table. Susan had the applicant's very detailed file, and clearly knew the family quite well.

This was the first time a member of the family would travel to Israel, though the student has traveled to other countries. Both parents had questions about medical care, finances, spending money, and host families. Very familiar with the trip and with the Israeli trip providers, Susan was able to pass on a lot of confidence and trust to the parents, who were satisfied and even humorous about their concerns.

Susan used a two-page contract, filled with references to Jewish values, to review expected behaviors and involvement of the student. At the end of the interview, the contract was signed by parents, student, and Susan, remaining in the student's file that will go to Israel with staff.

In the last part of the interview, Susan asked the parents and sibling to leave, and interviewed the candidate privately. This was a time for the applicant to share other concerns, and for Susan to review the physical nature of the trip—lots of hiking, and early wake-ups. The interview lasted into the first session of classes, and the younger sibling voluntarily left to go to class.

Interviews with parents confirmed their high satisfaction with the organization of the school in meeting their needs for their children's trip. One parent recounted:

> The other thing I must say is the preparation that they are doing for the Israel trip with teaching us what's going to occur, meeting people's concerns, giving a packing list. Having these meetings . . . Having kids come from Israel to talk to the other kids. Having kids from the last trip talking to them . . . I think it's great! I mean they're really preparing. I've had enough already. [Laughter] And there's one other meeting coming next week. And they have people who were trained, who've been there before tell you . . . we didn't know where to go buy a rolling duffle bag, it was helpful with that. I'm very impressed with them.

Parents also appreciated the flexibility provided in paying for the trip. They were pleased that both their own synagogues and the Jewish Federation each provided subsidies. The High School also administered interest-free loans to families to cover the necessary balance. Parents reported that loans were given "without judgments or '[bad] vibes.' It's just 'do the best you can' and it will all be okay."

## The Year of Preparation

Education and exposure to Israel is carefully built into the curriculum at Western Hebrew High. The curriculum is set up so that eleventh grade students enroll in a special Israel class for a full year previous to their departure. Clearly it is easier to motivate and engage kids in a class about the history and contemporary issues of Israel and Poland when the students know they will be traveling to these locales in a few short months. We had the chance to observe one of these Israel preparation classes in the spring of 2007. In this particular class a documentary film on the Warsaw Ghetto was shown. The students were clearly engrossed in the film. The teacher emphasized the fact that they will be traveling to Warsaw to the current site of the ghetto. Students were instructed to write themselves a letter reflecting on their thoughts about what they learned from the film. The students will then read their own letters when they arrive in Warsaw later that summer. We see this exercise as having good potential for connecting classroom material to real life. Through experiential learning the students will have the opportunity to make a personal connection to cognitive information they have absorbed in school.

What do the students actually gain or learn from their Israel trip? Researchers of Jewish educational programs know well that educational effectiveness in terms of specific educational outcomes is often quite difficult to assess. As JESNA researcher Leora Isaacs[7] writes, "in order to do so, educational goals must be clearly articulated in measurable terms and valid and reliable methodologies and instruments must be devised to assess achievement levels." Longitudinal data tracing the future attitudes and behaviors of participants would also be useful. Although these types of assessment were beyond the scope of this project, respondents provided anecdotal assessments of the impact of the trip on the students.

Tara, the current principal, attests to the power of the Israel trip as an important example of affective learning:

> I see it as being an excellent experience. I see it as altering these kids' lives for the better; a growing experience for them; a "putting it all together." It really is. That's when the light bulb goes off, that's when oh yeah, I remember that Chabad rabbi who taught me about the *ba'al Tshuvah* movement when I was in tenth grade and I didn't care but now this is cool; [this is real] life . . . there is this land . . . They start to put it all together when they are in Israel. For me, my goal is Jewish continuity. I'm pretty invested in that, and I [know] that this really helps to achieve that.

A survey[8] we conducted of thirty-four senior students in the spring of 2007 offers some more supporting evidence of the strong personal and educational impact of the Israel trip. It revealed that a large majority of respondents (more than 75%) claim that they are now "*much* more knowledgeable about Israel." Of the five central subject areas that make up the Western Hebrew High curriculum, discussed in more detail in the next section, students reported that they have gained considerably more knowledge about Israel than any other subject area.

In a separate section exploring Jewish attitudes, the survey asked students to report how their attitudes may have changed "as a result of their experiences at Hebrew High." Attitudes about areas such as "Jewish identity," belief in God, importance of marrying Jewish, importance of charity, among others, were solicited. The area that showed by far the most positive Jewish change was the theme of Israel, where more than 70 percent of respondents reported that they felt "a *much* stronger connection to Israel."

The fact their children were going to Israel also had an impact on the parents. As we know from the seniors' dinner, one parent reported that the trip was "life changing" for his daughter. Another gushed about his own feelings about the upcoming trip: "My family is from Israel. They were born in Tiberius and my daughter is going to get to see these places and I'm just thrilled. I can't put into words or convey how rich and deep I feel. So they're studying this for the year. My daughter comes home and tells me [about] this person and that pop item . . . and she can't wait to go. And the fact that that's where my blood is from—at least half — to me it's priceless and it's wonderful."

## Post-trip Programming

A key piece of the Israel trip is the post-trip programming. All participants of the trip are asked to speak in their home synagogues about their summer experiences in Israel and Poland. This serves the purpose of informing and connecting the general community to current events in Israel as well as encouraging potential students to attend Western Hebrew High and participate in the trip. In addition, a fall reunion for all participants is arranged each year where the Israeli staff is invited back to the United States for a full week of programming in several different synagogues and other venues. We were struck by the levels of student attendance at the 2007 main reunion party. Of the seventy central campus students who participated in the summer 2007 trip, sixty-four of them attended the reunion (even though only forty had continued into twelfth grade at the school). We know from Birthright Israel trips that the post-trip follow up programming plays an important role in maintaining the youths' connection to Jewish life. Ideally, this programming would continue on a regular basis, though this becomes increasingly difficult as the youth move into college life.

While the Israelis are visiting the city, the school facilitates a program where they make several visits to local public schools, thus linking their Jewish program to the wider community. This is a unique undertaking among programs following travel to Israel. Vera Becker describes it as follows:

We have the Israelis in the public schools during the week, which is the most amazing piece—that they get to educate in world religion classes, social studies classes, and geography classes. And in some of these schools in [our state] there are one or two Jewish kids there. So it's amazing for the Jewish kids to be there and say, "oh, there's an Israeli in my school." But it's more important for the non-Jewish kids to hear an Israeli perspective on what's going on. It's particularly important this year with the Lebanese war as almost all of our male staff got drafted back into the war until they could come back and talk to these classes here and say "I was in Lebanon. Here is what was actually happening." It was really important because that was clearly not a perspective they were getting here.

Another way that returning students from the summer trip are able to continue to engage in the ideas and feelings they have accumulated from their experience is the school's participation in the State Holocaust Remembrance Week. Students are asked to put their thoughts on the Holocaust in writing and this is passed on to a State Representative who introduces a joint resolution in the House and the State Senate. Students are invited on the House Floor and in the Senate as State Representatives read some of the students' writings.

## Other Experiential Education

Beyond the Israel and Poland trip the school facilitates other nonformal, out-of-classroom programs to promote experiential learning. In order for the students to experience *tikkun olam* first hand, for example, the school became involved in the local community's *Mitzvah-palooza* program. The school set up a class for freshman where they worked as a group to develop a number of charity/social action programs of their own to be implemented on a particular Sunday called Mitzvah Day. Some of the activities included ice skating with Special Olympians, participating in the city's "plant a million trees project," and visiting senior citizens in an old-age residence. After the program the groups convened with supervisors to process what they had learned and experienced.

Another *tikkun olam* initiative of the school is the *B'nai Tzedek* charity program. As the school website exclaims, "No matter what you've been told, teens can and do make a difference in the world!" *B'nai Tzedek* allows students to establish a personal endowment fund with an initial contribution of $250. The money is then matched by the city's Jewish Community Foundation so that the opening balance is $500. Students attend three educational programs throughout the school year on the subject of charity and philanthropy, and each spring donate 5 percent of their account to a Jewish nonprofit agency that speaks to their personal interests.

Another clear example of experiential learning, the school promotes the program as an "amazing opportunity to become the next generation of Jewish philanthropists and make a real difference in your community."

Finally, upon one of our visits to the school we had the opportunity to witness the school's Meet the Mayor night. As part of the central agency's "Political Engagement Series," Western Hebrew High arranged for a school-wide assembly to meet the city's popular and populist mayor. A student of the school was invited to introduce the mayor. In a large modern gymnasium in one of the local Jewish day schools more than 250 students—their teachers sitting among them—listened attentively to their personable mayor speak about the value of family, volunteering and giving back to your community, and personal integrity—values that the school certainly espouses. The sheer numbers of students were impressive given that a large public high school (where many Hebrew High students attend) was holding final exams that week. His inspirational words included the message that anyone can become a leader if they set their mind to it. After asking a series of intelligent questions, many students approached the mayor to engage in more discussion and to seek autographs. Energy levels ran high. Clearly this was a night at Hebrew High that the students would remember for a long time.

❖

Among the number of dynamic, out-of-classroom learning opportunities at Western Hebrew High, the Israel trip stands as a central pillar of the school. While this has helped the school achieve considerable success and longevity, there were some critical comments about the trip gathered from respondents. First, the design of the trip could benefit from more collaboration with local rabbis, so as to maintain wider community involvement, rather than being a project of the central agency alone. One rabbi lamented that the trip has "lost some of its soul" in terms of the traditional Judaica content. As the price of the trip continues to rise (over $8000 in 2007), the option of pursuing alternative trips (such as the free Birthright trip) becomes more attractive. Another concern is the fact that the trip does not always plant the seeds for students to return to Western Hebrew High after the trip for senior year. There is a significant decrease in enrollment between eleventh and twelfth grade (33% decrease in the 2006–07 year). Finally, with the school putting such a strong emphasis on the Israel trip, when this trip is cancelled, as it was in 2002, the total enrollment in the school can significantly decrease. This raises the question of the role of the trip in relation to the rest of the school curriculum.

# Curriculum and Professional Development

A recent study by JESNA[9] on Jewish supplementary High Schools in the United States reported that, "At schools with positive reputations among educational professionals, the educational approach is aligned with the schools' mission, vision, and goals (p. 15)." It also stated that: "Unfortunately, professional development, supervision, and guidance regarding content and pedagogic techniques were limited at most schools (p.13)."

Throughout its history Western Hebrew High has faced the same challenges as the majority of supplementary schools in the country. In addition to those mentioned above, its challenges include maintaining competitive salaries and recruiting and retaining qualified teachers. Teacher turnover can become the norm rather than the exception. As a result, schools can sometimes face the difficult choice of hiring staff that do not have the full complement of knowledge and skill sets necessary for the job. Especially at the high school level, if teachers are seen to have the valued skills of engaging and exciting Jewish teenagers—not an easy task—they are considered a hot commodity, and sometimes hired regardless of whether what they are able to teach fits within the larger curricular vision of the school. Other teachers may have high levels of knowledge in Jewish areas deemed essential for a school's curriculum, but they may have poor teaching skills.

In the last five years the central campus of Western Hebrew High has gone to considerable effort to address these common challenges. They have sought to address the issues of aligning their school mission with their curricular design and providing professional development for their teachers. The process started when a number of Western Hebrew High teachers participated in a three-year training workshop for supplementary school teachers conducted by local Jewish educational consultants. Using the well regarded *Understanding by Design* (Wiggins and McTighe, 2005) model of education, the use of "backwards design" was encouraged, by which the desired results of a class or a course are developed first, and the means to achieve these results subsequently follow. The training sessions also taught the importance of teaming novice teachers with more experienced mentors or "master" teachers and building a trusting working relationship between them. High degrees of accountability between team members ensured a deep learning experience for each.

Tara, a senior teacher at the time participating in the workshop, described with excitement what this training provided to some of the school's junior teachers: "We taught the teachers how to plan a lesson. We taught them how to filter for essential information in terms of what would be nice and what's essential for the bulk of the class. And we taught them how to plan. We taught them about development, appropriate activities to use at school, to get those lessons across. We taught them how to assess their lessons. We taught teachers to be more effective. We taught them to focus on what the student is learning, rather than just teaching and getting out of there!"

Through this immersion in teacher training, the school administration became inspired to continue the process of improving their school. In addition to higher staff quality, the school's main objective was to develop a more comprehensive educational vision for the school and to implement the necessary curricular changes to bring about this vision. A senior administrator in the central agency described the passion of Tara's predecessor, who initiated this process: "[The previous principal] . . . believed in his heart what we were trying to get him to believe about staff development. About how you retain your staff if they are part of building the institution, and how teachers' meetings are not about academic details . . . they are more about what our enduring understandings [are] and what do we want the kids to really gain out of this and how you build the school day and how do you build the curriculum properly."

With a private grant for this purpose, the central agency was later able to privately commission the educational consultants to assist the school in its objectives. The first step was to help the school articulate a coherent vision and set of goals. In the words of the consultants, the key question to ask was: "What do we want the student [to know]? . . . How can we point to a student who went to [Western Hebrew High] and point to a student who didn't and know the difference? That's basically what you are asking and that's what we want to do."

The consultants describe their process as follows: "[We] put together what's called the world café, we've used it a number of times, which is set up as a café model with people sitting down with the checker board table cloths and the candle in the middle and we had a menu. And the purpose of this was to go from "Do schools need goals?" to walking away saying "Yes, [Western] Hebrew High needs goals." And we had 20-some people attend. The 20-some people, the lay members, the principal. One of the things that really worked well is the principal here is one of the components. She wasn't standing aside."

It is worthwhile to reiterate here that the principal was one of the participants—a team member—in this process of clarifying the goals of the school. Tara, the new principal by this time, was perfectly placed to be involved in this initiative. She had served as a senior teacher in the three year workshop conducted previously, thus was intimately familiar with the educational philosophy being employed. By participating in the goals exercise she demonstrated to the teachers that the administration will support the teachers' efforts to achieve these goals. The Head of School thus becomes one of the crafters of the "Proof Text Document" and the teachers' concerns are valued so the goals can be closely based on actual "work in the field." From the world café a working committee of eight people—comprising school staff, central agency professionals, local rabbis, and lay people—formed to continue the process.

This visioning process helped the school to transform its mind-set from a school that revolved around an eleventh grade Israel trip accompanied by a "light," loosely based curriculum to a more intentional curriculum closely aligned with the school vision. The curriculum was redesigned around five key areas of concentration (see table 9.1) and, similar to a college system, students were asked to choose an area of specialization or "major" while also fulfilling the minimum requirements within the other core areas of concentration. The new school handbook explains, "your personal Jewish journey" over the next four years will allow you to "travel through five areas of study as you uncover things you never knew about your Jewish heritage." Employing professional vernacular, the handbook explains that these five areas of instruction encapsulate the school's belief or "enduring understanding" that it is providing students the "opportunity to grow in understanding, appreciation and application of Jewish knowledge, practice and values, empowering them to be more informed Jews and solidifying their Jewish identity."

Table 9.1 gives a taste of some of the curriculum of the school, with the five areas of concentration and a statement about the ways in which each can offer an opportunity for personal meaning and growth. A quick glance at the course titles should demonstrate the relative lack of "classical Judaica" content at the school in terms of elective courses. This approach is in keeping with the school's philosophy of offering "fun" courses that help students find personal meaning. It is also likely a function of the limited availability of staff qualified to teach traditional Judaica. As mentioned, most students at the school are affiliated with local synagogues and are therefore involved in their synagogue confirmation programs (eighth through tenth grade) through the school. It is in these courses that students are exposed to more traditional types of themes taught by congregational rabbis. Hebrew language is taught at the school, but this is not a particularly popular class. An attempt a number of years ago to make Hebrew language mandatory was met with considerable resistance by students and parents.

**Table 9.1**
*Elective Courses at Western Hebrew High*

| Area of Concentration | Sample of Some Courses |
| --- | --- |
| • JEWISH HISTORY AND PHILOSOPHY<br>Discover how to thrive as a Jew in a changing world | • Kabbalah and You<br>• Comparative Religion<br>• Sects Ed<br>• *Bal Shem Tov*: The Life, Stories and Teachings of the Founder of Chasidism |
| • ISRAEL<br>Develop a personal relationship to the Land, State, and People of Israel | • IDF: More than Just an Army<br>• Israeli Pop Culture<br>• Israeli Dance<br>• Israeli Issues and the Media |
| • TEXT<br>Build a foundation for making informed decisions about how to live as a Jew | • Beyond this Life: What Jews Do and Believe about Death<br>• *B'reisheit* in Conflict: Torah's Magnificent Contradictions<br>• Sex, Drugs, and Integrity: Jewish Wisdom for the 21st Century Teenager<br>• Jewish Dreams 101 |
| • ARTS AND CULTURE<br>Explore Jewish creativity and express your Jewish identity | • Kosher Cooking around the World<br>• Klez Garage Band<br>• The Holocaust in Film<br>• Art and Judaism |
| • JEWISH LIVING<br>Experience how Jewish tradition and cycles add meaning to your life | • The Jewish Lens: Exploring Values and Community through Photography<br>• Respect Me: Building Healthy Relationships<br>• "Jewpardy": The Making of a Jewish Game Show<br>• Tastes of Judaism: Jewish Culture through Food |

In keeping with the "best practices" recommendation of educational researcher Barry Holtz,[10] all teachers were assigned to one of the five areas of concentration and expected to work in teams supervised by more experienced teachers who serve as team/section leaders. New teachers that arrive at the school are similarly placed and mentored within a team structure. The educational consultants were committed to delegating these team leaderships as a crucial piece of the program's success. They understood that by establishing teams of teachers with team leaders they were building capacity within the school for its own future processes of strategic planning. This embedded planning process was designed to better connect enduring understanding to the school year (lesson planning, individual students, school goals).

Dividing staff into smaller teams helps teachers feel a sense of belonging in the school and creates an atmosphere conducive to personal growth. Tara was proud to tell us that teacher turnover has decreased and attendance at faculty meetings has increased. She spoke of the new energy at the faculty meetings: "And just sitting around with that group of people is a great time. It's an excellent educational conversation. It's a philosophic conversation, it's a "what are we doing well." And light bulbs go off and people's eyes are wide open. They are meeting each other. They are talking to each other more. They are learning about one another and a camaraderie is starting to build. I think that they are really noticing a difference in their teaching. They are enjoying being at school more."

It is perhaps not surprising to hear that while in theory the new curriculum and team structure is strong, in practice it is still a work in progress. The structure is still quite new and teachers will need to be continually nurtured and supported in the curriculum so as to become more knowledgeable in content areas and to fully "buy in." One teacher giving a class on Jewish Life Skills was unsure which teacher team she belonged to when we asked her. The smaller school campus did not participate in the curricular restructuring and teacher training programs. In terms of course selections this campus has chosen not to place any restrictions at this time on which classes their students take. Because the smaller campus is located within a more isolated Jewish community, the principal has taken a more lenient approach on this issue so as not to dissuade any students from attending. Neither campus currently has tools in place for formal written assessments of teachers.

Student surveys of seniors reveal that to date there are uneven results among the five areas of concentration. As mentioned, students report being "much more knowledgeable" about the subject of Israel, but considerably less so in the other areas. They also reported that some classes were disorganized and lacked structure. Despite some efforts at teacher training, the reality is that some of the staff are still relatively inexperienced and do not necessarily have clear expertise in their subject areas.

Interestingly, most parents we spoke to at the main campus were not aware of the curricular changes at their children's school. Some that were aware of it were concerned about the curriculum becoming too rigid with too many restrictions on how many courses a student can take in one area of concentration. Happy that their kids will participate in any type of organized Jewish program, they were concerned that their children would be turned off from the school and lose their desire to come. This group of parents does not want the school to become too "serious" and stray away from what they see as the primary value of the school: to be a social place where Jewish teenagers can interact with other Jewish teenagers.

Finally, despite the decrease in turnover in the teachers, Tara herself resigned after one year as head of school. We know from the recent JESNA report (2007) that turnover of school leaders emerged as a major challenge among Hebrew highs in the country. This, combined with the departure of the hired educational consultants—the grant money came to an end and their contract was not renewed by the central agency—leaves us to wonder whether the strong momentum built in this area can sustain itself.[11]

## Students Love to Come to School: "The Classes Are Cool, The Teachers Are Cool and They Learn Some Stuff"

One of the school staff enthusiastically conveyed to us: "These kids are so committed to [Western] Hebrew High. It's amazing! I've literally never seen [this level] of support. These kids are telling their parents how much they want to be here. They are coming to us in their soccer uniforms straight from practice, straight from play rehearsal. They haven't eaten. They are with us till 8:30 at night and then they go home and then they start their homework." Students actually like to come to school! This statement alone is a clear testament to things this school is doing very well, especially in light of the poor reputations from which supplementary schools often suffer.

When we asked Susan Parsons what aspect of the school she is most proud of she replied: "It's the power of seeing these two hundred kids come every week and just glad to see each other." As a past parent of two Western Hebrew High students herself she knows how pleased parents are that their kids want to go to Hebrew school, especially since many of the parents have negative memories of their own Hebrew school experiences: "Parents are thrilled. You know, "I can't believe he stayed home from school today because he had [a] scratchy throat but he's going to Hebrew High." And from my own personal experience my kids were the same way. They fought and kicked and screamed, 'I'm not going, I'm not going.' I said, 'Look, I paid the tuition, just go once or twice and see if you like it.' That was it, they wouldn't miss it. They wouldn't care if they had term papers or exams the next day. It was, 'Oh, it's just an hour and a half. We'll be back. We can do it later.'"

Rabbi Hillberg, who teaches at the school and has a child in the school, described the school as "a magnet for identified Jewish kids in the community. I think its social nexus is what's so appealing. It's the place to be. Youth groups in the community don't do stuff on Monday nights because they know it's head-to-head with Hebrew High. I think that's a wonderful thing."

All this praise for the school raises the obvious question as to what is it exactly about the school that accounts for this great popularity among students? Rabbi Hillberg provides a clue when he refers to its "social nexus." Student comments within the school handbook highlighted this theme repeatedly:

- Hebrew High is a chance to be connected with friends.
- I made so many new and awesome friends.
- What I have gained from Hebrew High is friendships and relationships that will last a lifetime.
- The friends I already had I got a lot closer with.

This concentration of Jewish friends creates an important sense of Jewish community for the students, many of whom attend public schools where there are few Jews.[12] One mother described the situation of her daughter, who left Western Hebrew High to enroll in college out of town one year early. When she decided she was not yet ready to start college, she returned home and desired to participate again in a Jewish youth organization of some sort. The mother explained the importance of the school as a portal to Jewish community: "[W]e belong to the Beth Tefillah Synagogue and I begged the rabbi to let her back into USY, but they wouldn't let her in because they say she already 'graduated.' But [Western Hebrew High] let her come back. And I cannot tell you what a big deal that was, not just for us because we never got to see her graduate or anything. But for her it kept her connected to the Jewish kids and the Jewish community where the rest of the Jewish community like the synagogues said tough luck."

When we spoke to Corey Engel, the director of the city's central agency we intended to discover what it is about the school that is engaging these students beyond the social experience of spending time with good friends or the sense of community the school provides. We were somewhat surprised to receive the following response: "The question is 'what brings in [the students]?' What makes it worthwhile? Is it the phenomenal academics? No. Is it that they know that by staying connected to the school they are going to be better Jews? No. It is that they want to see their friends and they want to connect with their friends and this is an exciting way to do it. And, by the way, the classes are cool, the teachers are cool and they learn some stuff. So I wouldn't say academics is the most important piece of the program."

In our examination of the school we wanted to challenge—or at least probe a little deeper into—the perspective that Mr. Engel provided. What does it mean that "the classes are cool, the teachers are cool and they learn some stuff"? We set out to unpack these ideas. A hint came in our discussions with Rabbi Lowenstein, another Rabbi who teaches in the school, who explained: "There seems to be a reputation that you go to [Western] Hebrew High for a social life. You meet other Jewish kids . . . they are young, have fun, and do not have consequences for being there. In other words, homework and evaluations are in a much more relaxed environment, so the kids automatically tend to associate more with the social aspects of it. But I know that some of what's going on there is on a very good level of exposure to different parts of Jewish life."

As we have seen (table 9.1), many of the course titles and subject areas are "hip" and "funky," appealing to a liberal Jewish teenage crowd immersed in the popular culture around them. "Sects Ed" is a clever name for a course on the four major Jewish movements or sects. "Politics Shmolotics" explores Jewish perspectives on civic duty and responsibility. The school shows considerable skill in connecting to today's teenager. The school handbook is full of photographs and comments of the students, past and present. The course descriptions are casual, creative, and inviting, making sure to explain how the class will be personally relevant and meaningful to the student. Here is the description of the "Kaballah and You" course:

> Would you like to build your own Golem? Cook up love potions? Exorcize dybbuks and demons? If so, this class is NOT for you. But if you are looking for ways to make sense of a seemingly chaotic world, give this class a try. We'll talk about the idea of G-d connecting to everything in the world, what prayer (tefillah) really is, Jewish ideas about reincarnation and other questions you were afraid to ask or didn't even know how to ask, We'll ground our discussions in traditional Jewish mysticism. Bring all your questions—all points of view welcome.

In keeping with their desire to stay relevant to new interests and reach out to a religiously diverse student body, the school often develops new courses and modifies its current courses. Barbara Steiner has a son in senior year at the school. She appreciates the school's flexibility:

> The thing that's really cool about this program is that they offer so many different classes. They appeal to a wide variety of interest. If something

doesn't work they either try to make it work or they change it a little bit and they ask the kids for input, the parents for input. They are always adding new kinds of classes and trying different things. I think it's very dynamic compared to [another local school] which is what my kids had experience with. It was really rigid. I mean you did this, and you did this. You know if it was too easy that was too bad. It was too hard it was too bad. It was just everybody did everything by grade, do you know what I mean?—So that's really it.

Besides the catchy names and inviting descriptions what else makes the classes "cool"? Rabbi Lowenstein described a course in the school called "Respect Me" that impressed him. Taught by a social worker, the course explores "male-female relationships and issues around respect and decency." Rabbi Lowenstein contributes to the course by offering some Jewish context to these issues. The course provides another example of how the school's programs go beyond the purely cognitive dimension as the instructor "does a remarkable job of preparing the students to be peer counselors." By connecting them to real life concerns beyond the classroom with many role-playing exercises, the rabbi considers the course important "life preparation" conducted in a Jewish context.

A big part of what makes classes so cool for teenagers are cool teachers. In our observations of the school we came across a handful of "magnet" or "signature" teachers who enjoy great popularity with the students for their highly engaging and personable style. Personable does not mean academically "light," however, as we discovered from Susan Parsons. She described her son's attraction to a past teacher named Marty Goldenberg (who later served as one of the school's educational consultants). Marty has a graduate degree in Jewish Education and many years of senior leadership in the field. Susan told us the school thrives in part because of the presence of "a couple of those magnet teachers. Marty Goldenberg was my kids' teacher—they just loved [him]. My son would only take a class with one teacher. He was one of these attentive kids, and he loved this one teacher who was very strict in his text study and just made them think philosophically and intellectually. He would only accept a certain number of kids in his class and he hand-picked those kids."

We found the smaller, more informal campus of the school to have a particularly energetic and vibrant atmosphere. Students seemed genuinely excited to be there. As described above, the smaller school is more loosely structured, where the new curricular design of the central campus has not (yet?) been implemented. The principal of the smaller campus, Kyra Yermus, articulated to us the central mantra of Hebrew highs in America: "I find the better the teacher, the more kids. I've had university teachers and they . . . don't always work with high school kids, it just depends. I need a balance. *I need a really incredible charismatic teacher with a really cool subject.*

To Kyra's credit she has succeeded in gathering a handful of dynamic, charismatic teachers in her school to whom students are drawn. Lionel Machtinger is such a teacher. A man in his mid-30's—he looks much younger—with an earring in his ear, Lionel is a star teacher to many of the one hundred students in the school. In fact he is something of a rock star, performing with his band all over the United States. Kyra allows him a flexible schedule so he can combine his teaching with his music career. Coming from the Midwest with a degree in Music Education, Lionel began teaching music in the public school system while also serving as the city's Director of BBYO programming. He quit the public school after a short time. Working with youth is his passion, so he began teaching at Western Hebrew High. He has been there five years. He confirmed for us the more laid back approach of his campus: "I think formality is not where this school wants to go. I think that part of its strength is that these kids can just come here and just hang—and they learn while they're here, wow!"

We observed Lionel's "Relationships" class and were struck by how the students became immersed in Lionel's story of his conflict with his younger brother. The conflict revolved around whether Lionel should attend his non-observant brother's bachelor party or attend synagogue services for Rosh HaShanah. Lionel weaved the familial considerations with the personal religious considerations in a way that the students could identify and apply to similar dilemmas they have faced in their own lives. The classroom decorum was extremely informal. Students were eating and lounged in their desks, sometimes with their feet resting on chairs. Knowing the context, we understand this to be a signal that the students felt comfortable and relaxed in the classroom, rather than a sign that they were bored and did not respect their teacher. The teenagers listened intently. Their eyes were glued to the speaker. They look up to Lionel and respect what he has to say. In our conversation with him he articulated his teaching philosophy of caring:

> With a teenager you've got to connect first. It's always true. For me that's what makes a good teacher. You've got to connect with your audience no matter what. But with a teenager I believe much more in the mentorship style than any other style when it comes to teaching. I spend the majority of my time letting them know that I care about them and that's why I'm teaching them. Not because I have a list of

things that I need to impart and then smack them until they learn it, but that I care about you. And I think these things are really going to make a huge difference in your life and you're going to feel better about yourself if you learn it. And look, here's how it has helped me. This is all stuff that I learned. It's very much a mentorship model.

We see here the school's strength in connecting with the students in a way that provides personal meaning for them. Anna Jessin, another young, dynamic teacher on the campus whom we met earlier, is also very skillful in engaging and exciting her students. She comes to Western Hebrew High with an impressive list of credentials. She holds a master's degree in Jewish Environmental Education, has served several years as Judaic Director of a summer camp, has taught at a Jewish day school and is a fellow of the North American Alliance for Jewish Youth (NAA).

Anna's signature class is her senior seminar. With only a total of one hundred students on the smaller campus, it is not unusual to have fewer than ten seniors enrolled at the school. When we observed her class in the early spring of 2007 seven were enrolled (in our subsequent visit in the 2007–08 school year there were sixteen students). Anna and her students held their class on couches in the lobby of the Jewish Community Centre. Though the front door of the building, with its bell, opened often for passing students, the students were oblivious to this, focusing on Anna and each other. Her course was designed in large part by the topics of interest generated by the students themselves in the first week of class. Based on readings the students had done from Rabbi Lawrence Kushner's Kabalistic *River of Light*, the class explored complex Jewish perspectives on consciousness, *tehiyat hameytim* (resurrection of the dead) and the "unity of souls." The students were intellectually engaged, posing thoughtful questions and comments. She is clearly well read on the subject and is able to promote critical thinking among her students.

After class we had a chance to talk to Anna about her passion for teaching. Her commitment to helping students on their own Jewish journeys to self-discovery highlights a great strength of the school:

I know I was put on this earth to be a teacher and specifically just taking kids out of the traditional western mode where they're being lectured at and then having to regurgitate information to someone. And being able to really allow them to think and giving them the opportunity to allow them to come to conclusions and research things deeper and to really investigate for themselves. I love that this is a teenage age group because I feel like this is when *they're really trying to formulate who they are and how they want to be in the world. And being able to give them the real tools and the time and the space to do that, I think is enormous.* We do some unbelievable things in my senior seminar that I feel like adults would [wonder]" this is what you're teaching seventeen-year-olds? Can they do that?" I feel like adults underestimate kids in high school. And so getting to really be able to delve into some really neat stuff with them and watching them make these connections and watching them get involved and get so excited. They are talking over each other because they're so excited to be able to share.

We have already had a taste of the enthusiasm of this small, tight group of senior seminar students at their seniors' dinner in the opening page of this chapter. Let us now go back to that Wednesday evening in April 2007. After the students had completed their presentations to their parents and had a bite to eat, they decided they would—as a group—visit the current eleventh grade class and share with them their thoughts of how much they enjoyed their senior year. We grabbed our tape recorder and chased the students through the strange labyrinth of trailers that constituted the Jewish Community Centre. Could there be a more powerful testament to the satisfaction of students than their voluntarily speaking to their junior cohort to encourage them to stay on at the school for their upcoming senior year? Standing in front of the cluttered classroom the seven students, in turn, addressed the eleventh graders who were lounging on chairs and couches. The seniors raved about the great value of the senior seminar which they had just completed. Here are some of the ideas they conveyed:

- We have great discussions; everyone is involved and contributes.
- You get to decide what you learn.
- It is very intellectually stimulating; we explored mature topics like life-after-death and the stream of consciousness.
- You can look at things in your own way; you don't have to tow the party line.
- It's spiritual.
- It will be your favorite class; you will have Anna as a teacher.

As we made our long drive in our rental car back to the local airport we were charged by the energy of what we had just witnessed. These students were excited about what they learned and what they experienced. Without this Hebrew High in this somewhat isolated locale, these teenagers would have very little outlet to explore their Jewishness. In our estimation this is a place making a meaningful Jewish impact on its students.

What is the nature of this "meaningful Jewish impact"? As we have said, researchers of Jewish educational programs know that specific educational outcomes are difficult to assess. Our survey administered to senior students may offer some useful data in this regard. The survey revealed that "as a result of [their] experiences at [Western] Hebrew High:

- More than 70% of respondents reported that they feel "a *much* stronger connection to Israel."
- 35% of respondents reported that they "feel a *much* stronger sense of Jewish identity."
- Just under 40% of respondents have become "*quite a bit* more active in Jewish organizations."

In terms of their attitudes for the future:

- Almost 45% report that they are "quite a bit more likely to become involved in Hillel or take Jewish Studies courses at college."
- More than 25% of respondents reported that they "feel *much* stronger about the importance of marrying a Jewish person."
- Almost 60% reported that they are "*much* more likely to provide [their] future children with a Jewish education."

## Conclusion

There is much that we can learn from Western Hebrew High, in terms of both its strengths and its shortcomings.

We have noted the lack of a school board of directors. Research has shown[13] that effective governance by professional and volunteer leadership is an important ingredient in creating a positive school culture. The principals of Western Hebrew High have very large responsibilities and little in the way of outside support. The disconnect we discovered between the school and the central agency exacerbates this challenge. These principals have grown accustomed to handling much of their workload by themselves. Directors of schools sometimes need mentoring around appreciating the valuable contributions of caring and committed lay leaders. Strong lay leaders who are regularly involved in crafting vision, articulating and carrying out mission, and formulating strategy can be effective advocates in good times and bad, at times of growth and shrinkage.

We discovered that, lacking this support, Tara felt "stifled, anxious and reserved" in her job. The energy she needed to exert to negotiate central agency politics drained her of her natural motivation and creativity. She accepted an attractive offer (better salary and benefits) to return to the site of her previous work as youth director of a local synagogue. There she supervises the youth programs in the synagogue's brand new youth activities building, which she helped develop.[14] From the perspective of Western Hebrew High, we see here a missed opportunity to nurture and support a talented young Jewish professional.

In addition to supportive governance, we know that a key piece of the structural integrity of a school is the active engagement of the parent body. To this point we do not see a large amount of this type of engagement. The administration revealed that parents are generally heard from when there is a problem, but are otherwise fairly quiet, remaining on the sidelines. As mentioned, interviews with parents revealed that they are not very familiar with the new curriculum design nor do they have many specific expectations of the school other than that their child enjoys themselves and spends time with Jewish friends in a "Jewish environment." The lack of a school board obviously impedes the active participation of parents and other lay leaders in the workings of the school.

Parents report satisfaction with the weekly email report they receive describing the current news in the school. We learned of plans to institute a new program next year called "Hebrew Heroes," which will involve a group of parents meeting at the same time and place as their kids to design and implement a fund-raising project for the school. More attempts at parent involvement in the school are recommended. Parents are major stake holders in a school. They can be better engaged to help ensure the future sustainability of schools.

Amid these challenges, the school exhibits a number of strengths. As a community school with little competition from other supplementary high schools in the area, the school plays a central role in this medium-sized Jewish community. Its strong relationship with local synagogues provides a structure to sustain a number of congregational confirmation programs, some of which were suffering within their own institutions. With its long history and strong reputation, the school's annual Israel trip has become tightly embedded in the fabric of the Jewish community and is a source of much pride for this community. The students enroll in the school in great anticipation of the six-week trip, and our anecdotal evidence suggests they come back more mature people, more personally engaged Jews, and much more connected to Israel. For some it is "life changing." The school facilitates a variety of post-Israel programming that interacts with the wider Jewish community. This model of a supplementary school as community magnet, a gathering place for the various Jewish youth of a city, is a system that works well here and can be replicated.

To its credit, after our research concluded we learned that the central agency has developed a more cohesive "youth programs committee" to oversee policy and procedure for the high school, the Israel trip, and the *B'nai Tzedek* charity program. We recommend continued efforts to develop and sustain this type of governing body.

The school should be commended for its sustained efforts at professional development and curricular redesign. We were impressed by the candor and thoughtful self-reflection by Tara on these matters. By participating in serious teaching workshops and privately commissioning educational consultants, the school has clearly gone further than most other schools in trying to improve its product. Although the outside educational consultants who worked with the school for a significant amount of time did not get the renewed contract they desired from the central agency, the agency did allocate funds for a new internal professional development consultant and began the procedure of paying teachers extra (up to $180 a semester) for their time spent in professional learning.

Overall, the school has succeeded in sharpening its curriculum to align it more closely with its mission to "empower its students" to be more informed Jews and solidify their Jewish identity." Developing team/section leaders has allowed for novice teachers to benefit more easily from the support and mentoring of experienced teachers. This does not mean that we witnessed only excellent teaching in our observations. In fact we witnessed examples of the same type of mediocre teaching environments that can be found in almost any school: inability to keep unruly students focused and engaged, inaccurate information presented, lack of sustained discussion to allow students to process information, classes too large to connect to all students, etc.

On the whole, however, we were struck by the school's ability to design a product that so excited and invigorated Jewish teenagers. The creative class topics resonate with liberal teenagers deeply engrossed in the secular culture around them and are packaged in inviting and engaging ways. The school has recruited a number of dynamic and charismatic teachers that are highly skilled at intellectually engaging their pupils while also caring for them and mentoring them. Outside the classroom the school provides social action programs, charity programs, political engagement series, Holocaust remembrance presentations, and other opportunities for nonformal, experiential education. Through this the school demonstrates that it understands how to connect with the Jewish sensitivities of its consumers. It strives to help its students develop personal meaning from the Jewish knowledge and concepts they are absorbing. They can thus be in a position to start to think about how Judaism fits into their lives. By providing a casual and comfortable environment in which to think and grow, the school helps these young people move forward on their ongoing Jewish life journeys.

It is not difficult to see the success of the social dimension of the school—students scattered across several public schools clearly love spending time with their Jewish friends, and the school actively promotes opportunities for this Jewish community building. In addition to this, however, we think we have gathered substantial evidence to reasonably suggest that there is more here than purely a good social experience with friends. We have argued that the intellectual and experiential dimensions of the school's program can make deep *personal* impressions on students and thus make a difference in how they understand their world and how they construct and understand their Jewish identities. We think this fusion of providing a place for Jewish social belonging with offering an opportunity to discover personal Jewish meaning is indeed a powerful combination—and is the secret of the success of Western Hebrew High.

## Notes

1. Steven M. Cohen and Arnold M. Eisen, *The Jew Within: Self, Family, and Community in America* (Bloomington: Indiana University Press, 2000).

2. Demographers generally describe millennials as those who are coming of age in the first decade of the new millennium (2000–2010).

3. Bethamie Horowitz. "Reframing the Study of Contemporary American Jewish Identity," *Contemporary Jewry* 23 (2002), pp. 14–34.

4. This includes the 15-minute break time.

5. One prominent community rabbi argued, however, that the school still has some way to go in deepening its relationship with local rabbis.

6. This may not be considered expensive in some major East Coast cities, but it is to some in this western region of the country. One of the issues is that the $800 provides two hours and fifteen minutes of instruction for twenty-four weeks a year, but not any extras such as food and transportation.

7. Leora Isaacs, "Jewish Education Center of Cleveland—Evaluation of Funded Positions Initiative," Jewish Educational Service of North America (JESNA), May 2003; http://www.jesna.org.

8. While we must be cautious with these types of survey results (small sample, only one year cohort surveyed, possible response bias, no longitudinal dimension), we still

think they hold some value in identifying how the students describe what they have learned and the impact of the school on their own Jewish lives.

9. "Making Jewish Education Work: Community Hebrew High Schools," *JESNA*, 2007; http://www.jesna.org.

10. Barry W. Holtz, ed., *Supplementary School Education* (Mandel Foundation, 1995).

11. After completing our research we learned that Tara's job was not refilled. Instead Susan Parsons, the administrator, added the role of principal to her portfolio. In addition, a curriculum consultant as well as professional development professional was hired on a part-time basis. The professional development for teachers no longer includes the Understanding by Design method, however.

12. Teachers also spoke about the way the school serves as an important source of Jewish community for them. One teacher told us, "if I went only to my temple on Shabbat, I would not know all these people and all this was going on."

13. "Making Jewish Education Work: Community Hebrew High Schools," *JESNA*, 2007; http://www.jesna.org.

14. This new youth center will clearly provide competition in the future for Western Hebrew High.

CHAPTER 10

# Putting the School Back into the Supplementary Jewish High School

JACK WERTHEIMER WITH SERENE VICTOR

$T$he field of supplementary Jewish education has struggled in recent decades to reconcile what actually happens in most settings with the potentially unrealistic expectations raised by their self-identification as "schools." Some educators, in fact, passionately deny their programs are schools in any meaningful sense. In their view, the limited number of hours available in Jewish settings as compared to full day schooling inevitably sets up supplementary programs for invidious comparisons. There is just so much that can be taught in so short a time span.[1] Moreover, the goals of supplementary education are both broader and narrower than those of full-time schools: broader because such programs seek to "enculturate" young Jews, to impart a strong sense of Jewishness, to connect them to the life of the Jewish people and often to a particular religious congregation[2] *in addition to* engaging in cognitive learning; more narrow, because only a limited amount of time is devoted to school-like subjects and tasks. Some educators, therefore, employ a different model entirely to describe what goes on in supplementary schools, preferring instead the label of informal learning.

East Coast Community High School has taken a different path. It has self-consciously adopted many of the formal trappings of schools precisely in order to win the respect of its students and parent-body. Among the most telling features of this program that lend it the feel of a school are:

• a Judaically well-educated and experienced faculty, many of whom have education degrees;

- a senior and associate school administrator who both have advanced degrees in either Judaica or education;
- clearly articulated attendance and tardiness policies;
- a requirement that students who miss five class sessions must make up the time by writing an additional paper—if they do not, they will not pass their courses for the year;
- a wide range of course offerings from which students select their programs;
- a fair number of courses that include strong textual components—required readings, use of Rabbinic texts, comparative analyses of texts, and written forms of assessment;
- a curriculum geared to be of "high interest and meaningful" to high school students;
- classroom dialogue between and among students and their teachers as the dominant instructional approach;
- a requirement of each teacher to provide a course description, syllabus, and final exam for each course (a common formatting and structure in these documents adds to the cohesiveness of the program);
- assigned homework in some classes;
- a commitment to assessing student learning through graded formal papers and/or exams.

Even as the school enforces these polices, it simultaneously attends to the affective and social dimensions of Jewish identity formation through a deliberately cultivated set of group experiences. Rather than cram every moment of its Sunday morning program with classes, the school sets aside a 35-minute break each week for students to socialize and participate in clubs over a bagel breakfast. Some classes are devoted to Israeli dance and dramatic improvisation—i.e. nonacademic subjects. And most important, the high school runs an extensive program of extracurricular activities all year long to bring students together for social action, religious gatherings, and recreational activities. The school thus balances formal study with community building and social engagement. It is the mix of the formal and informal that makes this school so interesting, even as the formal trappings set it apart from most other supplementary schools.

## The Ambience

East Coast Community High School is located in a Middle Atlantic state, not all that distant from a large city. Established as a communal institution under the auspices of a federation of Jewish philanthropy, the high school recruits students from a range of populations and claims support of 25 congregations: close to two-thirds of the students are drawn from Conservative congregations, 5 percent each are from Reform and Reconstructionist synagogues, and over 20 percent from unaffiliated homes. According to the estimates of the school administration between 20 and 25 percent of children have at least one Israeli-born parent, an extraordinarily high figure. In addition 20 percent of students attended Jewish day schools prior to enrolling in the high school, with the rest coming from synagogue religious schools. The Israeli and day school children (some pupils are both), however, make it possible for the high school to offer advanced classes that are quite unusual in a supplementary setting—e.g., an advanced Hebrew class in which the instructor and most students primarily speak to one another in Hebrew (here the children of Israelis play a disproportionate role) and a Talmud course in which students study the original text with medieval rabbinic commentaries (*Rishonim*).

The ambience of the school is religiously traditional. Boys are expected to wear a head covering, and food that is overtly from non-Kosher eateries is not permitted in the building. The Orthodox influence is particularly evident in the orientation of the tutors (to be discussed later) who work with small groups of students: all are Orthodox.[3] As we shall see, the faculty is also skewed heavily toward a modern Orthodox orientation. Unlike most elementary supplementary schools, this high school does not include prayers (*tefillah*) in its Sunday morning schedule.

The high school has been in existence for thirty-five years and for over twenty-five of those it has been run by the same school head. This kind of continuity is quite unusual and has a number of consequences. The school has been able through trial and error to fine-tune its program, but at the same time it has maintained fidelity to the guiding vision of its school head, a vision of a high school that, in his words, "is structured as a school—with late passes, bathroom passes, and exams—because otherwise the kids will not recognize it as a school." The principal's longevity has also insured that he has a strong hand in making decisions; by comparison, the board is marginal and addresses mainly fiduciary questions.[4] More generally, the school does not involve parents very actively. True, it invites parents to sit in on classes at an "open house" scheduled for one day during the year, and it involves a small number as volunteers who put out food at events. But it relates to parents primarily when they need to be kept informed of their children's academic and social progress, and does not regard them as decision makers in curricular matters or school governance. This high school may give pause to those who are convinced that an active school committee and parental involvement are necessary for running a good supplementary school.

## Recruitment and Retention

Since the high school's founding, enrollment numbers have gone through a number of ups and downs. Soon after the school's founding, the student population stood at 160 students, but then it suffered a steep decline within a decade, reaching a nadir of 20 students. After hiring its current school head, the school experienced rising enrollment numbers, peaking at over 300 students. Recently, though, the numbers have begun to slip. Where once incoming eighth grade classes could count on close to 100 students, now the figure is closer to 65. The school currently enrolls 270 students between grades 8 and 12. The larger context for this decline is the contraction of the Conservative movement from which the school draws the majority of its students. Most local religious schools run by Conservative synagogues are shrinking, a trend evident on the national level too.[5] With only two exceptions, the Conservative synagogues in the area now have fewer than 100 students each. Thus the pool of potential students for the high school is contracting.

Attrition is also a major source of concern within the school. The drop off after eighth grade is the steepest, and, by the time students reach twelfth grade, half of their entering class has withdrawn from the school. (In recent years, roughly 40 students have graduated annually from the twelfth grade.) Overall, the loss through attrition and lower levels of recruitment has resulted in an enrollment decline of 100 students compared to four years ago. The school does not have a clear explanation for this decline or a strategy to combat it.

All this places a heavy burden on the school to recruit among sixth and seventh graders in area synagogues and to find ways to retain students who are enrolled. East Coast Community High School received a Legacy Heritage grant to intensify its recruitment in several congregations and run experimental programs of particular appeal to seventh graders, thereby wooing them to the high school. Some congregational rabbis and school heads serve as strong allies in these efforts; others keep aloof. Here the school's weak board leadership may well be a factor: without strong professional and lay leadership from within congregations, the recruitment of new students falls entirely on the shoulders of the school administration.

It could potentially be a shared burden were the high school truly perceived as an upward extension of the synagogue schools.

From the perspective of the administrative leaders, the strongest allies in recruitment are parents who insist on their child enrolling and staying in the school for at least the eighth grade; unfortunately, in the view of the two school heads, the number of such parents is dwindling. With the multiple tugs on their children's time and perhaps a lack of appreciation for the value of ongoing Jewish education, many parents refrain from pressing the issue and leave it to their children to decide. According to the estimates of the school administration, the high school now attracts a quarter of the potential pool of children in its catchment area, where it once drew roughly a third of such students.[6]

Because the school runs classes only on Sunday mornings and is communal in nature, it never acquired its own building, relying instead on renting space at other educational institutions. Currently, its classes are held in a non-Jewish public facility, while its offices are housed in a professional building a few miles from the classroom site. This arrangement has inconvenienced administrators and discomfited students. The former must cart equipment such as a copy machine, files, and other supplies to and from the school building every Sunday morning and then oversee a clean-up at the end of the school day. In its present facilities, the school lacks an auditorium or large space for assemblies. The absence of such a central place to hold gatherings is felt by some students as a loss, especially for those who remember the previous building, which did include an auditorium. It deprives the school of opportunities to mark holidays with assemblies and host other types of large gatherings during school hours.

## Faculty and Administration

A principal and an assistant principal administer the school. The former, as noted, has led the school for twenty-five years and comes with educational training and experience in school administration; the latter, a female Conservative rabbi, joined the administration a few years ago. They make a good team, serving as contrasting role and gender models and also offering an Orthodox and a Conservative perspective that undoubtedly enrich the school.

During school hours, both are constantly in motion: when they are not patrolling the halls to insure the smooth functioning of the school or monitoring where students are and getting them where they ought to be, they step into classrooms unannounced and observe the flow of the class discussion. These impromptu class observations frequently spark later discussions between the administrators and specific teachers about problem areas. The administrators also call parents when students miss classes and insure that teachers contact parents when students are not doing well. They also review all class syllabi and every exam sheet distributed to students, checking everything from the nature of the curriculum to the grammatical correctness of the writing. Like other school heads, they also are actively involved in the hiring of faculty and the recruitment of students. And they deal with local rabbis and board members. In their monitoring of students, they are assisted by a professional guidance counselor who devotes two-thirds of his time to working with teens requiring special attention. This type of staffing is unusual for a supplementary school. In addition, a full-time director of student activities organizes extracurricular programming.

The faculty consists of twenty teachers drawn from a mix of denominations, but more than half are modern Orthodox. Contrary to expectations, the teachers are not primarily engaged in Jewish education during the rest of the week. Few teach in day schools. A number work as Jewish professionals or teach in public schools, while some of the younger teachers are pursuing degrees in Jewish studies. Some teachers spend their weekdays in activities far removed from Jewish study or education. They claim to enjoy the chance to contribute to Jewish education by teaching in this once-a-week high school.

An unusual pattern among the teachers is the longevity of their connection to the school. A few have taught in the high school for over fourteen years and most have at least seven years of experience in this school. The other surprising characteristic of the faculty is the preponderance of male teachers. The school head attributes this to the difficulty of finding women who would be satisfied teaching in a Sunday morning program only, when other supplementary schools offer two and three day-a-week teaching opportunities (and thereby the chance to earn a higher salary). How this gender imbalance affects both male and female students could not be ascertained but is worthy of study.

When interviewed separately and in small groups, faculty members express appreciation for the school's academic orientation, a fact that should not be surprising considering that teachers were recruited to the school for their ability to offer serious, high-level classes—that is, they were hired because of their compatibility with this particular school model. Still, because most teachers have taught in other Jewish educational settings, they do not take the virtues of this kind of high school for granted. As one teacher put it: "the more you ask from kids, the more they deliver. We don't have lateness, and don't have terrible absence problems. I came from a school that was much more of a model of informal education; I adjusted and like it much better here. The kids want their Hebrew school to resemble their secular high school." Another chimed in: "In my last school, kids referred to 'real school' and this place. Then they would catch themselves . . . Last year at a different school 50 percent absenteeism was typical. Here a bad day is 20 percent." The first teacher then added: "This is far closer to the day school than I imagined . . . They moved organically from the Solomon Schechter Day School to a Sunday Solomon Schechter school. They come to school on time, don't leave in the middle. I find there is no big break in the way they look at school. Obviously there is less demanded but there is a feeling that this is a serious place." At this point, the second teacher adds: "I tried to give creative homework. I created a blog, but I asked too much of them."

This exchange probably highlights the impact of former day school students on the school ambience and the willingness of children to take the high school program seriously, despite its once-a-week nature. Still, the teacher acknowledges the limitations of what his colleagues feel they can ask of their students. (The high school, we should note, is not associated with any day school.) Most important, the teachers are quite conscious of the benefits of teaching in a school largely devoid of discipline problems: the school culture fosters respect for teachers and learning; students generally do not act out in class; attendance is considerably better than at comparable schools; and relatively little class time is wasted on teachers struggling to get the students' attention. Teachers in this school know how fortunate they are compared to peers teaching in some other Jewish supplementary schools.

The school, in turn, asks a fair amount of its teachers. One member of the faculty explains how the system works: "There are penalties for tardiness, and we [also] get docked . . . if we come late to the Israel Parade. [The school expects a] monthly review, anecdotal reports, summaries of problem incidents that arise; finals have to be handed to [the school head] before they go to the students. [He] reads them before they're administrated. Sometimes [he alerts us] if the totals don't add up; or if the exam is too content-oriented, he asks us to give more of a thought question [on the test]." The school trappings in other words directly affect the teachers too. The principal reviews every exam before it is administered and holds teachers to other kinds of expectations. The teachers hasten to add that the school head is open to experimentation. In some classes, exams have been replaced by a portfolio review. Some exams now take the form of role playing, and other ways of eliciting what students have learned in classes have now been introduced, especially in courses more oriented toward the exploration of how Jews approach ethical choices.

Teachers also meet with some regularity with the principal to review their curricular plans and the progress of students. Several meetings occur before the beginning of the school year and then each teacher meets for forty-five minutes with the school head once a semester. What are these meetings like? One teacher reports: "This is the third school like this that I've been in. [The school head] gives it his personality. I already met with [him] to talk about this [Fall] semester and the Spring semester. He goes through my class list [and I] give a report on all the kids. Sometimes I might say I really don't have a handle. Sometimes we talk about the syllabus, but the interesting thing is we are dealing with each kid. That's what is interesting here." Another teacher adds: "[The school head] conveys that he takes it very, very seriously. I taught here for two years, and then was a Hebrew school principal [at another school] for two years. I thought I would use this experience, but all my teachers [at the other school] looked at me and said—'This is Hebrew school!' [In other words: don't expect so much of us.] I came back here." A third teacher commented as follows about the school head: "The man is a saint, a superstar. I give him all the credit. He always finds good people. He gets us to come back. He's always thinking out of the box. It filters down. He has high expectations of us. Syllabi, exams, lesson plans, contact with parents." At this point, a colleague interjects: "He backs us with discipline. It doesn't matter if the parents have influence as at other schools. He's behind the teacher." Still another teacher describes how well the school is organized to hit the ground running the moment the school year begins. Whereas other schools, in his experience, gear up slowly in September as a result of the High Holidays, the high school maximizes each school day. He adds about the school head, "he's relentless." His colleagues concur, and another adds: "He also takes chances. One or two kids were suicidal. He spoke with the therapist. He will stretch to the limit for a child." At least for these teachers, the structure created at the high school is appealing. In their view, the expectations of the school head keep them and their students in line and push the teachers to strive.

This is evident both in the level of serious instruction and in the attention paid to the needs of individual children. Teachers are held responsible for following up with students who require special attention, and some report interacting with their students outside school hours and at events other than school-sponsored extracurricular activities. One teacher describes the time a student who had missed some classes came to his home for follow-up. Some teachers also maintain ongoing contact with students after they have gone off to college. A popular teacher, according to some alumni, "keeps in touch for years afterward with former students." The school also enrolls students with special needs, who are not always welcomed in other Jewish schools. Teachers report on the presence of some students who suffer from Asperger's syndrome and ADD, as well as psychiatric disorders, who are integrated into the school and given special attention. The guidance counselor develops individual educational plans (IEPs) for these students and consults with teachers about implementing these plans.

The teachers' investment of themselves and sense of élan are all the more striking given the relatively low salaries offered by the school. According to the school head, until a few years ago, the school ranked in the bottom quarter of pay offered by supplementary schools across the country. "Three years ago, we went from the 25 percent [bracket] to 60–70 percent in the country compared to regular synagogue schools." The high school now has an official pay scale and does not cut deals with individual teachers. Those coming with no experience receive not much above $100 per school session. (The day, let us note, begins for teachers at 8:50 and ends at 12:30; teachers must prepare syllabi, lesson plans, and grade papers on their own time.) At the upper end, the more experienced teachers may earn close to $200 per session, a respectable level of compensation compared to many other supplementary schools.

Every Sunday, teachers assemble for twenty minutes before classes commence. The meetings tend to be perfunctory, focusing on upcoming special events, "good" and "welfare" announcements, and pep talks. Teachers are enlisted in talking up extracurricular activities and helping recruit students for *Shabbatonim* or other special events. At times, more substantive matters are raised. During open house day, some parents complained that their children, especially the eighth graders, find the thirty-five-minute break fraught with tension. Because the newly enrolled students are drawn from many different synagogues or are unaffiliated, many feel somewhat lost because they do not know other children; as a result, the parents complained, they hang around not knowing how to break into the group. To remedy this problem, the school offers several club activities during the break and has organized icebreaker activities, but they have been insufficient, the parents complain. At one teachers' meeting, the two principals raise this issue and elicit suggestions for additional clubs the school may run during the break. It is not a very active conversation, and outside observers were left wondering about the missed opportunity to include the teachers in more in-depth problem solving.

The teachers, in fact, have not been welded into a faculty that reflects together on the school culture, but are valued for what they can bring as classroom teachers. They confirm that their relationship with each other is formal. One teacher reports: "We are cordial, but we don't know each other." Another adds, "We are pretty professional, not collegial." "On *Shabbatonim* [Sabbath retreats] we get to know each other," remarks a third. And a fourth adds: "the time I worked most with other teachers was on the Israel trip . . . That's where I work closely with the other faculty." Given the once-a-week nature of the teaching at this school, it is perhaps not surprising that the teachers have only limited contact. Still, one wonders what it would take to remunerate teachers to participate in faculty conversations about school culture, teaching, and learning, and whether the goals of the school could be better attained if the teachers saw each other as partners in a common educational venture.

Instead, the emphasis is on individual teaching and building a personal connection with students. Perhaps the most sought-after class in the school, offered by the same teacher in all three class slots in order to accommodate all the takers, is a course on "Jewish Views of the Afterlife." An outsider cannot help but be struck by the numbers of students who spend time between classes and even during their longer break hanging out with the instructor of this course. Teachers also invite groups of students to spend Shabbat with their families. And then there are teachers who attend the *Shabbatonim* and various other extracurricular events, cultivating and getting to know the students. The emphasis on keeping parents informed about student progress also focuses teachers on their young charges, as does the investment of the school in a guidance counselor. The school's two administrators also track students carefully and call each child who is absent as a way to connect and also to intervene in case a child is contemplating dropping out. Despite the fact that it meets only one day a week, the school strives to cultivate relationships with its students, and teachers are at the front lines in this effort.

In addition to its teaching staff, the school also utilizes eight college students to serve as tutors in a program called "Teen Torah Center." The purpose of this program is not remedial but to offer students the option to spend one class session of their school day studying in small groups of anywhere from one to four peers matched with a tutor. The topics of these tutorials range from Bible to Kabbalah, from contemporary Jewish issues to rabbinic views of modesty, from the close reading of a text by Maimonides to Jewish self-help texts. A number of the tutors are alumni of the high school. Even more striking: every tutor identifies as Orthodox.[7]

When asked to define what they hope to accomplish, the tutors articulate a strong sense of Jewish mission: "I want each student to come out a step ahead in relationship to *Hashem* [God], other people, growth." "I try to give students exposure to something holy every week." The catchphrase of the Teen Torah Center last year, it is reported, was to give students a "positive Jewish experience."

Given that the student body is drawn mainly from Conservative synagogues and unaffiliated families, with very few Orthodox students, it is striking to observe that more than half the teaching staff and all the tutors are Orthodox. (The best estimate is that no more than a dozen teenagers in the school come from families that pray in an Orthodox or Chabad synagogue, constituting under 3 percent of the student body.) And yet, remarkably, this orientation is dismissed as little more than happenstance. Asked about his teachers, the school head says: "We have one Reform Jew; one Reconstructionist who will be back next year. Two or three teachers, I can only guess if they are Orthodox. I'm not interested in that: [I want my teachers to be] good with kids, passionate with their subject. I want open teachers. Closed people are in all movements." But more than half of his teachers are Orthodox, as are *all* the tutors. The students are certainly aware of the role models presented by their teachers, and parents, too, speak openly (and positively) of their children having an exposure to Orthodox religious services for the first time through their attendance of school *Shabbatonim*. The reasons for this imbalance may be more pragmatic than ideological: students from the Teen Torah Center seem prepared to work for scant remuneration; and there is the educational outlook of the school head, which may tend to attract more classically oriented teachers who focus on textual study rather than other types of class exercises. Still, the weight of the teaching staff cannot but shape the school culture.

When interviewed, the tutors acknowledged the religious gap between them and their students: "I'm not trying to make a clone of myself," one contends; "I want Judaism to be a value to them." Another adds: "My goal is not to make them *shomrei mitzvot* [ritually observant Jews]. The idea is not to demonstrate you must be like me but that there is a whole world that is not accessible to you." The tutors strive to be "tolerant and pluralistic." But they also want to "demonstrate that Orthodox Jews are normal and not closed-minded." "We want kids to see that you can be observant and cool at the same time," another adds, in what may be the unexpressed motto of the school.

The tutoring program and the extracurricular opportunities, including invitations to students to spend Shabbat in the home of an Orthodox teacher, are enriching programs. A small number of students become Orthodox as a result of their exposure; each year a few graduates opt to spend their gap year at an Israeli (Orthodox) *yeshiva*; others apparently are moved to continue their Jewish studies at college as a result of their positive experiences. A few also have gone on to study at the Jewish Theological Seminary. Nonetheless, the school pretends not to notice its own slant.

From an outside perspective, the heavy reliance of this high school on Orthodox faculty is a reflection of the inattention of the school's Conservative feeder congregations. Rather than subvent the high school properly so that it can afford to hire Conservative teachers, local Conservative synagogues have allowed it to limp along with a meager budget; rather than offer to pay tutors drawn from the Conservative movement, they apparently turn a blind eye to the fiscal challenges faced by the school.[8] Beyond that, it is not clear how much attention the congregations pay to students they are sending to the high school. They offer only a modest scholarship, and it is not clear how much they encourage the students, let alone take pride in their achievements. They don't seem to feel a sense of ownership, a distance the school probably has helped to widen by not involving lay leaders or congregational rabbis more actively. One has to wonder what would happen if the Conservative rabbis and religious school directors were really paying attention to the school; and whether the school could draw more help if it worked harder to involve local rabbis and lay leaders.

On the other side of the ledger is the story of the proactive behavior of Orthodox groups. An Orthodox program trains and sends tutors to the school, providing them with a way to approach the students. And Orthodox teachers in the school seem highly motivated by a sense of Jewish mission to work with teenagers of a different Jewish religious outlook. They apparently are intent on winning their young charges over to Judaism, and they are prepared to do so not only in the classroom but also at extracurricular programs. As noted, some teachers maintain contact with former students for years afterward. The high school should not be faulted for the failings of its feeder schools or for embracing highly motivated teachers. It is to be commended for assembling a dedicated cadre of teachers who care about their students and are prepared to give of themselves.

It should also be commended for creating a school culture with expectations of learning, which, in turn, has a direct impact on the school's success in attracting well-qualified teachers who take their work with students seriously.

## Professional Development and Teacher Learning

Even though it provides as many if not more staff workshops and more supervision than most other supplementary schools,[9] the school could be even better if it had a more sophisticated approach to professional development. The faculty members meet with the administration to discuss students and specific classroom issues, but do not engage regularly in reflective conversations about teaching and learning, or in evaluation of teaching. It is not hard to imagine why the school administration may feel constrained to ask its teaching staff to invest even more of its time on in-service and other forms of professional development when the demands on their time are already great and they are asked to be involved in extracurricular activities, all on a salary that is fairly low by the standards of other schools. Still, the good teaching on display could become excellent if teachers spent more time together planning curriculum, integrating the extracurricular and classroom learning, and reflecting on their own teaching practices. Much of the teaching corps exhibits skill and talent in the classroom, but the school counts on the teachers to ratchet up their skills on their own, without helping them to move to the next level. Given that this high school wants to see itself as a "school," it is all the more noteworthy that, unlike other "good schools," this one offers relatively few opportunities for teachers to be critical colleagues who engage in reflective conversations about teaching and learning, the very essence of good professional practice and development. Here again the seeming indifference of the congregational feeders to the needs of the school deprives the high school of the resources to enrich its teaching.

## Extracurricular Programs

Complementing the formal school program on Sunday mornings is an elaborate set of extracurricular activities held on Sunday afternoons, entire weekends, and during other nonschool hours designed to offer students a range of opportunities to interact with one another. The school attaches so much importance to these activities that it has hired a full-time coordinator who is solely responsible for the extracurricular programming. Some of these activities are merely recreational, such as going to a bowling alley or an amusement park, spending an afternoon snow tubing, ice skating, or go-karting. A further effort to stimulate social interaction comes in the form of trips to sporting events and the theater. Other programs engage students in social action, ranging from an after school visit to a Jewish senior citizens' residence to participation in Mitzvah Day. The latter is sponsored by the local federation and involves various kinds of projects, such as cleaning up a Jewish cemetery and helping out in facilities for the destitute and infirm. Other community service programs involve student participation in Super Sunday, a telephone fund-raising effort to support the local federation. And then there are special drives for *Tomchei Shabbos*, designed to deliver kosher food to needy families prior to the onset of the Sabbath, and a Hanukkah Toy Drive for Jewish children in need. These activities often require some training and also initiate young people into the life of the larger Jewish community. They are presumably designed to build a sense of responsibility in younger people for Jews who are in need. A further incentive for students is that they yield community service credits to meet high school or college requirements.

The third type of extracurricular activity consists of a mix of the social, recreational, and religious. The most sustained and developed such program run by the school is an annual ten-day trip to Israel scheduled for eleventh and twelfth graders in February of each year. Students prepare for the trip by taking a course on Israel and then process their trip in the same course upon their return. The trip is a high point for students and, as we have seen, for some of the teachers too. During the year we studied the school, however, the Israel trip was canceled because of insufficient enrollment. The prevailing explanation for the low enrollment is that the trip was a casualty of the success of Birthright Israel. Parents resisted spending $1,000 to cover their share of the expenses because they knew their child would be eligible two years later for a free trip sponsored by Birthright Israel. A secondary reason for the collapse of the trip was that the local Solomon Schechter school had recently instituted such a trip for eighth graders and quite a few of the eligible high school students had visited Israel just a few years earlier. The federation subvention, moreover, was insufficient to keep the cost as low as in previous years. For these and perhaps other reasons, a capstone event for the students, one often central to Jewish high school programs, was dropped.

Among the highlights of the school year are a weekend *Shabbaton* during the winter and a second weekend at a summer camp held toward the end of the school year. Undoubtedly, these weekend trips offer a chance to build a shared sense of community, connect students to some of their teachers, and strengthen the social ties between students, something eagerly sought by the young people, as we shall see. In the view of the school's director of student life, the goal of the *Shabbaton* is "primarily to create community for Jewish teens . . . so that we can retain them." These weekends, however, also pose some challenges to the administration. Let us recall that the school itself does not sponsor prayer services on school days. But over the Jewish Sabbath, prayer cannot be ignored. Here the Orthodox orientation of some of the teachers clashes with the egalitarian experiences of the students and the influence of the assistant director, who is a Conservative rabbi.[10] The school has experimented with two services: an early morning one for those who wish to participate in an Orthodox service and an egalitarian one held a bit later for the rest of the group. To make matters even more complex, some of the students, generally the day school products, tend to favor a more complete prayer service, whereas others have limited patience for prayer and have expressed a preference for the option of a discussion group in place of the religious services. These circumstances have made the religious services fraught with tension: some of the students are very attracted to the Orthodox services; others are repelled. Some want spirited prayer, others want to talk about prayer.

By all accounts, however, the *Shabbatonim* are a great success, enjoyed by students and faculty. But they also expose some of the inner tensions within the school:

- Its orientation slants heavily Orthodox, even as students are drawn almost exclusively from non-Orthodox homes; this is particularly evident when prayer services are held and the school must choose whether to require attendance and whether to offer an egalitarian and nonegalitarian option.
- The school tends to favor more cerebral activities (which in some ways are more neutral than religious ones), but these stand in tension with the recognition that it must offer rich social and community building opportunities.
- The school's standards sometimes stand in tension with its vigilance about enrollment attrition and therefore it goes out of its way to offer students an appealing program.

All of these dilemmas eventually spill out in discussion with faculty and administrators, some of whom privately wish the school would devote far more *school hours* to informal educational activities even as others seek to protect the existing school model geared to intensive academic study; some of the staff want a stronger Conservative presence, whereas others attribute the school's success in winning children over to greater Jewish religious engagement to the strong Orthodox influence; some are convinced the school can draw Jews into knowledgeable engagement by exposing them to the breadth of Jewish civilization, and others seem convinced that the school's model may have been appropriate "twenty to twenty-five years ago but today is unrealistic; now we should be happy if kids know they are Jewish and if we don't lose them between Bar/Bat Mizvah and marriage. It's not reasonable to expect a lot of kids going for an academic program." Thus, beneath the surface, this even-keeled, well-run school is staffed by strong-minded people who differ sharply in their views. One has to assume that the school principal chose these people knowingly and is prepared to manage areas of tension, regarding them as a source of strength rather than as a hindrance.

## The Students

Given the perennial student recruitment campaign and the ongoing struggle against attrition, the school has invested considerable energy trying to understand why students choose to attend. There is widespread consensus that the initial impulse owes much to the insistence of parents that their child give the school a try for the duration of the eighth grade; once they are enrolled, pupils choose to stay on, it is thought, mainly for social reasons—that is, because they have friends in the school. So strong is the social factor, the administration feels, that those teenagers who have an active social life with Jewish friends outside the school are the most apt to drop out along the way, whereas those who have few Jewish friends outside the school are more likely to remain if they have successfully befriended some of their classmates.

Conversations with students initially suggest the correctness of this analysis. One student reports that he attended because his parents made him go and because an older brother had "loved it." This student reports that on the first day he "hated it"; what still sticks in his mind two years later is that the bagels were hard that day and there was no more lox available! But he eventually stayed because he liked the *Shabbatonim* and by extension the friends he made who attend other public schools. A female student also noted her parents forced her to go, and expresses appreciation that they did so because she "made lots of friends." Still another student, an eighth grader, elaborates: "I really enjoy this program, unlike in [public] school where you are forced to go. Even though I've been out late [on Saturday nights], I still get up to come. I have a lot of friends. I still feel like it is family. I have a lot of friends in other grades. Not like [public] high school . . . not shoving stuff down my throat. Even though I don't have strong religious views, I still enjoy it. I like how we face problems with other points of view." Embedded in this response are hints that more than the social aspect attracts these students.

A different perspective is offered by a tenth grade student as he describes the school: "I like the classes better than the social aspect. The classes are more relaxed . . . I can ask questions. Like the teachers are a lot more approachable than in public schools. [He refers to two teachers.] You can learn more from them. Socially we are kind of isolated in our own groups. In break we sit with the people from [other schools]. Also, it looks good for college. It has changed my views on Judaism. Before I was a reluctant Jew. Taking the Afterlife class . . . it makes sense. I'm taking the Israel Highway and I like our politics. I'm a vegetarian." Once we get beyond the somewhat jumbled views and non-sequiturs, it is apparent that this student is captivated by some of his teachers and enjoys the learning ambience of the school, far more than its social qualities, which may be off-putting to him. His remarks allude to an effort to make sense of matters of belief and politics.

And he is not unique. A classmate offered a seemingly contradictory answer when asked why he attends: "I got involved in Jewish Student Union [JSU], which is organized for teens.[11] I ended up staying the next semester. I liked the *Shabbaton* and trips. I have friends that I know from other schools, and see them here. I come here to see my friends, to talk to the teachers. I'm not great in the classes, but [enjoy it more] during the break. I've met a lot of people since I started coming here . . . I'm not that religious and JSU recognized that. Instead of praying in the morning, we would talk about it and what it meant. I liked the old school [building] better because I get to meet kids from other schools. My brother goes here, he loves it. I love it."

Clearly, this student, as do others, has multiple reasons for staying in the school. While he is mainly attracted by the opportunity to socialize with friends he has made who attend other public schools, he also acknowledges some of the conversations that have shaped his thinking. Finally, like some of the other students, he speaks with nostalgia about the way the school had been before its move to new quarters where the fraternizing had been somewhat easier. (Other students lament the loss of religious spirit compared to previous years.) And then a senior chimes in: "The school has obviously changed a lot. A lot more religious than when I started. I still enjoy it. Lot of kids dropped out by my sophomore year. I went to Israel: it was probably my best experience. Want it back to what it used to be: the building kept us as a family. It's still a fun place to come on Sunday. The teachers are amazing."

These diverse views highlight the range of considerations shaping decisions about whether to attend and remain enrolled. True, students are quick to emphasize the social dimension as critical. But when they get beyond that, they talk about the impact of teachers and thought-provoking class discussions.

Students currently enrolled in the Teen Torah Center, the tutoring program, were particularly outspoken about the benefits of small group study. Student 1: "[We talked about] a lot of things . . . you wouldn't really learn about [in regular classes]. Customs, different things you might never have heard about. Why people laugh . . . Every week we have a different aspect of life, sort of explains simple things with spiritual meaning." Student 2 explains why he took a class reading Rashi, the preeminent Bible exegete: "Because it is chill . . . We aren't forced to learn one thing; we can learn whatever we want at our own pace. There is no time limit."

A conversation between five students about why they believe the tutors bother to work in the school:

G: It's fun.

A: They learn from us, too. It's not a set class; they don't know exactly what they are going to say. It's a conversation. We are equal.

S: My tutor said when she was a student at this school she had a lot of questions about Judaism and it changed [her mind]. She became Orthodox and religious. They had a lot of questions.

D: My teacher said when she was in a school she really didn't like learning in the eighth, ninth and tenth [grades]. Something hit her and she wanted to start learning about Judaism.

What begins to emerge from this exchange is the sheer curiosity driving some students to understand their tutors and the extent to which some students enjoy the chance to discuss unconventional topics that pique their interests.

This is not to suggest that idealism and imagination are their only motivators, any more than is the quest of some students to enlarge their social circle. Some teenagers are quite alert to the practical benefits of enrollment in the high school. About one third of the students send their Jewish supplementary high school transcripts to colleges, along with their general studies transcripts, and ask their teachers in this Jewish school for letters of recommendation. Some of the community service programs in which the students participate also yield certificates of attendance students can use to fulfill some requirements at their public high schools.

Students also seem appreciative of the elective system that gives them the choice to build their own schedules. One student likened the system to what one can expect to find in college. Despite the school-like ambience, students regard the structure as more grown-up than what they encounter in their public schools. This may not be the key factor drawing them to the school, but it may well play a role in keeping them enrolled.

It appears that multiple factors and attractions motivate students to attend the high school. Perhaps, it is the mix of formal and informal study that stimulates them. (Significantly, the teens claim not to find the Sunday mornings burdensome or an added stress factor.) Some are won over by the small group opportunities to study with college-aged tutors; others by their teachers; and still others by the social opportunities. Certainly, the academic approach of the school does not seem a major deterrent for these students, although admittedly we do not know why 50 percent of their peers drop out before graduating.

## Classes

The school day runs from 9:15 to 12:30 on Sunday mornings. This time is then divided into three periods of fifty minutes each plus a half hour break and time to change classes. During each period roughly a dozen classes are offered and students choose which they prefer to take. Perhaps, because school administrators are concerned about attrition and also attuned to the developmental needs of their younger students, they do not allow eighth and ninth graders to enroll in text courses, such as Bible or Talmud; rather they take classes on questions of Jewish ethics and values, dance, improvisational acting connected to Jewish themes, the use of photography to explore Jewish questions, and other thematic issues suitable for class discussion. Observing these classes, it is hard not to wonder whether the school has missed an opportunity by not offering more content-rich classes to younger students. Some of the latter have attended day school where they are used to such courses; others may well rise to the challenge of reading texts. The school is missing an opportunity to deepen the learning experience of its youngest students because it fears they will be turned off and leave.

A count of all courses offered in the fall of 2007 yields the following breakdown: nine are content-rich courses in subjects such as Bible, Talmud and Jewish thought; three are Hebrew language *ulpanim* (immersion classes); eight fall into the category of advocacy and identity building, courses on Jewish current events, contemporary Israel, and the arts; and six tend to emphasize moral dilemmas and problem solving loosely based on Jewish perspectives. In short, the courses are balanced. Because of the school's policy of steering younger students away from text courses, the content-rich ones tend to be taken by the tenth to twelfth graders.

Roughly a dozen separate classes are offered in each of the three teaching periods (most are repeated in at least two periods) plus eight Teen Torah Center tutorials (some of the latter are text oriented). Over the course of several visits to the school, virtually every class was observed, but the following analysis will of necessity focus sharply on a small number.

Among the weakest of the classes were the so-called *Ulpan* Hebrew classes. This is not unusual. Hebrew language instruction tends to be weak across the board in Jewish schools. It is hard to find teachers who are successful and a curriculum that works. And when a teacher seems to have success, it is unlikely that the progress achieved will be built upon effectively the following year as the students move to the next grade. The two classes observed at the high school were a study in contrasts. One was a Beginners *Ulpan.* The class employed a respected textbook, *Ivrit Mi'bereisheet,* and the teacher worked hard to engage the students in a drill of verb/noun agreement (*ani omed, at omedet, anachnu omdim,* etc.). Students took notes. But there was little life to the class session. More surprising was the elementary level at which the class was conducted: eighth and ninth graders, who had all studied in synagogue religious school and had celebrated a Bar or Bat Mitzvah that presumably involved reading some Torah and certainly Haftorah, struggled with—and generally failed to grasp— the most basic rules of conjugation and could barely read the teacher's clearly written Hebrew script. This is not the fault of the students but says a great deal about the learning goals and limited effectiveness of their previous schools as purveyors of Hebrew language skills.

A second Hebrew class, this one billed as an Advanced *Ulpan,* had an entirely different flavor. Here the teacher spoke mainly Hebrew and students responded in Hebrew. They spoke in sentences and employed a sophisticated vocabulary. To be sure, the students in this class all had attended a day school before coming to the high school and a fair number grew up in a home with Israeli parents. They were also motivated either because their parents insisted upon their taking the *Ulpan* and/or because they wanted to learn to communicate with Israeli relatives.

The school offers a range of classes addressing ethical questions or other matters that lend themselves to discussion. One class for eighth graders is called "You Be the Judge" and aims to spark discussion about resolving potentially difficult dilemmas from a Jewish perspective. The subject for discussion in one particular session was "Is Squealing a *Mitzvah*?" Two students were invited to debate the issue and asked to step out of the room to decide who would argue for and who against the proposition. The teacher worked hard to engage the twenty-two students in the class, equally divided between males and females, who managed to segregate themselves by sex, in a discussion. The class employs a textbook with the same title, published by Torah Aura Publications. To bring the question closer to home, the teacher introduced a particular scenario: imagine that a student at a Jewish school is caught shoplifting. Who should be told? And who should do the telling? In the course of the ensuing discussion, virtually every student spoke up. The teacher cited a *responsum* by the Orthodox rabbinic decisor Rabbi Moshe Feinstein, who ruled that a yeshiva should not compel a student to tattle on his fellow students. Some other texts were brought into the discussion, and inevitably a student referred to the Golden Rule (and misquoted it).

In another class for tenth to twelfth graders the subject is "Hot Topics" (named after the textbook on the subject issued by ARE Publications). The subject for the day was school violence, which the teacher introduced by asking students to reflect on their own experience of violence in the school setting. One student spoke about someone who had been killed in a high school and another about weapons brought into a local public school. Interestingly, at first only the girls spoke up. The teacher then moved directly in front of the area where the boys were clustered and in short order almost all of the males joined the discussion. Several rabbinic texts that reflect on violence, including one on the so-called rebellious son (*Ben Sorer U'Moreh*) were read in English translation and discussed. The teacher then steered the conversation to the question of human character: "Is the potential for good and evil in every one of us?" As the students responded, he insisted they talk about themselves rather than imagine what their peers believe—"Tell me whether you see yourself as capable of both good and evil, not whether you think others are?"

The most popular class in the school, as noted above, deals with "Jewish Views of the Afterlife." In contrast to virtually all of his colleagues, the teacher conducts the class entirely while *seated* behind his desk. The discussion focuses on some English translations of rabbinic texts and wanders into the realm of reincarnation, heaven, hell, and even Dybbuks. Five minutes after the class discussed "phantom limb syndrome" a male student blurts out a question about the phenomenon; he clearly had tuned out the entire previous discussion. Rather than rebuke the student, the teacher quietly expresses his amazement that he has heard of the syndrome whereas he, the teacher, only learned of it through the textbook, and then the teacher gently says, "We're not going to talk about your having missed the conversation."

While all these classes employ a textbook of one kind or another, some classes for older students engage in close reading of Jewish texts. A class on the Book of Numbers is perhaps the most frontal in the school. The teacher sits at his desk and students are arrayed along a large table. The subject at hand is the account of Miriam's defamation of Moses and Tziporah and her eventual punishment for engaging in *lashon ha'ra*, gossip. The teacher asks each student in turn to read a passage from the Bible or a commentary. Everything read is in English translation.

A new course created for the present school year in response to student demand examines Talmudic texts. In this class of eight students, more than half are males, the exchange between teacher and students is rapid-fire and nonstop. It ranges from students reading the text of the Talmud to analyzing a commentary by the eleventh-century medieval exegete and legal scholar, the Rif, Rabbi Isaac ben Jacob Alfasi. The teacher explains how the latter understood the Talmudic text under discussion (from the Tractate *Ketubot*), a discussion of the punishment for rape. And the students actively engage him in the analysis. Simultaneously, they also offer a running commentary, giving vent to their skepticism. As the teacher explains why it is important to understand the reasoning of the majority and minority opinions cited in the Talmudic discussion, some students question the entire enterprise. "Orthodoxy gives too much credit to the rabbis of the past," one student complains. Another, assuming a thick East European Jewish accent, replies sarcastically, "You don't know how wise the rabbis were."

The teacher continues to talk through the static and then addresses the students' concerns. He calmly explains that if one is prepared to work within the system of rabbinic law, it is important to understand the reasoning leading to the majority and minority views. "If you don't want to work within the Jewish legal framework that is your prerogative." The interaction about the Talmud and the sidebar commentary continues. Several aspects of the class are remarkable. One is the high level of Talmudic study. The students can work with the original text under the teacher's guidance. The other is the good-natured banter. At no point does the teacher get defensive. As the class concludes and the next session is about to begin with the same teacher, a class on Israeli Supreme Court decisions, the majority of students stay in place; they have elected to take two courses with the same teacher. (See below for a discussion of exam papers submitted for the second course.)

In a course entitled the "Jewish Lens: Exploring Values and Community through Photographs," students examine and interpret photographs by the Israeli photographer Zion Ozeri to learn how photography can be used to express Jewish values, identity, community, and tradition. The teacher projects images via computer onto a screen and asks his eighth and ninth graders to respond. In one discussion, the teacher prods the class to work in small groups to consider the nature of community. One group offers a working definition: "People care for each and feel a sense of responsibility—not obligations." A second student adds: "You would willingly do something for other people." The teacher then underscores the element of choice embedded in this definition. A second group focuses on: "People help each other to do things—to pray, to get by in life together, to help in bad times." And then a third group of students offers its definition: "Community is like an extended family—just like a family has stuff in common, so does a community." With that the teacher asks the class: "Why do you come here?" A student replies, "because I have friends here." This then opens to a conversation about the basis of relationships: "What is more important," the teacher asks, "shared relationships or shared values?" He clearly alerted students to the role of values in the making of community, something they had not raised in their discussion. Finally, the teacher asked: "How does the Talmudic pronouncement, 'all of Israel is responsible one for the other,' apply to the picture?" It is the first time that a Jewish text figures in the discussion. When asked to offer examples of how Jews act responsibly toward one another, a student blurts out "*nichum avelim*" (comforting the mourners). The causal way she made this reference was all the more dramatic because she naturally drew upon a basic Jewish category in its Hebrew original, something no other student offered. (The student, it turns out, is not a product of a Jewish day school, but comes from a family closely connected to the high school.)

In a second class session, the way students learn in this class was dramatized during the discussion about a photograph called "Summer Camp."

*Teacher:* So what's the point of the trees, the lake and the Torah? That's really what you're focusing on: four elements . . . trees, lake, Torah and all the fingers pointing, of all the people. What's the point here? . . .

*Student:* All the fingers on the hands lead you to the Torah. It's like showing the importance of the Torah.

*Teacher:* Somebody else? Something totally different:

*Student:* The beauty of the Torah and the beauty of nature.

*Teacher:* It's an issue of spiritual versus physical beauty. Excellent. What else do we have? A third thing. Somebody who has not had a chance. We have the centrality of Torah; we have physical versus spiritual beauty. What else do we have? One more thing . . . Any ideas? What does the photograph say? . . . What's the point?

*Student:* It's the balance between people, God, and nature.

*Teacher:* Excellent. Nature, people, God. Excellent.

The discussions in this class conform to the pattern observed in a number of other courses that aim to spur students to consider Jewish values, as opposed to a close reading of Jewish texts. Classes on Jewish ethics and the like tend to pose "what do you think?" types of questions to students and expose them to only a limited amount of traditional Jewish thinking. In fact, some classes employ textbooks that seem to delight in telling students what the traditional rabbinic perspective on an issue has been and why it is now challenged by new approaches—that is, we used to think of this issue one way, but now we tend to be wiser. Among them is the textbook for Hot Topics. Indeed, the Jewish textual basis for many of these discussions is quite flimsy. Even in the class on photography, the teacher is using a curriculum package accompanying *The Jewish Lens* that only pays lip service to Jewish texts. It includes a section in the manual with textual references, but doesn't integrate them into the general lessons. Instead it asks the most generic questions about the nature of community, peoplehood, and identification.

These ethics and identity focused courses could be vastly richer if students would confront Jewish texts rather than their own and their peers' half-formed notions. The prevailing approach is very much in sync with the emphasis in supplementary schools on getting students to reflect on their own experiences and beliefs, rather than broaden their knowledge of the world by exposing them to Jewish ideas at times radically different from their own ways of thinking. Presumably, schools take such an approach to help students problem solve when it comes to moral reasoning, but that reasoning is only thinly informed by Jewish values. It remains to be seen whether such an approach succeeds in stimulating real thinking or, alternatively, serves as a means to avoid the laudable goal announced by one of the tutors—to expose students to a world of Judaism they have never encountered before, to ground them in perspectives *different from their own.*

## The Exams[12]

One way to answer this question is by examining student responses to exam questions. The high school under study is unusual because it requires students to complete formal tests and in some cases write papers or compile portfolios. These artifacts provide entrée to aspects of learning usually kept invisible in Jewish supplementary schools. For the most part, such schools lack written evidence to judge what their students are learning; they only know that children work their way through a system and seem to master certain skills. But schools also need more tangible ways of understanding how students think about the material presented to them. The work samples produced by students in this high school offer a glimpse into the minds of the students to gain some insight into how they engage with the content they have encountered in classes.

By making these artifacts available for scrutiny, the school provided researchers with an extraordinary opportunity. What follows are a number of excerpts from student exam papers and in one case an oral examination. These examples are not offered as representative of the school or even of an entire class, but rather they illustrate some learning that took place in specific courses. We should note that exams had both recall and thought questions. The samples were taken from exam questions that asked students to analyze and reflect, rather than respond to recall questions. This analysis is most concerned with the sense students made of what they were exposed to in classes.

"Who Wrote the Bible" is offered as a course for students in grades 10 through 12. The course introduced students to multiple sources, both classical and more contemporary, that reflect on ways to understand the origins of the Torah. On the exam, students were asked whether their beliefs had changed as a result of taking the course and to substantiate any of their assertions by citing texts they had read while taking the course. To a person, students denied they had changed their views as a result of the course. Their exam papers, however, offered evidence of a deepening of their thinking and a new awareness of the range of perspectives on the question of the Bible's authorship. (The following excerpts are presented verbatim and intentionally include spelling and grammatical errors.)

*Student A*

. . . Personally, my views have not changed. I do not believe that there was not any sort of divine intervention, and that the Bible was authored by different people. But this class has helped me understand greatly the other sides. I have learned that such prominent rabbis, like Heschel, do not believe in a literal translation, yet still remain observant Jews.

Before coming to the class, I mainly thought that [one] has believe that the Torah had to be completely inspired and written by God or had to be completely written by people. This class has taught me the "middle ground" opinions, such as Rosenzweig's and Heschel's opinions. I found Rosenzweig's idea that the Torah is a response to God's will and love very interesting. On the hand, I was also able to understand Lamms' view better, and of one could accept the Torah literally. This class helped me to understand the reasons for why there are different opinions and beliefs on who wrote the bible.

*Student C*

My views haven't changed, but it was interesting to study how other people think.

*Student J*

My view has not changed. Although I understand other viewpoints, I really like my beliefs and I will stick with them.

In this class I have learned how to better analyze passages from religious books. I have taken into consideration many different view points of scholars and Rabbis. I still have trouble arguing with the "orthodox" way of understanding the Bible, however . . .

*Student G*

Honestly Rabbi [ . . . ], they haven't really changed that much. I still believe that God wrote the 10 commandments, Moses wrote the Bible and Joshua took over when he died. I don't know why, but thats always what I believed. I do, however, now hold a clearer understanding of how much involvement God had in the Torah . . . The Lamm, Heschel and Rosenzchweig discussion was very interesting to me. Is the Torah God's words or not? I side with Heschel: the middle man. I believe the Torah reflects God's will, but is not his exact words. Yay.

*Student CY*

> My views about what Judaism teacher us has not changed because Judaism teaches us to keep in mind many opinions and make decisions on what we learn.

In contrast, the student also writes . . .

> My views might have changed slightly because I liked the idea that if God used words we could understand (human language) then it presents God as a human figure, which I don't agree with.

"Jewish Law in the State of Israel" is another course offered to students in the upper classes. As noted in the course syllabus, the teacher aspires to introduce students to an understanding of legal and halachic reasoning for the purpose of preparing them to analyze thorny legal issues from a Jewish perspective. Students were asked to apply their learning to cases they studied—for example, "Assuming that there is a distinction between 'legal truth' and the 'historical truth' . . . , according to the Supreme Court decisions we studied, with which kind of truth does Jewish law concern itself? What lesson of a famous Talmudic story (the oven of Achnai) did the Supreme Court cite to support its conclusions?" They were also asked to read and interpret a case they had *not* previously studied, the controversial appeal of the Jewish-born Christian convert, Brother Daniel (Oswald Rufeisen), a monk. A Holocaust survivor, Rufeisen came to Israel in the 1950s and applied for automatic Israeli citizenship under the Law of Return. Eventually, the case came before Israel's Supreme Court, which issued an historic ruling in 1962.[13]

The following excerpts from the final exam illustrate that students were learning to take *halacha* into account as they constructed their arguments about a case they had not encountered during the course:

*Excerpt from Student A's response*

> [In this response, the student takes into the account the *purpose* of the law and an *interpretation of halacha*.]

> To answer this, we must examine what the purpose of the law of return was to begin with. I believe it was . . . to increase the Jewification of the Israeli population. The purpose was to increase the number of practicing and self-identifying Jews in the state, to add to the general cohesiveness of the population. But being a self-identifying Jew is not enough; one must be recognized as Jewish by the rest of one's commu-

nity. Therefore, I believe the law of return should apply only to self-identifying Jews who can also prove that they are halachically Jewish.

## Excerpt from Student T's response

[In this response, the student relies on the *halachic definition* of "who is a Jew" to construct an argument. He also considers challenges to the halachic definition (i.e., the fact that Rufeisen was a Catholic Priest and his acts of heroism).]

Oswald is religiously a Jew. His mother is Jewish so he counts as a Jew . . . On the other hand, he is a Catholic priest which is very unJewish like. This could be countered by his account of heroics during the holocaust. He is still religiously a Jew. I would rule: Jewish, let him in.

## Excerpt from Student E

[In this response, the student writes about the possible *implications of setting a precedent.*]

They [opponents of admission under the Law of Return] may also argue that by granting citizenship to Rufeisen, the Israeli government opens itself up to future claims of non-Jews that their heroic deeds merit privileges reserved for Jews in the state of Israel.

## Excerpt from Student A

[Another student suggests this case warrants an *exception* to the general law.]

By this reckoning, Daniel should not be allowed in: He is halachically Jewish but not self-identifying. However, I think there is one situation where a non-self identifying Jew should be let in and that is in the case of a righteous gentile. I think Daniel should be let in under the Law of Return.

## Excerpt from Student B

[Here a student identifies the *halacha* and includes self-identity as a criterion for entry under the Law of Return. The student concludes that the Brother Daniel case does not meet the stated criteria. He argues that an exception cannot be made based on righteous actions, but offers an alternative legal option to reconcile the issues.]

To my knowledge as far as the state is concerned one must process Jewish familial roots as well as being a self identified Jew these criteria seem satisfactory. While what a Jew is can [be] decided differently under different circumstances, the two points listed above are relevant. While halachically he is a Jew, I would say he does not meet the "Right of Return" standards. Therefore, the court must deny his claim. This does nothing to detract from his admirable heroism for which the court grants him a favored party status thereby assisting his immigration.

These are hardly rote answers to memorized questions. The course expects students to apply legal reasoning and to balance the judgment of Jewish law with other considerations.

In "The Bible as Literature," the class read the Joseph cycle, the David narrative, and some of the Psalms of David. To get them to read more self-consciously and analytically, the teacher distributes a list of "Eight Habits of a Proficient Reader." These habits include: (1) activating prior knowledge, (2) visualizing, (3) questioning, (4) determining importance, (5) predicting, (6) inferring, (7) retelling and summarizing, and (8) monitoring for meaning.[14] Students are expected to apply these ways of reading to specific Biblical texts and to keep a "Double Entry Journal" to record their thoughts, reactions, questions, insights, and speculations about the texts they read. At the start of each lesson, the teacher collected the journals to use as a springboard for class discussion. Tables 10.1 to 10.6 give excerpts from a selection of double entries.

In one class students engaged in comparative analysis, looking at the Joseph narrative in the Hebrew Bible and contrasting it with the Qur'an's account of Joseph. The teacher modeled for students how to draw out key differences and account for them, constantly asking students to speculate as to authorial intention: Why did the author of each account emphasize certain developments or downplay others? For example, the teacher asked, why did the Biblical narrative stress God's favoritism toward Jacob, as opposed to the Qur'an's emphasis on Jacob's preference for Joseph? Why does the Bible portray Joseph as a tattletale, but the Qur'an does not? Why does the Bible attribute important decisions to the role of *human agency*, whereas the Qur'an introduces Satan as an actor in the outcome?

Double entry assignments completed by students illustrate how they used some of the "8 Habits of Proficient Reading" as they read the Biblical Jewish texts. Students raise questions about Joseph's feelings toward his brothers—"*Why is Joseph forgiving to his brothers, if they hate him?*"— and about possible inconsistencies in the text: "*This seems to say Pharaoh*

**Table 10.1**
*Student A*

| Biblical Passage | Student Commentary |
|---|---|
| She caught hold of him and screamed lie with me! But he left his garment in her hand. (39,13) | I think the story of Joseph can be related to the story of David. King David, although extreme enemies with Saul had very much love and respect for him. Here Joseph is respecting Potiphar. |
| So Joseph's master had put him in prison where the king's prisoners were confined. (39,21) | Potiphar decides to put Joseph in jail because he knows that his wife had been lying and Joseph doesn't deserve to die. |
| The chief jailer didn't supervise anything that was in Joseph's charge, because the Lord was with him and whatever he did the Lord made successful. (39,23) | It says in Genesis that the Lord was with Joseph but did Joseph know he was with the power of the Lord? |

acknowledged the God of Joseph. How could that be if the Pharaoh believed in the Egyptian gods and had a "god-like" status among the Egyptians?" Examples of monitoring for meaning include observations such as: "What is Israel meaning when he says this? Does Pharaoh literally speak to God? How is Joseph able to rise up the ladder so quickly, as there are other people who have been in Pharaoh's court much longer?" In response to Genesis 39:11, "He took a liking to Joseph," a student notices a recurring theme: "I found it interesting how Joseph is being favored for a second time, first by Jacob and now by the pharaoh."

**Table 10.2**
*Student B*

| Biblical Passage | Student Commentary |
|---|---|
| Asking about, he saw his brother Benjamin, his mother's son . . . he went into a room and wept. 41 (2) 37 middle part of passage. | Not exactly sure, but in this state I believe it is Benjamin who realizes who Joseph is. |
| The famine spread out all over the world | Why in no other parts of the Bible or ancients books is there talk of this near apocalyptic famine? |

**Table 10.3**
*Student C*

| Biblical Passage | Student Commentary |
|---|---|
| So his brothers wrought up at him and his father kept the matter in mind. | Joseph's father tells him to be quiet about his dream but knows he is right. |
| Stay as a widow in your father's house until my son Shelah grows up. | He thinks that if Shelah gets married God won't take his life. |

Students enrolled in "The Jewish Lens" were asked to prepare a portfolio and then engage individually with the teacher in a conversation about their work. What follows is one student's conversation with the teacher about two photographs in her portfolio.

*Teacher:* Tell me about your four photographs.

*Student:* Ummm . . . it's a bunch of shoes, obviously. It sort of represents community and how everyone in the community is different but still we are tied together and we are all the same in some ways. We all have feet and we all have shoes and we are all coming together for this picture. Umm is that all you need to know about this?

*Teacher:* Whatever you want to tell me.

*Student:* Ah . . . I took it during class so it sort of represents this community

The conversation continues with the student interpreting a second photo, this one taken during a visit to Arlington Cemetery.

**Table 10.4**
*Student C*

| Biblical Passage | Student Commentary |
|---|---|
| Chapter 39<br>The Lord was with Joseph and he was a successful man. | The Lord's presence blessed Joseph and made him advantageous. |
| The Lord was with Joseph, and disposed of the chief jailer before him. | God gets a more lenient jailer to supervise Joseph, but orders him to do nothing because he knows the Lord is with him. |

**Table 10.5**
*Student C*

| Biblical Passage | Student Commentary |
|---|---|
| The chief steward assigned Joseph to then [*sic*] and he attended them | They heard about Joseph's success and productivity because his g-d was with him. |
| But the . . . cup bearer did not think of Joseph, he forgot him. | What does this mean? |
| God has told Pharoah what he has to do. | Does Pharoah literally speak to God? |
| Since God has made this known to you, there is not so discerning as you. | Since he has this skill, no one is better than him at anything. |

**Table 10.6**
*Student D*

| Biblical Passage | Student Commentary |
|---|---|
| 39:11 he took a liking to Joseph | I find it interesting how Joseph is being favored for a second time, first by Jacob and now by the pharaoh. |
| 40:22–23 But the chief baker he impaled—just as Joseph had interpreted to them. Yet the chief cupbearer did not think of Joseph, he forgot him. | How . . . baker remember Joseph, at this transition from . . . to the second one implies that? |
| 41:1–7 Pharaoh's dream | Does a dream that is able to predict the future mean it was told by God to the dreamer? Seeing as pharaoh had such a . . . dream, it would seem strange . . . such a connection between him and God. Why would God then let the Chief baker he was going to die then? |
| 41:33 Accordingly, let Pharaoh find a man of discernment and wisdom, and set him over the land of Egypt. | Is Joseph implying himself to do this? This would seem like an obvious . . . Joseph giving to Egypt ??? |

*Student:* I happened to be at Arlington cemetery a couple of weeks ago and I saw this photo and this was graves behind it. And I thought, I mean Jews, a lot of people joke that Jews are always in mourning that we are always sad and even though that's not true, it is a true Jewish value that we always respect the dead and that we believe in their memory and we do a lot of remembering. So I thought that the sign that everyone at this cemetery should be silent was very respectful toward the dead so, um, I decided to take this photo with this being in the foreground; that was the real Jewish value and the graves behind it express that we remember and we remember our dead and we remember our ancestors and our forefathers, so . . .

*Teacher:* Arlington—you are aware that it is not a Jewish cemetery?

*Student:* Yes.

*Teacher:* But there are Jews buried at Arlington.

*Student:* Yes . . . I have a couple of photos, ones you can see it on the gravestone they have the Jewish star on top.

The assessment of the student's portfolio offers only slim evidence of serious engagement with the Jewish dimension ostensibly under discussion: the lens may be Jewish but the Jewish content is quite thin.

Tests administered by the high school serve in microcosm to illustrate some of the dilemmas of assessment in supplementary schools. The insistence of the school on testing students already places it in an unusual category: such testing is hardly commonplace. But the motive for doing so already suggests limitations: when asked why there are tests, the principal is clear that the exam process was instituted "because we are a school." He is convinced that students draw invidious comparisons between what they call "real school"—that is, all day public or private schooling—and Jewish supplementary school. The exams, in short, serve primarily as a means of demonstrating to the students how serious the school is about its work (this is why the principal scrutinizes exam questions for each course in order to insure that they are free of typos, misspellings, and grammatical errors: exam papers should "look professional," the principal notes); secondarily, the exams are part of a process of rewarding the serious students with good grades based on some assessment instrument. The school, we should note, issues report cards with letter grades and comments by teachers.

Beyond that, the exams currently serve no real role. Because exams are taken on the last day of each semester, many students never get their graded exam papers back from the teachers. At the beginning of the new semester, some teachers seek out their former students in order to return their papers, but this is far from universal. Thus, the role exam papers could play as part of a feedback loop to students is not actualized. Moreover, exam papers are apparently not used by teachers for self-assessment. In some years when a teacher has given uniformly poor grades, the principal has questioned teachers on why so many students apparently did not master the material. But here, too, the exam papers are rarely used for real assessment.

To note these missed opportunities is not to dismiss the value of the examination process. Potentially, exam papers and other assessment tools can serve as a remarkable means to learn more about how students think about the material they have covered. If a school had the resources to test students at the outset of each year in order to create a baseline of their knowledge, it might be possible to measure learning. That is probably beyond the means of most supplementary schools. But even the kinds of exams administered by this high school open a window to the minds of students. They offer glimpses of how students have processed some information, how they have retained it, and, most important, the sense they are able to make of new perspectives—how they apply what they have learned to new questions.

The exams, then, can provide students with tangible evidence of their learning and vital feedback to teachers. Jewish supplementary schools generally seem fearful of burdening students with exams and written assignments; they fail to grasp that exam papers and other artifacts can make visible and sometimes concrete to students that they have spent their time working through certain types of texts and ideas. Having some record of their work can help students measure their own progress. Thus when students in the Bible class deny their beliefs have changed in light of the class, their exam paper can remind them how much their thinking has deepened, regardless of whether they actually revised their beliefs.

For the school, too, the artifacts of learning can shed some light on how well students have made sense of the material covered. The double entry system in the literature class, for example, provides examples of how students applied new tools for reading to the Biblical text. The teacher and the administration can better gauge how successfully the basic concepts of the class translated into student thinking.

Finally, the tests can also illuminate weaknesses in the curriculum. For example, when exam papers in a class on "Going to the Movies" elicit barely a mention of any real Jewish context, let alone text, the feedback may result in a rethinking on the part of the teacher about the curriculum for this particular course, and on the part of the school as to whether students' precious time once a week is well spent discussing movies with only the flimsiest connection to anything Jewish. Similarly, when students in a course on "The Jewish Lens" only connected photographs to Jewish issues in a cursory fashion, the school might ask whether the course package it purchased delivers the kinds of contextual and textual depth the students deserve. The creation of learning artifacts, in short, holds great promise, but that promise remains to be more fully realized in this high school.

## Conclusion

With all the constraints it faces, the high school examined in this essay can draw upon resources other schools can only imagine. It is situated in a part of the country with a large reservoir of well-educated Jews—some drawn from the ranks of professional Jewish educators, others inclined to teach as an avocation. It also is located in an area where it can draw upon a sufficiently large pool of students to experiment with a form of Jewish schooling that may appeal to only a limited number of takers. These two circumstances, alone, set the school apart and make it difficult to replicate exactly in other areas of the country.

We have noted how the school, for all its considerable strengths, has missed some opportunities. By failing to build a strong board leadership and forge better ties with its feeder congregations, it has lost out on the chance to bring additional resources to bear. The high school should be able to insist on greater financial and recruitment support from its feeder congregations, and if the school were better connected it would have a stronger claim on the local Federation for support of its communal program. The high school also has been so careful not to expose its youngest students to textual courses that it may be losing an opportunity to push them to more serious forms of learning. And the school could do much more in-service work, welding the faculty together in their joint effort.

None of this detracts from the considerable achievements of the East Coast Community High School. The principal's guiding assumption that the high school should be as much like a school as possible flies in the face of much conventional wisdom about supplementary Jewish education—yet it seems to work. By insisting upon discipline, the trappings of a "real" school, clearly articulated course syllabi and goals, and formal assessment of students at the end of each semester, the school offers students a model they know from their public school experiences. This academic orientation, we should note, does not come at the expense of social activities; the principal makes it amply clear he sees no dichotomy between academic study and experiential learning. Both co-exist in this school. Admittedly, the more serious academic approach will not appeal to all teens. But in communities of sufficient size, there ought to be a Jewish high school option with academic course offerings. In large and medium-sized communities, such a school might be "a school within a school," complemented by another that emphasizes social action and community building, and still another that focuses on identity formation. This school demonstrates there is a market for an academic Jewish supplementary high school—all the more reason such schools deserve communal support from the federation and local synagogues on a far more substantial basis than what this school has received.

A high school with a strong academic orientation can serve as a magnet, attracting not only certain kinds of students, but also faculty members of a certain stripe. Interesting people from a variety of backgrounds are drawn to teach in this school because it is serious about teaching, discipline, and expectations. Teachers are attracted because they know they can devote their Sunday mornings to teaching and not leave frustrated by student inattention and discipline problems. The choice of teachers fielded by a school, in turn, can have an important impact on the outlook of students. At this school, teens repeatedly talked about the "influence" teachers had upon them. An environment where teachers are respected and care about their students can have a profound impact on the Jewish outlook and lives of teens.

Another striking feature of the school worthy of emulation is its Teen Torah Center. By fielding tutors, the school provides students with the option of small-group learning. Here students can explore in a more casual way questions that are on their minds about a broad range of Jewish issues. The tutors seem to serve as big brothers and sisters to the students. But where might one find a cohort of tutors? In this instance, an Orthodox organization was established for the express purpose of providing Jewish experiences to public school students; it does so by preparing a cadre of college students to volunteer in the community high school. Such a program can be replicated by the Conservative and Reform movements and perhaps also some of the Zionist youth movements.

There is reason to believe that with vision, a sense of mission, and realistic expectations, other Jewish communities around the country can engage teens in serious high school study and Jewish exploration. This high school, for all its inner tensions and struggles, demonstrates that it is realistically possible to put the school back into the supplementary high school.

## Notes

1. See, for example, David Resnick, "Jewish Supplementary Schooling Misperceived," *Contemporary Jewry* 13 (1992), pp. 14–17. See also Norman L. Friedman, "On the 'Non-Effects' of Jewish Education on Most Students: A Critique," *Jewish Education* (Summer 1984), pp. 30–34.

2. See Isa Aaron, Sara Lee, and Seymour Rossel, *A Congregation of Learners: Transforming the Synagogue into a Learning Community* (New York: UAHC Press, 1995).

3. When asked about this, the administrators note ruefully that they cannot afford to pay high tutoring fees and the only takers are Orthodox individuals. The tutors, in turn, speak of their work as mission-driven: they strive to help fellow Jews become better Jews. One wonders whether it would prove difficult to find some qualified tutors who are not Orthodox.

4. The school budget is based on three components: half comes from tuition revenues; another 20 percent from the federation; and the rest must be raised annually. It is not clear how actively board members support the school financially. They are not selected for their philanthropic largess. Because the school enjoys only a limited relationship with feeder synagogues, it cannot call upon them to help finance its operation—even though it is educating youth from those synagogues.

5. See Jack Wertheimer, *A Census of Jewish Supplementary Schools* (New York: Avi Chai Foundation, 2008), pp. 12–13.

6. A demographic survey conducted by the federation sponsoring the school found that two-thirds of children in its catchment area received no formal Jewish education during their high school year, a figure that would be significantly higher were Orthodox day school students excluded from the survey. The pool of students for the high school consists mainly of teens from Conservative and unaffiliated homes; teens from Reform homes attend high school in Reform institutions, if they are enrolled at all.

7. The school administrators attribute this slant to the unwillingness of Conservative college students to work as volunteers in the school. The Orthodox tutors are paid a token $15 per morning; and the school administration contends it cannot get anyone else to work for such meager payment. But if the tutors are not remunerated financially, they are drawn by other considerations, principally a sense of religious mission.

8. We should note in this context that the school policy is not to hire pulpit rabbis to teach in the school, presumably because that would then place it in a position of choosing between rabbis and possibly rejecting some who do not measure up to its standards. The school does employ two Conservative rabbis who do not hold congregational positions.

9. It should be noted that the school runs four in-service programs a year for teachers at which an outside guest speaker addresses broader questions in education, such as how to motivate teens to learn, how to build a curriculum, alternatives to frontal learning, and what teachers should know about the types of experiences high school students are apt to encounter in public school that influence their thinking. Lasting

for two hours over lunch on four Sunday afternoons a year, these sessions begin to address generic issues, but do not necessarily help improve the way teachers handle their Judaica classes. Individual teachers are helped by the school to attend conferences devoted to topics that can strengthen their teaching.

10. The school pays teachers and tutors a minimal sum to participate in the *Shabbatonim*, so little that according to the school administration it is impossible to recruit Conservative students or teachers to staff the event. Orthodox tutors attend, however. One wonders whether the school cannot find more creative ways of attracting non-Orthodox personnel.

11. This national effort is under Orthodox auspices and offers programs for Jewish students enrolled in public high schools to inspire them "to do something Jewish." See www.jsu.org.

12. Dr. Rhonda Cohen, a specialist in curricular instruction whose research interests focus on teacher education and artifacts of classroom teaching, served as a consultant during our examination of student tests and papers. The following discussion draws upon her analysis.

13. For a probing analysis of the case, see Michael Stanislawski, "A Jewish Monk? A Legal and Ideological Analysis of the Origins of the 'Who is a Jew' Controversy in Israel," Eli Lederhendler and Jack Wertheimer, eds., *Text and Context: Essays in Modern Jewish History and Historiography in Honor of Ismar Schorsch.* (New York: JTS Press, 2005), pp. 547–77.

14. A growing body of literature has appeared in recent years, providing tools to develop "habits of proficient reading." See, for one example, Jeff Zwiers, *Building Reading Comprehension Habits in Grades 6–12: A Toolkit of Classroom Activities* (Menlo Park, Calif.: International Reading Association, 2004).

# Conclusion

Our portraits of ten schools have introduced readers to a range of programs differing in size, geographic setting, and affiliation. All have strengths; some more than others. Each suggests that, under the proper conditions, supplementary schools are able to give children positive Jewish experiences, teach them a modicum of Hebrew and other Judaic skills, stimulate them to reflect on religious and ethical questions from a Jewish perspective, and foster attachment to Israel and the Jewish people. What, then, are those conditions? What can we extract from these portraits about the key traits of effective schools?

## Building a Jewish Community within the School

The best schools *intentionally* develop a community among their students, staff and parents. They begin with the assumption that learning cannot be separated from context, and that to a large extent the school's most important message is embedded in the culture and relationships it fosters. Hence, they devote much time to building a community that attends to the needs of individual children; embraces them in an environment where their classmates become their good, often their best, friends; and connects them to the larger congregational body, if the school is housed in a synagogue, or to another Jewish sub-community if it is not. No less importantly, the community fostered by the school not only is warm and hospitable, but also establishes norms explicitly identified as distinctly Jewish. Although denominational orientation affects what these norms are, good schools across the spectrum focus particularly on the interpersonal, teaching young people through example and open discussion how to treat one another. Put in a more traditional Jewish idiom, they stress *mitzvot bein adam leḥavero*—i.e., proper behavior toward others.

We have seen examples of this approach in virtually every school included in this study. At the Chabad Hebrew School, the director and staff members not only strive to be attuned to each child, but also work to reinforce learning with rewards and compliments. When the rabbi of Beit Knesset Hazon assumed his position, he announced to the staff that, "If your kids know the *alef-bet* before everyone's name in the class, everyone gets an F. Don't even open the book the first class." The school head explains: "We work hard to help faculty understand that it's not all about the content. The content is important, but the community building is also really critically important. . . . If we're going to have a feeling of warmth and welcoming and family, we have to dedicate some serious time to helping kids know each other." Education at the Reconstructionist congregation is deliberately designed to extend beyond the classroom. The synagogue's leaders want children in the religious school to have a Jewish "neighborhood" experience that no longer exists in the place where they actually live.

The operative word here is *Jewish* community. For the education to have an impact on the identity of young people, the setting must reinforce uniquely Jewish dimensions. At Tikvah Synagogue School, such community is built by engaging members and children actively in prayer. As one parent put it: "On a week-to-week basis, it really feels like a community. Just on a regular, ongoing basis the people really want to be [there], not just to drop the kids off for Sunday school. It's really being there, and the parents being partners."

Kehilla builds Jewish community by emphasizing *kavod*. Both in its approach to human interactions and its vocabulary for teaching proper behavior, the school conveys what it stands for—and the basis of its commitments. As we have seen, one class devoted three weeks to creating a class *brit,* or covenant. The teacher explained what they did:

> The first week we talked about the three different kinds of *kavod* (respect): *kavod le'atzmi* (respect for oneself), *kavod le'aherim* (respect for others), and *kavod la-sviva* (respect for the environment). We took these categories and tried to decide what was important to the students. We did this in various ways. For example, we had everyone write down on a sheet some of the rules and boundaries. We also used a text from the Rambam as a springboard. It took a while to figure exactly how to phrase [our *brit*], to see that it was rooted in a text. By attending to traditional Jewish texts, the school highlighted what is distinctively Jewish in its approach.

High school programs particularly can have a profound impact by emphasizing community building and attending to the needs of the individual learner, coupled with a stress on how the Jewish approach differs. We have seen how students at the high school of Kehilla were able to portray the school's special ambience as a safe haven. While their secular schooling was a source of pressure to perform, they said, their Jewish schooling offered a respite from the stresses. One high school student described how Kehillah helped to get one through middle school. "We were all so self-conscious and insecure. . . . Kehillah always supported you through those days. . . . At [my public] school a lot of the time, it's a place where teachers are in authority and have a lot more power over the students. . . . And the teachers take your respect without giving it. But here it's more mutual respect. . . . Kehillah is a diverse community. People are actually truly respected here for their differences. . . . They don't want us to memorize things. They want us to learn things. . . . There is always an undertone of happiness. It's really a happy place."

At Western Jewish High School, a teacher clearly sees the opportunity she has to stimulate reflection on what Judaism means to her students: "My objective is to get them to really begin the road to figure out who they are and where Judaism is going to fit in their life. . . . You're born Jewish whether you like it or not; you're sort of in this. So why don't you investigate? . . . Something is there, some connection. Why don't you spend the rest of your life, a piece of it, finding that out?"

The answers students devise to these questions will change over the course of their lives, but the exercise of thinking seriously about their own Jewish identity and their relationship to Jewish texts can establish a foundation for later reflection—all the more reason Jewish supplementary high schools carry a heavy responsibility and the Jewish community can ill afford to allow most of its young people to drop out of Jewish schooling at the age of thirteen or fourteen.

## Engaging with Judaism at a High Level

Good schools place an emphasis on taking Jewish study seriously. Admittedly, some schools are far stronger at engaging students in discussions about Jewish values and issues than in the intensive study of texts. But regardless of the emphasis, good schools have developed a sophisticated curriculum that goes beyond rote learning, examining Jewish content so that it "sticks." To do so, most of the schools in this study work at engaging the minds of their students, getting them to mull over texts and issues. Class discussions press students to analyze, evaluate, and compare texts, ideas, and ethical dilemmas.

We may recall how an avocational teacher at Tikvah synagogue school explained the difference between teaching on the Sabbath and holidays, as compared to weekdays. Suddenly, she had to forgo the usual accoutrements of schooling—chalk, notebooks, coloring books—and instead focus on a text. The result in her estimation was a deeper exchange about the meaning of the texts to her students.

At the Chabad Hebrew School, fourth graders devote the year to learning about the Jewish home, with its requirements for dietary observance and affixing a mezuza to doorposts. The stress was on how intricately complex these observances are even as they may be joyful. A teacher at Kehilla put it well by rejecting the need to simplify: "In order to accommodate the developmental level of your students, it doesn't mean making a complex thing simple. It makes a complex thing apprehendable [*sic*]. But if you do that by stripping out all of the sophistication, all of the complexity, the kids will be left feeling that this is a simple thing that they have mastered and there's nothing else there. . . . That's one of the most difficult tightropes that we walk here, and sometimes we overreach."

Some of the schools worked hard at teaching students about Jewish prayer and also *how* to pray. These are not simple matters, but schools cannot ignore prayer if they conceive of themselves as religious institutions, as most do. Attention to prayer is also vital if a congregational school is to nurture a new generation of synagogue participants. The school at Beit Knesset Hazon works at this, with apparently positive results. Observing the sixth and seventh graders during tefillah, our researchers were impressed with the level of participation: "At an age where students can be quite cynical about praying, especially in a public setting, the level of participation and apparent *kavanna* were impressive. One never knows really what is in the heart of another, but all of the students had their eyes covered at the transition to *Shema*, and it appeared that all were concentrating on the words. It was quite a sight—preadolescents, in a school setting, engaged in *tefillah*."

As part of their commitment to serious learning, a number of the schools we studied hold students accountable. Despite the part-time nature of the enterprise, they engage in formal assessment. At Kehilla, teachers send home an "assessment rubric," highlighting the degree of proficiency the student has achieved in each of the goals for that level. Those children who do not master the basic goals and objectives of their grade repeat that level the following year (one student spent three years at the same level). The staff speaks of this in matter-of-fact terms. The East Coast Jewish Community High School, which deliberately cultivates a strong academic ambience, requires students to submit papers and sit for final exams in most courses. Generally, exams go well beyond asking for responses to memorized questions. Students are expected to apply their knowledge, much as they are asked to do in their public or private school classes. These schools take themselves seriously as learning environments and take their subject matter seriously.

Simultaneously, good schools nurture the affective component by providing a range of Jewish experiences. These may include special Shabbat programs and retreats, *hesed* programs which enable young Jews to give of themselves to the Jewish elderly or the local soup kitchen or the cleanup of a Jewish cemetery, dance and musical activities to engage students in forms of Jewish artistic expression, fairs and parades highlighting a connection to Israel, and deliberate efforts to cultivate Jewish prayer and other opportunities for children to explore matters of the spirit. This experiential component, in tandem with formal learning, is vital; it provides students with the opportunity to live their Judaism and not only to learn about it.

## Aligning the Curriculum and Teaching Staff with School Goals

Good schools understand the need to align all their efforts with school goals. Principals and lay leaders often play a critical role in clarifying the school's goals and working with teaching staff to align what goes on in the classroom with the broader objectives of the school. Beyond the classroom, budgets, governance, leadership, and other facets of the school also are directed to attain goals.

To take but one example, the principal at the Chabad school reviews curricular goals with each teacher and observes classes whenever the school is in session. At most of the schools in our study, directors play a critical role in clarifying the school's goals and working with teaching staff to align what goes on in the classroom with the broader objectives of the school. In several schools, teachers spoke about how the school had deliberately jettisoned earlier methods of teaching in favor of more calibrated and serious approaches. At Beit Knesset Hazon, we have seen how older students have come to envy the enriched programs—not available when they took certain classes currently in place for the lower grades.

## Valuing the School, Valuing Students

In most of the schools under study, discipline was achieved primarily by attending closely to the needs of individual children. Not surprisingly, students respond positively when they feel valued. There are many examples of how good schools manage to achieve this. A teacher at Kehilla described the school's approach to students like this: "Teaching here isn't just teaching *Yahadut* [Judaism], just teaching *Ivrit* [Hebrew]. We talk about this all the time, that teaching begins from the moment the kids get off the bus or the moment they are dropped off from their car pool. From the moment you are asking them *ma nishma* (how are things going?), your teaching has begun." At this school, a teacher who was having difficulty with a student was assigned to watch that student during breaks and free time, so she could come to better understand him.

Sometimes respect for students must extend to those who opt to leave the school. Let us recall the approach taken by the principal of Temple Reyim, as she saw a child who was transferring out of her school depart. Rather than berate him, she gently invited him to visit whenever he wanted and not to feel embarrassed if he sees her outside of the school setting. She left the door open and validated his desire to try a different school, surely an act of respect.

## Engaging Families in the Educational Process

When properly enlisted, parents in these schools serve as allies; conversely, when schools fail to engage students, parents give up on the school. At the Chabad Hebrew School, for example, parents recounted how trying it had been when their children had attended other supplementary schools and every Sunday morning they had to drag their children to school. By contrast, this school had won the children over; they no longer resisted coming to the religious school. Not surprisingly, the parents were deeply appreciative. Parents also described how they were then drawn into the Chabad Center by their children, whose enthusiasm for programs was infectious and a welcome change from their previous unhappiness at other schools.

All of these schools worked to involve parents in the educational process. Clearly reflective in her work, the head of school at Adath Shalom actively engages parents and students by running a blog.

> I send an e-mail to the parents, "check the new information on the blog and see what Johnny did." They'll go on; they can ask a question. They can see what their kids are interested in. I want them to know what's happening in Hebrew school because when a kid comes home, he doesn't [necessarily] talk about Hebrew school. So the idea is to engage

the parent in what the kid is doing. . . . And all of a sudden I have a parent letting me know that Johnny is not coming to Hebrew School because he is playing saxophone. [So now I can figure out what I can do to keep him caught up.]

At most, if not all, of the schools studied, parents became more engaged with Jewish living as a result of their children's exposure to experiences in supplementary schools. Ben, a parent at Kehilla, reflected on what his older daughter, now in Tichon, has learned: "I think the biggest success has been cultural and spiritual. . . . My daughter loves prayer. She leads *tefillah* in the evening, a *Ma'ariv* (evening) service for the kids in Tichon. She's very comfortable in synagogue with the ritual part of it. . . . She has gotten a much better Jewish education than I did. In fact I'm now inspired: I'm going to enroll in [a city-wide adult education] program; my kids have left me in the dust from a knowledge standpoint. They can discuss things I don't know what they're talking about, put aside the Hebrew part of it." A parent at Temple Shalom appreciated the impact of the school's *Havdala* study program: "For our family the *Shabbaton* program has a huge social component. We also joined a *havurah* in the congregation. . . . Our *havurah* is in *Shabbaton*. We often go out to dinner after *Shabbaton* together, so we are spending from 3:30 to 8:30 together on a Saturday."

When adults have participated in serious family education or other Jewish study programs, it is not at all unusual that they become strong advocates for the improvement of the school. Two parents in Beit Knesset Hazon reflected upon their growth as a result of adult education: "The adult learning that a lot of us were engaged in put the pressure on the religious school, because suddenly we had an experience that was positive and phenomenal. . . . We realized that what our kids were getting was so old-school . . . and that there was another way to go about this." As another graduate of a Federation program notes: "[It] gives you this really deep understanding of Torah and history, and then you see that your kids are coloring apples for Rosh Hashanah." Both of these parents became advocates for higher standards in their children's school.

The real work of building an effective supplementary school is not only to actualize each of these aspirations so that they become real, but also to hold them in balance. No single one alone will ensure a strong program. It is the combination of traits that forges a strong school.

In order to develop these traits, schools have worked hard to reshape their own culture. In fact, all the schools in our sample either have undergone significant transformation over the past decade or have continually reworked their programs and approaches. They have put in place a series of building blocks to make improvement possible. What are the key enabling factors for developing and maintaining a good supplementary school?

## A Clear Vision

Ideally, such a vision includes both an image of its ideal graduate and a plan for educating and forming such a student. In the current educational vocabulary, this means in the first instance an "existential vision"—"a conception of the kind of person and community that the process of education should strive to realize." In addition, this vision must be sufficiently clear to provide guidance to stakeholders in the school: in short, it must include "a process of education . . . organized to realize the ideals identified in the vision with the particular populations that are to be educated, given cultural, economic, and technological realities."[1] In truth, few of the schools we observed have such a fully developed vision. Instead, many have a strong sense of the atmosphere they seek to foster and some learning goals. They are clear about the ambience they seek to create and to some extent what they do not want to stress. It is far harder to pin them down on what they would like their students to learn and experience by the time they graduate. Supplementary schools would benefit from investing more time in developing a vision.

At two of the schools, educators were explicit about their learning goals. From the website of Kehilla we learn of its objectives:

> Through the proficiency approach, language becomes relevant to the learners. At Kehilla, this learner-centered approach emphasizes the ability to function in Hebrew, to actually be able to use the language playing soccer and board games, having snacks, in social interactions with staff and other kids. The kids are divided into groups that are based on proficiency and developmental appropriateness. Unit themes are designed to be relevant to the kids' lives, such as the Kehilla environment, family, home, things we do in the home, Holidays and Israel. The students revisit these themes each year with a variation on the theme at a higher proficiency level in all the skill areas: reading, writing, speaking, listening and grammar. All proficiency levels work on the same themes at the same time, creating an environment of cohesiveness.

Kehilla, in short, is very clear about its proficiency goals and invites the parents to celebrate their children's progress. By contrast, the school head adamantly rejects Bar/Bat Mitzvah preparation as a school goal: "I'm much more interested in what does it mean to be thirteen and make Jewish choices, and have a Jewish vocabulary, and know your history and what that means to you now, and feel like a speaker of the language. That's who I want thirteen-year-olds to be." Kehilla serves as a model of how a supplementary school can devise clear learning objectives and stay focused on those goals, despite pressures to waver.

The Western Hebrew High School has worked to align its curricular design with its mission. The process started when a number of educators at the school participated in a three-year training workshop for supplementary school teachers conducted by local Jewish educational consultants. Using the well-regarded method of "backwards design," the school first defined desired results for classes and then developed a plan to achieve these results. This visioning process helped the school to transform itself from a program mainly revolving around an eleventh grade Israel trip accompanied by a "light," loosely structured curriculum to a more intentional curriculum closely aligned with the school vision.

Most other schools in our sample defined their goals far more loosely. This is how Beit Knesset Hazon states its mission:

> We know that each person has a story; each person is on a journey. We assist and enrich the lives of our members and our congregation by providing a wide range of learning opportunities, and multiple gateways, enabling individuals to make choices that are the best next steps for them personally and at the same time help them connect with our community. Jewish learning is a lifelong endeavor and we seek to engage all learners from preschool through adult, from novice to expert.
>
> We know that there are many ways to learn and that real learning happens best when it is connected with experience. Consequently our learning programs integrate formal and informal learning, joining academic and experiential approaches . . .

Even though her school pioneered an innovative program for building Hebrew decoding skills and innovative approaches to teasing out Jewish values from practices and texts, the director of the Chabad school primarily defines her goals in affective terms: "Our job is to ignite their souls, teach the Torah as relevant and sophisticated . . . It's not my job to do the whole job. We are here to inspire them. God takes care of the rest. It's not my job to finish it. I have them a few hours a week, [and try to] make every minute as rich as possible." And at Temple Shalom, educational leaders are even more direct in stressing the affective above all else. In describing their vision, educators and lay leaders alike repeatedly return to the desire to "build community" and foster "feeling good." "Content is secondary," an educator notes. "We strive to have kids learn; we can be most successful in having kids love being Jewish."

When it comes to clarifying learning goals, then, these ten schools array themselves on a spectrum. Most tend to limit their aspirations to exposing students to good Jewish experiences and fostering a positive Jewish outlook among their children. Of course, they also provide content, but they don't worry as much about curricular objectives. Only a few try to develop learning goals, let alone align their curriculum and classes with those goals. Yet at the same time, they offer classes in Hebrew language and content. It is not that they are averse to Jewish learning. Rather, they seem to shy away from defining what they expect their students to learn.

## Creating a Culture of Self-Reflection

Stronger schools strive to create a culture of self-reflection aimed at recalibrating their programs based on a critical examination of what is working and what is not—i.e., along with self-reflection comes a commitment to experiment. In order for such re-thinking to take hold, it is necessary to forge collaborative leadership, harnessing the talents of a variety of players in a common effort. Good schools tend not to rely too heavily on any single individual. Contrary to conventional wisdom, the synagogue rabbi does not have to be a central figure for a school to work well. As to school heads, we found that those directors who concentrated all decision making in their own hands tended to be overwhelmed by the immensity of the task and harmed the school, even as they and everyone else imagined that they were single-handedly carrying the school on their shoulders.

## Making the Most of Resources

Even when schools are autonomous institutions, they do not operate in isolation. A school's congregational or communal base of support is critical to its success, and certainly to its finances. Beyond their immediate funding support, several schools in this study drew upon the wider community for expertise and grants. There is little doubt that schools located in areas where there is a large potential pool of educators, where a school of Jewish education trains teachers, where a bureau of Jewish education has a broad and creative agenda, and where communal funding is available through federations, have great advantages. Schools, in short, have to consider potential internal and external resources, then plan to make maximal use of both. In this regard, size is not necessarily the key point. Both large and small schools have to be clear about their circumstances and act wisely to benefit from their environment.

Two of the smallest schools in our sample were especially adept at harnessing resources. Tikvah Synagogue School has the smallest enrollment of those we studied but has been able to bring its students to high levels of synagogue skills, Hebrew reading ability, and comprehending Jewish texts through the creative use of local personnel. Necessity forced this school to seek out unusual teachers and to develop them as Jewish educators. The Chabad School is also small but it benefits greatly from the larger Chabad network. Most of the teachers are part of an extended family, and each year a volunteer or two from Brooklyn or other faraway communities comes to help out. Moreover, the central Chabad office runs an online service for *shluchos* and Hebrew school directors who seek each other's advice. The *shluchos* also gather annually to compare notes. Even though their schools are small, Chabad educators can gain access to a national (if not an international) network, thereby overcoming their isolation.

Some schools, particularly communal ones, can serve as a resource even as they benefit from support from other institutions. The possibilities for reciprocity are highlighted by Western Hebrew High School's central role in its community. As a community school with little competition among other supplementary high schools in the area, Western plays a central role in its medium-sized Jewish community. Its strong relationship with local synagogues provides a structure to sustain a number of congregational confirmation programs, some of which had languished within their own institutions until they joined with the high school. Over time, the school's annual Israel trip has become tightly embedded in the fabric of the Jewish community and is a source of much local pride. Students enroll in the school in great anticipation of the six-week trip, and anecdotal evidence suggests they come back more mature, more personally engaged as Jews, and much more connected to Israel. The school facilitates a variety of post-trip programming that interacts with the wider Jewish community. This model of a supplementary school as community magnet—a gathering place for the various Jewish youth of a city—is a system that works well for the school and community, and can be replicated.

# Developing a Common Purpose with Lay Leaders and Parents

One of the truisms of school change in Jewish supplementary schools is that it is vital to involve lay leaders—board members and others—in the life of the school, and to work cooperatively with them to refine the objectives of the school. Several of the schools we studied worked hard to bring lay leaders on board, an effort that yielded long-term benefits. In fact, the drivers of change and innovation in a few of the schools in our sample were parents and other concerned lay leaders who sustained change efforts even when school heads and teachers came and went. Lay leaders, in short, provide continuity in schools that might suffer greatly at times of personnel turnover.

# A Staff Imbued with a Strong Jewish Mission

Inspired teachers matter. When asked, students and parents can immediately identify which teachers have made an impression: teachers and school heads who are personally invested in Jewish life and in their teaching serve as powerful role models to children. When, as is the case at some schools, students spend break time hanging out with teachers, they are voting with their feet. It is also evident which teachers give of themselves at retreats or invite students to spend Shabbat in their homes. For the best teachers, Jewish education is a mission. Nothing can substitute for a teacher's sense of Jewish mission to help young people find their way as Jews.

One way such commitment is measured is through the wise use of time. Based on the knowledge that class hours are few, and difficult decisions must be made to prioritize how that time will be used most effectively, the best educators feel a sense of urgency. During the course of our research we learned of a calendar hanging in the teachers' area of a Chabad Hebrew school that counts the days and hours of classes until the end of the school year. It's purpose is not to raise teacher morale by counting down to the end of the year, but to dramatize how little time is left—and therefore to heighten the sense of urgency. This sense of urgency has led some schools to insist on better planning so as to maximize class time. Quite a few of our schools are also using nonschool days far more effectively by running Shabbat and holiday programs, scheduling programs and retreats on school vacation days, and drawing students to extracurricular activities on weekends. Creative use of time serves as an auxiliary to formal class hours. Finally, schools maximize the use of time by eliminating programs that have little connection to the school's stated goals. This requires a tough-minded approach to separate the essential from the extraneous.

Based on the ten schools examined in this volume, we may also draw some larger conclusions pertinent to the considerations of policy makers within synagogues and schools, federations of Jewish philanthropy, central agencies for Jewish education, denominational agencies and funders.

- Change must be multi-levered. It must draw upon multiple resources and strive to affect different aspects of the school. Too many schools focus on a single arena, believing that by improving curriculum or intensifying professional development or forging a strong bond between the synagogue and the school they can redirect the entire school enterprise. Each of these is important. But schools are complex institutions and require a series of interventions to turn them around. So many components of school life are interrelated; therefore, fixing one aspect will have only limited impact if others are amiss. For the most part, the rich schools—those with financial resources and a critical mass of concerned lay leaders—are getting richer because they draw upon multiple resources, rather than relying on a single action. Small schools, which constitute the majority within the supplementary system, will have to find ways to harness resources so that they too will be able to engage in a broad-gauged process of renewal.
- Supplementary Jewish education lacks a mechanism for helping educators make informed curricular decisions. Due to the highly decentralized nature of the field, many schools shape their own curriculum. Some schools employ or adapt curricula devised by denominational education arms, such as the Chai curriculum prepared by the Department of Lifelong Jewish Learning at the Union for Reform Judaism. Others base their teaching largely on textbooks devised by commercial publishers. The existing national bodies do not currently reach into most schools; and local central agencies have limited impact, particularly at a time when many have been stripped of their budgets and authority to provide direct services. In addition, teachers often arrogate decision-making authority, changing curricula to suit their own interests and tastes. The result is a chaotic situation in which each school (and sometime each teacher) fends for itself—and often wastes a great deal of time in reinventing the proverbial wheel.
- This, in turn, highlights the paucity of champions for the field of supplementary Jewish education. It is easy to blame the national organizations or the central agencies for the unhappy state of affairs, but upon closer

inspection it is evident that these institutions often lack the capacity, the personnel, and the authority to help schools. In the absence of such resources, there is only so much they can accomplish. Just as donors are banding together to aid day schools, summer camps, early childhood programs, birthright Israel, and other educational enterprises, the field of supplementary Jewish education will also need an infusion of money and energetic leadership. The creation of PELIE is a step in the right direction, but it is beginning quite modestly.

• Who will help the small schools? With 60 percent of Jewish supplementary schools enrolling fewer than 100 students, it would be wise not to overlook this niche. In some cases, schools left to their own devices have developed highly creative and effective programs. Tikvah Synagogue in our sample is a dramatic case in point. But while necessity as well as strong rabbinic leadership may have propelled Tikvah forward, few even know of its approach. Moreover, the school leadership is resentful of its neglect by the large national agencies, especially from its own movement. The model of the Institute for Southern Jewish Life may offer one useful approach: circuit-riding educators who visit small communities. It is possible to conceive of a section in denominational offices or other national agencies dedicated to small schools, as well as an initiative like the Mandel Teacher Education Institute designed expressly for teachers in small schools. Alternatively, the needs of small schools might be well served by a program to help local central agencies work specifically with them.

• The field would benefit from having a clearinghouse for good ideas. Some of the national organizations such as CAJE (the Coalition for Advancing Jewish Education), try to play this role. But here, too, budgetary constraints limit impact. Moreover, it is not enough to disseminate ideas for programming. Schools need guidance in how to adapt curricula, programs, and initiatives from other settings. Absent the infrastructure, communal support, and trained personnel, the models we have described above may not fit in other schools. It is not only ideas, then, that must be exchanged, but also guidance about *how* to adapt them.

• The culture of supplementary Jewish education would be enriched through the fostering of hard thinking about the objectives of schooling, self-reflection on how well these objectives are being met, and serious work on reorganizing programs based upon these considerations. Even some of the better schools in our study have made only limited progress in thinking through what they hope to accomplish, what their ideal graduate will have mastered and experienced, and how they define their short-term and long-range goals. By their own admission, many schools are most interested in giving students positive Jewish experiences. While they also devote time to teaching skills and content, this often occurs without a clear sense of the ends they wish to achieve.

There is no shortage of reasons for this situation. The part-time nature of the enterprise leaves little room for thinking through what the school hopes to accomplish. The limited time available with students encourages a scattershot approach to many different aspects of Jewish culture and religion. The broad range of learners suggests to some that we cannot determine a single set of goals, because individual students will take away different lessons based on their own interests, temperaments, family backgrounds and personalities. In addition, some educators argue, the goal ought to be to give students good feelings about being Jewish so that they will become lifelong Jewish learners. Indeed, the purpose of supplementary schooling may be to ignite a spark of Jewish enthusiasm, rather than fill young Jews with a great deal of content they may not retain for long.

Though no agency can dictate to schools what they ought to be doing, we can hope to stimulate conversation about the objectives they wish to set for themselves and the means they use to engage in self-evaluation. This does not mean that schools should necessarily rely upon standardized testing or externally imposed criteria for success. It does mean that supplementary schools, like all educational efforts, would do better if they were clear about their goals and honest with themselves about how well they are succeeding. As matters currently stand, standards of success are subjective at best. Both educators and the lay leaders who support their work may feel much better about the enterprise if they are clear on their objectives and measures of success. Certainly, students are likely to benefit from well-focused and well-executed formal and informal Jewish education offered by supplementary schools.

Here, then, are some of the broader implications we may draw from our school portraits. They are offered in the hope that educators and interested lay leaders will learn from the experiences of other supplementary programs as they re-conceive their own schools. Given the urgency of the moment and the strong sense that the field must reinvent itself, school leaders seem more receptive to change. They also are aware, perhaps as never before, that a single silver bullet will not suffice. In order to improve a supplementary school, a combination of factors must be put in place. When the "perfect storm" arrives, schools can right themselves and succeed as settings for a good Jewish education—which is all the more reason to learn from the ten schools in this study.

## *Notes*

1. Daniel Pekarsky, "Vision-Guided Jewish Education," in Roberta Louis Goodman, Paul A. Flexner, and Linda Dale Bloomberg, eds., *What We Now Know About Jewish Education: Perspectives on Research and Practice.*" Los Angeles: Torah Aura Productions, 2008, p. 27.

# Index

A Package From Home fundraiser, 153
Abel, 32
Abraham, 15, 135, 211, 265–66
Achnai, 334
Adam, 32, 61, 98
Adath Shalom: Bar/Bat Mitzvah at, 147,
150, 152–53, 156, 160–61, 165, 171,
173; budget at, 148, 167, 172–73;
challenges at, 164–68, 173; *chavurot*
at, 171–72; community, creation of at,
149, 153, 158–60, 165, 170–72, 174;
Conservative Judaism at, 145–75; curriculum potential at, 147–48, 150–59,
161–62, 166–67, 169–70, 173–75;
egalitarianism at, 147; enrollment statistics of, 147; evaluation at, 152, 154,
167–68; experimentation at, 167; Federation, work with at, 150; fundraising
at, 167; God, learning about at, 149;
governance at, 151, 166–69, 173; Hebrew, knowledge of at, 149, 151–56,
159, 161–66, 174; high school programs at, 164, 170, 172, 174–75; history, learning about Jewish at, 149,
164; holidays, learning about at, 149,
152, 154; Holocaust, learning about
at, 153, 161; identity, learning about
Jewish at, 158, 174; informality at,
152, 170–72, 175; intermarriage at,
147; Israel, learning about at, 149,
153, 161, 163; and Jewish involvement after Bar/Bat Mitzvah, 157; law,
learning about Jewish at, 153; learning
from model of, 171–75; a look at,
145–47; mission, defining at, 153,
158, 167, 170; Orthodox Judaism at,
149, 159; parental and family education at, 148–50, 152, 161, 163, 169,
172–73, 352–53; Passover, learning

about at, 152, 154–57; pedagogy at,
151, 174; prayer at, 149, 151–53, 156,
164–65; religious school of, 147–48;
rituals, learning about at, 149; Shabbat at, 147–49, 152, 158, 165–66,
173; staff, role of at, 150–51, 154, 160,
167–69, 171, 173; Sunday school at,
147–48; Sunday school model replaced
with Shabbat model at, 150; teachers,
expectations of at, 151, 154–56, 159–
64, 172; teen experiences at, 157–59,
170; Torah, learning at, 149, 152, 162,
165; Traditional Judaism at, 147; transitions for, 168–71; tuition at, 148,
167; *tzedakah* (charity), learning about
at, 153; values, exposure to Jewish at,
149, 152–53, 174; vision, educational
at, 148–50, 153, 159–60, 166, 169–71,
173; *yahadut,* knowledge of at, 151,
156, 159
ADD/ADHD, 245, 316. *See also* Special-
needs students
Adler, Cyrus, 232
Afterlife, 98–99, 301–2, 317, 324, 328
Akiva, Rabbi, 31, 251
*Al Kol Eileh,* 164
*Alef bet,* 45, 130
*Alef-Bet* choir, 236
Aleph Champ, 93–96, 106
Alfasi, Rabbi Isaac ben Jacob (the Rif),
329
Allen, Morris, 64
Allen, Woody, 119
Ambience: at Chabad schools, 80–83,
104, 106; at East Coast Community
High School, 309–11, 314, 326, 350;
at Kehillah, 349; at supplementary
schools, 354; at Temple Reyim, 180–83,
204

American Council on the Teaching of
Foreign Languages, 22
Amichai, Yehuda, 59
*Amidah*, 54, 126, 142
Amnesty International, 256
Ancient Near East, 63
Animals, treatment of, 64–65, 74, 97
Antisemitism, 130, 142, 221
Application of Jewish learning, 32–33
ARE Publications, 328
Arlington Cemetery, 338, 340
Artscroll, 97
*Ashrei*, 164
Asperger's syndrome, 316. *See also*
Special-needs students
Assessment. *See* Evaluation
Avi Chai Foundation, xiv
*Avodah*, 270

*Ba'al teshuvah* movement, 287
Bagels on the *Bimah*, 123
*Bal tashchit*, 117
Balaam, 210
Bar Mitzvah Adventure (BMA), 249–50,
254–58, 267–68
Bar/Bat Mitzvah: at Adath Shalom, 147,
150, 152–53, 156, 160–61, 165,
171, 173; adult, 177; associating Jewish education with, xii; at Beit Knesset
Hazon, 241, 249–50, 253–58; at
Chabad schools, 89, 93, 97, 101, 105;
counterculture in Reform Judaism,
207, 212, 215–16, 219–21, 227; differences between, 99–100, 104; ending
Jewish education with, xii; family
*d'var Torah* at, 131–34; Hebrew
schools as mills, 84; individualized
planning for, 68; Jewish involvement
after: at Adath Shalom, 157; at Beit
Knesset Hazon, 249, 253; counterculture in Reform Judaism, 216–17; at
East Coast Community High School,
323; at Reconstructionist schools,
134; at supplementary schools, 349;
at Temple Reyim, 184, 194, 196, 201,
204; at Tikvah Synagogue School, 52,
56, 58; at Western Hebrew High, 278;
learning about prayer before, 54; performance at, xi; post- in Tamid program, 52; pre- and post- as prayer
leaders at Tikvah Synagogue School,

52; preparation not part of Kehillah
curriculum, 33, 40, 43, 355; reading
Hebrew at, 21, 28, 193, 327; at
Reconstructionist schools, 114–16,
119–21, 127, 141; Reconstructionist
schools, class before, 129–31; for
special-needs students, 196; at Temple
Reyim, 177, 183, 199
BBYO (B'nai Brith Youth Organization),
300
Becker, Vera, 283–85, 288
*Bedikat chametz*, 155
Behrman House, 152
Beit Knesset Hazon: assumptions of,
243–49; Bar/Bat Mitzvah at, 241,
249–50, 253–58; budget at, 245–46,
248, 269; challenges at, 247, 269–70;
*chavurot* at, 237, 243, 247, 250–51,
269; community, creation of at, 234,
239–41, 244, 248, 250–51, 253–54,
259, 264–66, 271, 348; curriculum
potential at, 238, 242, 247, 249–67,
269, 351; enrollment statistics of, 239,
249–50, 253, 258; ethics, learning
about Jewish at, 254; evaluation at,
248–49; experiential learning at, 243–
44; experimentation at, 239, 248–49;
Federation, work with at, 237–40,
242, 246, 248, 251, 271–72; goals
of, 240–42; governance at, 239, 245;
Hebrew, knowledge of at, 236, 242,
244, 254, 256, 258, 262–63; high
school programs at, 249–54; history,
learning about Jewish at, 243, 251–52,
254; identity, learning about Jewish at,
238; informality at, 243, 250, 355; Israel, learning about at, 236, 243, 251,
270; and Jewish involvement after
Bar/Bat Mitzvah, 249, 253; learning
from model of, 270–72; a look at,
236–37; mission, defining at, 239,
253, 271, 355; *mitzvot*, learning about
at, 253–55; and multiple intelligences,
theory of, 244; Orthodox Judaism at,
266; parental and family education
at, 236–37, 240, 246, 251, 254–56,
258–60, 264, 267, 269–70, 353; as
a perfect storm, 237–40; prayer at,
252–54, 262, 267–69, 350; Reform
Judaism at, 236–73; rituals, learning
about at, 244; Shabbat at, 237, 250,

252, 258, 269; special-needs students at, 244–45, 247, 258, 260; staff, role of at, 236, 240–41, 247–49, 252–53, 261–62, 269, 271–72, 348; Sunday school at, 236, 244, 261, 270; Talmud, learning at, 236, 251, 255; teachers, expectations of at, 236, 238, 244–45, 247–48, 256–61, 263–64, 266–67; and *tikkun olam*, 242, 255, 257, 271; Torah, learning at, 236, 238–39, 242, 254, 265, 270; trip to Israel with, 242; tuition at, 246, 269; *tzedakah* (charity), learning about at, 255, 258; values, exposure to Jewish at, 234, 253–54, 256, 260, 264, 266, 271; vision, educational at, 234–73
*Beit Midrash*, 215–16, 219, 227
Ben and Jerry's, 39
Ben Bag Bag, 30
*Ben Sorer U'Moreh*, 328
*Benayim* (middle school) programs at Kehillah, 21, 32–34, 39
Benjamin, 131, 337
Ben-Peretz, Miriam, 25
Berg, Miriam, 7, 10–11, 18–19, 21, 31, 33, 40–42
Beth Tefillah Synagogue, 297
Bialik, 61
Bible. *See* Torah
*Bikkur cholim*, 266
Birthright Israel, 288, 290, 321, 360
Blum, Kineret, 242, 244–45, 247–48, 261–62, 268, 270
*B'nai Tzedek*, 289, 305
Board of directors. *See* Governance
*Book of Legends, The*, 61
*Brachot*, learning, 3–4, 7
Brandeis University, 283
*Brit* (covenant): class at Kehillah, 348; creation of a classroom, 20; between God and Israel, 25, 32; theme of *Shabbaton*, 224; of *Tsevet* members, 18
*Brit milah*, 224
Brother Daniel, 334–36
Budget: at Adath Shalom, 148, 167, 172–73; addressing problem of, xii–xiii, xvi; at Beit Knesset Hazon, 245–46, 248, 269; at Chabad schools, 89–90, 357; counterculture in Reform Judaism, 210, 231; at East Coast Community High School, 319; making the

most of resources, 183–87, 202–3, 356–57, 359–60; at Reconstructionist schools, 116, 140; at Temple Reyim, 199; at Tikvah Synagogue School, 357, 360; at Western Hebrew High, 357. *See also* Fundraising; Scholarships; Tuition
Bureau of Jewish Education, 227, 261
Bush, George W., 257
*B'Yachad*, 122–27, 136, 138, 141–42

Cain, 32
CAJE (Coalition for the Advancement of Jewish Education), 76, 88, 150, 282–83, 360
Camp JRF, 113, 129, 143
Candle lighting, 127
Cantor Sam, 115, 120, 125–29, 134, 138
Catholicism, 335
Chabad schools: ambience at, 80–83, 104, 106; assessment of, 106–9; Bar/Bat Mitzvah at, 89, 93, 97, 101, 105; budget at, 89–90, 357; community, creation of at, 83, 90–91, 347; Conservative Judaism at, 79, 88, 100–103; curriculum potential at, 92–96, 351; as emissaries of God, 85; ethics, learning about Jewish at, 92, 97; evaluation at, 88; experimentation at, 87–88, 108; extracurricular programs at, 82, 101, 358; fundraising at, 79–80; God, learning about at, 92; Hebrew, knowledge of at, 85, 90–96, 106–7, 355; history, learning about Jewish at, 92, 97; holidays, learning about at, 92, 96; Holocaust, learning about at, 98; identity, learning about Jewish at, 84, 103; informality at, 81–82; intermarriage at, 102, 105; Israel, learning about at, 87, 89, 92; kosher, keeping at, 85, 97, 99, 103, 350; lack of board of directors at, 82, 108; law, learning about Jewish at, 84–85, 97, 99, 105, 107; a look at, 79–80; mission, defining at, 79–109; *mitzvot*, learning about at, 86, 97; morals, learning about Jewish at, 92; and multiple intelligences, theory of, 83; no egalitarianism at, 99–100, 104; Orthodox Judaism at, 79–109; parental and family education at, 81–82, 86–88, 90, 95, 101–9, 352;

Chabad schools (*continued*)
Passover, learning about at, 82, 86; pedagogy at, 91–92, 107; prayer at, 92–93; Purim, learning about at, 81, 101; Reconstructionist Judaism at, 103; Reform Judaism at, 88, 100–105; rewards at, 81–82, 94–96, 101, 107, 348; rituals, learning about at, 92, 101, 103, 105–6; setting the tone at, 80–90; Shabbat at, 87–88, 97, 101, 103; staff, role of at, 87, 90–92, 96, 106, 347; structure of, 90–101; students at East Coast Community High School from, 318; Sunday school at, 82, 85, 90, 93, 96, 100; Talmud, learning at, 98; teachers, expectations of at, 80–88, 90–92, 96, 98–99, 107–9, 350, 358; Torah, learning at, 85–87, 92, 96–97, 99, 107, 355; tuition at, 89; *tzedakah* (charity), learning about at, 97; values, exposure to Jewish at, 92, 97–98, 101, 105; vision, educational at, 85

Chai curriculum, 119, 121, 135–36, 359

Challenges: at Adath Shalom, 164–68, 173; at Beit Knesset Hazon, 247, 269–70; counterculture in Reform Judaism, 213, 232; at East Coast Community High School, 319; at Kehillah, 18; at Temple Reyim, 184–85, 198–200; at Tikvah Synagogue School, 69–72, 75–76; at Western Hebrew High, 291, 296, 304

*Chametz*, 155

Charity. *See Tzedakah* (charity), learning about

*Chavurot*: at Adath Shalom, 171–72; at Beit Knesset Hazon, 237, 243, 247, 250–51, 269; counterculture in Reform Judaism, 225; at Temple Reyim, 353; at Tikvah Synagogue School, 72

*Chesed* programs, 351

*Chet* (sin), 38

Chomsky, William, 114, 139

*Chosen, The*, 59, 253

Christ, crucifixion of, 220

Christianity, 334

*Chug HaSefer*, 237, 246, 249–50, 258–60, 273

*Chugim*, 221, 243

Citizen Schools, 10

Coalition for the Advancement of Jewish Education (CAJE), 76, 88, 150, 282–83, 360

Cohen, Leora, 55, 62, 66, 69

Cohen, Steven, 279

Cohn, Ethan, 242

Columbus, Christopher, 252

Community, creation of: at Adath Shalom, 149, 153, 158–60, 165, 170–72, 174; at Beit Knesset Hazon, 234, 239–41, 244, 248, 250–51, 253–54, 259, 264–66, 271, 348; at Chabad schools, 83, 90–91, 347; counterculture in Reform Judaism, 209–15, 217–20, 223–24, 228, 230–32; at East Coast Community High School, 309, 312, 321, 330–31, 338; and educational vision, 354; in high school programs, 348–49; *kavod*, through, 7–9, 13, 18, 20, 28–29, 34–38, 348; at Kehillah, 4, 7–9, 12–13, 18, 20, 30, 32, 37, 39–43, 348–49; at Reconstructionist schools, 113–24, 128, 133, 136–43, 348; at supplementary schools, 347–49; at Temple Reyim, 180–82, 186, 192, 195, 199, 202–3, 205, 356; at Tikvah Synagogue School, 50–52, 55–60, 66–69, 71–73, 75–76, 348; at Western Hebrew High, 280–81, 284–85, 288–90, 297, 303–6, 349, 357. *See also Kehillah kedoshah*, creation of

Confirmation program at Western Hebrew High, 280–81

Connection to Jewish people, personal, xi

Connections program, 136

Conservative Judaism: at Adath Shalom, 145–75; at Chabad schools, 79, 88, 100–103; at East Coast Community High School, 310–12, 318–19, 322, 343; at Kehillah, 10; at Reconstructionist schools, 122; at Temple Reyim, 176–78, 180; at Tikvah Synagogue School, 47, 50; at Western Hebrew High, 280

"Consumer Judaism", 83–84, 105–6

Content classes at Chabad schools, 96–100

Conversion. *See* Jews-by-choice

Counterculture in Reform Judaism: and Bar/Bat Mitzvah, 207, 212, 215–16, 219–21, 227; and budgets, 210, 231; and challenges, 213, 232; and *chavurot*,

225; and community, creation of, 209–15, 217–20, 223–24, 228, 230–32; and curriculum potential, 212–13, 215–16, 219–28; and educational program, 213–19; and enrollment statistics, 216; and ethics, learning about Jewish, 218, 220–21; and evaluation, 221; and experimentation, 228–29, 233; and governance, 230; and *havdalah* ceremonies, 209, 219, 224, 226; and Hebrew, knowledge of, 209, 211, 213, 215, 218, 221–24, 229; and history, learning about Jewish, 219–20, 223; and holidays, learning about, 218–19; and Holocaust, learning about, 220; and identity, learning about Jewish, 208–9, 221, 223; and informality, 214; and intermarriage, 214, 224; and Israel, learning about, 210–11, 219, 223; and Jewish involvement after Bar/Bat Mitzvah, 216–17; and law, learning about Jewish, 230; learning from model of, 231–34; a look at, 207–9; and mission, defining, 226, 228, 232–33; and *mitzvot*, learning about, 219–20; and morals, learning about Jewish, 220; and parental and family education, 207–9, 214–19, 222–26, 232–33; and prayer, 209–10, 212–13, 215, 222–23, 227; and Purim, learning about, 222; and rewards, 220; rituals, learning about at, 215, 220, 224, 230; and Shabbat, 207–12, 214–15, 218–19, 223–26, 229–30, 232; and special-needs students, 212, 214, 227; and staff, role of, 208–14, 216–19, 221–34; and Sunday school, 215–16, 222–24, 226–27, 229; and Sunday school model replaced with Shabbat model, 215; surroundings of, 209–13; and Talmud, learning, 213–14; and teachers, expectations of, 211, 216–17, 220, 226–27, 229–33; and *tikkun olam*, 218; and Torah, learning, 214, 217, 219–21; and tuition, 230; and values, exposure to Jewish, 211–15, 217–24, 228, 230–32; and vision, educational, 218, 232–33

Creation, 263, 266

Cremation, 98–99

Cremin, Lawrence, 232

Criticism of supplementary schools, xiii–xiv

Cross-grade groupings, 56, 67, 118, 120, 124, 129

Curriculum potential: at Adath Shalom, 147–48, 150–59, 161–62, 166–67, 169–70, 173–75; at Beit Knesset Hazon, 238, 242, 247, 249–67, 269, 351; at Chabad schools, 92–96, 351; counterculture in Reform Judaism, 212–13, 215–16, 219–28; at East Coast Community High School, 309–10, 313, 315, 320, 326–32, 341–42; at Kehillah, 25–26, 30–32, 43; at Reconstructionist schools, 119–22, 135–36; at supplementary schools, 349, 351, 356, 359; at Temple Reyim, 178, 185–90, 192–93, 197, 199, 203–5; at Tikvah Synagogue School, 52–60, 66, 73–75; at Western Hebrew High, 281, 283–84, 286–87, 290–96, 299, 304–5, 355

Dancing, Israeli, 59

Darfur, escape from, 16

David, King, 336–37

Davids, Beth, 11, 18–19, 38

Davids, Rabbi Tamara, 252–54, 261, 267

Dead, resurrection of the, 98–99, 301–2, 317, 324, 328

Dewey, John, 139, 143, 243

Diversity, religious, 280, 298, 349

*Divrei Torah*, 115–16, 120, 131–34, 189, 216, 254

Donations, running Chabad schools using, 89–90

Dybbuks, 208, 298, 328

East Coast Community High School: ambience at, 309–11, 314, 326, 350; budget at, 319; Chabad schools, students from, 318; challenges at, 319; community, creation of at, 309, 312, 321, 330–31, 338; Conservative Judaism at, 310–12, 318–19, 322, 343; curriculum potential at, 309–10, 313, 315, 320, 326–32, 341–42; egalitarianism at, 322; enrollment statistics of, 311; ethics, learning about Jewish at, 315, 326, 328, 331; evaluation at, 309, 320, 340–42, 350–51; exams at, 332–42, 350–51; experiential learning at,

East Coast Community High School
(*continued*)
343; extracurricular programs at, 309,
313, 315–17, 319–23; Federation, work
with at, 310, 321, 342–43; goals of,
332; governance at, 310–11; Hanukkah, learning about at, 321; Hebrew,
knowledge of at, 310, 327; identity,
learning about Jewish at, 309, 327,
330–31, 334–36, 343; informality at,
309; Israel, learning about at, 321,
324, 327, 330, 334–36; and Jewish involvement after Bar/Bat Mitzvah, 323;
kosher, keeping at, 310; law, learning
about Jewish at, 329, 334–36; learning
from model of, 342–43; a look at,
308–9; mission, defining at, 318–19,
343; *mitzvot*, learning about at, 328;
no parental and family education at,
311; no prayer at, 310, 322; Orthodox
Judaism at, 310, 312, 318–19, 322, 325,
329, 343; pluralism, learning about
at, 318; professional development
and teacher learning, 320; Reconstructionist Judaism at, 310, 318; recruitment and retention, 311–12; Reform
Judaism at, 310, 318, 343; Shabbat
at, 316–19, 321–24; special-needs
students at, 316; staff, role of at, 312–
20, 323; students at, 323–26; Sunday
school at, 309–10, 312–14, 316, 320,
324, 326, 343; Talmud, learning at,
310, 326, 329–30, 334; teachers, expectations of at, 309, 312–20, 325,
330–31, 340; Torah, learning at, 310,
317–18, 325–27, 329–33, 336–39,
341, 343; trip to Israel with, 317, 321,
324; values, exposure to Jewish at,
318, 326, 330–31, 340; vision, educational at, 310, 343
Efraim, 31
Egalitarianism: at Adath Shalom, 147; at
East Coast Community High School,
322; not present at Chabad schools,
99–100, 104; at Tikvah Synagogue
School, 49
Eisen, Arnold, 279
Eisner, Elliot, xiv
Ellis Island, 252
*Elohai Neshama*, 123, 128, 141
Enculturation, 229–30

Engel, Corey, 297–98
Enlightenment, 25
Enrollment statistics: at Adath Shalom,
147; at Beit Knesset Hazon, 239,
249–50, 253, 258; counterculture in
Reform Judaism, 216; at East Coast
Community High School, 311; at
Kehillah, 12; problem at supplementary schools, xii, xiv; at Reconstructionist schools, 118; at Temple Reyim,
178–79, 204; at Tikvah Synagogue
School, 56; at Western Hebrew High,
280, 290
Entrepeneurship, combining with Jewish
mission, 79–109
Epstein, Leslie, 39
Esau, 256
*Eshet Hayil*, 99–100, 104
Esther, Queen, 29
Ethics, learning about Jewish: at Beit Knesset Hazon, 254; at Chabad schools, 92,
97; counterculture in Reform Judaism,
218, 220–21; at East Coast Community High School, 315, 326, 328, 331;
expectations of supplementary schools,
xi; at Kehillah, 25–26; at supplementary schools, 347, 349; at Tikvah
Synagogue School, 54, 63, 65–66
Ethiopia, escape from, 15
Evaluation: at Adath Shalom, 152, 154,
167–68; at Beit Knesset Hazon, 248–
49; at Chabad schools, 88, 106–9;
counterculture in Reform Judaism,
221; at East Coast Community High
School, 309, 320, 340–42, 350–51; at
Kehillah, 350; problem at supplementary schools, xv; at Reconstructionist
schools, 117, 120, 136; at Temple
Reyim, 190, 196–98, 200–201, 203;
at Tikvah Synagogue School, 69, 76;
at Western Hebrew High, 295, 298
Eve, 32
Expectations of supplementary schools:
ethics, learning about Jewish, xi;
Hebrew, knowledge of, xi; history,
learning about Jewish, xi; holidays,
learning about, xi; mission, defining,
xi–xii, xv; rituals, learning about, xi;
of school heads, xvi; synagogue skills,
learning, xi; Torah, learning, xi; values, exposure to Jewish, xi

Expectations of teachers. *See* Teachers,
    expectations of
Experiential learning: at Beit Knesset
    Hazon, 243–44; at East Coast Com-
    munity High School, 343; at supple-
    mentary schools, 351; types of, xvi; at
    Western Hebrew High, 280, 283–90,
    306
Experimentation: at Adath Shalom, 167;
    at Beit Knesset Hazon, 239, 248–49;
    at Chabad schools, 87–88, 108; coun-
    terculture in Reform Judaism, 228–29,
    233; at Reconstructionist schools, 115–
    16, 118, 121–22, 140; at supplemen-
    tary schools, 356; at Tikvah Synagogue
    School, 56
Extracurricular programs: at Chabad
    schools, 82, 101, 358; at East Coast
    Community High School, 309, 313,
    315–17, 319–23; at Reconstructionist
    schools, 120

Family education. *See* Parental and family
    education
Family Education at Synagogue Today
    (FEAST) program, 52–58, 60, 62–63,
    67–70
Federation: Adath Shalom, work with,
    150; Beit Knesset Hazon, work with,
    237–40, 242, 246, 248, 251, 271–72;
    East Coast Community High School,
    work with, 310, 321, 342–43; Kehillah,
    work with, 41; parental and family
    education, work with, 353; supple-
    mentary schools, work with, 357,
    359; Temple Reyim, work with, 187;
    Western Hebrew High, work with,
    282, 285–86
Feinstein, Rabbi Moshe, 328
Feld, Shimon, 3–4, 7, 9, 11, 27–28,
    30–31, 34, 42
*Fiddler on the Roof*, 133
Fisher, Esther, 253, 269
Five Books of Moses. *See* Torah
*Four Hundred Blows*, 161
Franchise, Chabad as a, 88–90
Frankenstein, 69
Fried, Melanie, 5, 8–11, 39–40, 42
*Frisco Kid, The*, 253
Fundraising: at Adath Shalom, 167; at
    Chabad schools, 79–80; for Israel,
    153, 171; at Kehillah, 39; at Tikvah
    Synagogue School, 49; at Western
    Hebrew High, 304. *See also* Budget;
    Scholarships; Tuition

*Gan Ami*, 215
Gan Shalom, 114, 119, 122–23
Gardner, Howard, 18, 244
*Gates of Prayer*, 212
*Gemeinschaft* model, Tikvah Synagogue
    School a, 51, 72
*Gesellschaft* model, moving away from
    the, 51, 72
Gibson, Bina, 8, 13–15, 17, 20
Gibson, Mel, 220
Glaser, Sam, 251
*G'milut chasadim*, 119–20, 135, 255, 270
Goals. *See* Mission, defining; Vision, edu-
    cational
God: Adath Shalom, learning about at,
    149; always with people, 100, 337;
    balance with man and nature, 331;
    belief in, 287; *brit* between Israel and,
    25, 32; Chabad as emissaries of, 85;
    Chabad schools, learning about at, 92;
    communicating through Torah, 26–27,
    30, 265; conception of, 123; connec-
    tion with to everything, 298; listening
    to, 266–67; love of, 62; man in image
    of, 242, 262–64, 271; mentioned in
    the Torah, 336, 338–39; nature of, 66;
    partnership of Jews with, 224, 227;
    Reconstructionism, unnecessary in,
    113; relationship with, 318; role of,
    118; splitting the Red Sea, 121; teach-
    ers as messengers of, 355; Temple
    Reyim, developing relationship with
    at, 185–86, 188–93; and *tikkun olam*,
    257–58; Torah as words of, 333–34;
    wrestling with, 220–21
*God's Favorite*, 251
Goldenberg, Marty, 299
*Golem*, 69
Golems, 69, 298
Goodman, Barry, 164
Governance: at Adath Shalom, 151,
    166–69, 173; at Beit Knesset Hazon,
    239, 245; Chabad schools, lack of
    board at, 82, 108; counterculture in
    Reform Judaism, 230; developing
    common purpose with parents, 358;

Governance (*continued*)
  at East Coast Community High School,
  310–11; at Kehillah, 39–40; at supple-
  mentary schools, 351; at Tikvah Syna-
  gogue School, 55; at Western Hebrew
  High, 284, 303–4
Gratz College, 114
Green, Brad, 15
Greenfield, Jerry, 39
Gresham's Law, 84

*Hachnasat orchim*, 29
*Hagaddah*, 157
*Hagigah*, 215, 228, 231
*Halacha. See* Law, learning about Jewish
Halloween, 146
Haman, 29
Hanukkah, learning about: at East Coast
  Community High School, 321; at Ke-
  hillah, 25, 29; at Reconstructionist
  schools, 125, 130, 133, 142; at Tikvah
  Synagogue School, 58
Hartman Institute, 231
*Hatikva*, 223
*Havayah* program, 240, 243, 245,
  249–54, 269
*Havdalah* ceremonies: counterculture in
  Reform Judaism, 209, 219, 224, 226;
  at Kehillah, 41; at Reconstructionist
  schools, 137–38; at Temple Reyim,
  353; at Tikvah Synagogue School, 56,
  58, 73
*HaZamir*, 158
Hearing-impaired, working with the, 180,
  187, 195–96. *See also* Special-needs
  students
Hebrew, knowledge of: at Adath Shalom,
  149, 151–56, 159, 161–66, 174;
  addressing problem of, xvi, 49; at
  Bar/Bat Mitzvah, 21, 28, 193, 327;
  at Beit Knesset Hazon, 236, 242, 244,
  254, 256, 258, 262–63; at Chabad
  schools, 85, 90–96, 106–7, 355; counterculture in Reform Judaism, 209,
  211, 213, 215, 218, 221–24, 229; at
  East Coast Community High School,
  310, 327; expectations of supplementary schools, xi; Israel, outside of, 90,
  96; at Kehillah, 5–9, 11–15, 17–18,
  20–24, 28, 32, 34–38, 41–45, 352,
  354–55; at Reconstructionist schools,

  120–22, 125–26, 136; at supplemen-
  tary schools, 347, 356; at Temple
  Reyim, 176–77, 186–92, 196, 201;
  at Tikvah Synagogue School, 57–62,
  65, 73, 357; at Western Hebrew High,
  280, 293
Hebrew Association of the Deaf (HAD),
  195–96
*Hebrew Primer, The*, 152
Hebrew Union College, 218, 229
Hebrew University, 11
Hecht, Brenda, 237–38
*Henai Matov*, 113
Hertzberg, Arthur, 79
Heschel, Abraham Joshua, 74, 129, 333
*Hesed* programs, 351
High Holy Days, 114, 196, 214, 315
High school models: East Coast Commu-
  nity High School, 308–43; Western
  Hebrew High, 277–306
*High School Musical*, 127
High school programs: at Adath Shalom,
  164, 170, 172, 174–75; at Beit Knesset
  Hazon, 249–54; and community, crea-
  tion of, 348–49; at Kehillah, 12, 34–35,
  37–38; turf battles in supplementary,
  xiii, xvi, 90. *See also* Teen experiences
Hillberg, Rabbi, 296–97
Hillel, 10, 69, 303
Hirsch, Rabbi Peter, 176–77, 181, 184, 200
History, learning about Jewish: at Adath
  Shalom, 149, 164; at Beit Knesset
  Hazon, 243, 251–52, 254; at Chabad
  schools, 92, 97; counterculture in
  Reform Judaism, 219–20, 223; expectations of supplementary schools,
  xi; at Kehillah, 25, 31, 355; at Reconstructionist schools, 137, 142; at supplementary schools, 353; at Temple
  Reyim, 187; at Tikvah Synagogue
  School, 58–59, 73; at Western Hebrew
  High, 286, 294
Hitler, Adolf, 15–16
Holidays, learning about: at Adath Shalom,
  149, 152, 154; at Chabad schools, 92,
  96; counterculture in Reform Judaism,
  218–19; expectations of supplementary schools, xi; at Kehillah, 25, 32,
  40, 354; at Reconstructionist schools,
  122, 137; at Tikvah Synagogue School,
  51, 56, 58

Holocaust, learning about: at Adath Shalom, 153, 161; at Chabad schools, 98; counterculture in Reform Judaism, 220; at Kehillah, 25; at Reconstructionist schools, 126, 130; from a survivor, 334; at Temple Reyim, 192–93; at Tikvah Synagogue School, 59; at Western Hebrew High, 289, 305

Holtz, Barry, 294

Horowitz, Bethamie, 279

Identity, learning about Jewish: at Adath Shalom, 158, 174; at Beit Knesset Hazon, 238; at Chabad schools, 84, 103; counterculture in Reform Judaism, 208–9, 221, 223; at East Coast Community High School, 309, 327, 330–31, 334–36, 343; at Kehillah, 14; at Reconstructionist schools, 142; at supplementary schools, 349; at Temple Reyim, 205; at Western Hebrew High, 279, 287, 293, 303, 305–6

Idolatry, 32

Improvement of supplementary schools, xiv

Independence Day, 227

Individual educational plans (IEP), 316

Informality: at Adath Shalom, 152, 170–72, 175; at Beit Knesset Hazon, 243, 250, 355; at Chabad schools, 81–82; counterculture in Reform Judaism, 214; at East Coast Community High School, 309; at Kehillah, 6–7, 12, 42–43; at Reconstructionist schools, 119; at Western Hebrew High, 289, 299–300, 305

Inquisition, 25

Institute for Southern Jewish Life, 360

Interdenominationalism, 280

Intermarriage: at Adath Shalom, 147; at Chabad schools, 102, 105; counterculture in Reform Judaism, 214, 224; at Kehillah, 5; at Reconstructionist schools, 123, 132, 139; at Temple Reyim, 177, 181; at Western Hebrew High, 280

Intifada, 284

Involvement after Bar/Bat Mitzvah, Jewish: at Adath Shalom, 157; at Beit Knesset Hazon, 249, 253; counterculture in Reform Judaism, 216–17; at East

Coast Community High School, 323; at Reconstructionist schools, 134; at supplementary schools, 349; at Temple Reyim, 184, 194, 196, 201, 204; at Tikvah Synagogue School, 52, 56, 58; at Western Hebrew High, 278

Isaac, 134

Isaacs, Leora, 287

Isaacs, Sarah, 239, 249–50, 253–54

Israel. *See also* Zionism

Israel, learning about: at Adath Shalom, 149, 153, 161, 163; appreciation for, gaining, xi; at Beit Knesset Hazon, 236, 243, 251, 270; *brit* between God and, 25, 32; at Chabad schools, 92; counterculture in Reform Judaism, 210–11, 219, 223; culture of, 23–24; dancing, 59; day at Chabad schools, 87, 89; at East Coast Community High School, 321, 324, 327, 330, 334–36; fundraiser for, 153, 171; geographical placement of, 66; Independence Day, 227; at Kehillah, 3, 33, 354; leadership training program, 158, 170; and learning Hebrew outside of, 90, 96; literature, 59; meanings of, 13–17; sabbatical in, 5; and students' parents from, 310, 327; and studying in, 63; at supplementary schools, 347, 351; and teachers representing, 55, 59; at Temple Reyim, 176, 186–87; through trip: with Beit Knesset Hazon, 242; with East Coast Community High School, 317, 321, 324; with Temple Reyim, 178; with Western Hebrew High, 279–80, 283–90, 293, 304–5, 355, 357; at Tikvah Synagogue School, 73; walk for, 153, 171; at Western Hebrew High, 279–80, 283–90, 293–95, 303–5; year in, 10, 319

Israel, Sylvia, 270

*Ivrit Mi'bereisheet*, 327

Jacob (Ya'akov), 13–15, 100, 127, 131, 133, 256, 336–37, 339

JESNA, 287, 291, 296

Jessin, Anna, 278–79, 301–2

Jewish Actors' Workshop (JAWS), 237, 251

Jewish Camping Initiative, 240

Jewish Community Center (JCC), 10, 42, 301–2

Jewish Community Foundation, 289
Jewish Community Relations Council, 240, 251
*Jewish Lens, The*, 331
Jewish Organizing Initiative, 11
Jewish Student Union (JSU), 324
Jewish Theological Seminary of America, 232, 319
Jewish Youth Directors Association, 282
Jews-by-choice, 59, 62, 64, 205, 214, 224
Job, 251
Jones, Lilly Cohen, 177–78, 180–85, 187–90, 192–200, 203–4
Joseph, 127, 131, 336–39
*Joseph and the Amazing Technicolor Dreamcoat*, 251
Joshua, 267, 333
Judah, 127, 131

Kabbalah, 74, 298, 301, 317
Kadima, 158
Kaplan, Jill, 169
Kaplan, Mordecai, 113–15, 117, 124, 129, 139, 143
Kaplan, Rhonda, 283
Katrina, Hurricane, 141, 171
Kaufman, Ellen, 54, 62
*Kavannah* (intentionality) of prayer, 190, 268, 350
*Kavod*, community building through: at Kehillah, 7–9, 13, 18, 20, 28–29, 34–38; at supplementary schools, 348
*Keeping Up With the Steins*, 220
Kehillah: ambience at, 349; Bar/Bat Mitzvah preparation not part of curriculum at, 33, 40, 43, 355; challenges at, 18; community, creation of at, 4, 7–9, 12–13, 18, 20, 30, 32, 37, 39–43, 348–49; Conservative Judaism at, 10; curriculum potential at, 25–26, 30–32, 43; enrollment statistics of, 12; ethics, learning about Jewish at, 25–26; evaluation at, 350; facts about, 5–6; Federation, work with at, 41; fundraising at, 39; governance at, 39–40; Hanukkah, learning about at, 25, 29; *havdalah* ceremonies at, 41; Hebrew, knowledge of at, 5–9, 11–15, 17–18, 20–24, 28, 32, 34–38, 41–45, 352, 354–55; high school programs at, 12, 34–35, 37–38; history, learning about Jewish at, 25,

31, 355; holidays, learning about at, 25, 32, 40, 354; Holocaust, learning about at, 25; identity, learning about Jewish at, 14; informality at, 6–7, 12, 42–43; intermarriage at, 5; Israel, learning about at, 3, 33, 354; kosher, keeping at, 4; learning from model of, 41–45; a look at, 3–4; middle school program at, 21, 32–34, 39; *mitzvot*, learning about at, 25–26; and multiple intelligences, theory of, 18–19; parental and family education at, 40–41, 43, 353; Passover, learning about at, 28–29; pluralism, learning about at, 33; prayer at, 33, 40, 353; Purim, learning about at, 25, 29, 39; Reform Judaism at, 11, 33; rituals, learning about at, 25, 32, 38; Shabbat at, 29, 31, 41; staff, role of at, 6, 8–12, 17–20, 34, 37, 40, 42; Talmud, learning at, 26–32; teachers, expectations of at, 8–9, 12–20, 350; Torah, learning at, 26–33; Traditional Judaism at, 3–45; *tzedakah* (charity), learning about at, 25, 29; values, exposure to Jewish at, 25–26; vision, educational at, 4, 6–9, 11, 13, 25, 354–55; *yahadut*, knowledge of at, 6–9, 11–12, 18, 20–21, 25–32, 36–37, 42–43, 352
*Kehillah kedoshah*, creation of, 240–42, 264–66, 271. *See also* Community, creation of
Kehillat Ha'ir, 3–6, 10–13, 18, 27, 32, 34, 37–40
Kehillat Haparvar, 5–8, 10, 12–13, 15, 39–41
*Kibud av v'em*, 37, 152
*Kiddush*, 97
King, Jennifer, 49
*Kippot*, wearing, 106–7, 127, 176
*Kol YIsrael Areivim Zeh B'Zeh*, 153. *See also* Community, creation of
Kosher, keeping: at Chabad schools, 85, 97, 99, 103, 350; at East Coast Community High School, 310; eco-, 59, 63–65; at Kehillah, 4; needy families, 321; struggle with, 14
Krasnianski, Devora, 83
Kress, 160, 163, 165
Kushner, Rabbi Harold, 255
Kushner, Rabbi Lawrence, 301

Laban, 100
*Ladies Home Journal*, 202
*Lamed-Vavniks*, 196
Lamm, 333
Large schools: Adath Shalom, 145–75; Beit Knesset Hazon, 236–73; counterculture in Reform Judaism, 207–34; Reconstructionist, 113–43; Temple Reyim, 176–205
*Lashon hara*, 152, 329
Law, learning about Jewish: at Adath Shalom, 153; at Chabad schools, 84–85, 97, 99, 105, 107; counterculture in Reform Judaism, 230; at East Coast Community High School, 329, 334–36; at Reconstructionist schools, 140; at Tikvah Synagogue School, 64
Law of Return, 334–36
Learning, types of, xvi
Learning disabilities. *See* Special-needs students
Learning from models: Adath Shalom, 171–75; Beit Knesset Hazon, 270–72; counterculture in Reform Judaism, 231–34; East Coast Community High School, 342–43; Kehillah, 41–45; Reconstructionist schools, 139–43; supplementary schools, 347–61; Temple Reyim, 200–202; Tikvah Synagogue School, 72–73, 76–77; Western Hebrew High, 303–6
*Lecha Dodi*, 177
Lechner, Ariel, 154
Legacy Heritage Foundation, 58, 311
Levy, Dalia, 11
Levy, Irwin, 237
Lightfoot, Sara Lawrence, xiv
*Limmud*, 76
Literature, Jewish, 59, 73
London Underground, 225
Lorch, Beth, 239–42, 245, 247–48, 254, 258, 260–62, 269–71
Lot, 265
Lowenstein, Rabbi, 298–99
Lubavitcher Rebbe, 80
Lyndon Johnson Public School, 145, 163

*Ma'achil re'evim*, 153
*Ma'asim tovim*, 236, 243, 254–56
Maccabees, Book of, 130
Maccabi Games, 128
Machtinger, Lionel, 300

Mad Cow disease, 64
*Madrichim*, role of, 217, 219, 225, 231, 247, 251
*Mah Tovu*, 209–10
Maimonides, 64, 98, 161, 238, 317, 348
Mandel Teacher Education Institute, 360
Mandela, Nelson, 256
*Ma'nishtanah*, 156
*Matanot l'evyonim*, 25
Maximizing time spent in supplementary schools, xvi
Mead, Margaret, 256
Meier, Deborah, 72
Melton Adult Mini School, 150–52
Menasheh, 31
Messiah, 98
*Mezuzot*, 97, 350
*Mi Kamocha*, 33, 61
*Middot. See* Values, exposure to Jewish
*Mikraot Gedolot*, 30–31
Miriam, 329
Mirsky, Cory, 245, 247, 254, 256–58
*Mishkan* (tabernacle), 189, 265
*Mishloach manot* project, 39
*Mishpacha* program, 236, 240, 270
*Mishpachot*, 224–25
Mission, defining: at Adath Shalom, 153, 158, 167, 170; at Beit Knesset Hazon, 239, 253, 271, 355; at Chabad schools, 79–83, 103, 106; counterculture in Reform Judaism, 226, 228, 232–33; at East Coast Community High School, 318–19, 343; expectations of supplementary schools, xi–xii, xv; at Reconstructionist schools, 124, 126; and teachers/staff, expectations of, 358–61; at Temple Reyim, 185–88, 192–93, 199, 201, 205; at Western Hebrew High, 291–93, 303, 305, 355
Mitkadem, 120–22, 136
Mitzvah Day, 289, 321
*Mitzvah* projects, 120, 132, 149, 152, 172
*Mitzvah*-palooza, 289
*Mitzvot*, learning about: at Beit Knesset Hazon, 253–55; at Chabad schools, 86, 97; counterculture in Reform Judaism, 219–20; at East Coast Community High School, 328; at Kehillah, 25–26; at supplementary schools, 347; at Temple Reyim, 198; at Tikvah Synagogue School, 61–62

*Modeh Ani*, 127
Morals, learning about Jewish, 92, 220
Moses, 29–31, 98, 155, 157, 229, 329, 333
*Motzie*, 127
Mourners, comforting, 330
Multiple intelligences, theory of, 18–19, 83, 244
*My Name is Rachamim*, 15
Mysticism, 74, 298, 301, 317

Nachshon, 121
*Nichum avelim*, 330
*Night*, 59
Nile River, 131
No Child Left Behind Act, 222
Noah, 32, 220
North American Alliance for Jewish Youth (NAA), 282, 301
NPR, 39

Obstacles impeding supplementary schools, xii–xiii
*Ometz lev*, 25
Orthodox Judaism: at Adath Shalom, 149, 159; at Beit Knesset Hazon, 266; at Chabad schools, 79–109; at East Coast Community High School, 310, 312, 318–19, 322, 325, 329, 343; at Reconstructionist schools, 127; at Tikvah Synagogue School, 48–49, 56, 71
OWLS, 154
Ozeri, Zion, 330

Palestinian mandate, 223
*Paper Clips*, 193
Parental and family education: at Adath Shalom, 148–50, 152, 161, 163, 169, 172–73, 352–53; at Beit Knesset Hazon, 236–37, 240, 246, 251, 254–56, 258–60, 264, 267, 269–70, 353; at Chabad schools, 81–82, 86–88, 90, 95, 101–9, 352; counterculture in Reform Judaism, 207–9, 214–19, 222–26, 232–33; and Federation, work with, 353; at Kehillah, 40–41, 43, 353; not at East Coast Community High School, 311; at Reconstructionist schools, 115, 118–20, 122–28, 131–34, 136–38, 140–42; at supplementary schools, xvi, 352–54; at Temple Reyim,

178, 180, 183, 192, 194, 196, 199–202, 204, 353; at Tikvah Synagogue School, 54–56, 60–70, 72; at Western Hebrew High, 285–86, 288, 304
*Parshat HaShavuah*, 115, 120, 131–32, 145, 221
Parsons, Susan, 282–83, 285–86, 296, 299
Passover, learning about: at Adath Shalom, 152, 154–57; at Chabad schools, 82, 86; at Kehillah, 28–29; lack of interest in, 49; at Reconstructionist schools, 125, 137, 142; seder comparison to Jewish education, 117; at Tikvah Synagogue School, 61
Passport to Israel, 187
Patriarchs, stories of the, 32
*Pay It Forward*, 255
Pedagogy: at Adath Shalom, 151, 174; at Chabad schools, 91–92, 107; at Temple Reyim, 178, 197, 199
Pekarsky, 186
PELIE, 360
Phantom limb syndrome, 329
Pharaoh, 131, 155, 336–37, 339
Philosophy, learning about Jewish, 278–79, 294
Pink, 256
*Pirkei Avot*, 242, 254, 259–60
Plautedition Torah, 212
Pluralism, learning about, 33, 114, 318
Poland, trip to, 284, 286, 288–89
Politics, learning about, 290, 298, 305
Portraiture, xiv
Posen, Rabbi Barry, 146, 148, 150–51, 159–60, 166–71
Potiphar, 337
Potok, Chaim, 59
Potter, Harry, 154
Powell, Heather, 63–65, 73
*Power of Their Ideas, The*, 72
Prayer: at Adath Shalom, 149, 151–53, 156, 164–65; attitudes toward, 74; before Bar/Bat Mitzvah, 54; at Beit Knesset Hazon, 252–54, 262, 267–69, 350; at Chabad schools, 92–93; counterculture in Reform Judaism, 209–10, 212–13, 215, 222–23, 227; *kavannah* (intentionality) of, 190, 268, 350; at Kehillah, 33, 40, 353; kids' interest in, 21; love of, 32, 38; not at East Coast

Community High School, 310, 322; at Reconstructionist schools, 122–23, 126–29, 136, 142; at supplementary schools, 351; at Temple Reyim, 186–93, 200; at Tikvah Synagogue School, 52, 54, 56–58, 60–62, 65–66, 68–69, 73, 348; at Western Hebrew High, 298

Principal's Forum, 150

Problems at supplementary schools, xii–xiii, xv–xvi, 49. *See also* Challenges

Professional development. *See* Teachers, expectations of

Project Kehillah, 116, 122, 134, 136–41

Prophets, messages of the, 32, 266–67

Proverbs, Book of, 99, 104

*Prozdor*, 157–58

Psalms, 213, 336

Purim, learning about: at Chabad schools, 81, 101; counterculture in Reform Judaism, 222; at Kehillah, 25, 29, 39

Purpose, leaders and parents developing common, 358

Quinn, Denise, 248–49, 253

Qur'an, 336

Rabbi Abby, 114–16, 118–29, 132–37, 141–42

Rabbi Tom, 115–17, 131–34, 136–39, 141

Rael, Elsa Okon, 259

Rahab, 267

*Raiders of the Lost Ark*, 107

Rak Shabbat, 243, 245

Rambam (Maimonides), 20, 64, 98, 161, 238, 317, 348

"Rap with the Rabbi" program, 159, 182

Rashi, 259–60, 325

Ravnitsky, 61

Rebecca, 131

Reconstructionist Judaism: at Chabad schools, 103; at East Coast Community High School, 310, 318; schools of, 113–43; at Temple Reyim, 176; at Western Hebrew High, 280

Reconstructionist Rabbinical College, 132

Reconstructionist schools: Bar/Bat Mitzvah at, 114–16, 119–21, 127, 141; budget at, 116, 140; Chai and Mitkadem, 135–36; community, creation of at, 113–24, 128, 133, 136–43, 348; Conservative Judaism at, 122; curriculum potential at, 119–22, 135–36; enrollment statistics of, 118; evaluation at, 117, 120, 136; experimentation at, 115–16, 118, 121–22, 140; extracurricular programs at, 120; family *d'var torah*, 131–34; Gan Shalom and Bagels on the Bimah, 122–23; goals of, 117–22; God, unnecessary in, 113; Hanukkah, learning about at, 125, 130, 133, 142; *havdalah* ceremonies at, 137–38; Hebrew, knowledge of at, 120–22, 125–26, 136; history, learning about Jewish at, 137, 142; holidays, learning about at, 122, 137; Holocaust, learning about at, 126, 130; identity, learning about Jewish at, 142; informality at, 119; intermarriage at, 123, 132, 139; and Jewish involvement after Bar/Bat Mitzvah, 134; law, learning about Jewish at, 140; learning from model of, 139–43; a look at, 113–16; mission, defining at, 124, 126; Orthodox Judaism at, 127; parental and family education at, 115, 118–20, 122–28, 131–34, 136–38, 140–42; Passover, learning about at, 125, 137, 142; pluralism, learning about at, 114; prayer at, 122–23, 126–29, 136, 142; pre-Bar/Bat Mitzvah class at, 129–31; project Kehillah, 136–39; Reform Judaism at, 119–20, 122, 125; rituals, learning about at, 119; Shabbat at, 115–16, 118, 121–26, 128, 131–33, 137; Shabbat school and *B'Yachad*, 123–29; special-needs students at, 141; staff, role of at, 114–26, 132, 136–38, 140, 143; Sunday school model replaced with Shabbat model at, 118, 121–26; teachers, expectations of at, 115–16, 120–21, 129–30, 135, 141; teen experiences at, 134–35; and *tikkun olam*, 137; Torah, learning at, 115, 125–26, 135, 142; vision, educational at, 117–24, 129, 140–42

Red Sea, 33, 121, 155

Reform Judaism: at Beit Knesset Hazon, 236–73; at Chabad schools, 88, 100–105; counterculture in, 207–34; at

Reform Judaism (*continued*)
East Coast Community High School,
310, 318, 343; at Kehillah, 11, 33; at
Reconstructionist schools, 119–20,
122, 125; at Temple Reyim, 176–205;
at Tikvah Synagogue School, 47–49, 57,
61, 71; at Western Hebrew High, 280
Reimer, Joseph, 199
Reincarnation, 298, 328
Resources, making the most of, 183–87,
202–3, 356–57, 359–60
Resurrection of the dead, 98–99, 301–2,
317, 324, 328
Rewards: at Chabad schools, 81–82,
94–96, 101, 107, 348; counterculture
in Reform Judaism, 220
Rif, the (Rabbi Isaac ben Jacob Alfasi), 329
Rituals, learning about: at Adath Shalom,
149; at Beit Knesset Hazon, 244; at
Chabad schools, 92, 101, 103, 105–6;
counterculture in Reform Judaism,
215, 220, 224, 230; expectations of
supplementary schools, xi; at Kehillah,
25, 32, 38; at Reconstructionist schools,
119; at Temple Reyim, 200; at Tikvah
Synagogue School, 73
*River of Light*, 301
Rosen, Linda, 59, 73
Rosenberg, Ellen, 177
Rosenzweig, 333
Rosh Chodesh programs, 134–35, 158, 243
Rosh HaShanah, 69, 239, 300, 353
Rubenstein, Rabbi, 146
Rufeisen, Oswald, 334–36

Sarah (Sarai), 15, 266
Satan, 336
Saul, King, 337
Schachter-Shlomi, Zalman, 64
Schedule, daily at Kehillah schools, 6
Schein, Edgar, 8
Scholarships, 230, 246, 319. *See also*
Budget; Fundraising; Tuition
School heads, expectations of, xvi
Schools, synagogue programs not consid-
ered as, xii–xiii, xvi
Seder, 117, 126, 155, 157
*Sefer HaAgadah*, 61
Self-reflection, creating culture of, 356
Senge, Peter, 141–42
*S'fatai Tiftah*, 57

Shabbat: at Adath Shalom, 147–49, 152,
158, 165–66, 173; at Beit Knesset
Hazon, 237, 250, 252, 258, 269; at
Chabad schools, 87–88, 97, 101, 103;
counterculture in Reform Judaism,
207–12, 214–15, 218–19, 223–26,
229–30, 232; at East Coast Community High School, 316–19, 321–24; at
Kehillah, 29, 31, 41; model replaced
by Sunday school model: at Adath
Shalom, 150; counterculture in Reform
Judaism, 215; at Reconstructionist
schools, 118, 121–26; at Tikvah Syna-
gogue School, 48–50, 52–54, 56–58,
60, 62–63, 66–67, 70–73; at Recon-
structionist schools, 115–16, 118,
121–26, 128, 131–33, 137; at supple-
mentary schools, 351, 358; at Temple
Reyim, 180, 183, 192, 195–96, 204,
353; at Tikvah Synagogue School, 50,
52–54, 56–58, 60, 62–63, 66–67,
70–73, 350
Shabbat *B'Yachad*, 183, 204
*Shaliach Tzibor*, 149
*Shalom bayit*, 118
*Shalosh Regalim*, 155, 157
Sharon, Ariel, 130
Shavuot, 13, 27, 36
*Shechita*, 99
*Sheheheyanu*, 130
Shelah, 338
*Shema*, 26–27, 65–66, 97, 128, 135, 212,
268–69, 350
*Sherut*, 237, 240, 247, 251
SHINE, 158–59
*Shoah. See* Holocaust, learning about
*Siddur*, reading the. *See* Prayer
*Siddur Kol HaNoa*, 128
Siegal, David, 50, 55, 58–59, 61, 65–66,
69–71, 74–75
Siegal, Sarah, 50, 56
*Simchat Torah*, 259
Simon, Neil, 251
Sin, 38
Sinai, giving Torah at, 32, 131
Singer, Isaac Bashevis, 59
Slavery, 252
Small schools: Chabad schools, 79–109;
Kehillah, 3–45; Tikvah Synagogue
School, 47–77
Sodom and Gemorrah, 265

*Sofer*, learning to be a, 97
Solomon Schechter Day School, 314, 321
*South Park*, 220
Spain, Golden Age of, 25
Special Education (SPED) program,
    194–95, 198
Special Olympics, 289
Special-needs students: ADD/ADHD, 245,
    316; Asperger's syndrome, 316; Bar/
    Bat Mitzvah for, 196; at Beit Knesset
    Hazon, 244–45, 247, 258, 260; coun-
    terculture in Reform Judaism, 212,
    214, 227; at East Coast Community
    High School, 316; hearing-impaired,
    180, 187, 195–96; at Reconstruction-
    ist schools, 141; at Temple Reyim,
    179–80, 187, 194–96, 198
Staff, role of: at Adath Shalom, 150–51,
    154, 160, 167–69, 171, 173; at Beit
    Knesset Hazon, 236, 240–41, 247–49,
    252–53, 261–62, 269, 271–72, 348;
    at Chabad schools, 87, 90–92, 96,
    106, 347; counterculture in Reform
    Judaism, 208–14, 216–19, 221–34; at
    East Coast Community High School,
    312–20, 323; at Kehillah, 6, 8–12,
    17–20, 34, 37, 40, 42; mission, defin-
    ing, 358–61; at Reconstructionist
    schools, 114–26, 132, 136–38, 140,
    143; at supplementary schools, 351;
    at Temple Reyim, 177–79, 181, 187,
    192–93, 195, 197, 199–205, 352; at
    Western Hebrew High, 281–85,
    288–89, 291–93, 295
Star Foundation, 148
State Holocaust Remembrance Week, 289
Stein, Karen, 39
Steiner, Barbara, 298
Steiner, Tom, 7, 18–19
Stern, Wendy, 238
Stodolosky, 174
Stone *Chumash*, 97
*Story of Anne Frank, The*, 251
Strassfeld, Michael, 162
Study, overview of supplementary school,
    xiv–xvii
Sukkot, 118
Sunday school: at Adath Shalom, 147–48;
    at Beit Knesset Hazon, 236, 244, 261,
    270; at Chabad schools, 82, 85, 90,
    93, 96, 100; counterculture in Reform

Judaism, 215–16, 222–24, 226–27,
    229; at East Coast Community High
    School, 309–10, 312–14, 316, 320,
    324, 326, 343; replaced with Shabbat
    model: at Adath Shalom, 150; counter-
    culture in Reform Judaism, 215; at Re-
    constructionist schools, 118, 121–26;
    at Tikvah Synagogue School, 48–50,
    52–54, 56–58, 60, 62–63, 66–67,
    70–73, 348; at supplementary schools,
    352; at Temple Reyim, 177–78, 187,
    196, 200
Super Sunday, 321
Supernaturalism, rejection of, 113
Synagogue 2000 (program), 148, 238
Synagogue skills, learning, xi
Synaplex Synagogue, 148

Tabernacle, 189, 265
*Talit*, 93, 127–28, 176
Taller, Carl, 237
Talmud, learning: at Beit Knesset Hazon,
    236, 251, 255; at Chabad schools, 98;
    counterculture in Reform Judaism,
    213–14; at East Coast Community
    High School, 310, 326, 329–30, 334;
    at Kehillah, 26–32
TAMID program, 52–53, 56–60, 62–70
Tastes of Judaism, 251
Teachers, expectations of: at Adath Shalom,
    151, 154–56, 159–64, 172; at Beit
    Knesset Hazon, 236, 238, 244–45,
    247–48, 256–61, 263–64, 266–67; at
    Chabad schools, 80–88, 90–92, 96,
    98–99, 107–9, 350, 358; countercul-
    ture in Reform Judaism, 211, 216–17,
    220, 226–27, 229–33; defining Jewish
    mission, 358–61; at East Coast Com-
    munity High School, 309, 312–20, 325,
    330–31, 340; Israel, representing, 55,
    59; at Kehillah, 8–9, 12–20, 350; as
    messengers of God, 355; parents as at
    Tikvah Synagogue School, 54–56,
    60–67; at Reconstructionist schools,
    115–16, 120–21, 129–30, 135, 141;
    at supplementary schools, 351–52; at
    Temple Reyim, 179–81, 188–204; at
    Tikvah Synagogue School, 69–70,
    73–74, 349–50; unfairly compensat-
    ing, xii, xvi; at Western Hebrew High,
    278–79, 283, 291–96, 300–302, 305

Teen Council at Adath Shalom, 170

Teen experiences, 134–35, 157–59, 170. *See also* High school programs

Teen Torah Center, 317–18, 325, 327, 343

*Tefilin*, 93, 103

*Tefilla Breira*, 116, 128–29, 142

*Tefillah. See* Prayer

*Tehiyat hameytim* (resurrection of the dead), 98–99, 301–2, 317, 324, 328

Tel Aviv University, 11

Temple, Holy, 130, 243–44

Temple Reyim: accessing available resources, 183–87, 202–3; ambience at, 180–83, 204; Bar/Bat Mitzvah at, 177, 183, 199; budget at, 199; challenges at, 184–85, 198–200; *chavurot* at, 353; community, creation of at, 180–82, 186, 192, 195, 199, 202–3, 205, 356; Conservative Judaism at, 176–78, 180; curriculum potential at, 178–80, 185–97, 199, 203–5; enrollment statistics of, 178–79, 204; evaluation at, 190, 196–98, 200–201, 203; Federation, work with at, 187; God, developing relationship with at, 185–86, 188–93; *havdalah* ceremonies at, 353; Hebrew, knowledge of at, 176–77, 186–92, 196, 201; history, learning about Jewish at, 187; Holocaust, learning about at, 192–93; identity, learning about Jewish at, 205; intermarriage at, 177, 181; Israel, learning about at, 176, 186–87; and Jewish involvement after Bar/Bat Mitzvah, 184, 194, 196, 201, 204; learning from model of, 200–202; a look at, 176–80; mission, defining at, 185–88, 192–93, 199, 201, 205; *mitzvot*, learning about at, 198; parental and family education at, 178, 180, 183, 192, 194, 196, 199–202, 204, 353; pedagogy at, 178, 197, 199; prayer at, 186–93, 200; questions, lingering about, 202–5; Reconstructionist Judaism at, 176; Reform Judaism at, 176–205; rituals, learning about at, 200; Shabbat at, 180, 183, 192, 195–96, 204, 353; special-needs students at, 179–80, 187, 194–96, 198; staff, role of at, 177–79, 181, 187, 192–93, 195, 197, 199–205,

352; Sunday school at, 177–78, 187, 196, 200; teachers, expectations of at, 179–81, 188–204; trip to Israel with, 178; values, exposure to Jewish at, 186, 194, 198, 204–5; vision, educational at, 178, 185–86, 355–56

Temple Torah, 177, 181

Ten Commandments, 333

Tepper, Rabbi Joseph, 238–39, 241–42, 249–50, 253–54, 260, 270

Teutsch, David, 132

*Tichon* (high school) programs at Kehillah, 12, 34–35, 37–38

*Tikkun olam*, learning about: at Beit Knesset Hazon, 242, 255, 257, 271; counterculture in Reform Judaism, 218; and God, 257–58; at Reconstructionist schools, 137; at Tikvah Synagogue School, 63–64, 73; at Western Hebrew High, 289

Tikvah Synagogue School: budget at, 357, 360; challenges at, 69–72, 75–76; *chavurot* at, 72; community, creation of at, 50–52, 55–60, 66–69, 71–73, 75–76, 348; Conservative Judaism at, 47, 50; creation of community at, 348; curriculum potential at, 52–60, 66, 73–75; egalitarianism at, 49; enrollment statistics of, 56; ethics, learning about Jewish at, 54, 63, 65–66; evaluation at, 69, 76; experimentation at, 56; fundraising at, 49; governance at, 55; Hanukkah, learning about at, 58; *havdalah* ceremonies at, 56, 58, 73; Hebrew, knowledge of at, 57–62, 65, 73, 357; history, learning about Jewish at, 58–59, 73; holidays, learning about at, 51, 56, 58; Holocaust, learning about at, 59; Israel, learning about at, 73; and Jewish involvement after Bar/Bat Mitzvah, 52, 56, 58; law, learning about Jewish at, 64; learning from model of, 72–73, 76–77; a look at, 47–51; *mitzvot*, learning about at, 61–62; Orthodox Judaism at, 48–49, 56, 71; parental and family education at, 54–56, 60–70, 72; Passover, learning about at, 61; prayer at, 52, 54, 56–58, 60–62, 65–66, 68–69, 73, 348; prayer leaders around age of Bar/Bat Mitzvah, 52; Reform Judaism at, 47–49,

57, 61, 71; rituals, learning about at, 73; Shabbat at, 50, 52–54, 56–58, 60, 62–63, 66–67, 70–73, 350; Sunday school model replaced with Shabbat model at, 48–50, 52–54, 56–58, 60, 62–63, 66–67, 70–73, 348; teachers, expectations of at, 69–70, 73–74, 349–50; teachers, parents as at, 54–56, 60–67; and *tikkun olam*, 63–64, 73; Torah, learning at, 57–58, 60, 63, 68, 73–74; Traditional Judaism at, 47–77; values, exposure to Jewish at, 57, 73
Tishah b'Av, 214
*Tizmoret*, 211
TNP, 216–17, 219, 221, 229
*Toledot*, 216
*Tomchei Shabbos*, 321
Tonnies, Ferdinand, 51
Torah: at Adath Shalom, 149, 152, 162, 165; at Beit Knesset Hazon, 236, 238–39, 242, 254, 265, 270; at Chabad schools, 85–87, 92, 96–97, 99, 107, 355; counterculture in Reform Judaism, 214, 217, 219–21; at East Coast Community High School, 310, 317–18, 325–27, 329–33, 336–39, 341, 343; expectations of supplementary schools, xi; family *d'var torah*, 131–34; God, communicating through, 26–27, 30, 265; God mentioned in, 336, 338–39; at Kehillah, 26–33; at Reconstructionist schools, 115, 125–26, 135, 142; from Sinai, 32, 131; at supplementary schools, 353; at Tikvah Synagogue School, 57–58, 60, 63, 68, 73–74; as words of God, 333–34
Torah A Midrash Identity Divrei Hayamim (TAMID), 52–53, 56–60, 62–70
*Torah and You*, 152
Torah Aura Publications, 328
*Torah lishmah*, 228
Touro College, 91
Tower of Babel, 30–32
Traditional Judaism, 3–45, 47–77, 147
Triangle Shirt Company, 252
*Trope* (cantillation), learning: at Beit Knesset Hazon, 262; counterculture in Reform Judaism, 216; at Temple Reyim, 182, 193; at Tikvah Synagogue School, 58, 69
*Tsevet* (staff). *See* Staff, role of

*Tshuvah* (repentance), 38
Tuition: at Adath Shalom, 148, 167; at Beit Knesset Hazon, 246, 269; at Chabad schools, 89; counterculture in Reform Judaism, 230; at Western Hebrew High, 281, 284. *See also* Budget; Fundraising; Scholarships
*Tzavta*, 215, 226, 229
*Tzedakah* (charity), learning about: at Adath Shalom, 153; at Beit Knesset Hazon, 255, 258; at Chabad schools, 97; at Kehillah, 25, 29; at Western Hebrew High, 287, 289–90, 305
*Tzedek*, 223
*Tzelem Elohim*, 242, 262–64, 271
Tziporah, 329
*Tzitzit*, 128, 166

*Ulpan*, 149, 159, 164. *See also* Hebrew, knowledge of
*Understanding by Design*, 66, 135, 139, 188, 291
Union for Reform Judaism, 47, 119, 257, 359
Unitarian church, Reconstructionism founded in, 114
United Synagogue of America (United Synagogue of Conservative Judaism), 50, 70
Upward Bound, 10
URJ, 242
USY (United Synagogue Youth), 157–58, 297

Values, exposure to Jewish: at Adath Shalom, 149, 152–53, 174; at Beit Knesset Hazon, 234, 253–54, 256, 260, 264, 266, 271; at Chabad schools, 92, 97–98, 101, 105; counterculture in Reform Judaism, 211–15, 217–24, 228, 230–32; at East Coast Community High School, 318, 326, 330–31, 340; expectations of supplementary schools, xi; at Kehillah, 25–26; at supplementary schools, 349, 351–52; at Temple Reyim, 186, 194, 198, 204–5; at Tikvah Synagogue School, 57, 73; at Western Hebrew High, 285, 290, 293
Victor, Rabbi Bruce, 238
Victor, Serene, 95

Violence in school, 328
Vision, educational: at Adath Shalom, 148–50, 153, 159–60, 166, 169–71, 173; at Beit Knesset Hazon, 234–73; at Chabad schools, 85; and community, creation of, 354; counterculture in Reform Judaism, 218, 232–33; at East Coast Community High School, 310, 332, 343; at Kehillah, 4, 6–9, 11, 13, 25, 354–55; at Reconstructionist schools, 117–24, 129, 140–42; of supplementary schools, 354–56; at Temple Reyim, 178, 185–86, 355–56; at Western Hebrew High, 284, 291–93, 295, 303, 355. *See also* Mission, defining
Vogel, Naomi, 246–47, 259–60

Wagman, Tania, 278
Walk for Israel, 153, 171
Warsaw Ghetto, 286–87
Waxman, Rachel, 145–47, 150–51, 153–54, 159–60, 164–70, 172–75
Weinstein, Tara, 282–83, 287, 291–92, 295–96, 304–5
Western Hebrew High: budget at, 357; challenges at, 291, 296, 304; community, creation of at, 280–81, 284–85, 288–90, 297, 303–6, 349, 357; Confirmation program at, 280–81; Conservative Judaism at, 280; curriculum potential at, 281, 283–84, 286–87, 290–96, 299, 304–5, 355; enrollment statistics of, 280, 290; evaluation at, 298; experiential learning at, 280, 283–90, 306; Federation, work with at, 282, 285–86; fundraising at, 304; goals of, 292–93, 295; governance at, 284, 303–4; Hebrew, knowledge of at, 280, 293; history, learning about Jewish at, 286, 294; Holocaust, learning about at, 289, 305; identity, learning about Jewish at, 279, 287, 293, 303, 305–6; informality at, 289, 299–300, 305; intermarriage at, 280; Israel, learning about at, 279–80, 283–90, 293–95, 303–5; and Jewish involvement after Bar/Bat Mitzvah, 278; lack

of assessments at, 295; learning from model of, 303–6; a look at, 277–80; mission, defining at, 291–93, 303, 305, 355; parental and family education at, 285–86, 288, 304; philosophy, learning about Jewish at, 278–79, 294; politics, learning about at, 290, 298, 305; prayer at, 298; Reconstructionist Judaism at, 280; Reform Judaism at, 280; staff, role of at, 281–85, 288–89, 291–93, 295; students loving, 296–303; teachers, expectations of at, 278–79, 283, 291–96, 300–302, 305; and *tikkun olam*, 289; trip to Israel with, 279–80, 283–90, 293, 304–5, 355, 357; tuition at, 281, 284; *tzedakah* (charity), learning about at, 287, 289–90, 305; values, exposure to Jewish at, 285, 290, 293; vision, educational at, 284, 291–93, 295, 303, 355
*When Zaydeh Danced on Eldridge Street*, 259
World to Come, 98
World War II, 114, 176

*Yahadut,* knowledge of: at Adath Shalom, 151, 156, 159; at Kehillah, 6–9, 11–12, 18, 20–21, 25–32, 36–37, 42–43, 352
*Yanshoofs*, 154–55
Yermus, Kyra, 277–78, 282, 299–300
*Yeshiva*, study in, 319, 328
*Yesod* program, 236, 240, 242–44, 247–51, 253, 258–67, 269–70
Yom Haazmaut, 227
Yom HaShoah, 192
Yom Kippur, 38, 117, 214
*Yotzer Or*, 65
Young Judaea, 5, 9, 11
Youth Choir, 251
Youth Commission at Adath Shalom, 170

Zeus, 130
Zionism, 25, 33, 114, 223, 343. *See also* Israel
*Zman Likro*, 154
*Zmirot*, learning, 58

Question for
Jodi

1. Changes over
    last 3
         years.

2. Accurate?
   Anything
        missing?

3. Rebuild
   project 2
        years later

4. [scribble] How many
        students?
           families.

5. Lee SH temple.

6. New challenges.

7.     Old Recon--- dress,